Using Basic Personality Research
to Inform Personality Pathology

Using Basic Personality Research to Inform Personality Pathology

EDITED BY DOUGLAS B. SAMUEL

AND

DONALD R. LYNAM

OXFORD
UNIVERSITY PRESS

OXFORD

UNIVERSITY PRESS

Oxford University Press is a department of the University of Oxford. It furthers
the University's objective of excellence in research, scholarship, and education
by publishing worldwide. Oxford is a registered trade mark of Oxford University
Press in the UK and certain other countries.

Published in the United States of America by Oxford University Press
198 Madison Avenue, New York, NY 10016, United States of America.

© Oxford University Press 2019

Library of Congress Cataloging-in-Publication Data
Names: Samuel, Douglas B., 1978– editor. | Lynam, Donald R., 1967– editor.
Title: Using basic personality research to inform personality pathology /
edited by Douglas B. Samuel and Donald R. Lynam.
Description: New York, NY : Oxford University Press, [2019] |
Includes bibliographical references and index.
Identifiers: LCCN 2018034602 (print) | LCCN 2018037528 (ebook) |
ISBN 9780190227081 (UPDF) | ISBN 9780190668570 (EPUB) |
ISBN 9780190227074 (hardcover : alk. paper)
Subjects: LCSH: Personality disorders. | Personality.
Classification: LCC RC554 (ebook) | LCC RC554 .U85 2019 (print) |
DDC 616.85/81—dc23
LC record available at https://lccn.loc.gov/2018034602

9 8 7 6 5 4 3 2 1

Printed by Sheridan Books, Inc., United States of America

CONTENTS

SECTION IV Biological Bases of Personality

Douglas B. Samuel, PhD, is Associate Professor of Clinical Psychology at Purdue University. His research focuses on investigating dimensional models—particularly the five-factor model of personality—for improving the conceptualization of psychopathology. He is particularly interested in integrating multiple sources (e.g., clients, therapists, informants) and methods (e.g., EEG, ecological momentary assessment) to better assess and diagnose mental illness.

Donald R. Lynam, PhD, is Distinguished Professor of Psychological Sciences at Purdue University. His research examines the contribution of individual differences to psychopathology and deviance across the life course. Much of his work uses general models of personality to conceptualize and assess more complex constructs (e.g., psychopathy, narcissism, impulsivity, and so on).

Xia Allen
Department of Psychology, University of Notre Dame, Notre Dame, Indiana

Elizabeth Mayfield Arnold
Department of Psychiatry and Behavioral Medicine, Wake Forest School of Medicine, Winston-Salem, North Carolina

Steve Balsis
Department of Psychological and Brain Sciences, Texas A&M University, College Station, Texas

Nadia Bounoua
Department of Psychology, University of Maryland, College Park, Maryland

Turhan Canli
Department of Psychology, Stony Brook University, Stony Brook, New York

John P. Capitanio
California National Primate Research Center and Department of Psychology,
University of California, Davis, California

Lee Anna Clark
Department of Psychology, University of Notre Dame, Notre Dame, Indiana

Elizabeth J. Daly
Department of Psychology, University of Notre Dame, Notre Dame, Indiana

Rodica I. Damian
Department of Psychology, University of Illinois, Champaign, Illinois

William Fleeson
Department of Psychology, Wake Forest University, Winston-Salmen, North Carolina

R. Michael Furr
Department of Psychology, Wake Forest University, Winston-Salmen, North Carolina

Kathrin Herzhoff
Department of Psychology, University of Houston, Houston, Texas

Christopher J. Hopwood
Department of Psychology, Michigan State University, East Lansin, Michigan

Thomas Kingsbury
Department of Psychology, University of Notre Dame, Notre Dame, Indiana

Shauna C. Kushner
Department of Psychology, University of Toronto, Toronto, Ontario, Canada

Stephanie Larew
Department of Psychology,
 University of Notre Dame,
 Notre Dame, Indiana

Carl W. Lejuez
Department of Psychology,
 University of Maryland,
 College Park, Maryland

William A. Mason
California National Primate Research
 Center and Department of
 Psychology, University of
 California, Davis, California

Alexis Matusiewicz
Department of Psychology,
 University of Maryland,
 College Park, Maryland

Joshua D. Miller
Department of Psychology,
 University of Georgia, Athens,
 Georgia

Malek Mneimne
Department of Psychology, Wake
 Forest University, Winston-Salmen,
 North Carolina

Hallie Nuzum
Department of Psychology, University
 of Notre Dame, Notre Dame,
 Indiana

Thomas F. Oltmanns
Department of Psychological and
 Brain Sciences, Washington
 University in St. Louis, St. Louis,
 Missouri

Aaron L. Pincus
Department of Psychology,
 Pennsylvania State University,
 University Park, Pennsylvania

Kathleen W. Reardon
Department of Psychology, University
 of Houston, Houston, Texas

Eunyoe Ro
Department of Psychology, Southern
 Illinois University Edwardsville,
 Edwardsville, Illinois

Brent W. Roberts
Department of Psychology, University
 of Illinois, Champaign, Illinois

Jaime L. Shapiro
Department of Psychology, University
 of Notre Dame, Notre Dame,
 Indiana

James Soldinger
Department of Psychology, University
 of Maryland, College Park,
 Maryland

Jennifer L. Tackett
Department of Psychology, University
 of Houston, Houston, Texas

Thomas A. Widiger
Department of Psychology, University
 of Kentucky, Lexington, Kentucky

Aidan G. C. Wright
Department of Psychology, University
 of Pittsburgh, Pittsburgh,
 Pennsylvania

Using Basic Personality Research
to Inform Personality Pathology

Introduction to Personality Disorders

Historical Overview of Personality Disorders

THOMAS A. WIDIGER ∎

The purpose of this chapter is to provide a brief history of the diagnosis of personality disorder as provided within the American Psychiatric Association's (APA) *Diagnostic and Statistical Manual of Mental Disorders* (*DSM*). It is perhaps self-evident that an authoritative, common language for the classification of personality disorder is necessary for clinical practice. Imagine the chaos if clinicians were free to use whatever personality disorder classification they preferred. Even if they used the same diagnosis (which is unlikely), they would probably use very different diagnostic criteria. The primary purpose of a diagnostic manual is to facilitate reliable (and valid) diagnostic practice for clinicians and professional agencies.

A common language is also advantageous to scientific research (Widiger, 2012b). It would be quite difficult to accumulate a body of knowledge regarding a respective personality disorder if each researcher used his or her own idiosyncratic nomenclature. Of course, an authoritative nomenclature, such as the APA's *DSM*, might in principle hinder creativity, innovation, and progress if it stifled alternative conceptualizations. Hyman (2010), past director of the National Institute of Mental Health (NIMH), argued passionately against the predominance for research purposes of the *DSM*. This is now somewhat ironic, given that NIMH has since indicated that researchers should adhere to their own newly developed NIMH diagnostic system to obtain funding (Insel, 2013).

In any case, it is debatable if the APA nomenclature has actually stifled scientific research. The APA nomenclature has served as a useful foil, a common point of comparison. Researchers have been free to assert through argument and empiricism their own version of a diagnostic construct, such as psychopathy (Crego & Widiger, 2015; Hare & Neumann, 2008) and even fundamental paradigm shifts (Clark, 2007; Widiger & Trull, 2007).

This chapter will cover the first through the fifth editions of the APA's diagnostic manual (Millon, 2011; Widiger, 2012b), although emphasis will be given to the more recent editions. The chapter concludes with suggestions for future editions.

ICD-6 AND DSM-I

The World Health Organization (WHO) accepted the authority to produce the sixth edition of the *International Classification of Diseases* (*ICD*), due in large part to the inability of clinicians from different countries to be able to communicate effectively when treating the psychological casualties of World War II (Kendell, 1975). *ICD-6* attempted to be responsive to the needs of the war veterans. One specific absence, though, was a diagnosis of passive-aggressive personality disorder, which, curiously, might have been the most frequently diagnosed personality disorder during the war, accounting for 6% of all admissions to Army hospitals (Wetzler & Jose, 2012). The first edition of the *DSM* (*DSM-I*; APA, 1952) was America's version of *ICD-6*, and it was largely successful in providing a common, authoritative nomenclature for American psychiatry (Kendell, 1975). However, fundamental objections and criticisms regarding the reliability and validity of psychiatric diagnosis were being raised (e.g., Zigler & Phillips, 1961).

DSM-II AND ICD-8

ICD-6 was revised to *ICD-7* in 1955, but there were no revisions to the mental disorders section. In 1965, the APA appointed the Committee on Nomenclature and Statistics to revise *DSM-I* to be compatible with *ICD-8* and yet also be suitable for use within the United States. Spitzer and Wilson (1968) summarized the changes. Shifted out of the section for personality disorders were substance dependencies and sexual deviations. Deleted entirely was the passive-dependent variant of the passive-aggressive personality trait disturbance (Wetzler & Jose, 2012). New additions were the explosive, hysterical, and asthenic personality disorders (APA, 1968).

Mental disorder diagnosis though remained fundamentally controversial (e.g., Rosenhan, 1973). A significant problem continued to be the absence of support for their reliability, let alone their validity. Researchers though had by now developed more specific and explicit criterion sets to increase the likelihood of replicable research. The most influential of these efforts was provided by Feighner et al. (1972), who developed specific and explicit criteria for 14 conditions (as well as secondary depression), one of which was antisocial personality disorder.

DSM-III (AND ICD-9)

In 1974, the APA appointed a task force to revise *DSM-II* in a manner that would be compatible with *ICD-9* but would also incorporate many current innovations.

DSM-III was published in 1980 and did indeed include many innovations (Spitzer, Williams, & Skodol, 1980). Four of the *DSM-II* personality disorders were deleted (i.e., aesthenic, cyclothymic, inadequate, and explosive) and four were added (i.e., avoidant, dependent, borderline, and narcissistic; APA, 1980; Frances, 1980; Spitzer et al., 1980). Each of the personality disorders was also provided with relatively specific and explicit diagnostic criteria.

An innovation of *DSM-III* was the placement of the personality disorders in a distinct section (i.e., Axis II) to ensure that they would not be overlooked by clinicians whose attention was typically drawn to more florid and immediate concerns of (for instance) anxiety, mood, or substance use. The effect of this placement was indeed a boon to the diagnosis of personality disorders, dramatically increasing their clinical recognition. Loranger (1990) compared the frequency of personality disorder diagnoses in the last 5 years of *DSM-II* with the first 5 years of *DSM-III*. The percent receiving a personality disorder diagnoses went from 19% with *DSM-II* to 49% with *DSM-III*. The multiaxial system though has been deleted in *DSM-5*. It would be of interest to determine if this results in a decrease in the recognition of personality disorders in general clinical settings.

DSM-III-R

A difficulty for *DSM-III* was an absence of much research to guide the construction of the criterion sets, including the personality disorders (with the exception of antisocial, and perhaps borderline). The APA therefore authorized the development of a revision to *DSM-III*. The manual was to be revised only "for consistency, clarity, and conceptual accuracy" (APA, 1987, p. xvii). However, it was perhaps unrealistic to expect the authors of *DSM-III-R* to confine their efforts to simply refinement, given the acclaim and influence of *DSM-III* (Frances & Widiger, 2012).

It was not difficult to find persons who wanted to be involved in *DSM-III-R*, and everyone wanted to have a significant impact. There were in fact many more persons involved in providing the *DSM-III-R* refinements to the personality disorders (i.e., 38 work group members) than had been involved in its original construction (i.e., 10). Not surprisingly, there were many proposals for significant revisions and even new additions, despite the limited mandate.

The threshold for the inclusion of new diagnoses in *DSM-III* and *DSM-III-R* was also quite liberal. As expressed by Spitzer, Sheehy, and Endicott (1977), "if there is general agreement among clinicians, who would be expected to encounter the condition, that there are a significant number of patients who have it and that its identification is important in their clinical work, it is included in the classification" (p. 3). Approved for inclusion in *DSM-III-R* by the personality disorders work group and the task force were two new diagnoses, the masochistic and sadistic personality disorders. However, both proposals were rejected by the APA Board of Trustees due to their controversial nature and questionable empirical support (Widiger, Frances, Spitzer, & Williams, 1988).

DSM-IV AND *ICD-10*

By the time work was completed on *DSM-III-R*, work had already begun on *ICD-10*. In May 1988 the APA Board of Trustees appointed a *DSM-IV* Task Force. Mandates for *DSM-IV* were to be more compatible with *ICD-10*, more user-friendly for the clinician, and more explicitly empirically based (Frances, Widiger, & Pincus, 1989).

With respect to the third mandate, one of the more common concerns regarding *DSM-III* and *DSM-III-R* was the extent of its empirical support. It was often suggested that the decisions were more consistent with a priori wishes of work group members than with the published research. Gunderson (1983), chair of the *DSM-IV* personality disorders committee, suggested that "for most of the personality disorder categories there was either no empirical base (e.g., avoidant, dependent, passive-aggressive, narcissistic) or no clinical tradition (e.g., avoidant, dependent, schizotypal); thus their disposition was much more subject to the convictions of individual Advisory Committee members" (p. 30). Millon (1981) criticized the *DSM-III* criteria for antisocial personality disorder for being too heavily influenced by Robins (1966), a member of the *DSM-III* personality disorders committee. Gunderson (1983) and Kernberg (1984), in turn, criticized the inclusion of avoidant personality disorder for being too heavily influenced by Millon (1981), another member of the same committee.

The primary authors of *DSM-IV* suggested that "the major innovation . . . will not be in its having surprising new content but rather will reside in the systematic and explicit method by which DSM-IV will be constructed and documented" (Frances et al., 1989, p. 375). The development of *DSM-IV* included three stages of empirical review, including systematic and comprehensive reviews of the research literature, reanalyses of multiple data sets, and field trials. It was emphasized that the intention and focus of the literature reviews were not simply to make the best case for a respective proposal (Widiger, Frances, Pincus, Davis, & First, 1991). The authors were required to acknowledge and address findings inconsistent with their proposals (Frances & Widiger, 2012). An explicit method of literature search was required to maximize the likelihood that it would be objective and systematic, including the specification of the criteria for study inclusion and exclusion, thereby making it difficult to confine the review to a limited set of studies that were most consistent with the viewpoints of the authors (Widiger et al., 1991). Each review was also submitted for critical review by persons likely to oppose the proposals.

In sum, the approach taken in *DSM-IV* was considerably more conservative than it had been for *DSM-III* and *DSM-III-R* (Frances & Widiger, 2012). The sadistic and self-defeating personality disorders (included in an appendix to *DSM-III-R*) were deleted. Proposed for *DSM-IV* was a dimensional trait model, but it was eventually reduced to simply an acknowledgment of the existence of this perspective (Widiger & Sanderson, 1995). The personality disorder that was the most frequently diagnosed by clinicians during World War II (passive-aggressive) was downgraded to an appendix (Wetzler & Jose, 2012). A new diagnosis though, depressive, was added to the appendix (Bagby, Watson, & Ryder, 2012), and the diagnostic criterion sets were also significantly revised in an effort to improve discriminant validity.

DSM-IV-TR

No substantive changes were made to the personality disorders in *DSM-IV-TR* (APA, 2000). *DSM-IV-TR* revisions (at least for the personality disorders) were confined simply to updating the text (First & Pincus, 2002). There was initially a plan to publish a documentation of the empirical support for the text. In the end, the text for some of the personality disorders (e.g., antisocial) was updated, but not all of them. It was decided not to publish the documentation, largely because it was incomplete and inconsistent in quality.

DSM-5

The principal authors of *DSM-5* intended this next revision to provide a "paradigm shift" (Kupfer, First, & Regier, 2002, p. xix); more specifically, toward a dimensional classification of psychopathology. "We have decided that one, if not the major difference, between DSM-IV and DSM-V will be the more prominent use of dimensional measures" (Regier et al., 2009, p. 649).

The development of *DSM-5* was preceded by a series of preparatory conferences, each one focused on shifting the personality disorders to a dimensional trait model. The first "DSM-V Research Planning Conference" was held in October 1999. The Nomenclature Work Group of this conference concluded that it would be "important that consideration be given to advantages and disadvantages of basing part or all of DSM-V on dimensions rather than categories" (Rounsaville et al., 2002, p. 13). This work group suggested that this shift was most clearly suited for the personality disorders. "If a dimensional system of personality performs well and is acceptable to clinicians, it might then be appropriate to explore dimensional approaches in other domains" (Rounsaville et al., 2002, p. 13).

The Personality Disorders and Relational Disorders Work Group summarized the research in support of shifting the personality disorders to a dimensional trait model and identified the primary alternatives (First et al., 2002). They recommended that *DSM-5* revise "the classification of personality disorders using a dimensional approach that avoids the artificiality of the current categorical approach and facilitates the identification and communication of the patient's clinically relevant personality traits" (First et al., 2002, p. 179).

This initial *DSM-5* preparatory conference was followed by a series of international conferences. The first, "Dimensional Models of Personality Disorder: Etiology, Pathology, Phenomenology, & Treatment," was held in December 2004. Its purpose was to review the literature and set a research agenda "that would be most effective in leading the field toward a dimensional classification of personality disorder" (Widiger, Simonsen, Krueger, Livesley, & Verheul,

2005, p. 315). An integration of existing models was proposed, consisting of the four domains of emotional dysregulation versus emotional stability, extraversion versus introversion, antagonism versus compliance, and constraint versus impulsivity. It was suggested though that a fifth broad domain, unconventionality versus closed to experience, would be necessary to be fully comprehensive. Unconventionality versus closedness was not within the integrative model because it is was not included within some of the predominant systems, such as Livesley's four-dimensional model, assessed by the Dimensional Assessment of Personality Pathology-Basic Questionnaire (DAPP-BQ; Livesley & Jackson, 2009), and Clark's three-factor model, assessed by the Schedule for Nonadaptive and Adaptive Personality (SNAP; Clark, Simms, Wu, & Casillas, in press). Unconventionality versus closedness though was included within the five-factor model (FFM; Widiger & Trull, 2007).

The seventh conference of this series was devoted to redefining much of the entire manual, including the personality disorders, to fundamental dimensions. The dimensional model of Livesley and Jackson (2009) was provided as an illustration for the personality disorders (Krueger, Skodol, Livesley, Shrout, & Huang, 2008).

The *DSM-5* Personality and Personality Disorders Work Group (PPDWG) began work in 2007 (Krueger & Markon, 2014). Skodol, Morey, Bender, and Oldham (2013) indicated that "for the first year or so, 'everything was on the table,' with no a priori limitations on the extent of changes that *DSM-5* could incur" (p. 344). "Work group members were encouraged to 'think outside the box'" (Skodol et al., 2013, p. 344). This liberal mandate led to quite a few proposals, well beyond just shifting to a dimensional trait model (Widiger & Oltmanns, 2017).

Initial *DSM-5* Personality Disorder Proposals

The initial *DSM-5* PPDWG proposals were extensive, to say the least. As indicated by Skodol (2010), "the work group recommends a major reconceptualization of personality psychopathology" (para. 1). The proposals included the deletion of five diagnoses; a revision to the definition that was coordinated with the inclusion of an assessment of a level of personality functioning; the replacement of the specific and explicit criterion sets with narrative paragraphs; and the inclusion of a dimensional trait model (APA, 2010; Skodol, 2010). Not surprisingly, these extensive revisions were met with considerable objection. A special section of the *Journal of Personality Disorders* included six critical reviews (i.e., Bornstein, 2011; Clarkin & Huprich, 2011; Paris, 2011; Ronningstam, 2011; Widiger, 2011a; Zimmerman, 2011); a special section of *Personality Disorders: Theory, Research, and Treatment* included three more (Pilkonis, Hallquist, Morse, & Stepp, 2011; Pincus, 2011; Widiger, 2011b). Five additional critical reviews were published independently of these special sections (i.e., Gunderson, 2010a, 2010b; Miller, Widiger, & Campbell, 2010; Shedler et al., 2010; Zimmerman, 2012). There was even a critical review by a work group member (i.e., Livesley, 2010). Each proposal will be discussed in turn.

DELETION OF FIVE DIAGNOSES

The *DSM-5* PPDWG initially proposed to delete half of the diagnoses (i.e., histrionic, narcissistic, dependent, paranoid, and schizoid) largely to reduce diagnostic co-occurrence (Skodol, 2010). Diagnostic co-occurrence has been a significant problem (Clark, 2007; Trull & Durrett, 2005; Widiger & Trull, 2007), but sacrificing fully half of them to address this problem might have been rather draconian (Livesley, 2013; Widiger, 2011b). Lack of adequate coverage has also been a problem of comparable magnitude (Verheul & Widiger, 2004).With the removal of the histrionic and dependent personality disorders, essentially half of all manner of maladaptive interpersonal relatedness would no longer have been represented (Pincus & Hopwood, 2012; Widiger, 2010). The credibility of the field of personality disorder might have also suffered from the fact that the *DSM-5* PPDWG decided that literally half of the disorders that had been recognized, discussed, and treated over the past 30 years lacked sufficient utility or validity to remain within the diagnostic manual (Pilkonis et al., 2011; Widiger, 2011b).

Skodol et al. (2011) had also concluded that the narcissistic, dependent, histrionic, schizoid, and paranoid diagnoses had inadequate empirical support. There is much less research on the histrionic, paranoid, and schizoid personality disorders than for the borderline, antisocial, and schizotypal (Blashfield & Intoccia, 2000; Blashfield, Reynolds, & Stennett, 2012; Hopwood & Thomas, 2012). The proposal to delete the dependent and narcissistic diagnoses, however, was more difficult to defend (Bornstein, 2011, 2012; Gore & Pincus, 2013; Ronningstam, 2011; Widiger, 2011b). There might in fact be as much, if not more, research to support the validity and utility of the dependent and narcissistic personality disorders than for the avoidant and obsessive-compulsive (Gore & Pincus, 2013; Miller et al., 2010; Mullins-Sweatt, Bernstein, & Widiger, 2012; Widiger, 2011b). As expressed by Livesley (2010), a work group member, "well-studied conditions that represent important clinical presentations, such as dependent and narcissistic personality disorders, are slated for elimination, whereas obsessive–compulsive personality disorder, which is often associated with less serious pathology, will be retained" (p. 309).

Bornstein (2011) and Livesley (2013) suggested that the proposals for retention and deletion were biased in favor of the personality disorders included within the heavily funded and widely published Collaborative Longitudinal Study of Personality Disorders (CLPS; Skodol et al., 2005). The CLPS project was confined largely to the avoidant, schizotypal, obsessive-compulsive, and borderline diagnoses. Zimmerman (2012) suggested that the *DSM-5* PPDWG, prominent members of which were also principal investigators for CLPS, argued to retain the avoidant and obsessive-compulsive because they were the focus of CLPS. It would indeed have been difficult for Skodol et al. to delete the disorders that were the focus of over 10 years of NIMH funding.

However, CLPS may not have actually yielded much research that was concerned with issues of specific or unique importance for understanding and validating the avoidant and obsessive-compulsive personality disorders. The typical CLPS publication was concerned with more generic issues that applied to all of the personality disorders (e.g., temporal stability, factor structure, and external correlates). This is not the case for a good part of the research concerning the dependent and narcissistic personality disorders, both of which have generated a considerable body of findings devoted to questions and issues specific to them (Bornstein, 2011, 2012; Campbell & Miller, 2011; Gore & Pincus, 2013).

LEVEL OF PERSONALITY FUNCTIONING

DSM-IV included a brief criterion set for the presence of a personality disorder, consisting of dysfunction in cognition, affectivity, interpersonal relatedness, and/ or impulse control (any two of which were required; APA, 1994). The PPDWG proposed a substantial broadening of this definition, coordinating it with a lengthy assessment of level of personality functioning tied to the theory that deficits in the sense of self (with respect to identity and self-regulation) and interpersonal relatedness (with respect to empathy and intimacy) are fundamental to the presence of a personality disorder (Bender et al., 2011; Kernberg, 2012; Pincus, 2011).

The proposal was criticized for its complexity (Clarkin & Huprich, 2011; Pilkonis et al., 2011; Widiger, 2011b). One might also question an alignment of the definition with psychodynamic theory (Widiger & Oltmanns, 2017). One of the innovations of *DSM-III* was shifting away from any particular theoretical model toward a more neutral perspective, one that could be comfortably used by persons who did not share the theoretical perspective of work group members (Spitzer et al., 1980). Yet the *DSM-5* PPDWG proposed shifting toward psychodynamic constructs (Bender et al., 2011; Kernberg, 2012; Pincus, 2011). This might not have been well received, particularly as the rest of psychiatry is shifting toward a neurobiological perspective (Hyman, 2010; Insel & Quirion, 2005).

NARRATIVE PROTOTYPE MATCHING

Another proposal was to abandon the well-established specific and explicit criterion sets for lengthy narrative paragraphs. As expressed by Kendler, Munoz, and Murphy (2010), the "interest in diagnostic reliability in the early 1970s— substantially influenced by the Feighner criteria—proved to be a critical corrective and was instrumental in the renaissance of psychiatric research witnessed in the subsequent decades" (p. 141). One of the benefits of this renaissance was CLPS (Skodol et al., 2005). CLPS would not likely have been funded if they had proposed abandoning this form of assessment for subjective matching to narrative paragraphs.

There is, however, support among some personality disorder clinicians and researchers for a shift to narrative matching (e.g., First & Westen, 2007; Huprich, Bornstein, & Schmitt, 2011; Shedler et al., 2010). One of its attractive features is its simplicity. "Clinicians could make a complete Axis II diagnosis in 1 or 2 minutes" (Westen, Shedler, & Bradley, 2006, p. 855) because they would no longer have to assess systematically each of the sentences included within a criterion set or the narrative description. "Diagnosticians rate the overall similarity or 'match' between a patient and the prototype . . . considering the prototype as a whole rather than counting individual symptoms" (Westen et al., 2006, p. 847).

It would seem self-evident though that clinicians would not likely provide reliable diagnoses if they assessed a lengthy three-paragraph description of borderline personality disorder (for instance) in just 1–2 minutes through a subjective impression of an overall gestalt (Livesley, 2010; Pilkonis et al., 2011). The narratives proposed for *DSM-5* would probably be even less reliable than had been the case for *DSM-II* (APA, 1968) because they were much longer and more complex.

DIMENSIONAL TRAIT MODEL

Krueger et al. (2012) stated that in the development of the dimensional trait model "our focus was initially on identifying and operationalizing specific maladaptive personality falling within five broad domains" (p. 1180). "If the work group members had ample opportunity to contribute (e.g., in describing a wide range of personality disorder characteristics), and the data pointed to the well-replicated structure of personality pathology, it would be hard for work group members to argue that somehow the empirical model was imposed from the outside" (Krueger, 2013, p. 359). In other words, using the work group members' own nominations, "one hope was that . . . we would arrive at essentially the same well-replicated empirical structure of personality pathology delineated by Widiger and Simonsen (2005)" (Krueger, 2013, p. 350).

However, the initial proposal was for a six-domain model (i.e., negative emotionality, introversion, antagonism, disinhibition, compulsivity, and schizotypy) that was explicitly distinguished from the FFM; more specifically, that compulsivity and schizotypy did not align with any FFM domain (i.e., Clark & Krueger, 2010). In the end, the dimensional trait model was said to be aligned with the FFM (Krueger & Markon, 2014), but it was presented in its initial years as if it was created de novo, not aligned with any established model (Livesley, 2013). This provided considerable fuel to those who opposed the dimensional trait perspective. As expressed by Shedler et al. (2010) in their *American Journal of Psychiatry* editorial in opposition to the proposal, "the resulting model no longer rests on decades of research, which had been the chief rationale for including it" (p. 1027).

Final *DSM-5* Proposals

All of the proposals were revised to varying degrees (Skodol, 2012). The proposal to delete narcissistic personality disorder was withdrawn. Dependent personality disorder, however, remained slated for deletion. The narrative prototype matching proposal was withdrawn due in large part to its questionable reliability and inadequate empirical support (Livesley, 2010; Pilkonis et al., 2011; Widiger, 2011b; Zimmerman, 2011). However, the work group did not return to the specific and explicit criterion sets of *DSM-IV-TR*. Instead, they cobbled together, with relatively little time remaining, a new hybrid model of personality disorder diagnosis (Skodol, 2012) which combined psychodynamically oriented deficits in self and interpersonal functioning obtained from the level of personality functioning proposal (Bender et al., 2011; Kernberg, 2012; Pincus, 2011) with maladaptive personality traits obtained from the dimensional trait proposal, which had been reduced from a six-domain, 37-trait model to a five-domain, 25-trait model on the basis of factor analyses by PPDWG members (Krueger et al., 2012).

By the time the hybrid model was completed, three *DSM-5* oversight committees had been formed. They were developed through the course of *DSM-5* in response to concerns being raised across the diagnostic manual with respect to a number of provocative proposals (Greenburg, 2013). There was the Oversight Committee, which served in part as an advisor to the APA Board of Trustees, who have ultimate veto power over the *DSM-5* Task Force. There was also the Clinical and Public Health Review Committee (CPHC), which was concerned with implications for public health care. Finally, there was the Scientific Review Committee (SRC; chaired by Drs. Kenneth Kendler and Robert Freedman), which was concerned with extent of empirical support for the proposed revisions.

Kendler, Kupfer, Narrow, Phillips, and Fawcett (2009) had developed guidelines for revisions that were quite conservative and demanding. Any change to the diagnostic manual had to be accompanied by "a discussion of possible unintended negative effects of this proposed change, if it is made, and a consideration of arguments against making this change" (p. 2). Kendler et al. further stated that "the larger and more significant the change, the stronger should be the required level of [empirical] support" (p. 2).

Many of the *DSM-5* literature reviews did appear to meet the spirit of Kendler et al. (2009), but others did not (First, 2014; Frances & Widiger, 2012; Widiger & Crego, 2015). Quite a few concerns (e.g., Livesley, 2010; Widiger, 2011b; Zimmerman, 2011) were raised with respect to the initial personality disorder literature reviews and continued to be raised (e.g., Blashfield & Reynolds, 2012; Miller & Lynam, 2013; Widiger, 2013) with respect to the final literature review.

For example, Blashfield and Reynolds (2012) systematically reviewed the reference list provided in the final PPDWG review and concluded that it was slanted heavily toward papers and studies published by work group members and/or their close colleagues. They noted only one reference to FFM research despite it being the "dominant dimensional approach in the personality literature" (p. 826). They indicated as well that "Cleckley and Hare are well-known authors who defined how psychopathy is currently conceptualized; neither was referenced in the *DSM-5* rationale" (Blashfield & Reynolds, 2012, p. 826).

Skodol et al. (2013) acknowledged an awareness of the Kendler et al. (2009) guidelines, but they suggested that the PPDWG did not expect that they would actually have to adhere to them. "The problems with the existing 10-category system for diagnosing personality disorders seemed so severe, and the advantages of a hybrid system as gauged against . . . traditional validity markers . . . so substantial, that a reduced threshold for change seemed warranted" (Skodol et al., 2013, p. 345). Apparently, in the end, this did not turn out to be the case.

The final literature review by the PPDWG was submitted to the *DSM-5* Task Force, who approved the proposals. The review was then forwarded to the CPHC and the SRC. Regrettably, the CPHC and SRC reviews of the proposals have not been made publicly available. As indicated by Skodol et al. (2013), "the review by the CPHC primarily raised concerns about the decision . . . not to specify four of the DSM-IV personality disorders" (p. 348), as presumably they were still of interest to clinicians. The CPHC also felt that the new method proposed for diagnosing the personality disorders was "too complicated and unfamiliar for immediate use by psychiatrists" (Skodol et al., 2013, p. 348). Skodol et al. (2013) also summarized the conclusions of the SRC: "Predictive validators and familial aggregation were given special weight. Because such data had not been gathered on the specific model proposed by the [work group] . . . the proposal was viewed as not strongly supported by the published research at the time" (p. 347). In sum, the CPHC and SRC recommended to the APA Board of Trustees to reject all of the proposals. The Board of Trustees agreed with the SRC and CPHC.

Krueger (2013) suggests that the rejection of the PPDWG's proposals was the result of "political processes" (p. 355). There was likely a considerable amount of backchannel communication against the proposals that might have indeed been very influential. However, it does appear to be the case that the opinion of the SRC (Kendler, 2013) was that the PPDWG proposals lacked adequate empirical support (First, 2014; Skodol et al., 2013), consistent with the review by Blashfield and Reynolds (2012). It should also be noted that there was considerable amount of compelling objection within the field to virtually every proposal (i.e., Bornstein, 2011; Clarkin & Huprich, 2011; Gunderson, 2010a, 2010b; Miller et al., 2010; Paris, 2011; Pilkonis et al., 2011; Pincus, 2011; Ronningstam, 2011; Shedler et al., 2010; Widiger, 2011a, 2011b; Zimmerman, 2011, 2012). Two work group members even resigned in frustration over the process and content of the PPDWG proposals (Livesley, 2012; Verheul, 2012).

In the end, all of the *DSM-IV-TR* personality disorders were retained, along with their *DSM-IV* criterion sets. Regrettably, none of these criterion sets, now more than 20 years old, were revised to improve their validity. It would have been helpful, for instance, if the PPDWG had made some improvement to the criterion sets that are still being used in clinical practice and research. For example, a potential innovation of *DSM-IV* was that most of the diagnostic criteria were presented in a descending order of diagnostic value based on the existing research (Gunderson, 1998). Clinicians often fail to systematically consider all of the diagnostic criteria, given the limited amount of time available to them. If they are not going to consider all of the criteria, then it would be useful if they were told which criteria are most diagnostic (Mullins-Sweatt & Widiger, 2009). The existence of this information, however, was never noted within *DSM-IV* in part because there was insufficient research concerning the new diagnostic criteria (all of whom were therefore placed at the bottom of the list). By the time work began on *DSM-5*, however, a substantial body of research was now readily available to provide a meaningful rank order for all of the diagnostic criteria, thereby facilitating the obtainment of more reliable and valid clinical assessments.

The PPDWG proposals were placed in a section of *DSM-5* for "emerging measures and models" (APA, 2013, p. 729). A special section of *Personality Disorders: Theory, Research, and Treatment* was devoted to a postmortem review of what went wrong and what should perhaps happen next (i.e., Gunderson, 2013; Krueger, 2013; Skodol et al., 2013; Widiger, 2013).

FUTURE EDITIONS

The proposals for *DSM-5* were placed in Section III of *DSM-5* to stimulate research and perhaps set the stage for the next edition. As expressed in *DSM-5*, dimensional approaches will "supersede current categorical approaches in coming years" (p. 13). However, what is in store in the future for the *DSM* personality disorders is not really clear.

DSM-5 shifted from a Roman numeric (e.g., *DSM-IV*) to Arabic (i.e., *DSM-5*) in part because it is anticipated that future revisions will occur more frequently and will at times be confined to one or more particular sections of the manual (First, 2014). However, the timetable was not specified, nor is it even clear that there will be a personality disorders work group. Proposals for revision by individuals (or collections of individuals) could instead be proactively submitted to a standing committee who might in fact make decisions without obtaining critical review, or even alerting the wider scientific community (First, 2015). A few issues that should perhaps be considered will be suggested herein.

Dimensional Trait Model

The dimensional trait model component of the hybrid model is receiving a considerable amount of research attention. Krueger and Markon (2014) summarized the results of 25 studies, and many more have since been published. Two issues worth noting in particular about this particular model are its coverage and unipolar structure.

COVERAGE
The dimensional trait model was not initially constructed with the expectation that its traits would become part of the diagnostic criterion sets. If that had been the case, perhaps the list would have been more inclusive. In the final posting on the *DSM-5* website, there were only two traits listed for the obsessive-compulsive and narcissistic personality disorders (two more from the proposed model were subsequently assigned for obsessive-compulsive), and only three for dependent, leading some to question the adequacy of coverage (e.g., Bornstein, 2011; Ronningstam, 2011). In the final posting, the traits for antisocial covered well the *DSM-IV-TR* criterion set but did not include any representation of the more heavily researched construct of psychopathy (Lynam & Vachon, 2012). Three additional traits were subsequently assigned to provide a psychopathy specifier (APA, 2013). However, low anxiousness, low social withdrawal, and high attention seeking may be, at best, weak proxy measures for the constructs of fearless-dominance and boldness that they purportedly represent (Crego & Widiger, 2014). In sum, an important

area for future research will be whether the list of 25 traits should be expanded to provide additional coverage.

BIPOLARITY

A predominant view of the FFM of personality disorder is that there are maladaptive variants of all 10 poles of all five domains (Samuel, 2012; Widiger, 2011a). For example, with respect to the domain of agreeableness versus antagonism, there are maladaptive variants of agreeableness (e.g., gullibility, meekness, subservience, selflessness, and self-denigration) as well as maladaptive variants of antagonism (e.g., arrogance, greed, exploitativeness, aggression, and callousness). The *DSM-5* dimensional trait model, in contrast, is largely unipolar (Krueger et al., 2012). Opposite to the domains of negative affectivity, detachment, psychoticism, antagonism, and disinhibition is normal personality; more specifically, emotional stability, extraversion, lucidity, agreeableness, and conscientiousness, respectively (APA, 2013). There are two exceptions. The dimensional trait model includes rigid perfectionism (opposite to disinhibition) and restricted affectivity (considered in *DSM-5* to be opposite to negative affectivity, although coded primarily within detachment). Krueger et al. (2011, 2012) suggested that there is limited empirical support for the bipolarity, yet it is evident in a large body of factor analytic studies by members of the PPDWG (Widiger, 2011a) and it was apparent in most every study posted on the *DSM-5* website that provided a structural model of personality disorder (e.g., Markon et al., 2005; O'Connor, 2005; Saulsman & Page, 2004; Watson et al., 2008; Widiger & Simonsen, 2005). Even those who oppose the presence of maladaptive variants of both poles include a significant representation of this bipolar maladaptivity within their own dimensional traits models (e.g., Simms et al., 2011).

The inclusion of the bipolarity though would have increased the complexity of the proposal, which was already meeting with substantial opposition (e.g., Gunderson, 2010a; Shedler et al., 2010). Nevertheless, the absence of the bipolarity is problematic (Samuel, 2012). For example, because the model does not include maladaptively low neuroticism, it is less able to include psychopathic fearlessness and glib charm (Lynam & Widiger, 2007), relying instead on reverse-keying anxiousness and social withdrawal (Crego & Widiger, 2014). Because there is no maladaptive high agreeableness, there is no ability to recognize the self-denigration, meekness, gullibility, and self-sacrifice of the dependent (Gore & Pincus, 2013; Lowe, Edmundson, & Widiger, 2009). Because the model does not include maladaptive conscientiousness, there is only limited coverage of the compulsivity traits integral to obsessive-compulsive personality disorder (Crego, Samuel, & Widiger, 2015).

Research Domain Criteria

As the construction of *DSM-5* was drawing to a close, NIMH announced that it no longer wished to fund studies that used the APA nomenclature. "It is critical to realize that we cannot succeed if we use DSM categories" (Insel, 2013, para. 4). NIMH has become frustrated with the rate at which researchers have been able to identify specific etiologies, pathologies, and treatments and blames much of this on a diagnostic system that relies on overt features rather than assessing for an underlying pathology.

However, a difficulty with an emphasis on underlying pathology is that there are alternative theoretical models for the pathology of mental disorders: neurobiological, cognitive, interpersonal, and psychodynamic (Berenbaum, 2013). NIMH appears to have embraced one particular theoretical model: the neurobiological. "Mental disorders are biological disorders involving brain circuits that implicate specific domains of cognition, emotion, or behavior" (Insel, 2013, para. 3). This is in contrast to the *DSM-5* hybrid model proposal, wherein the self and interpersonal deficits are aligned with a psychodynamic perspective (Bender et al., 2011; Kernberg, 2012; Pincus, 2011).

NIMH is likely to give preference to its own neurobiologically oriented nomenclature, the Research Domain Criteria (RDoC), consisting of five broad domains: negative valence, positive valence, cognitive, social processes, and arousal/modulatory systems (Insel, 2013). These five domains parallel to some extent the five domains of the FFM and *DSM-5* dimensional trait models (Widiger, 2012a).

Negative valence (anxiety, fear, threat) aligns well with FFM neuroticism (or *DSM-5* negative affectivity). Positive valence (reward, approach) aligns well with FFM extraversion (or *DSM-5* low detachment), as positive affectivity is the driving temperament for extraversion (Clark & Watson, 2008). Social processes align with FFM antagonism and introversion because these are the two fundamental domains of all manner of interpersonal relatedness. The RDoC domain of cognitive systems would include the psychoticism of *DSM-5*, which aligns with FFM openness (otherwise known as intellect). RDoC arousal regulatory systems align with FFM conscientiousness (or constraint; *DSM-5* low disinhibition), because this domain concerns regulatory constraint (Clark & Watson, 2008).

The alignment of RDoC with the FFM and *DSM-5* dimensional trait models is perhaps a stretch in some cases. However, the dimensional trait models do at least appear to be more commensurate with the NIMH RDoC than the *DSM-5* Section II (i.e., *DSM-IV-TR*) or *DSM-5* hybrid model diagnostic categories (Skodol, 2014, however, suggests that the self and interpersonal deficits are aligned with RDoC social processes).

ICD-11

As the *DSM-5* PPDWG struggled with dissension, controversy, and pushback, the *ICD-11* personality disorders work group has progressed without a comparable level of attention or apparent controversy, yet the proposal for *ICD-11* has been comparably radical (Tyrer et al., 2011). The official proposal for *ICD-11* is to delete all of the categories, including the borderline and antisocial, and replace them with a global rating of level of severity and a five-domain dimensional trait model, albeit in the end a borderline pattern qualifier was added.

The severity rating concerns four levels: personality difficulty, personality disorder, complex personality disorder, and severe personality disorder (Tyrer et al., 2011). The proposed severity rating aligns conceptually with *DSM-5* level of personality functioning, but it is considerably less complex and does not include inferences with respect to deficits in the sense of self (these deficits were added in the final version but they only constitute a minor component of the severity rating).

The *ICD-11* dimensional trait model has varied. One version consisted of four domains: internalization, externalization, schizoid, and compulsivity (Mulder, Newton-Howes, Crawford, & Tyrer, 2011). A subsequent version consisted of five domains: emotionally unstable, anxious/dependent, asocial/schizoid, dissocial, and obsessional/anankastic (Tyrer et al., 2011). The latest version (to date) consists of a revised set of five domains: negative emotionality, schizoid/detached, dissocial/externalizing, obsessional/anankastic, and disinhibition that resulted from "negotiations" (Tyrer et al., 2014) and is more closely aligned with the *DSM-5* trait model, albeit does not include psychoticism (the WHO [1992] considers schizotypal to be a form of schizophrenia rather than a personality disorder), and has disinhibition and obsessional/anakastic as independent domains, consistent with the original Clark and Krueger (2010) proposal. Given the rejection in the final hour of the *DSM-5* proposal, it would not be terribly surprising for the *ICD-11* proposal to meet a similar fate, although may indeed meet with final approval. If approved, this would put considerable pressure on the APA to make a comparable shift toward a dimensional trait model.

CONCLUSIONS

The construction of a diagnostic manual is a difficult task, in large part because it represents simply the opinions of its authors (Frances & Widiger, 2012). There is no gold standard for what constitutes a mental disorder (Widiger & Crego, 2015). This task is further complicated when there are strongly felt differences of opinion within the field. It has been suggested that there is consensus within the field of personality disorder (Skodol, 2014), but there may in fact be sharply divided factions (Widiger, 2013). The authors of the next edition of the diagnostic manual may face a formidable task in navigating the many disputes.

REFERENCES

American Psychiatric Association. (1952). *Diagnostic and statistical manual. Mental Disorders*. Washington, DC: Author.
American Psychiatric Association. (1968). *Diagnostic and statistical manual of mental disorders* (2nd ed.). Washington, DC: Author.

American Psychiatric Association. (1980). *Diagnostic and statistical manual of mental disorders* (3rd ed.). Washington, DC: Author.

American Psychiatric Association. (1987). *Diagnostic and statistical manual of mental disorders* (3rd ed., rev. ed.). Washington, DC: Author.

American Psychiatric Association. (1994). *Diagnostic and statistical manual of mental disorders* (4th ed.). Washington, DC: Author.

American Psychiatric Association. (2000). *Diagnostic and statistical manual of mental disorders. Text revision* (4th ed., rev. ed.). Washington, DC: Author.

American Psychiatric Association. (2010, February 10). *Personality disorders*. Retrieved from http://www.dsm5.org/ProposedRevisions/Pages/PersonalityandPersonalityDiso rders.aspx.

American Psychiatric Association. (2013). *Diagnostic and statistical manual of mental disorders* (5th ed.). Washington, DC: Author.

Bagby, R. M., Watson, C., & Ryder, A G. (2012). Depressive personality disorder. In T. A. Widiger (Ed.), The *Oxford handbook of personality disorders* (pp. 628–647). New York, NY: Oxford University Press.

Bender, D. S., Morey, L. C., & Skodol, A. E. (2011). Toward a model for assessing level of personality functioning in *DSM-5*, Part I: A review of theory and methods. *Journal of Personality Assessment, 93*, 332–346.

Berenbaum, N. (2013). Classification and psychopathology research. *Journal of Abnormal Psychology, 122*, 894–901.

Blashfield, R. K., & Intoccia, V. (2000). Growth of the literature on the topic of personality disorders. *American Journal of Psychiatry, 157*, 472–473.

Blashfield, R. K., & Reynolds, S. M. (2012). An invisible college view of the *DSM-5* personality disorder classification. *Journal of Personality Disorders, 26*, 821–829.

Blashfield, R. K., Reynolds, S. M., & Stennett, B. (2012). The death of histrionic personality disorder. In T. A. Widiger (Ed.), *The Oxford handbook of personality disorders* (pp. 603–627). New York, NY: Oxford University Press.

Bornstein, R. F. (2011). Reconceptualizing personality pathology in *DSM-5*: Limitations in evidence for eliminating dependent personality disorder and other DSM-IV syndromes. *Journal of Personality Disorders, 25*, 235–247.

Bornstein, R. F. (2012). Illuminating a neglected clinical issue: Societal costs of interpersonal dependency and dependent personality disorder. *Journal of Clinical Psychology, 68*, 766–781.

Campbell, W. K., & Miller, J. D. (Eds.). (2011). *Handbook of narcissism and narcissistic personality disorder: Theoretical approaches, empirical findings, and treatments.* New York, NY: Wiley.

Clark, L. A. (2007). Assessment and diagnosis of personality disorder: Perennial issues and an emerging reconceptualization. *Annual Review of Psychology, 57*, 227–257.

Clark, L. A., & Krueger, R. F. (2010, February 10). *Rationale for a six–domain trait dimensional diagnostic system for personality disorder*. Retrieved from http://www. dsm5.org/ProposedRevisions/Pages/RationaleforaSix-DomainTraitDimensional DiagnosticSystemforPersonalityDisorder.aspx.

Clark, L. A., Simms, L. J., Wu, K. D., & Casillas, A. (in press). *Manual for the Schedule for Nonadaptive and Adaptive Personality (SNAP-2)*. Minneapolis: University of Minnesota Press.

Clark, L. A., & Watson, D. (2008). Temperament: An organizing paradigm for trait psychology. In O. P. John, R. W. Robins, & L. A. Pervin (Eds.), *Handbook of personality: Theory and research* (3rd ed., pp. 265–286). New York, NY: Guilford.

Clarkin, J. F., & Huprich, S. K. (2011). Do *DSM-5* personality disorder proposals meet criteria for clinical utility? *Journal of Personality Disorders, 25*, 192–205.

Crego, C., Samuel, D., & Widiger, T. A. (2015). The FFOCI and other measures and models of OCPD. *Assessment, 22*, 135–151.

Crego, C., & Widiger, T. A. (2014). Psychopathy, *DSM-5*, and a caution. *Personality Disorders: Theory, Research, and Treatment, 5*, 335–347.

Crego, C., & Widiger, T. A. (2015). Psychopathy and the DSM. *Journal of Personality, 83*, 665–677.

Feighner, J. P., Robins, E., Guze, S. B., Woodruff, R. A., Winokur, G., & Munoz, R. (1972). Diagnostic criteria for use in psychiatric research. *Archives of General Psychiatry, 26*, 57–63.

First, M. B. (2014). Empirical grounding versus innovation in the *DSM-5* revision process: Implications for the future. *Clinical Psychology: Science and Practice, 21*, 262–268.

First, M. B. (2015, May 24). *DSM-5*.x: The plan for interim revisions of the DSM. In D. Samuel (Chair), *The future of diagnosis: Substance and form*. Symposium conducted at the Annual Meeting of the Association for Psychological Science, New York, NY.

First, M. B., Bell, C. B., Cuthbert, B., Krystal, J. H., Malison, R., Offord, D. R., . . . Wisner, K. L. (2002). Personality disorders and relational disorders: A research agenda for addressing crucial gaps in DSM. In D. J. Kupfer, M. B. First, & D. A. Regier (Eds.), *A research agenda for DSM-V* (pp. 123–199). Washington, DC: American Psychiatric Association.

First, M. B., & Pincus, H. A. (2002). The DSM-IV text revision: Rationale and potential impact on clinical practice. *Psychiatric Services, 53*, 288–292.

First, M. B., & Westen, D. (2007). Classification for clinical practice: How to make ICD and DSM better able to serve clinicians. *International Review of Psychiatry, 19*, 473–481.

Frances, A. J. (1980). The DSM-III personality disorders section: A commentary. *American Journal of Psychiatry, 137*, 1050–1054.

Frances, A. J., & Widiger, T. A. (2012). Psychiatric diagnosis: Lessons from the DSM-IV past and cautions for the *DSM-5* future. *Annual Review of Clinical Psychology, 8*, 109–130.

Frances, A. J., Widiger, T. A., & Pincus, H. A. (1989). The development of DSM-IV. *Archives of General Psychiatry, 46*, 373–375.

Gore, W. L., & Pincus, A. L. (2013). Dependency and the five–factor model. In T. A. Widiger & P. T. Costa (Eds.), *Personality disorders and the five–factor model* (3rd ed., pp. 163–177). Washington, DC: American Psychological Association.

Greenberg, G. (2013). *The book of woe: The DSM and the unmaking of psychiatry*. New York, NY: Blue Rider Press.

Gunderson, J. (1983). DSM-III diagnosis of personality disorders, in Frosch J (ed): Current Perspectives on Personality Disorders. Washington, DC, American Psychiatric Press, 1983, pp. 20–39.

Gunderson, J. G. (1998). DSM-IV personality disorders: Final overview. In T. A. Widiger, A. J. Frances, H. A. Pincus, R. Ross, M. B. First, W. Davis, & M. Kline (Eds.), *DSM-IV sourcebook* (Vol. 4, pp. 1123–1140). Washington, DC: American Psychiatric Association.

Gunderson, J. G. (2010a). Commentary on "Personality traits and the classification of mental disorders: Toward a more complete integration in *DSM-5* and an empirical model of psychopathology." *Personality Disorders: Theory, Research, and Treatment, 1*, 119–122.

Gunderson, J. G. (2010b). Revising the borderline diagnosis for DSM-V: An alternative proposal. *Journal of Personality Disorders, 24*, 694–708.

Gunderson, J. G. (2013). Seeking clarity for future revisions of the personality disorders in *DSM-5*. *Personality Disorders: Theory, Research, and Treatment, 4*, 368–378.

Hare, R. D., & Neumann, C. S. (2008). Psychopathy as a clinical and empirical construct. *Annual Review of Clinical Psychology, 4*, 217–246.

Hopwood, C. J., & Thomas, K. M. (2012). Paranoid and schizoid personality disorders. In T. A. Widiger (Ed.), *The Oxford handbook of personality disorders* (pp. 582–602). New York, NY: Oxford University Press.

Huprich, S. K., Bornstein, R. F., & Schmitt, T. A. (2011). Self–report methodology is insufficient for improving the assessment and classification of Axis II personality disorders. *Journal of Personality Disorders, 23*, 557–570.

Hyman, S. E. (2010). The diagnosis of mental disorders: The problem of reification. *Annual Review of Clinical Psychology, 6*, 155–179.

Insel, T. R. (2013). *Director's blog: Transforming diagnosis*. Retrieved from http://www.nimh.nih.gov/about/director/2013/transforming-diagnosis.shtml

Insel, T. R., & Quirion, R. (2005). Psychiatry as a clinical neuroscience discipline. *Journal of the American Medical Association, 294*, 2221–2224.

Kendell, R. E. (1975). *The role of diagnosis in psychiatry*. London, UK: Blackwell Scientific Publications.

Kendler, K. S. (2013). A history of the *DSM-5* scientific review committee. *Psychological Medicine, 43*, 1793–1800.

Kendler, K. S., Kupfer, D., Narrow, W., Phillips, K., & Fawcett, J. (2009). *Guidelines for making changes to DSM-V*. Unpublished manuscript. Washington, DC: American Psychiatric Association.

Kendler, K., Munoz, R. A., & Murphy, G. (2010). The development of the Feighner criteria: A historical perspective. *American Journal of Psychiatry, 167*, 134–142.

Kernberg, O. F. (1984). Problems in the classification of personality disorders. In *Severe personality disorders* (pp. 77–94). New Haven, CT: Yale University Press.

Kernberg, O. F. (2012). Overview and critique of the classification of personality disorders proposed for DSM-V. *Swiss Archives of Neurology and Psychiatry, 163*, 234–238.

Krueger, R. F. (2013). Personality disorders are the vanguard of the post–*DSM-5.0* era. *Personality Disorders: Theory, Research, and Treatment, 4*, 355–362.

Krueger, R. F., Derringer, J., Markon, K. F., Watson, D., & Skodol, A. E. (2012). Initial construction of a maladaptive personality trait model and inventory for *DSM-5*. *Psychological Medicine, 42*, 1879–1890.

Krueger, R. F., Eaton, N. R., Clark, L. A., Watson, D., Markon, K. E., Derringer, J., Skodol, A., & Livesley, W. J. (2011). Deriving an empirical structure of personality pathology for *DSM-5*. *Journal of Personality Disorders, 25*, 170–191.

Krueger, R. F., & Markon, K. E. (2014). The role of the *DSM-5* personality trait model in moving toward a quantitative and empirically based approach to classifying personality and psychopathology. *Annual Review of Clinical Psychology, 10*, 477–501.

Krueger, R. F., Skodol, A. E., Livesley, W. J., Shrout, P. E., & Huang, Y. (2008). Synthesizing dimensional and categorical approaches to personality disorders: Refining the research agenda for DSM-V Axis II. In J. E. Helzer, H. C. Kraemer, R. F. Krueger, H–U. Wittchen, P. J. Sirovatka, & D. A. Regier (Eds.), *Dimensional approaches to diagnostic classification. Refining the research agenda for DSM-V* (pp. 85–100). Washington, DC: American Psychiatric Association.

Kupfer, D. J., First, M. B., & Regier, D. A. (2002). Introduction. In D. J. Kupfer, M. B. First, & D. A. Regier (Eds.), *A research agenda for DSM-V* (pp. xv–xxiii). Washington, DC: American Psychiatric Association.

Livesley, W. J. (2010). Confusion and incoherence in the classification of personality disorder: Commentary on the preliminary proposals for *DSM-5*. *Psychological Injury and Law, 3*, 304–313.

Livesley, W. J. (2012). Tradition versus empiricism in the current *DSM-5* proposal for revising the classification of personality disorders. *Criminal Behavior and Mental Health, 22*, 81–90.

Livesley, W. J. (2013). The *DSM-5* personality disorder proposal and future directions in the diagnostic classification of personality disorder. *Psychopathology, 46*, 207–216.

Livesley, W. J., & Jackson, D. (2009). *Manual for the Dimensional Assessment of Personality Pathology—Basic Questionnaire*. Port Huron, MI: Sigma Press.

Loranger, A. W. (1990). The impact of DSM-III on diagnostic practice in a university hospital. *Archives of General Psychiatry, 47*, 672–675.

Lowe, J. R., Edmundson, M., & Widiger, T. A. (2009). Assessment of dependency, agreeableness, and their relationship. *Psychological Assessment, 21*, 543–55

Lynam, D. R., & Vachon, D. D. (2012). Antisocial personality disorder in *DSM-5*: Missteps and missed opportunities. *Personality Disorders: Theory, Research, and Treatment, 3*, 483–495.

Lynam, D. R., & Widiger, T. A. (2007). Using a general model of personality to identify the basic elements of psychopathy. *Journal of Personality Disorders, 21*, 160–178.

Markon, K. E., Krueger, R. F., & Watson, D. (2005). Delineating the structure of normal and abnormal personality: An integrative hierarchical approach. *Journal of Personality and Social Psychology, 88*, 139–157.

Miller, J. D., & Lynam, D. R. (2013). Missed opportunities in the *DSM-5* Section III personality disorder model. *Personality Disorders: Theory, Research, and Treatment, 4*, 365–366.

Miller, J. D., Widiger, T. A., & Campbell, W. K. (2010). Narcissistic personality disorder and the DSM-V. *Journal of Abnormal Psychology, 119*, 640–649.

Millon, T. (1981). *Disorders of personality. DSM-III: Axis II*. New York, NY: Wiley.

Millon, T. (2011). *Disorders of personality. Introducing a DSM/ICD spectrum from normal to abnormal* (3rd ed.). New York, NY: John Wiley & Sons.

Mulder, R. T., Newton-Howes, G., Crawford, M. J., & Tyrer, P. J. (2011). The central domains of personality pathology in psychiatric patients. *Journal of Personality Disorders, 25*, 364–377.

Mullins-Sweatt, S. N., Bernstein, D. P., & Widiger, T. A. (2012). Retention or deletion of personality disorder diagnoses for *DSM-5*: An expert consensus approach. *Journal of Personality Disorders, 26*, 689–703.

Mullins-Sweatt, S. N., & Widiger, T. A. (2009). Clinical utility and DSM-V. *Psychological Assessment, 21*, 302–312.

O'Connor, B. P. (2005). A search for consensus on the dimensional structure of personality disorders. *Journal of Clinical Psychology, 61*, 323–345.

Paris, J. (2011). Endophenotypes and the diagnosis of personality disorders. *Journal of Personality Disorder, 25*, 260–268.

Pilkonis, P., Hallquist, M. N., Morse, J. Q., & Stepp, S. D. (2011). Striking the (im) proper balance between scientific advances and clinical utility: Commentary on the

DSM-5 proposal for personality disorders. *Personality Disorders: Theory, Research, and Treatment, 2,* 68–82.

Pincus, A. L. (2011). Some comments on nomology, diagnostic process, and narcissistic personality disorder in the *DSM-5* proposal for personality and personality disorders. *Personality Disorders: Theory, Research, and Treatment, 2,* 41–53.

Pincus, A. L., & Hopwood, C. J. (2012). A contemporary interpersonal model of personality pathology and personality disorder. In T. A. Widiger (Ed.), *The Oxford handbook of personality disorders* (pp. 372–388). New York, NY: Oxford University Press.

Regier, D. A., Narrow, W. E., Kuhl, E. A., & Kupfer, D. J. (2009). The conceptual development of DSM-V. *American Journal of Psychiatry, 166,* 645–655.

Robins, L. N. (1966). *Deviant children grown up.* Baltimore, MD: Williams & Wilkins.

Ronningstam, E. (2011). Narcissistic personality disorder in DSM-V. In support of retaining a significant diagnosis. *Journal of Personality Disorders, 25,* 248–259.

Rosenhan, D. L. (1973). On being sane in insane places. *Science, 179,* 250–258.

Rounsaville, B. J., Alarcon, R. D., Andrews, G., Jackson, J. S., Kendell, R. E., Kendler, K. S., & Kirmayer, L. J. (2002). Toward DSM-V: Basic nomenclature issues. In D. J. Kupfer, M. B. First, & D. A. Regier (Eds.), *A research agenda for DSM-V* (pp. 1–30). Washington, DC: American Psychiatric Press.

Samuel, D. B. (2012). Assessing personality in the *DSM-5*: The utility of bipolar constructs. *Journal of Personality Assessment, 93,* 390–397.

Saulsman, L. M., & Page, A. C. (2004). The five-factor model and personality disorder empirical literature: A meta–analytic review. *Clinical Psychology Review, 23,* 1055–1085.

Shedler, J., Beck, A., Fonagy, P., Gabbard, G. O., Gunderson, J .G., Kernberg, O., Michels, R., & Westen, D. (2010). Personality disorders in *DSM-5. American Journal of Psychiatry, 167,* 1027–1028.

Simms, L. J., Goldberg, L. R., Roberts, J. E., Watson, D., Welte, J., & Rotterman, J. H. (2011). Computerized adaptive assessment of personality disorder: Introducing the CAT-PD project. *Journal of Personality Assessment, 93,* 380–389.

Skodol, A. (2010, February 10). *Rationale for proposing five specific personality types.* Retrieved from http://www.dsm5.org/ProposedRevisions/Pages/RationaleforProposi ngFiveSpecificPersonalityDisorderTypes.aspx

Skodol, A. (2012). Diagnosis and *DSM-5*: Work in progress. In T. A. Widiger (Ed.), *The Oxford handbook of personality disorders* (pp. 35–57). New York, NY: Oxford University Press.

Skodol, A. (2014). Personality disorder classification: Stuck in neutral, how to move forward? *Current Psychiatry Reports, 16,* 480–490.

Skodol, A. E., Bender, D. S., Morey, L. C., Clark, L. A., Oldham, J. M., Alarcon, R. D., . . . Siever, L. J. (2011). Personality disorder types proposed for *DSM-5. Journal of Personality Disorders, 25,* 136–169.

Skodol, A. E., Gunderson, J. G., Shea, M. T., McGlashan, T. H., Morey, L. C., Sanislow, C. A., . . . Stout, R. L. (2005). The Collaborative Longitudinal Personality Disorders Study (CLPS): Overview and implications. *Journal of Personality Disorders, 19,* 487–504.

Skodol, A. E., Morey, L. C., Bender, D. S., & Oldham, J. M. (2013). The ironic fate of the personality disorders in *DSM-5. Personality Disorders: Theory, Research, & Treatment, 4,* 342–349.

Spitzer, R. L., Sheehy, M., & Endicott, J. (1977). DSM-III: Guiding principles. In V. Rakoff, H. Stancer, & H. Kedward (Eds.), *Psychiatric diagnosis* (pp. 1–24). New York, NY: Brunner/Mazel.

Spitzer, R. L., Williams, J. B. W., & Skodol, A. E. (1980). DSM-III: The major achievements and an overview. *American Journal of Psychiatry, 137,* 151–164.

Spitzer, R. L., & Wilson, P. T. (1968). A guide to the American Psychiatric Association's new diagnostic nomenclature. *American Journal of Psychiatry, 124,* 1619–1629.

Trull, T. J., & Durrett, C. A. (2005). Categorical and dimensional models of personality disorder. *Annual Review of Clinical Psychology, 1,* 355–380.

Tyrer, P., Crawford, M., Mulder, R., Blashfield, R., Farnam, A., Fossati, A., . . . Reed, G. M. (2011). The rationale for the reclassification of personality disorder in the 11th revision of the international classification of diseases (ICD-11). *Personality and Mental Health, 5,* 246–259.

Tyrer, P., Crawford, M., Sanatinia, R., Tyrer, H., Cooper, S., Muller-Pollard, C., . . . Weich, S. (2014). Preliminary studies of the ICD-11 classification of personality disorder in practice. *Personality and Mental Health, 8,* 254–263.

Verheul, R. (2012). Personality disorder proposal for DSM-5: A heroic and innovative but nevertheless fundamentally flawed attempt to improve DSM-IV. *Clinical Psychology and Psychotherapy, 19,* 369–371.

Verheul, R., & Widiger, T. A. (2004). A meta-analysis of the prevalence and usage of the personality disorder not otherwise specified (PDNOS) diagnosis. *Journal of Personality Disorders, 18,* 309–319.

Watson, D., Clark, L. A., & Chmielewski, M. (2008). Structures of personality and their relevant to psychopathology: II. Further articulation of a comprehensive unified trait structure. *Journal of Personality, 76,* 1485–1522.

Westen, D., Shedler, J., & Bradley, R. (2006). A prototype approach to personality disorder diagnosis. *American Journal of Psychiatry, 163,* 846–856.

Wetzler, S., & Jose, A. (2012). Passive–aggressive personality disorder: The demise of a syndrome. In T. A. Widiger (Ed.), The *Oxford handbook of personality disorders* (pp. 674–693). New York, NY: Oxford University Press.

Widiger, T. A. (2010). Personality, interpersonal circumplex, and *DSM-5*: A commentary on five studies. *Journal of Personality Assessment, 92,* 528–532.

Widiger, T. A. (2011a). The *DSM-5* dimensional model of personality disorder: Rationale and empirical support. *Journal of Personality Disorders, 25,* 222–234.

Widiger, T. A. (2011b). A shaky future for personality disorders. *Personality Disorders: Theory, Research, and Treatment, 2,* 54–67.

Widiger, T. A. (2012a). Future directions of personality disorder. In T. A. Widiger (Ed.), *The Oxford handbook of personality disorders* (pp. 797–810). New York, NY: Oxford University Press.

Widiger, T. A. (2012b). Historical developments and current issues. In T. A. Widiger (Ed.), *The Oxford handbook of personality disorders* (pp. 13–34). New York, NY: Oxford University Press.

Widiger, T. A. (2013). A postmortem and future look at the personality disorders in *DSM-5. Personality Disorders: Theory, Research, and Treatment, 4,* 382–387.

Widiger, T. A., & Crego, C. (2015). Process and content of *DSM-5. Psychopathology Review, 2,* 162–176.

Widiger, T. A., Frances, A. J., Pincus, H., Davis, W., & First, M. (1991). Toward an empirical classification for DSM-IV. *Journal of Abnormal Psychology, 100,* 280–288.

Widiger, T. A., Frances, A. J., Spitzer, R. L., & Williams, J. B. W. (1988). The DSM-III–R personality disorders: An overview. *American Journal of Psychiatry, 145,* 786–795.

Widiger, T. A., & Oltmanns, J. R. (2017). Alternative *DSM-5* model for personality disorders. In A. Wenzel (Ed.), *The SAGE encyclopedia of abnormal and clinical psychology* (pp. 139–142). Thousand Oaks, CA: Sage.

Widiger, T. A., & Sanderson, C. J. (1995). Towards a dimensional model of personality disorders in DSM-IV and DSM-V. In W. J. Livesley (Ed.), *The DSM-IV personality disorders* (pp. 433–458). New York, NY: Guilford.

Widiger, T. A., & Simonsen, E. (2005). Alternative dimensional models of personality disorder: Finding a common ground. *Journal of Personality Disorders, 19,* 110–130.

Widiger, T. A., Simonsen, E., Krueger, R., Livesley, W. J., & Verheul, R. (2005). Personality disorder research agenda for the DSM-V. *Journal of Personality Disorders, 19,* 315–338.

Widiger, T. A., & Trull, T. J. (2007). Plate tectonics in the classification of personality disorder: Shifting to a dimensional model. *American Psychologist, 62,* 71–83.

Zigler, E., & Phillips, L. (1961). Psychiatric diagnosis: A critique. *Journal of Abnormal and Social Psychology, 63,* 607–618.

Zimmerman, M. (2011). A critique of the proposed prototype rating system for personality disorders in *DSM-5*. *Journal of Personality Disorders, 25,* 206–221.

Zimmerman, M. (2012). Is there adequate empirical justification for radically revising the personality disorders section for *DSM-5*? *Personality Disorders: Theory, Research, and Treatment, 3,* 444–457.

2

The Current State of Personality Disorders Through the Lens of *PDTRT*

CARL W. LEJUEZ, ALEXIS MATUSIEWICZ, NADIA BOUNOUA,
AND JAMES SOLDINGER ■

The notion of personality—an individual's unique, enduring, and predictable patterns of thinking, feeling, and behaving that are relatively invariant across contexts—is an ancient one, first formalized by Hippocrates in the first century BCE. The term "personality disorder" refers to the maladaptive extremes of personality: patterns of relating to oneself and others that are pervasive and inflexible so as to cause extreme distress and disruption in role functioning (Dumont, 2010). Historically, personality disorders were distinguished from other clinical disorders by their persistence (vs. episodicity), resistance to treatment, ego syntonicity (i.e., symptoms are experienced as acceptable or even pleasurable), and environmental (vs. biological) origins. However, this perspective has been refuted by empirical work (New, Triebwasser, & Charney, 2008), and personality disorders have now come to be viewed by many similar in nature to other forms of psychopathology (Livesley, 2003; Widiger, 2003). In the United States, approximately 9% of adults meet diagnostic criteria for a personality disorder at some point in their lives and those with a diagnosis experience greater psychiatric severity, functional impairment, interpersonal problems, suicidality, and diminished social support relative to individuals without personality disorders (see Table 2.1; Trull, Jahng, Tomko, Wood, & Sher, 2011).

For much of the 20th century, the study of personality and personality disorders progressed independently. As Lenzenweger and Clarkin (2005) recount, personality disorders fell within the purview of psychiatry and clinical psychology, whereas academic psychologists developed models and measurement of normative personality. Personality psychology, which was concerned with typical

Table 2.1 DESCRIPTION AND LIFETIME PREVALENCE OF *DSM-IV* PERSONALITY
DISORDERS IN THE UNITED STATES

Disorder	Defining Characteristics	Prevalence
Paranoid	Extreme suspiciousness and mistrust of others; constantly on guard and reactive to real or perceived threats; tend to view themselves as superior and unique, and others as deceitful and untrustworthy	1.9%
Schizoid	Restricted range of affect, interpersonal indifference and isolation	0.6%
Schizotypal	Odd, eccentric behavior, distorted thoughts and perceptions, inappropriate affect, and discomfort with social relationships	0.6%
Narcissistic	Inflated self-importance, inability to empathize with others, and overemphasis on status	1.0%
Histrionic	Need to be center of attention, exaggerated or inappropriate emotionality, and seductiveness	0.3%
Borderline	Volatile interpersonal relationships, fear of abandonment, self-mutilation/suicidality, impulsivity, and emotional instability	2.7%
Antisocial	Aggressive interpersonal interactions, impulsivity, lack of remorse, and defiant disregard for safety of self and others	3.8%
Obsessive-compulsive	Preoccupation with adherence to rules, orderliness, and control	1.9%
Dependent	Persistent and pathological need to be with and gain approval of others	0.3%
Avoidant	Low tolerance for negative emotions, few close relationships, and fear of rejection or ridicule in interpersonal interactions	1.2%

SOURCE: Adapted from Jahng, S., Trull, T. J., Wood, P. K., Tragesser, S. L., Tomko, R., Grant, J. D., & Sher, K. J. (2011). Distinguishing general and specific personality disorder features and implications for substance dependence comorbidity. *Journal of Abnormal Psychology, 120*(3), Table 1.

personality processes in nonclinical subjects, had little bearing on the field of personality psychopathology, which emphasized clinical assessments of patient populations and was influenced strongly by biological psychiatry and psychoanalytic theory. To a large extent, scholarship on personality and personality disorder emerged as separate fields of study, with distinct objectives, theoretical models, and populations of interest, until the last decades of the 20th century.

More recent times have brought significant changes in the study of personality disorders, as psychological perspectives and research methods are increasingly brought to bear on the study of personality disorders. In the context of these changes, the field has relied on the *Journal of Personality Disorders* (*JPD*) to provide specialty coverage for research on personality disorders. Founded by Theodore Millon and Allen J. Frances in 1987, *JPD* provided a voice for the study of personality disorders that welcomed a broad range of psychiatric and psychologically focused research.

Given the explosion of work in the field over the past decade, *Personality and Mental Health* emerged to address the absence of specialty journal space, welcoming psychiatric and psychological perspectives on personality pathology and encouraging both basic and health services research. As the title suggests, the journal supports both work in personality disorders as diagnostic entities as well as more basic personality research and the link to psychopathology. The journal is sponsored by the Centre for Health and Justice within the Institute of Health based out of the University of Nottingham and provides a strong international outlet.

Even with the addition of *Personality and Mental Health*, the growth of high-quality empirical and theoretical work in personality disorders, as well as the growing buzz that was surrounding the *Diagnostic and Statistical Manual of Mental Disorders*, fifth edition (*DSM-5*) working group, demanded another specialty outlet. With a nod to the potential of dimensional models in the *DSM-5* as well as advancements in assessment and behavioral treatments for personality disorders, the most recent entry emerged from the American Psychological Association. The journal *Personality Disorders: Theory, Research and Treatment* (*PDTRT*) was founded by Carl Lejuez. The journal was developed to focus on empirical work with traditional options for standard full-length articles or brief reports. Two other sections were unique and timely.

First, the "Target Conceptual Article" and "Commentaries" sections were created to provide not only an opportunity for scholarly theoretical work but, more important, places for challenging discourse on that work. Although there are certainly examples of this in psychiatry and psychology more broadly, it was the first of its kind in the field of personality disorders. Critical to the success of this format was the emergent debate surrounding the *DSM-5* revisions. Kim Gratz, who was instrumental in the early development of the journal, was appointed as Section Editor to shepherd target articles through the process. Published Target Articles included papers on dimensional models and the personality disorders; the complex relationship between trait narcissism, often studied in analog samples using self-report measures, and the clinical construct of narcissistic personality disorder (NPD); the role of parenting in the pathogenesis of borderline personality disorder (BPD); a meta-analytic perspective on the Psychopathic Personality Inventory (PPI) nomological network; the use of a two-factor model of psychopathic personality drawing heavily upon the PPI; the place of behavioral genetics in the study of personality disorders and implications for diagnostic classifications; the impact of modern culture on the increase of narcissistic traits in society and its potential impact of the clinical disorder; and an upcoming piece on the development of a unifying framework for the choice and rapid response domains of impulsivity.

Given the early success of these target articles, several special sections (and, in some cases, full special issues) adopted the same approach. These included two special issues on the *DSM-5*. The first issue, edited by Drs. Joshua Miller and Kenneth Levy, was undertaken in the period leading up to the release of the *DSM-5*, with papers on the proposed overhaul to the Personality Disorders section. The second special issue was a reflection on the scientific process and administrative decisions that led to the surprising conclusion of *DSM-5* Personality Disorder revision. This much-needed postmortem was undertaken brilliantly by Tom Widiger and Bob Krueger. Although the overall discourse across both special issues was quite comprehensive, there were many issues that fell under the radar and toward this end *PDTRT* put together a special issue that was coedited by Alexis Matusiewicz on overlooked issues and unique perspectives on the *DSM-5* (Matusiewicz & Lejuez, 2012). This included a paper questioning the empirical support for aspects of the *DSM-5* proposal; the perilous state of particular personality disorders, including depressive personality disorder and antisocial personality disorder; and the absence of important personality dimensions, such as perfectionism, in the dimensional scoring scheme.

Other special issues have focused on an array of topics such as new perspectives in the diagnosis and treatment of NPD and mentalization, a psychoanalytic construct, in BPD from bench to bedside spearheaded by Carla Sharp and Peter Fonagy, illustrating *PDTRT*'s commitment to a broad range of theoretical perspectives. Finally, the journal highlighted its new partnership with the North American Society for the Study of Personality Disorders through a special issue from its inaugural conference. The partnership was ideal in many practical ways but also symbolic, as both *PDTRT* and the Society emerged as the new kids on the block with a lot to offer but also great urgency to show their utility in a space that was already well served.

Second, the Practice Reviews section was developed in line with *PDTRT*'s commitment to bridging science and practice. Practice reviews include the presentation of a personality-related issue from clinical practice, a review of relevant research, and development of a practical recommendation informed by research. A particularly unique requirement of the Practice Review was that it needed to be coauthored by at least one individual with a primary focus in clinical practice and at least one individual with a primary focus in research. This partnering of individuals with distinct professional emphases is crucial for practice reviews to provide a credible bridge between research and practice. Not everyone warmed up to this requirement. Many researchers argued that their clinical work, which often represented a small fraction of their time, was sufficient to provide both sides of this important coin, but the journal did not budge on this issue, and so the requirement remained. Four excellent Practice Reviews have been published since this requirement took effect. These have focused on the difficulty of applying a fairly straight view from the literature to the complex realities of clinical settings, including (the lack of) empathy in NPD and the prevailing theoretical perspective on dependent personality disorder (DPD). Other papers considered the challenges of treating patients with personality disorders in medical health care settings, and medical complications associated with personality disorders.

In the 5 years since its inception, *PDTRT* has published over 200 papers and has an impact factor of 3.67 (slightly increased from its first impact factor in the previous year of 3.54), ranking it along this metric as #1 in personality disorder journals and among the top 15% of all clinical psychology journals. Given its status, *PDTRT* provides an interesting opportunity to uncover current trends and dilemmas in personality disorder research. In doing so, we utilize data from the journal from submissions, publications, and editorial decisions.

METHOD

Article Inclusion

Based on a change in the system used to handle manuscripts and the desire to provide current trends, we covered the period from May 2012 to May 2014 (which was the time of the initial presentation of this work). In total, 183 manuscripts (brief reports, reviews, special issue articles, and articles) were included into the review, with the exclusion of commentaries. Two research assistants separately double-coded each article for the variables listed in the following.

Variables of Interest

EDITORIAL DECISION
The editorial decision of the article was coded as accepted or rejected. Articles sent out for revisions were coded as accepted.

PERSONALITY DISORDER CATEGORY
Personality disorders were categorized into the following groups: BPD, P/anti-social personality disorder (P/ASPD), NPD, schizotypal personality disorder (SPD), traits/general personality (Tr/GP), and articles that contained two or more disorders (Mult). An "Other" category was created to encompass articles relating to obsessive-compulsive disorder, avoidant personality disorder, and other disorders which occurred quite infrequently.

PERSONALITY DISORDER ASSESSMENT APPROACH
Each article was coded for the operationalization of the personality disorder of interest. The three possible types were categorical, continuous, or mixed. Manuscripts were coded as "categorical" in nature if participants in the study were scored as "disorder present" or "disorder absent." These judgments typically were made on the basis of a clinical interview or clinical cutoff on a symptom scale. Manuscripts were coded as "continuous" if personality disorder severity was

measured along a continuum, such as those that used symptom counts or dimensional trait scores.

POPULATION

Population types were coded into the following categories: adult clinical, adult healthy, college student, and youth. There were no cases of college student clinical or youth healthy in the sample of articles. Samples that were at risk such as incarcerated or in substance use treatment were coded as clinical.

GENDER INCLUSION

Articles were coded based on the sample composition: males only, females only, or both males and females.

STUDY TYPE

The next variable was used to characterize the type of research question. Manuscripts were coded as experimental psychopathology if the study examined the nature, course, or predictors of a personality disorder or personality disorder traits (Zvolensky et al., 2001). Manuscripts were coded as treatment research if the study addressed the effectiveness or efficacy of an intervention, predictors of treatment outcome, or moderators or mediators of treatment response. Manuscripts were coded as measurement if the study related to the development or validation of a personality disorder assessment method.

GENETIC OR BIOLOGICAL CORRELATES

Manuscripts were rated on the use of biobehavioral or genetic assays.

COUNTRY OF ORIGIN

Each article was coded as a study that took place internationally or in the United States.

RESULTS

Representation of Different Personality Disorders

The first question we asked is which personality disorders have the greatest market share among the studies submitted from 2012 to 2014.

As shown in the left panel of Table 2.1, the two most frequent submissions came from BPD and P/ASPD. Of note, this number was strongly driven by manuscripts on psychopathy, often with ASPD included only as a control variable. Possibly the most surprising example is the distinction of SPD and NPD from other lesser studied personality disorders. Papers covering multiple personality disorders were well represented, but this number may have been inflated due to the large number of conceptual pieces based on *DSM-5*. In line with the movement away from categorical diagnoses among some subsets of researchers, 15% of the papers focused on personality traits (including maladaptive trait models) without any reference to particular personality disorders. It is important to clarify that the distinction made here is not categorical vs continuous measurement, which we address in detail later, but the focus on either general personality dimensions or PD-specific maladaptive traits, independent of a specific PD diagnosis.

While admittedly impacted by the views of the Founding Editor of *PDTRT*, another key variable is the area of specialization for members of the editorial board. As indicated in Table 2.2, some interesting outcomes are seen when comparing the board composition to the percentage of papers received—in some cases an almost perfect correspondence occurred and in other the lack of correspondence has a fairly logical explanation. First, the number of board members with expertise in BPD resulted from my early expectation that this would be the *Journal of Borderline Personality Disorder*. I based this initial estimate on the proportion of articles on BPD published in *JPD* and without considering the number of psychopathy papers that may have been going to other outlets (e.g., *Journal of Abnormal Psychology* or *Psychological Assessment*). This missed prediction also is compounded for psychopathy by the relatively small number of researchers and therefore eligible reviewers for this work. Although the number of reviewers with expertise in BPD has remained relatively stable, the number of psychopathy reviewers has risen over the years to meet the demand. And while there certainly are some excellent researchers not on the board, the available pool to add to the board is simply less in this area. If this were not the case, the number of board members with expertise in psychopathy would be even greater by this point in *PDTRT,* to reflect submissions related to psychopathy. The correspondence between editorial board members and number of submissions is quite striking for other areas, including NPD and SPD. As demand for reviewers has risen to accommodate the larger-than-anticipated number of submissions on these topics, I have been able to increase the number of board members in these areas.

Following from the distinction between studies focused on disorder type and traits, it also is helpful to examine the type of data utilized. In line with trends in

Table 2.2 DISTRIBUTION OF ACCEPTED MANUSCRIPTS AND EDITORIAL
BOARD MEMBER EXPERTISE BY FOCAL PERSONALITY DISORDER:
PDTRT, 2012–2014

Disorder	% Submitted	% Board Members
Psychopathy/antisocial	25	15
Borderline	28	34
Schizotypal	7	6
Narcissistic	6	7
Multiple personality disorders	16	11
Other	3	6
Traits/general personality	15	28

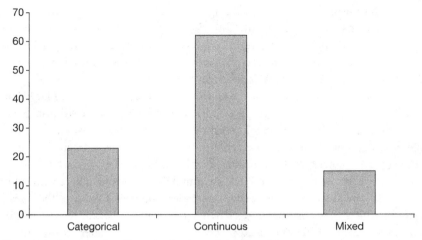

Figure 2.1. Percent of studies submitted as a function of data type.

the field, even studies focused on specific disorders have shown an emergence of work utilizing dimensional/continuous data. This is borne out in our data as shown in in Figure 2.1.

Indeed, while a large number of studies still focus on discrete personality disorders as indicated in the previous section, almost two thirds included a primary focus on continuous measurement opposed to categorical assessments. This proportion rises to 75% when we consider manuscripts that use multiple assessment methods (e.g., categorical with continuous). It is wise to caution against overinterpreting the lower percentage of studies using categorical data without keeping in mind that in some cases this may be less likely a philosophical choice and more a result of constrained resources to conduct research, since there are relatively low rates of clinical impairment in most convenience samples.

Just over half of the studies submitted on BPD used categorical diagnosis, whereas that number drops to just under one third for SPD and NDP. This trend seems to reflect the fact that many studies of SPD employ student samples. About two thirds of studies with a focus on multiple personality disorders or less common personality disorders used categorical diagnoses, suggesting a greater focus on the disorders themselves than on underlying traits. Alternately, there may be fewer validated assessment tools available to measure these constructs dimensionally, and these studies may be more likely to come from clinical, rather than student samples.

As is clear in this discussion, it is useful to consider the types of populations studied. We examined the percentage submitted studies that employed community samples (64%) and clinical populations (36%). Among these groups, college students were almost exclusively in the healthy category and studies focused on this group accounted for 36% of the submitted papers. Samples comprised of adolescents and young adults made up 12% of the papers and were equally

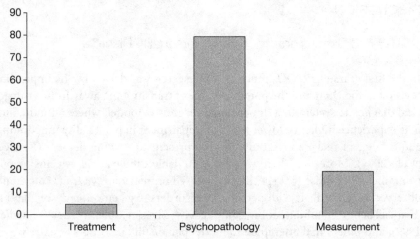

Figure 2.2. Percent of studies submitted as a function of study type.

represented in the clinical and community groups, with most of the former associated with at-risk samples in P/ASPD and the latter in BPD. One notable finding was that all papers for SPD used nonclinical samples and 75% of those were limited to college students.

Finally, we considered study type in the categories of treatment, psychopathology, or assessment (Figure 2.2). One purpose in the creation of *PDTRT* was to provide a space for psychosocial intervention research, but this represents the least common type of research published in the journal. Assessment-focused and measure development papers were represented 18%, leaving psychopathology-focused papers covering about 78% of the manuscripts.

With regard to type of manuscript, there appears to be a meaningful difference in the rate of papers accepted from each category. Specifically, about one third of psychopathology papers and under 10% of treatment papers were accepted, while more than 50% of assessment-focused/measurement development papers were accepted. Of the treatment papers submitted, almost all involved BPD, however, only 10% of papers on BPD were treatment based; even fewer BPD paper (<5%) were in the assessment/measure development category). Assessment papers were most common among studies of multiple personality disorders and general traits, with both at about 33% of the papers submitted for those categories.

Other interesting data points suggest the field of personality disorder research is expanding. Almost one third of the papers come from teams led by an international author. Additionally, about 15% of the papers included some form of biological assessment; about 10% included genes or neural assessment specifically. Not surprisingly, the preponderance of studies included both genders. However, it is notable that the traditional exclusion of women in studies of psychopathy/ASPD and men in BPD appears to have softened, with only 32% of the former including only men and 21% of the latter including only women.

DISCUSSION

DSM-5 and Dimensional Models of Personality Disorder

In the first years of *PDTRT*, much of the research was driven by the impending revision of the *DSM* and the potential value of transitioning away from a categorical diagnostic system to a dimensional diagnostic model, where an individual may experience higher or lower levels of impairment in personality functioning, and a range of maladaptive traits may be present to varying degrees (Krueger et al., 2007). Moreover, there were several viable dimensional systems to pull from, including those that specifically focused on maladaptive traits commonly observed in individuals with personality disorders (e.g., emotion dysregulation, dissocial behavior, inhibitedness, compulsivity; Livesley, 2006; Westen & Shedler, 1999), and others that attempted to model personality disorders as extremes of traits that underlie normal personality functioning (e.g., "The Big 5"; Costa & McCrae, 1990; Schroeder, Wormsworth, & Livesley, 2002). Others made use of established symptom scales (e.g., PAI-BOR; Morey, 1991) but eschewed clinical cutoffs in favor of continuous scores. As mentioned earlier, *PDTRT* published a precursor on the topic of dimensional models as the first Target Conceptual Article by Krueger and Eaton, which currently is the most highly cited paper in the short history of the journal (though no longer with the highest average cites per year). Then it followed with the first special issue leading up to the *DSM-5* with several highly cited papers, including the lead article from the working group which currently has the highest average per year number of citations at *PDTRT* (Skodol et al., 2011).

Despite the energy and enthusiasm some brought to the possibilities of a dimensional approach, there was no shortage of detractors for reasons ranging from limited real-world practicality to questions about the depth of the empirical base to support all aspects of the potential new approach. Nevertheless, it was quite a shock when the announcement was made that the proposed dimensional changes would not be represented in the personality disorder sections of the *DSM-5*. Thus, it was reasonable to expect that the postmortem series that *PDTRT* published within months of the decision would generate significant citations. Although the papers have been heavily downloaded, the citation numbers have been more modest—good but not through the roof, as I expected. This suggests that the field may be ready to move on—at least until there is movement toward the next version, where many of these issues will certainly re-emerge.

Controversies Associated With Psychopathy

Without question, the biggest surprise in editing *PDTRT* was the activity surrounding the construct of psychopathy. The high number of manuscripts submitted was particularly surprisingly when compared to the relative absence of any material on ASPD.

Possibly in a more psychology-focused journal this was to be expected because psychopathy avoids the common critique of ASPD as being too behavioral in its measurement. Moreover, psychopathy provides multiple methods of assessments, whereas few assessment approaches are available for diagnostic criteria. Particularly with the rise in popularity of the triarchic model (Patrick, Fowles, & Kreuger, 2009), psychopathy research was moving out of purely incarcerated samples of men and providing a dimensional perspective on issues that the categorical options available for ASPD simply weren't meeting. Many of these were nicely fleshed out by Lynam and Vachon (2012).

The editorial process for psychopathy papers was a bit complicated and often contentious. Interestingly, P/ASPD accounted for well over 80% of the cases where a request was made by an author to "avoid" a particular reviewer, and in those cases it typically included several names. Psychopathy research accounted for all of the cases in which the editor chose to contact reviewers to ask them to remove the ad hominem attacks embedded in their critiques. To their credit all three reviewers graciously complied with the request.

One of the most cited papers published in *PDTRT* was one that was rejected at another journal after multiple rounds of incredibly extensive and challenging reviews. The author had shared the reviews with me and asked if I would consider the paper despite the pages and pages of critique that it generated. Based on the reviews from that journal, the decision was made to immediately publish the paper and invite reviewers from earlier submissions. After the dust had settled, it was one of the most well received target articles at *PDTRT*. It generated a commentary and rejoinder that each were almost as long as the original manuscript (and would have been even longer without some intervention on the part of the journal), served as a useful template for clearly laying out where the differences in opinion existed, and allowed the evaluation of solid data and theory by readers who could develop their own decisions about where they stood on the issues.

Gender Bias in Diagnosis of Borderline and Antisocial Personality Disorder

Evidence for gender differences in the diagnosis of personality disorders is inconclusive. Some have reported that women are more likely to be diagnosed with BPD and men are more likely to be diagnosed with ASPD (Trull et al., 2011), but findings are inconsistent in this regard (Grilo et al., 1996; Kringlen, Torgensen, & Cramer, 2001). Regardless of overall prevalence, little is known about potential gender differences in the expression or course of personality disorders. Until recent years disorders such as BPD and P/ASPD excluded one gender (males in the former and females in the latter). As noted in the earlier analyses, this practice is becoming less common. Moreover, the field has started to expand to work directly in exploring gender differences (e.g., Mager, Bresin, & Verona, 2014), the conditions under which these differences are and aren't evident, and the mechanisms for these differences. A meaningful understanding of the role of gender across personality disorders will require continued progress in this regard.

Studying Personality Disorder Traits in Nonclinical Samples

Historically, the study of personality disorders largely was conscribed to clinical samples of psychiatric patients; however, there is growing interest in examining personality disorders in the general population. Although rates of personality disorders certainly are higher in patient populations, personality disorders are represented in nonclinical settings, including community members and college students. There are practical and conceptual advantages of using nonpatient participants: They are often easier and less costly to recruit, which may facilitate larger scale studies and provide adequate statistical power to examine group and experimental effects, and identify moderators and mediators. The use of nonclinical samples may provide incremental understanding of precursors to and vulnerability factors for the development of personality disorders as they present in clinical settings (Tull, Bornovalova, Patterson, Hopko, & Lejuez, 2008). Finally, the phenomenology of personality disorders in the general population is of interest in its own right. However, a limitation of using community and/or students samples is that it remains unclear whether findings from nonpatient populations generalize to individuals with more extensive personality disturbance or greater clinical severity. Currently the journal is receiving a balanced number of papers with clinical and healthy samples, which provides opportunities to approach vulnerability and course of PD pathology in various ways. However, there is some resistance to considering findings form healthy samples as relevant to what we know about clinical samples. In the journal this issue has played out most extensively with NPD, where there are serious questions as to whether the wealth of findings on narcissistic traits is relevant for the clinical disorder.

Personality Disorders in Children and Adolescents

Since the concept of personality disorders was first proposed over a century ago, there has been empirical and theoretical interest in the developmental origins of the disorder. Contemporary models suggest that personality disorders emerge from a combination of inborn temperament and developmental experiences, particularly early childhood adversity (Crowell, Beauchaine, & Linehan, 2009; Johnson, Bromley, & McGeoch, 2009). Thus, most significant precursors to personality disorder are present in the earliest years of life and manifest throughout childhood and adolescence (Shiner, 2009). However, historically, there has been great reluctance to diagnose personality disorders in youth (Chanen & McCutcheon, 2008). Many have questioned the appropriateness and validity of personality disorder diagnoses in childhood and adolescence because personality formation is underway and is inherently unstable during these years (Crick, Murray-Close, & Woods, 2005; Shapiro, 1990). Likewise, some symptoms of personality disorder, which may be unusual or inappropriate later in life, may be normative during childhood and adolescence (e.g., concerns about separation, reckless behavior, identity disturbance). However, reservations about diagnosing juvenile personality disorders may be minimized by the clinical imperative to recognize and intervene when symptoms first emerge, rather than waiting to see if they "grow out of it" (Paris, 2014). In response to this need, there has been a tremendous surge in interest in research on personality disorders in children and adolescents (Sharp & Tackett, 2014). Accordingly, while 12% of submissions is not an incredibly large number, it is a step in the right direction with important lines of work being established with both clinical and healthy youth.

The Emergence of Narcissistic Personality Disorder/ Schizotypal Personality Disorder and the Forgotten Personality Disorders

At the onset of *PDTRT*, there were almost no papers submitted on NPD or SPD and almost no reviewers on the board who could handle these papers. At the same time, many personality disorders received almost no attention in the journal. Particularly surprising was the absence of Cluster C personality disorders. Our special series in 2013 attempted to draw attention to these areas with lesser focus. However, trends in the journal continue to suggest that the largest percentage of submissions continue in BPD and P/ASPD, with NPD and SPD the focus in a smaller but meaningful number of studies, while few other disorders have appeared with any regularity.

Passing of the Editorship

The completion of this chapter occurred at the time the leadership of *PDTRT* is transitioning from Carl Lejuez to Tom Widiger. This evolution bodes very well for the continued health of *PDTRT*. More important, this leaves the personality disorders with three outstanding sources and a great opportunity to continue the advancements in this area of work. As the controversy over *DSM-5* may have subsided a bit, there is now opportunities to further gather the data necessary for the continued progress of the field into *DSM-6* when the controversies can start anew.

REFERENCES

Chanen, A. M., & McCutcheon, L. K. (2008). Personality disorder in adolescence: The diagnosis that dare not speak its name. *Personality and Mental Health, 2*(1), 35–41.

Costa Jr, P. T., & McCrae, R. R. (1990). Personality disorders and the five-factor model of personality. *Journal of Personality Disorders*, 4(4), 362–371.

Crick, N. R., Murray-Close, D., & Woods, K. (2005). Toward a model of borderline personality in childhood: A developmental psychopathology approach. *Development and Psychopathology*, 17, 1051–1070.

Crowell, S. E., Beauchaine, T. P., & Linehan, M. M. (2009). A biosocial developmental model of borderline personality: Elaborating and extending linehan's theory. *Psychological Bulletin*, 135(3), 495.

Dumont, F. (2010). *A history of personality psychology: Theory, science, and research from Hellenism to the twenty-first century*. Cambridge: Cambridge University Press.

Grilo, C. M., Becker, D. F., Walker, M. L., Edell, W. S., & McGlashan, T. H. (1996). Gender differences in personality disorders in psychiatrically hospitalized young adults. *The Journal of Nervous and Mental Disease*, 184(12), 754–757.

Jahng, S., Trull, T. J., Wood, P. K., Tragesser, S. L., Tomko, R., Grant, J. D., & Sher, K. J. (2011). Distinguishing general and specific personality disorder features and implications for substance dependence comorbidity. *Journal of Abnormal Psychology*, 120(3), 656.

Johnson, J. G., Bromley, E., & McGeoch, P. G. (2009). Childhood Experiences and Development of Maladaptive and Adaptive Personality Traits. *Essentials of Personality Disorders*, 143.

Kringlen, E., Torgersen, S., & Cramer, V. (2001). A Norwegian psychiatric epidemiological study. *American Journal of Psychiatry*, 158(7), 1091–1098.

Krueger, R. F., Skodol, A. E., Livesley, W. J., Shrout, P. E., & Huang, Y. (2007). Synthesizing dimensional and categorical approaches to personality disorders: Refining the research agenda for DSM-V Axis II. *International Journal of Methods in Psychiatric Research*, 16(S1), S65–S73.

Lenzenweger, M. F., & Clarkin, J. F. (Eds.). (2005). *Major theories of personality disorder*. New York, NY: Guilford.

Livesley, W. J. (2003). Diagnostic dilemmas in classifying personality disorder. In K. A. Phillips, M. B. First, & H. A. Pincus (Eds.), *Advancing DSM: Dilemmas in psychiatric diagnosis* (pp. 153–189). Arlington, VA, US: American Psychiatric Association.

Livesley, W. J. (2006). Behavioral and molecular genetic contributions to a dimensional classification of personality disorder. In T. A. Widiger, E. Simonsen, P. J. Sirovatka, & D. A. Regier (Eds.), *Dimensional models of personality disorders: Refining the research agenda for DSM-V* (pp. 49–53). Arlington, VA: American Psychiatric Association.

Lynam, D. R., & Vachon, D. D. (2012). Antisocial personality disorder in DSM-5: Missteps and missed opportunities. *Personality Disorders: Theory, Research, and Treatment*, 3(4), 483.

Mager, K. L., Bresin, K., & Verona, E. (2014). Gender, psychopathy factors, and intimate partner violence. *Personality Disorders: Theory, Research, and Treatment*, 5, 257–267.

Matusiewicz, A., & Lejuez, C. W. (2012). Overlooked issues and unique perspectives on the DSM-5: Introduction to the special series. *Personality Disorders: Theory, Research, and Treatment*, 3, 442–443.

Morey, L. C. (1991). *Personality Assessment Inventory: Professional manual*. Odessa, FL: Psychological Assessment Resources.

New, A. S., Triebwasser, J., & Charney, D. S. (2008). The case for shifting borderline personality disorder to Axis I. *Biological Psychiatry*, 64(8), 653–659.

Paris, J. (2015). Clinical implications of biological factors in personality disorders. *Canadian Psychology/Psychologie Canadienne, 56*(2), 263–266.

Patrick, C. J., Fowles, D. C., & Krueger, R. F. (2009). Triarchic conceptualization of psychopathy: Developmental origins of disinhibition, boldness, and meanness. *Development and Psychopathology, 21*, 913–938.

Schroeder, M. L., Wormworth, J. A., & Livesley, W. J. (1992). Dimensions of personality disorder and their relationships to the Big Five dimensions of personality. *Psychological Assessment, 4*(1), 47.

Shapiro D. L. (1990). Standard of care in the prediction of violent behavior. *Psychotherapy in Private Practice, 8*, 43–53.

Sharp, C., & Tackett, J. L. (2014). Introduction: An idea whose time has come. In Sharp, Carla, Tackett, Jennifer L. (Eds.), *Handbook of borderline personality disorder in children and adolescents* (pp. 3–8). New York, NY: Springer.

Shiner, R. L. (2009). The development of personality disorders: Perspectives from normal personality development in childhood and adolescence. *Development and Psychopathology, 21*(3), 715–734.

Skodol, A. E., Clark, L. A., Bender, D. S., Krueger, R. F., Morey, L. C., Verheul, R., et al. (2011). Proposed changes in personality and personality disorder assessment and diagnosis for DSM-5 Part I: Description and rationale. *Personality Disorders: Theory, Research, and Treatment, 2*, 4–22.

Tull, M. T., Bornovalova, M. A., Patterson, R., Hopko, D. R., & Lejuez, C. W. (2008). Analogue research. In Dean McKay (Ed.), *Handbook of research methods in abnormal and clinical psychology* (pp. 61–78). Thousand Oaks, CA: Sage.

Westen, D., & Shedler, J. (1999). Revising and assessing Axis II, Part I: Developing a clinically and empirically valid assessment method. *American Journal of Psychiatry, 156*(2), 258–272.

Widiger, T. A. (2003). Personality disorder and Axis I psychopathology: The problematic boundary of Axis I and Axis II. *Journal of Personality Disorders, 17*(2: Special issue), 90–108.

Zvolensky, M. J., Eifert, G. H., & Lejuez, C. W. (2001). Emotional control during recurrent 20% carbon dioxide-enriched air induction: Relation to individual difference variables. *Emotion, 2*, 148–165.

3

Personality Disorders as Collections of Traits

JOSHUA D. MILLER ■

After more than 20 years of advocacy (Costa & McCrae, 1992; Frances, 1993; Livesley, Jackson, & Schroeder, 1992; Widiger & Trull, 1992), trait-based perspectives of personality disorders (PDs) have gained tremendous traction of late with the move to include a diagnostic model of PD that is based, in part, on traits in the *Diagnostic and Statistical Manual of Mental Disorders* (*DSM-5*; APA, 2013). Although this attempt ultimately failed, in that the proposed model was included in Section III of the *DSM-5* for "emerging measures and models," rather than Section II, this still represents an important move toward the ultimate integration of trait-based perspectives to the conceptualization, assessment, and diagnosis of PDs (Widiger, 2013). As the field moves toward the potential full-scale adoption of such an approach in future iterations of the *DSM* (e.g., *DSM-5.1; DSM-6*), it is important to review what is known to date about the success of such models, much of which has been done using general personality traits studied within a five-factor model framework (FFM). In what follows, the robust literature on the FFM of PD (e.g., Widiger & Costa, 2013) is reviewed and used as a roadmap for the work that is ongoing and yet to come on the *DSM-5* pathological FFM.

CHARACTERIZATION OF PERSONALITY DISORDERS AS COLLECTIONS OF *GENERAL* TRAITS

Expert Ratings

The description of PDs as collections of general traits from the FFM began most formally in 1994 when Widiger and colleagues translated the *DSM-III-R*

(APA, 1987) and *DSM-IV* (APA, 1994) PDs into the language of the FFM. The facets of the FFM were rated as being relevant (high or low) for each PD on the basis of the *DSM* symptoms and text, as well as the extant empirical literature associated with each PD. For instance, Widiger and colleagues (1994) rated the following FFM facets as being representative of borderline PD: anxiety (high), angry hostility (high), depression (high), impulsiveness (high), vulnerability (high), trust (low), compliance (low), and competence (low). Following a similar approach but in reference to psychopathic personality traits, Widiger and Lynam (1998) translated the Psychopathy Checklist-Revised (Hare, 1991), the instrument many consider to be the gold standard in the assessment of psychopathy, into the language of the FFM. Here the authors demonstrated the central role of traits from the domains of agreeableness-antagonism and conscientiousness-disinhibition, with smaller and more nuanced relations (i.e., high and low traits) for traits from the domains of neuroticism-emotional stability and extraversion-introversion in capturing psychopathic personality traits.

These initial attempts to characterize both *DSM* and non-*DSM* PDs using the language of the FFM set the stage for larger, more comprehensive projects where a greater numbers of expert ratings (researchers and clinicians) were collected. For instance, Miller and colleagues (2001; psychopathy) and Lynam and Widiger (2001; all 10 *DSM-IV* PDs) took this approach a step further by having a more inclusive list of expert raters (e.g., having published at least one article on the PD) describe a prototypical individual with a given PD using the 30 facets of the FFM on a 1 to 5 scale (rather than using binary ratings as used in the original Widiger et al., 1994 ratings). For example, Lynam and Widiger asked the expert raters to:

> describe the prototypic case for one personality disorder on a 1 to 5 point scale, where 1 indicates that the prototypic person would be extremely low on the trait (i.e., lower than the average person), 2 indicates that the prototypic person would be low, 3 indicates that the person would be neither high nor low (i.e., does not differ from the average individual), 4 indicates that the prototypic person would be high on the trait, and 5 indicates that the prototypic person would be extremely high on that trait. (p. 403)

Across the 11 PDs (10 *DSM-IV* PDs and psychopathy), the number of raters ranged from 10 (paranoid) to 24 (borderline) with a mean of 17. In both Miller et al. (2001) and Lynam and Widiger (2001), the expert ratings were averaged to create an FFM prototype for each PD. These ratings proved to be reasonably reliable across raters and, for the *DSM* PDs, were relatively consistent with initial ratings completed by Widiger et al. (mean $r = .71$). As an example, the expert-rated FFM psychopathy prototype compiled by Miller et al. was characterized by elevations (i.e., mean expert ratings of a 4 or higher) on impulsiveness, assertiveness, excitement seeking, and competence and low scores (i.e., mean expert ratings of 2 or lower) on all six facets of agreeableness (e.g., modesty, straightforwardness), dutifulness, self-discipline, deliberation, warmth, anxiety, depression, self-consciousness, and vulnerability. The academician ratings for psychopathy and the *DSM-IV* PDs can be found in Table 3.1.

A second set of FFM-*DSM-IV* PD prototypes were developed by Samuel and Widiger (2004) using the same approach except that clinicians were used as raters instead of academicians. The number of clinical raters for each *DSM-IV* PD ranged from 22 (narcissistic PD) to 39 (dependent PD) with a mean of 31. As with the academician ratings, the clinical ratings manifested good interrater agreement for all the PDs. This second set of FFM PD prototypes can also be found in Table 3.1.

Five-Factor Model–Personality Disorder Meta-Analyses

Following on the heels of the development of expert ratings for these 11 PDs, two meta-analyses were published that examined the FFM trait correlates of the *DSM* PDs (Samuel & Widiger, 2008) and psychopathy (Decuyper, De Pauw, De Fruyt, De Bolle, & De Clercq, 2009). Using data from 18 samples (n = 3,207), Samuel and Widiger (2008) documented the facet-level FFM relations with *DSM* PDs. For instance, borderline PD was characterized by significant positive correlations with all six neuroticism facets (e.g., depressiveness, angry hostility) and negative correlations with traits from agreeableness (e.g., trust, compliance), conscientiousness (e.g., competence, self-discipline), and extraversion (e.g., positive emotions). Similarly, Decuyper et al. compiled data from 26 independent samples (n = 6,913) to present the meta-analytic correlations between the 30 FFM traits and psychopathy scores. Psychopathy was most consistently negatively correlated with facets from agreeableness (e.g., straightforwardness, compliance) and conscientiousness (e.g., deliberation, dutifulness), and manifested both positive and negative correlations with neuroticism (*positive*: angry hostility, impulsiveness; *negative*: anxiety) and extraversion (*positive*: excitement seeking; *negative*: warmth). See Table 3.1 for the meta-analytically derived FFM profiles for the *DSM* PDs and psychopathy.

As can be seen at the bottom of Table 3.1, the academic and clinician FFM–PD profiles were highly correlated with one another (range: .90–.95; mean r = .94). Similarly both the academic ratings (range: .60 to .91; mean r = .80) and clinician ratings (range: .63 to .92; mean r = .80) were correlated with the meta-analytic profiles for the PDs. The only area of significant divergence was for dependent PD in which both sets of expert ratings characterized individuals with dependent PD using high levels of agreeableness (e.g., trust, compliance, modesty), whereas the empirical data do not support this relation (see Miller & Lynam, 2008, for a discussion of these issues). Instead, lower levels of conscientiousness (paired with high neuroticism) may better characterize this PD from the perspective of the FFM.

Table 3.1 FIVE-FACTOR MODEL PERSONALITY DISORDER PROTOTYPES

	Paranoid			Schizoid			Schizotypal			Antisocial			Psychopathy	
	AR	CR	MA	AR	CR	MA	AR	CR	MA	ARSW	CR	MA	AR	MA
NEUROTICISM														
Anxiety	3.60	4.25	.27	2.23	3.06	.13	4.25	3.85	.27	1.82	2.00	.00	1.47	-.15
Angry hostility	4.00	4.39	.41	2.54	2.84	.19	3.08	3.42	.29	4.14	3.93	.27	3.87	.29
Depression	3.30	3.64	.35	3.15	3.42	.28	3.58	3.62	.39	2.45	2.70	.12	1.40	.05
Self-consciousness	3.30	2.94	.29	3.31	3.37	.23	4.00	3.69	.32	1.36	1.63	.02	1.07	-.09
Impulsiveness	2.90	3.17	.15	2.08	2.03	.00	3.17	3.16	.17	4.73	4.22	.27	4.53	.24
Vulnerability	3.60	3.36	.22	3.31	2.97	.14	3.75	3.96	.25	2.27	2.07	.04	1.47	.00
EXTRAVERSION														
Warmth	1.30	1.61	-.28	1.08	1.19	-.42	1.58	1.58	-.28	2.14	2.00	-.13	1.73	-.20
Gregariousness	1.70	1.89	-.20	1.00	1.06	-.48	1.58	1.62	-.25	3.32	3.48	.02	3.67	.03
Assertiveness	2.90	3.25	-.08	1.54	1.90	-.22	2.17	2.04	-.13	4.23	4.07	.06	4.47	.16
Activity	2.90	3.19	-.08	1.92	2.00	-.25	2.25	2.23	-.13	4.00	4.00	.02	3.67	.07
Excitement seeking	2.20	2.42	-.01	1.38	1.71	-.21	2.17	2.12	-.04	4.64	4.30	.25	4.73	.31
Positive emotions	2.20	2.08	-.27	1.23	1.55	-.38	1.92	1.65	-.26	2.86	3.52	-.09	2.53	-.10
OPENNESS														
Fantasy	2.90	3.14	.00	3.23	2.81	-.05	3.83	4.00	.14	2.82	3.48	.10	3.07	.05
Aesthetics	2.20	2.54	-.05	2.77	2.42	-.06	3.17	3.31	.07	2.36	2.78	.00	2.33	-.01
Feelings	2.40	2.46	-.02	1.31	1.52	-.17	2.17	2.31	.03	2.27	2.41	-.02	1.80	-.10
Actions	2.00	2.37	-.10	1.62	2.13	-.13	2.42	2.81	-.06	4.23	4.07	.10	4.27	.09
Ideas	3.50	3.29	-.03	3.38	3.45	.00	4.33	4.38	.09	2.91	3.26	.04	3.53	.03
Values	1.90	1.69	-.05	2.31	2.42	-.05	2.42	2.81	.01	3.00	3.48	.08	2.87	.00

(continued)

Table 3.1 CONTINUED

	Paranoid			Schizoid			Schizotypal			Antisocial			Psychopathy	
	AR	CR	MA	AR	CR	MA	AR	CR	MA	ARSW	CR	MA	AR	MA
AGREEABLENESS														
Trust	*1.00*	*1.19*	-.45	2.38	*1.68*	-.28	2.08	2.04	-.31	*1.45*	*1.70*	-.22	*1.73*	-.34
Straightforwardness	*2.00*	*1.89*	-.24	2.77	2.42	-.09	3.00	2.46	-.16	*1.41*	*1.41*	-.37	*1.13*	-.61
Altruism	*1.90*	*1.86*	-.21	2.38	2.29	-.19	2.75	2.50	-.15	*1.41*	*1.41*	-.24	*1.33*	-.41
Compliance	*1.40*	*1.92*	-.27	3.00	2.77	-.08	2.50	2.65	-.13	*1.77*	*1.81*	-.32	*1.33*	-.48
Modesty	2.40	2.53	-.06	3.31	3.48	.08	3.08	3.27	.05	*1.68*	*1.70*	-.17	*1.00*	-.31
Tendermindedness	*1.80*	2.14	-.18	2.38	2.58	-.11	3.00	2.88	-.05	*1.27*	*1.52*	-.19	*1.27*	-.31
CONSCIENTIOUSNESS														
Competence	3.30	3.53	-.13	2.85	3.00	-.13	2.33	2.85	-.18	2.09	2.52	-.21	**4.20**	-.17
Order	3.70	3.56	.00	3.08	3.19	-.02	2.00	2.58	-.06	2.41	2.74	-.18	2.60	-.17
Dutifulness	3.40	3.39	-.10	3.00	3.16	-.08	2.50	2.77	-.10	*1.41*	*1.52*	-.29	*1.20*	-.32
Achievement striving	3.00	3.08	-.07	2.38	2.68	-.13	2.25	2.35	-.13	2.09	2.33	-.19	3.07	-.11
Self-discipline	3.50	3.19	-.14	3.15	3.10	-.12	2.67	2.77	-.18	*1.81*	*1.85*	-.25	*1.87*	-.22
Deliberation	3.80	3.56	-.09	3.23	3.71	-.02	2.67	3.73	-.10	*1.64*	*1.96*	-.38	*1.60*	-.38
Profile rs: AR-CR	.95*			.91*			.91*			.97*				
AR-MA/CR-MA	.71*	.75*		.73*	.81*		.80*	.79*		.80*	.79*		.77*	

*p < .01.

AR = academician ratings (Lynam & Widiger, 2001; Miller et al., 2001); CR = clinician ratings (Samuel & Widiger, 2004); MA = meta-analytically derived rs (Decuyper et al., 2009; Samuel & Widiger, 2008); OCPD = obsessive-compulsive personality disorder.

NOTE: Expert-rated items rated 2 or lower are italicized; items rated 4 or higher are in bold.

Table 3.1 Continued

	Borderline			Histrionic			Narcissistic			Avoidant			Dependent			OCPD		
	AR	CR	MA	AR	CR	MA	AR	CR	MA	AR	CR	MA	AR	CR	MA	AR	CR	MA
NEUROTICISM																		
Anxiety	4.04	4.25	.38	3.42	4.07	.00	2.33	2.71	.02	4.76	4.34	.41	4.32	4.46	.39	4.00	4.49	.16
Angry hostility	4.75	4.56	.48	3.42	3.55	.08	4.08	3.90	.23	2.81	2.90	.29	2.42	2.95	.18	3.00	3.24	.10
Depression	4.17	4.03	.50	2.68	3.27	-.06	2.42	2.75	.03	3.95	3.72	.53	3.63	4.03	.41	3.18	3.76	.09
Self-consciousness	3.17	2.94	.35	2.00	2.45	-.11	1.50	1.67	-.03	4.67	4.45	.56	4.16	4.42	.42	3.29	3.86	.13
Impulsiveness	4.79	4.38	.34	4.32	4.16	.17	3.17	3.57	.14	1.62	2.14	.14	2.32	2.49	.17	1.53	2.18	-.07
Vulnerability	4.17	4.03	.39	3.95	3.90	.01	2.92	2.76	-.01	4.52	3.90	.40	4.32	4.64	.43	3.12	3.49	.03
EXTRAVERSION																		
Warmth	3.21	2.69	-.20	3.89	3.50	.26	1.42	2.05	-.07	2.33	2.45	-.35	3.84	3.49	-.03	2.06	2.24	-.07
Gregariousness	2.92	3.28	-.12	4.74	4.32	.35	3.83	3.95	.04	1.29	1.45	-.42	3.26	2.54	-.03	2.18	2.40	-.16
Assertiveness	3.17	3.69	-.09	3.84	3.39	.27	4.67	4.00	.19	1.19	1.52	-.39	1.32	1.46	-.39	3.00	3.03	-.01
Activity	3.29	3.56	-.10	4.16	3.94	.25	3.67	4.14	.09	2.05	2.07	-.29	2.26	2.00	-.12	3.35	3.31	.03
Excitement Seek	3.88	4.06	.06	4.47	4.13	.27	4.17	4.10	.16	1.24	1.55	-.23	2.26	1.69	-.06	1.59	1.88	-.12
Positive emotions	2.63	3.16	-.26	4.16	3.80	.23	3.33	3.52	-.02	1.67	1.79	-.39	2.53	2.03	-.15	2.41	2.29	-.09
OPENNESS																		
Fantasy	3.29	4.00	.13	4.37	4.13	.16	3.75	3.82	.11	3.14	3.07	.00	3.05	2.95	.05	2.06	2.52	-.09
Aesthetics	2.96	3.19	.05	3.53	3.60	.10	3.25	3.32	.04	3.05	2.69	-.03	2.89	2.58	.01	2.59	2.56	.01
Feelings	4.00	3.84	.09	4.16	4.13	.18	1.92	2.68	.05	3.43	3.07	-.04	3.74	3.45	.05	1.82	2.22	.01
Actions	4.00	3.78	-.03	4.21	3.70	.12	4.08	3.36	.04	2.00	1.83	-.20	2.21	1.79	-.13	1.53	1.76	-.12
Ideas	3.21	3.69	-.01	3.11	3.30	.04	2.92	3.09	.07	3.19	2.69	-.05	2.84	2.26	-.12	1.76	2.48	.03
Values	2.88	3.00	.05	3.63	3.50	.04	2.67	2.68	-.01	2.57	2.34	-.05	2.89	2.05	-.04	1.76	1.82	-.09

(continued)

Table 3.1 Continued

	Borderline			Histrionic			Narcissistic			Avoidant			Dependent			OCPD		
	AR	CR	MA	AR	CR	MA	AR	CR	MA	AR	CR	MA	AR	CR	MA	AR	CR	MA
AGREEABLENESS																		
Trust	2.21	1.69	-.29	**4.00**	3.39	.05	1.42	1.86	-.20	2.24	2.39	-.29	**4.26**	3.95	-.07	2.65	2.20	-.08
Straightforwardness	2.08	1.94	-.21	2.32	2.29	-.10	1.83	1.91	-.31	2.90	2.82	-.06	3.11	2.90	.00	3.47	3.06	.04
Altruism	2.46	2.31	-.18	2.21	2.52	.02	1.00	1.73	-.20	2.90	2.93	-.12	3.95	3.85	.03	2.76	2.63	.04
Compliance	2.00	1.81	-.27	2.53	2.90	-.12	1.58	1.77	-.26	3.52	3.21	-.02	**4.68**	**4.50**	.10	3.18	2.82	.01
Modesty	2.83	2.56	.03	2.32	2.20	-.16	1.08	1.23	-.37	**4.33**	3.68	.20	**4.26**	**4.23**	.16	3.06	3.17	.02
Tendermindedness	2.79	2.47	-.09	3.05	3.00	.02	1.50	1.77	-.17	3.43	3.43	-.02	3.89	3.79	.09	2.82	2.76	.00
CONSCIENTIOUSNESS																		
Competence	2.71	2.78	-.29	2.37	2.68	-.01	3.25	3.00	.01	3.05	3.45	-.23	2.58	3.28	-.25	**4.53**	**4.41**	.19
Order	2.38	2.31	-.10	2.10	2.30	-.05	2.92	3.00	-.03	3.43	3.48	-.03	2.89	3.21	-.06	**4.76**	**4.59**	.25
Dutifulness	2.29	2.22	-.22	2.10	2.32	-.08	2.42	2.50	-.10	3.29	3.45	-.09	3.79	3.79	-.08	**4.76**	**4.20**	.25
Achievement striving	2.50	2.72	-.19	2.68	2.60	.04	3.92	3.18	.02	2.67	2.90	-.19	2.47	2.97	-.16	**4.29**	**4.03**	.25
Self-discipline	2.33	2.34	-.29	1.79	2.13	-.04	2.08	2.23	-.09	3.05	3.07	-.22	2.84	3.31	-.23	**4.53**	**4.06**	.21
Deliberation	1.88	2.09	-.27	1.74	1.94	-.16	2.25	2.45	-.13	3.43	3.62	-.01	3.00	3.36	-.06	**4.59**	**4.37**	.24
Profile rs: AR-CR	.93*			.95*			.95*			.96*			.90*			.94*		
AR-MA/CR-MA	.84*	.77*		.86*	.79*		.81*	.87*		.78*	.76*		.60*	.63*		.91*	.92*	

Prototype Matching via Similarity Analyses

Given that traits can be used to reliably and validly describe *DSM* and non-*DSM* PDs, the next question asked was whether personality traits scores on measures of the FFM could be used to assess PDs. To do this, two scoring techniques were developed that utilize the information gleaned from these expert ratings (these approaches usually use the profiles generated by the academician ratings [Lynam & Widiger, 2001; Miller et al., 2001] but clinician ratings and meta-analytic profiles can be used as well [e.g., Bastiaansen, Rossi, & De Fruyt, 2013]).

The first strategy used was a prototype matching approach in which an individual's scores on a measure of the FFM (typically but not always assessed with the Revised NEO Personality Inventory; NEO PI-R; Costa & McCrae, 1992) is compared to one or more of the FFM PD prototypes and the degree of similarity in the profiles is quantified using a double entryintraclass correlation (r_{ICC}). The r_{ICC} assesses the similarity of the two set of ratings (e.g., individual A's scores on the 30 NEO PI-R facets vs. the FFM PD prototype). This strategy takes into account the *absolute* similarity of the profiles with regard to shape and elevation. Although the r_{ICC} is the most frequent strategy used to assess profile similarity in this literature, a *Pearson r* also works well (McCrae, 2008) and is easier to compute.

Prototype Matching via Additive Count Technique

Another means of scoring an individual's FFM data with regard to the FFM PD prototypes is the additive count procedure (Miller, Bagby, Pilkonis, Reynolds, & Lynam, 2005), in which an individual's scores on the PDs are determined by simply summing scores on the FFM facets considered particularly relevant (low and high) for each PD. In this case, facets with a mean score of 4 or higher (indicating that a prototypic individual with a given PD would be high on this trait) or 2 or lower (indicating that a prototypic person with a given PD would be low on this trait) are included in the equation for any given PD (with facets rated as being prototypically low being reverse scored before being summed). Referring to the academician ratings presented in Table 3.1, the FFM borderline PD count involves summing the scores from the following facets (facets with a "-r" must be reverse scored prior to summation): anxiety, angry hostility, depression, impulsiveness, vulnerability, openness to feelings, openness to actions, compliance-r, and deliberation-r. The two scoring approaches for the FFM PDs yield scores that are highly correlated with one another (median *r* for *DSM-IV* PDs across two samples: .91; Miller, Bagby, Pilkonis, et al., 2005). Given the similarity of the resultant scores, the count approach is preferred primarily because the scores are easier to calculate.

Validity of the Five-Factor Model Personality Disorder Prototypes and Counts: Convergent Validity

Several studies have examined the correlations between the FFM PD similarity scores and/or counts and *DSM-IV* PD symptom counts using self-report data. Table 3.2 provides a meta-analytic review of the convergent validity correlations from these studies. The number of studies included ranged from 11 (psychopathy) to 20 (borderline) with total *N*s ranging from 3,094 (Cluster A PDs) to 4,394 (borderline). The studies used in this meta-analysis include those in which the FFM was scored via self-reported data from the NEO PI-R; interview data from the Structured Interview for the Five Factor Model (SIFFM; Trull & Widiger, 1997); clinician ratings from the Five Factor Model Scoring Sheet (FFMSS; Few et al., 2010); and PD symptoms scored via interview ratings, expert consensus ratings, and self-report measures. The unweighted mean correlations ranged from .17 (obsessive-compulsive PD [OCPD]) to .60 (avoidant PD) with a median of .46.

These convergent validity correlations are quite comparable to those found using explicit measures of the *DSM* PDs (i.e., measures designed to capture the DSM PDs; see Widiger & Boyd, 2009, for a review). The largest convergent validity correlations for the FFM PDs were for avoidant, borderline, and psychopathy,

Table 3.2 Meta-Analytic Review of Convergent Validity Correlations

	Unweighted Effect Size (*r*)	Total *N*
Five-Factor Model Personality Disorders		
Paranoid	.46	3,094
Schizoid	.49	3,094
Schizotypal	.35	3,094
Antisocial	.44	3,623
Psychopathy	.52	4,122
Borderline	.58	4,394
Histrionic	.35	3,142
Narcissistic	.47	3,624
Avoidant	.60	3,142
Dependent	.36	3,413
OCPD	.17	3,142

NOTE: Each study only contributed one effect size.
OCPD = obsessive-compulsive personality disorder.

whereas the smallest convergent validity effect sizes were found for OCPD, schizotypal, and histrionic PDs. It is interesting to note that for two of the three FFM PDs that manifested the poorest convergent validity scores—OCPD and histrionic—Samuel and Widiger (2008) found the greatest degree of heterogeneity in effect sizes (meaning that many of the mean effect sizes for the FFM–PD relations varied quite substantially across studies). This suggests that the failure to find large convergent correlations could reflect substantial variability in the personality profiles associated with these PDs, which may reflect difficulty scoring these PDs reliably or variability in how they are assessed across instruments. Overall, however, the convergent validity correlations for the FFM PDs are relatively strong when considering that they are similar in size to those found when comparing two explicit measures of DSM PDs, are derived from studies that utilize a wide array of methodologies to assess the FFM facets and the PDs, and most of the FFM scores were derived from instruments that were not written to assess pathological variants of these traits. When instruments that assess more pathological variants of the FFM are used, the PD scores more closely match the various *DSM* and non-*DSM* PDs (Lynam et al., 2011; Miller, Few, Lynam, & MacKillop, 2015; Samuel et al., 2013).

Discriminant Validity/Comorbidity

In addition to examining the convergent validity correlations, several studies have examined the discriminant validity of the FFM PD prototypes. In most cases (e.g., Bastiaansen, Rossi, & De Fruyt, 2013; Miller, Bagby, & Pilkonis, 2005; Miller et al., 2004; Miller, Lynam, et al., 2008), the FFM PD prototype scores manifested their strongest correlations with the convergent *DSM-IV* PD (e.g., FFM avoidant and *DSM-IV* avoidant). In the instances where this was not true, the FFM PD score typically manifested its strongest correlation with a *DSM-IV* PD from the same cluster (e.g., avoidant and dependent PD) or was found for PDs that are commonly found to co-occur (e.g., schizoid and avoidant; e.g., Zimmerman, Rothschild, & Chelminski, 2005). It is important to note that the discriminant validity of the FFM PDs is limited by the discriminant validity of the *DSM-IV* PDs that they were designed to assess. In fact, Lynam and Widiger (2001) demonstrated that FFM PDs prototypes successfully recreate the comorbidity found among *DSM-IV* PDs, suggesting that *DSM* PDs co-occur because they share similar underlying traits. For instance, antisocial and narcissistic PD co-occur, in part, due to the shared role of traits from the domain of antagonism (e.g., immodesty; oppositionality).

Similarity of Empirical Networks

A number of studies have tested whether the FFM PD scores recreate the nomological networks associated with specific *DSM-IV* PDs. To do this, one can compare the similarity of the sets of correlations generated by two scores (e.g., an FFM PD score vs. an explicit *DSM-IV* PD measure). One approach to doing this is to compare the trait profiles generated by the FFM PD similarity scores with those generated by *DSM-IV* PD scores. For instance, Miller and colleagues (2004, 2010) compared the trait profiles created by these two sets of PD scores using the 15 traits from Clark's (1993) Schedule for Nonadaptive and Adaptive Personality (SNAP) measure. Across these two studies, the average r_{ICC} for the SNAP trait profiles generated by the FFM and *DSM* PDs was .73, indicating substantial agreement in the traits measured via these two distinct approaches to assessing PDs.

The similarity of the empirical networks has also been examined using non-trait-based criteria. For instance, Trull, Widiger, Lynam, and Costa (2003) and Miller and colleagues (2012) compared the correlates of FFM borderline PD (BPD) scores with *DSM-IV* BPD scores in relation to a number of relevant constructs such as developmental history (e.g., child abuse, parental psychopathology), affective experience, informant-reported PD symptoms, and functioning, to name a few (see Table 3.3). Combining data from these two studies, a profile analysis of the external correlates of FFM and *DSM-IV* BPD scores demonstrates very substantial convergence (r_{ICC} = .87), despite the use of different methodologies to assess BPD (FFM BPD = self-report; *DSM-IV* BPD = semistructured interview/LEAD diagnoses). Similar results have been found for other PDs as well (e.g., antisocial PD; Gudonis, Miller, Miller, & Lynam, 2008). The substantial similarity in empirical correlates manifested by the FFM PDs with more explicit markers of *DSM* PDs is rather remarkable, given that the FFM PDs are scored using instruments that make no attempt to assess the diagnostic criteria associated with PDs and are typically written with little regard for the assessment of impairment.

Sex Differences

There exists a substantial literature examining sex differences among the *DSM* PDs with concerns noted that such differences may be due, in part, to sex biases. For instance, sex differences in PDs could be due to the inclusion of diagnostic criteria that are oriented more toward one sex (e.g., focus on physical aggression rather than relational aggression in antisocial personality disorder; focus on seductiveness in histrionic PD) or due to clinicians' beliefs about the likelihood that certain PDs manifest more frequently in one sex than the other. As noted and tested by Lynam and Widiger (2007), another possibility is that sex differences may not represent bias alone but instead may also be "reflections of the true state of affairs" (p. 384). Lynam and Widiger (2007) tested whether sex differences for *DSM* PDs could be modeled by sex differences on the facets of the FFM that may underlie these PDs. For instance, women tend to score higher on the facets of neuroticism, whereas men tend to score lower on the facets of agreeableness; as such, PDs characterized by high levels of neuroticism might be expected to be found more frequently in women (e.g., borderline), whereas PDs characterized by interpersonal antagonism might be expected to be found more frequently in men (e.g., antisocial). Lynam and Widiger (2007) correlated the expected sex differences for each trait-based FFM PD with the actual sex

	BPD	
	DSM-IV BPD	FFM BPD
	r	*r*
CHILDHOOD ABUSE		
Sexual [T]	.21*	.19
Physical [T]	.20	.20
PARENTAL PSYCHOPATHOLOGY		
Biological parent, any disorder [T]	.20	.26
Biological father, substance use disorder [T]	.14	.23
Biological father, mood disorder [T]	.10	.09
Biological mother, substance use disorder [T]	.06	.05
Biological mother, mood disorder [T]	.19	.21
PSYCHOLOGICAL DISTRESS		
Depression [M]	.58	.56
Anxiety [M]	.59	.58
Distress [M]	.54	.65
AFFECT		
Negative [M]	.41	.56
Positive [M]	−.29	−.44
ATTACHMENT STYLE		
Anxiety [M]	.48	.60
Avoidance [M]	.30	.29
INFORMANT-REPORT PERSONALITY DISORDERS		
Paranoid [M]	.46	.40
Schizoid [M]	.27	.23
Schizotypal [M]	.46	.45
Antisocial [M]	.54	.43
Borderline [M]	.53	.53
Histrionic [M]	.50	.36
Narcissistic [M]	.36	.28
Avoidant [M]	.33	.48
Dependent [M]	.41	.36
Obsessive-compulsive [M]	.22	.19

(*continued*)

Table 3.3 CONTINUED

	BPD	
	DSM-IV BPD	FFM BPD
	r	r
SELF-HARM		
No intent to die [M]	.45	.39
Intent to die [M]	.56	.36
AGGRESSION—PERPETRATION		
Aggression [M]	.38	.33
Assault [M]	.35	.20
AGGRESSION—VICTIMIZATION		
Aggression [M]	.31	.27
Assault [M]	.23	.21
INTERPERSONAL FUNCTIONING		
Interpersonal sensitivity [M]	.55	.73
Interpersonal ambivalence [M]	.38	.55
Aggression [M]	.47	.59
Need for approval [M]	.46	.59
Lack of sociability [M]	.44	.56
FUNCTIONING		
Distress [M]	.62	.64
Romantic [M]	.44	.39
Parental [M]	.58	.44
Occupational [M]	.54	.46
Social [M]	.54	.45
Distress on others [M]	.76	.59
Interpersonal [T]	.39	.53
Global dysfunction [T]	.39	.52
Profile similarity (r_{ICC})	.87*	

NOTE: [T] = data from Trull, Widiger, Lynam, & Costa, 2003; [M] = data from Miller et al., 2012

*$p < .01$.

BPD = borderline personality disorder; FFM = five-factor model.

differences (ds) found for the *DSM* PDs compiled via a meta-analytic review. In general, the two sets of data were substantially correlated ($r = .72$), suggesting that sex differences in PDs may be due, in part, to basic differences on the personality traits that comprise each PD.

Clinical Utility

There are several ways one might study the clinical utility of different approaches to the conceptualization, assessment, and diagnosis of PDs—one is to survey clinicians and ask about their preferences for various models of PD (e.g., *DSM*- vs. FFM-based models), and the second is to compare models with regard to their ability to provide important information of use in clinical settings. With regard to the former, several surveys have been undertaken to compare clinicians' preferences for *DSM*- vs. FFM-based conceptualizations (e.g., Rottman, Ahn, Sanislow, & Kim, 2009; Samuel & Widiger, 2006; Spitzer, First, Shedler, Westen, & Skodol, 2008; Sprock, 2003) with variable results. In general, the results generally favor trait-based approaches when studied by proponents of a trait approach, whereas the results generally favor *DSM*-based approaches when studied by proponents of the *DSM*-based nosology, suggesting the possibility of important allegiance effects. When comparable assessment methods are used, however, the FFM fares as well or better than the traditional *DSM*-based approach with regard to clinicians' preferences (Mullins-Sweatt & Lengel, 2012).

Another means of addressing clinical utility is to compare the degree to which each approach provides information that is clinically relevant. For example, Miller et al. (2010) examined the relations between the FFM PD prototypes, as measured by a brief clinician rating form, and several indices of impairment. In general, the FFM PD counts were significantly related to overall impairment, occupational impairment, social impairment, and distress caused to others, and consistently accounted for greater unique variance in the impairment scores than did *DSM-IV* PD symptoms. Similarly, Trull et al. (2003) and Miller et al. (2012) demonstrated that FFM BPD scores were significantly related to self-harm behavior and multiple ratings of impairment. These ratings are not limited to cross-sectional data either, as Stepp and Trull (2007) demonstrated that FFM PDs scores for antisocial and borderline PD predicted several externalizing behaviors across multiple years. Not only do the FFM PDs correlate and even predict variables of interest to clinicians, but there are some data that suggest that changes in FFM traits are related to changes in *DSM-IV* PD symptoms (e.g., Wright, Hopwood, & Zanarini, 2015), although the converse is not true (Warner et al., 2004). These data would suggest that personality variables might be appropriate targets of clinical interventions (Presnall, 2012).

CHARACTERIZATION OF PERSONALITY DISORDERS AS COLLECTIONS OF *PATHOLOGICAL* TRAITS: *DSM-5* SECTION III

As noted earlier, the recognition of the role of traits in the conceptualization, assessment, and diagnosis of PDs took a major leap forward in *DSM-5*, as traits now play a fundamental role in the assessment of *DSM-5* PDs in Section III of the manual. In what follows, the new alternative model is reviewed, along with initial empirical evidence as to its link to the FFM and ability to successfully recreate previous findings based on the FFM of PD.

Overview and Correspondence With the Five-Factor Model

The *DSM-5* Section III approach to diagnosing PD involves two major components: an evaluation/consideration of the presence of personality dysfunction in two domains (self and interpersonal) and documentation of the presence of pathological personality traits. These pathological traits can then be used in place of the previous criteria lists to diagnose 6 of the 10 *DSM-IV* PDs (schizotypal, antisocial, borderline, narcissistic, avoidant, OCPD) or to generate PD-trait specified diagnoses for cases where an individual manifests significant personality dysfunction paired with one or more trait elevations.

Although the *DSM-5* trait model and its description changed over the course of time (see Widiger, 2013, for a review), the final model comprises five broader domains (i.e., negative affectivity, detachment, antagonism, disinhibition, and psychoticism) and 25 more specific facets (e.g., eccentricity, callousness, separation insecurity). In *DSM-5*, the domains of the *DSM-5* trait model are now described as "maladaptive variants of the extensively validated and replicated model of personality known as the 'Big Five,' or Five-Factor Model of personality (FFM)" (APA, 2013, p. 773). Despite its recent development and publication, there are already several studies that have examined the relations between the *DSM-5* trait model and the FFM; to date, the *DSM-5* trait model is typically assessed using the Personality Inventory for *DSM-5* (Krueger et al., 2012; see Maples et al., 2015, for a briefer version as well). Averaging the correlations between the *DSM-5* and FFM domains across seven studies ($n = 2,471$), the convergent correlations range from .20 (psychoticism–openness) to .71 (negative affectivity–neuroticism) with a mean correlation of .56 (see Table 3.4). Despite differences in how these models were assessed across these studies, with regard to FFM-based instruments (e.g., NEO PI-R; Five Factor Model Rating Form) and raters (self; clinical ratings), the effect sizes did not vary dramatically except in the case of openness. For this domain, the convergent correlations ranged from −.18 to .46. Not surprisingly, there continues to be an ongoing debate as to the nature of the relations between these two dimensions (e.g., Chmielewski, Bagby, Markon, Ring, & Ryder, 2014; Edmundson, Lynam, Miller, Gore, & Widiger, 2011).

Table 3.4 CONVERGENT CORRELATIONS BETWEEN FIVE-FACTOR MODEL AND *DSM-5* DOMAINS ACROSS SEVEN SAMPLES

	Negative Affectivity	Detachment	Psychoticism	Antagonism	Disinhibition
		UNWEIGHTED *rs*			
Five-Factor Model					
Neuroticism	.71				
Extraversion		-.58			
Openness			.20		
Agreeableness				-.64	
Conscientiousness					-.56

NOTE: N = 2,471.

Expert Ratings of the *DSM-5* Section III Traits Associated With *DSM-IV/5* Personality Disorders

The *DSM-5* Personality and Personality Disorder (P & PD) Work Group specified the manner in which the 25 traits from the *DSM-5* model would be used to diagnose the *DSM-IV* PDs (see Table 3.5). For instance, the *DSM-5* Section III approach states that schizotypal PD is diagnosed using the following traits (in addition to evidence of both self and interpersonal dysfunction): suspiciousness, restricted affectivity, withdrawal, eccentricity, cognitive and perceptual dysregulation, and unusual beliefs and experiences. In addition to the ratings provided by the *DSM-5* P & PD Work Group, independent expert ratings of the relevance of *DSM-5* traits to each *DSM-IV* PD exist, which were collected by Samuel, Lynam, Widiger, and Ball (2012).

These ratings were collected by asking a larger group of experts (i.e., individuals who had published on the PD for which they provided ratings) to rate the relevance of all *DSM-5* traits in relation to a specific PD using a 0 (not at all or very little) to 3 (extremely descriptive) metric. These ratings were conducted on the original 37 traits put forth by the *DSM-5* P & PD Work Group but can be translated easily to the official 25-trait model following Krueger et al. (2012). See Table 3.5 for these expert ratings. In general, the *DSM-5* P & PD Work Group trait assignments were correlated (traits included in the *DSM-5* count were given a "1," those not included in a given PD diagnosis were given a "0") with Samuel et al. expert ratings with correlations ranging from .51 (paranoid) to .91 (schizoid) with a median of .73. A comparison of these two sets can help identify where the two sets of ratings diverge. For instance, the *DSM-5* P & PD Work Group chose only two traits for the diagnosis of narcissistic PD—grandiosity and attention seeking—whereas the Samuel et al. experts rated grandiosity (3.00), manipulativeness (2.38), and callousness (2.07) as being most emblematic of this disorder (attention seeking, which the *DSM-5* P & PD Work Group included, was given only a rating of 1.83 by the Samuel et al.).

Validity of the *DSM-5* Trait PD Counts: Convergent Validity

To date, there have been a few studies (e.g., Miller et al., 2015; Samuel et al., 2013) that have examined the correlations between the *DSM-5* Section III PD counts and Section II PD scores. Although there are a variety of ways one might calculate counts (see Samuel et al. for a review), the procedure used here is modeled after the one used in the FFM literature in which the scores for each relevant facet are simply summed (i.e., personality dysfunction scores were not included). Averaged across these two studies, the convergent validity correlations for the Section III PD counts and the Section II PD scores range from .46 (obsessive-compulsive) to .74 (borderline) with a median of .61 (see Table 3.6). The size of these correlations was relatively similar across the two samples despite differences in sample composition (Miller et al.: community participants in mental health treatment; Samuel et al.: undergraduates) and assessment of the Section II and III PDs

	PAR		SZD		SCT		APD		BPD	
	AR	D5	AR	D5	AR	D5	AR	D5	AR	D5
Submissiveness	0.11		0.38		0.43		0.09		1.43	
Depressivity	1.02		0.52		0.59		0.35		1.85	x
Separation insecurity	0.33		0.08		0.43		0.09		**2.69**	x
Anxiousness	1.33		0.85		1.64		0.23		1.93	x
Emotional lability	0.78		0.15		0.64		1.36		**2.79**	x
Suspiciousness	**3.00**	x	1.23		**2.50**	x	1.57		1.32	
Perseveration	1.33		0.77		0.62		0.14		0.45	
Restricted affectivity	**2.00**		**2.85**	x	1.93	x	1.62		0.29	
Withdrawal	**2.22**		**2.89**	x	**2.50**	x	0.93		0.39	
Intimacy avoidance	**2.00**	x	**2.77**	x	**2.29**		1.10		0.67	
Anhedonia	1.56		**2.38**	x	1.79		0.48		0.57	
Manipulativeness	1.11		0.00		0.29		**2.95**	x	0.95	
Deceitfulness	1.11		0.08		0.29		**2.67**	x	0.69	
Hostility	**2.39**	x	0.46		0.54		**2.50**	x	1.42	x
Callousness	1.89		0.66		0.47		**2.84**	x	1.24	
Attention seeking	0.11		0.00		0.36		1.43		1.10	
Grandiosity	1.44		0.46		0.50		**2.57**		0.55	
Irresponsibility	0.67		0.23		0.79		**2.76**	x	1.12	
Impulsivity	0.22		0.15		0.71		**2.62**	x	**2.48**	x
Distractibility	0.33		0.54		1.36		1.38		1.12	
Risk taking	1.11		0.96		1.50		**2.85**	x	**2.23**	x
Rigid perfectionism	1.67		0.92		0.74		0.19		0.52	
Eccentricity	1.06		1.31		**2.79**	x	0.24		0.96	
Cognitive/perceptual dysregulation	0.33		0.62		**2.00**	x	0.05		1.70	
Unusual beliefs/experiences	0.89	x	1.12		**2.90**	x	0.17		0.56	
Profile *rs*	.51*		.91*		.79*		.73*		.82*	

NOTE: Ratings of 2 or higher are bolded. Profile correlations calculated by replacing "x"s with 1 for the *DSM-5* ratings (and traits without an "x" were given a 0).
*$p < .01$.
AR = academician ratings (compiled from Samuel et al., 2012); D5 = *DSM-5* trait assignments; PAR = paranoid; SZD = schizoid; SCT = schizotypal; APD = antisocial personality disorder; BPD = borderline personality disorder; HIS = histrionic personality disorder; NPD = narcissistic personality disorder; AVD = avoidant personality disorder; DPD = dependent personality disorder; OCPD = obsessive-compulsive personality disorder.
SOURCE: Data compiled from Samuel, Lynam, Widiger, and Ball (2012).
Academician and *DSM-5* Ratings of Personality Disorders Using the *DSM-5* Trait Model

Table 3.5 CONTINUED

	HIS		NPD		AVD		DPD		OCPD	
	AR	D5	AR	D5	AR	D5	AR	D5	AR	D5
Submissiveness	1.12		0.14		**2.07**		**2.80**	x	0.54	
Depressivity	0.62		0.55		1.67		1.43		0.95	
Separation insecurity	1.76		0.62		1.07		**2.70**	x	0.54	
Anxiousness	1.24		0.83		**2.43**	x	**2.20**	x	1.62	
Emotional lability	**2.59**	x	1.28		0.43		1.15		0.33	
Suspiciousness	0.59		1.45		0.79		0.60		0.38	
Perseveration	0.24		0.38		0.29		0.50		**2.46**	x
Restricted affectivity	0.24		0.86		1.21		0.26		1.46	x
Withdrawal	0.03		0.36		1.79	x	0.48		0.93	
Intimacy avoidance	0.75		1.14		1.79	x	0.32		0.92	x
Anhedonia	0.12		0.41		1.36	x	0.37		0.85	
Manipulativeness	**2.06**	x	**2.38**		0.07		0.74		0.85	
Deceitfulness	1.65		1.59		0.07		0.42		0.31	
Hostility	0.90		1.69		0.07		0.37		0.96	
Callousness	1.09		**2.07**		0.00		0.14		0.79	
Attention seeking	**2.82**	x	1.83	x	0.00		0.95		0.23	
Grandiosity	**2.06**		**3.00**	x	0.36		0.42		1.00	
Irresponsibility	1.59		0.86		0.00		0.24		0.15	
Impulsivity	**2.18**		0.93		0.07		0.53		0.31	
Distractibility	1.94		0.17		0.50		0.53		0.46	
Risk taking	**2.21**		1.85		0.50		0.94		0.62	
Rigid perfectionism	0.28		0.83		0.55		0.59		**3.00**	x
Eccentricity	1.03		0.18		0.04		0.10		0.31	
Cognitive/perceptual dysregulation	1.35		0.07		0.07		0.50		0.23	
Unusual beliefs/ experiences	0.62		0.14		0.04		0.15		0.23	
Profile *rs*	.58*		.53*		.68*		.90*		.73*	

(Miller et al.: clinical ratings; Samuel et al.: self-reports). It is also noteworthy that the average convergent correlations manifested by the Section III PD counts and Section II PD scores were significantly correlated ($r = .70$, $p < .05$) with the number of traits used to assess each PD in the Section III approach (range: 2 [narcissistic] to 7 [antisocial; borderline]), suggesting that greater convergence may be attainable for several PDs if additional traits are added to the Section III *DSM-5* PDs.

Table 3.6 CONVERGENT CORRELATIONS AMONG DSM-5 PERSONALITY DISORDER TRAIT COUNTS AND SECTION II DSM-5 PERSONALITY DISORDERS

DSM PD Counts	Miller et al. (2015) (N = 109)	Samuel et al. (2013) (N = 1,025)	Mean r (N = 1,134)
Paranoid	.59	.61	.60
Schizoid	.67	.63	.65
Schizotypal	.56	.71	.64
Antisocial	.81	.61	.72
Borderline	.81	.66	.74
Histrionic	.60	.61	.61
Narcissistic	.53	.58	.56
Avoidant	.55	.60	.58
Dependent	.59	.60	.60
OCPD	.43	.49	.46

NOTE: OCPD = Obsessive-compulsive personality disorder.

Discriminant Validity/Comorbidity

Miller and colleagues (2015) examined the discriminant validity of the DSM-5 PD counts and found that for 7 of the 10 PDs they manifested their largest correlation (or tied for the largest) with the corresponding DSM-5 Section II PD. For two of the remaining three (paranoid and narcissistic) they manifested slightly higher correlations with PDs from the same cluster (schizotypal and histrionic, respectively). Much like the findings reported previously for the FFM PDs, one would expect that the DSM-5 Section III PD counts would also recreate the comorbidity found among the Section II PDs; Miller et al. found that this was the case as the patterns of relations among the two sets of PD scores were significantly correlated with one another ($r = .78$) and that the comorbidity among the DSM-5 Section III PD counts was significantly associated with the number of traits shared among the PDs ($r = .76$).

Similarity of Empirical Networks

Miller et al. (2015) also examined whether the DSM-5 Section II and III PDs manifested similar empirical networks with relation to general traits from the FFM. To do this, the two sets of DSM-5 PD scores were first correlated with the 30 facets of the FFM and the similarities between the two sets of correlations were

Table 3.7 PROFILE TRAIT SIMILARITIES AMONG ALL
10 *DSM-5* SECTION II AND SECTION III PERSONALITY
DISORDERS

DSM PD Counts	Miller et al. (2015) (N = 109)
	r_{ICC}
Paranoid	.95
Schizoid	.92
Schizotypal	.82
Antisocial	.93
Borderline	.98
Histrionic	.71
Narcissistic	.83
Avoidant	.91
Dependent	.96
OCPD	.59
Mean r_{ICC}	.90

NOTE: OCPD = obsessive-compulsive personality
disorder; PD = personality disorder.

SOURCE: Adapted with permission from Miller, J. D., Few,
L. R., Lynam, D. R., & MacKillop, J. (2015). Pathological
personality traits can capture DSM-IV personality
disorder types. *Personality Disorders: Theory, Research,
and Treatment, 6,* 32–40.

examined using a r_{ICC}. The intraclass correlations among these FFM trait profiles
for the 10 PDs ranged from .59 (obsessive-compulsive) to .98 (borderline) with a
mean of .90 (see Table 3.7). A review of the lowest and highest convergence can
help elucidate these findings (see Table 3.8 for Section II and III trait profiles for
obsessive-compulsive and borderline PDs). The trait profiles associated with the
two borderline scores were nearly identical, with both demonstrating substantial
positive correlations with facets of neuroticism, and negative correlations with
facets from conscientiousness, agreeableness, and extraversion.

There was a more moderate degree of overlap among the trait correlates of the
Section II and III OCPD scores; here, the correlations differed primarily in relation to facets from extraversion with the Section III trait-based OCPD score
manifesting substantially larger negative correlations with traits such as gregariousness, warmth, and positive emotions. It is worth nothing that the original
DSM-5 trait-based diagnosis of OCPD involved only two facets: perseveration and

Table 3.8 PROFILE SIMILARITY AMONG SECTION II AND SECTION III PERSONALITY
DISORDERS—HIGHEST AND LOWEST

	Borderline		OCPD	
	DSM-IV	*DSM-5* TC	*DSM-5* TC	*DSM-IV*
Anxiety	.41	.39	.25	.34
Angry hostility	.47	.53	.25	.24
Depression	.50	.50	.27	.26
Self-consciousness	.39	.36	.29	.23
Impulsiveness	.47	.48	−.03	.15
Vulnerability	.50	.52	.23	.28
Warmth	−.19	−.21	−.58	−.09
Gregariousness	−.18	−.14	−.45	−.19
Assertiveness	−.12	−.11	−.30	−.06
Activity	−.15	−.15	−.30	−.04
Excitement seeking	.11	.17	−.20	−.09
Positive emotions	−.16	−.20	−.49	−.21
Fantasy	.06	.00	−.19	.07
Aesthetics	.13	.04	−.22	−.08
Feelings	.08	.08	−.21	.15
Actions	−.09	−.20	−.37	−.21
Ideas	−.05	−.13	−.15	.08
Values	−.05	−.19	−.20	−.12
Trust	−.29	−.40	−.41	−.11
Straightforwardness	−.40	−.38	.02	−.10
Altruism	−.19	−.22	−.23	.02
Compliance	−.26	−.33	−.04	−.06
Modesty	.04	.00	.10	.11
Tendermindedness	−.13	−.11	−.19	−.07
Competence	−.46	−.50	−.12	−.02
Order	−.24	−.23	.14	.16
Dutifulness	−.47	−.44	.12	.09
Achievement striving	−.33	−.31	−.02	.04
Self-discipline	−.31	−.26	−.07	−.14
Deliberation	−.45	−.50	.21	.07
Profile match (r_{ICC})	.98*		.59*	

NOTE: OCPD = obsessive-compulsive personality disorder.
*$p < .01$.

SOURCE: Adapted with permission from Miller, J. D., Few, L. R., Lynam, D. R., &
MacKillop, J. (2015). Pathological personality traits can capture DSM-IV personality
disorder types. *Personality Disorders: Theory, Research, and Treatment, 6*, 32–40.

rigid perfectionism. However, this diagnosis was revised prior to inclusion in the *DSM-5* and two other traits were added: restricted affectivity and intimacy avoidance. Table 3.9 demonstrates the degree to which these newer traits are correlated with *DSM-5* Section II diagnoses of OCPD. The mean correlations across two

Table 3.9 REASONS FOR LIMITED CONVERGENCE OF *DSM-5* SECTION III OCPD COUNT

	DSM-5	AR	OCPD	
			Miller et al.	Hopwood et al.
Submissiveness		0.54	.23	.26
Depressivity		0.95	.15	.27
Separation insecurity		0.54	.09	.28
Anxiousness		1.62	.23	.42
Emotional lability		0.33	.32	.35
Suspiciousness		0.38	.17	.27
Perseveration	x	2.46	.41	.46
Restricted affectivity	*x*	1.46	.16	.23
Withdrawal		0.93	.24	.28
Intimacy avoidance	*x*	0.92	.11	.28
Anhedonia		0.85	.25	.22
Manipulativeness		0.85	.12	.23
Deceitfulness		0.31	.10	.19
Hostility		0.96	.21	.32
Callousness		0.79	−.02	.15
Attention seeking		0.23	−.08	.18
Grandiosity		1.00	.15	.25
Irresponsibility		0.15	.15	.15
Impulsivity		0.31	.03	.11
Distractibility		0.46	.27	.30
Risk taking		0.62	.07	−.07
Rigid perfectionism	x	3.00	.52	.54
Eccentricity		0.31	.19	.34
Cognitive/perceptual dysregulation		0.23	.30	.35
Unusual beliefs/experiences		0.23	.14	.31

NOTE: AR = Samuel et al. (2012) academician ratings. x = trait included in the *DSM-5* Section OCPD count.

SOURCES: Hopwood et al. (2012); Miller et al. (2015).

studies (Hopwood et al., 2012; Miller et al., 2015) for the two original facets of perseveration and rigid perfectionism were .44 and .53, respectively, compared to mean correlations of .20 and .20 for the two newly added traits of restricted affectivity and intimacy avoidance. Miller et al. (2015) demonstrated that removal of these two "new" traits from the Section III OCPD count resulted in an increased convergent correlation with the Section II OCPD scores (r = .56 for two traits vs. .43 for all four traits) and better convergence with the FFM profile generated by the *DSM-5* Section II OCPD scores (two traits: r_{ICC} = .78; four traits: r_{ICC} = .59).

Sex Differences

Mirroring the findings for the FFM, it is possible that the sex differences found for *DSM* PDs might be explained by sex differences on the pathological personality traits used to describe PDs in *DSM-5* Section III. Based on the gender differences found for the *DSM-5* traits in the Few et al. (2013) study, men had higher scores on risk taking, restricted affect, and eccentricity, whereas women had higher scores for traits such as emotional lability and depressivity. Similar to the Lynam and Widiger (2007) finding using FFM traits, sex differences on the *DSM-5* Section III PD Trait Counts were significantly correlated with the sex differences reported for the *DSM* PDs on the basis of Lynam and Widiger's meta-analytic review (r = .64). As with the FFM data, it seems that sex differences in PDs may be due, at least in part, to differences in pathological personality traits that comprise these disorders.

Clinical Utility

As with the FFM, there are now results that speak to the clinical utility of the *DSM-5* Section III approach from the perspective of clinicians' preferences, as well as data that examine these models in relation to clinically relevant outcomes. Morey, Skodol, and Oldham (2014) compared clinicians' preference for the *DSM-5* Section II and III PD models and found that for five of six outcomes (e.g., ease of use; communicating with patients; communicating with professionals; useful for formulating intervention plans), the *DSM-5* Section III trait model was seen as having greater clinical utility than the *DSM-5* Section II PD approach.

With regard to the latter conceptualization of utility, Few and colleagues demonstrated that the *DSM-5* Section III traits were substantially correlated with interview-based ratings of personality impairment, including impairments in identity (mean r = .48), self-directness (mean r = .46), empathy (mean r = .44), and intimacy (mean r = .50). The *DSM-5* Section III traits were also significantly correlated with *DSM-5* Section II PDs, as well as symptoms of anxiety, depression, and overall distress. With regard to incremental validity, the *DSM-5* traits provided twice the incremental validity in the impairment variables above and beyond the variance accounted for by the *DSM-5* Section II PDs (mean ΔR^2 = .11) as compared to that provided by the *DSM-5* Section II PDs above the Section III trait domains (mean ΔR^2 = .06). With regard to symptoms of depression and anxiety, as well as general distress, the *DSM-5* traits again accounted for additional variance over the Section II PDs (mean ΔR^2 = .08), although the PDs accounted for additional variance as well (mean ΔR^2 = .08).

CONCLUSIONS

Study the past, if you would divine the future.

—CONFUCIUS

The inclusion of a trait model in the *DSM-5* represents an important advance toward a more empirically based, valid, and useful approach to research and treatment of personality pathology. As documented here, there is a robust literature on the validity and utility of general trait models, much of which looks to generalize to the *DSM-5* pathological trait model. It has been argued elsewhere that the existing empirical base could have been used to provide a stronger empirical base for the *DSM-5* PD proposal (Miller & Lynam, 2013), but for some reason much of the literature was largely ignored in publications originally put out by the *DSM-5* P & PD Work Group (Blashfield & Reynolds, 2012; Lilienfeld, Watts, & Smith, 2012). The best chance that the *DSM-5* Section III PD model, or a similar trait-based model, has of eventually becoming the sole or primary diagnostic approach used in the future iterations of the *DSM* is to combine the existing literature on the FFM (and other trait models) approaches to PDs with the rapidly growing research on the *DSM-5* pathological trait model. The integration of the extant empirical literature on trait models of PDs with the burgeoning research on the *DSM-5* Section III model would go far in rebutting claims that the *DSM-5* Section III PD model, as least the trait portion, represents a brand new and untested model. Another important task will be to work toward building some consensus within the field, which will be a Herculean task, given the substantial criticisms that have been levied against various aspects of the *DSM-5* Section II PD approach (Gunderson, 2010, 2013; Livesley, 2012; Shedler et al., 2010). Unfortunately, many of the criticisms that have been made to date are inconsistent with empirical evidence (e.g., that the new PDs will be substantially different than the traditional PD constructs; that borderline and antisocial PDs are not well captured by trait approaches) and thus bring more "heat" than "light" to these important issues. Moving forward, it will be important that objective considerations of the existing data drive decisions as to how PDs are conceptualized, assessed, and diagnosed in the official diagnostic nosology.

REFERENCES

An asterisk (*) indicates that data from this study were included in the meta-analyses.
American Psychiatric Association. (1987). *Diagnostic and statistical manual of mental disorders* (3rd ed., rev. ed.). Washington, DC: Author.

American Psychiatric Association. (1994). *Diagnostic and statistical manual of mental disorders* (4th ed.). Washington, DC: Author.

American Psychiatric Association. (2013). *Diagnostic and statistical manual of mental disorders* (5th ed.). Washington, DC: Author.

Blashfield, R. K., & Reynolds, S. M. (2012). An invisible college view of the DSM-5 personality disorder classification. *Journal of Personality Disorders, 26*, 821–829.

*Cauffman, E., Kimonis, E. R., Dmitrieva, J., & Monahan, K. C. (2009). A multimethod assessment of juvenile psychopathy: Comparing the predictive utility of the PCL: YV, YPI, and NEO PRI. *Psychological Assessment, 21*, 528–542.

Chmielewski, M., Bagby, R. M., Markon, K., Ring, A. J., & Ryder, A. G. (2014). Openness to experience, intellect, schizotypal personality disorder, and psychoticism: Resolving the controversy. *Journal of Personality Disorders, 28*, 483–499.

Clark, L. A. (1993). *Manual for the Schedule for Nonadaptive and Adaptive Personality (SNAP)*. Minneapolis: University of Minnesota Press.

Costa, P. T., & McCrae, R. R. (1992). The five-factor model of personality and its relevance to personality disorders. *Journal of Personality Disorders, 6*, 343–359.

Costa, P. T., & McCrae, R. R. (1992). *Revised NEO Personality Inventory (NEO-PI-R) and NEO Five-Factor Inventory (NEO-FFI) Professional Manual*. Lutz, Florida: PAR, Inc.

*Decuyper, M., De Clerq, B., De Bolle, M., & De Fruyt, F. (2009). Validation of FFM PD counts for screening personality pathology and psychopathy in adolescence. *Journal of Personality Disorders, 23*, 587–605.

Decuyper, M., De Pauw, S., De Fruyt, F., De Bolle, M., & De Clercq, B. J. (2009). A meta-analysis of psychopathy-, antisocial PD, and FFM associations. *European Journal of Personality, 23*, 531–565.

*De Fruyt, F., De Clercq, B., De Bolle, M., Wille, B., Markon, K., & Krueger, R. F. (2013). General and maladaptive traits in a five-factor framework for DSM-5 in a university student sample. *Assessment, 20*, 295–307.

Edmundson, M., Lynam, D. R., Miller, J. D., Gore, W. L., & Widiger, T. A. (2011). A five-factor measure of schizotypal personality traits. *Assessment, 18*, 321–334.

Few, L. R., Lynam, D. R., Maples, J. L., MacKillop, J., & Miller, J. D. (2015). Comparing the utility of DSM-5 section II and III antisocial personality disorder diagnostic approaches for capturing psychopathic traits. *Personality Disorders: Theory, Research, and Treatment, 6*(1), 64–74.

Few, L. R., Miller, J. D., Morse, J. Q., Yaggi, K. E., Reynolds, S. K., & Pilkonis, P. A. (2010). Examining the reliability and validity of clinician ratings on the Five-Factor Model score sheet. *Assessment, 17*, 440–453.

*Few, L. R., Miller, J. D., Rothbaum, A., Meller, S., Maples, J., Terry, D., Collins, B., & MacKillop, J. (2013). Examination of the Section III DSM-5 diagnostic system for personality disorders in an outpatient clinical sample. *Journal of Abnormal Psychology, 22*, 1057–1069.

Frances, A. (1993). Dimensional diagnosis of personality––Not whether, but when and which. *Psychological Inquiry, 4*, 110–111.

*Gaughan, E. T., Miller, J. D., *Pryor, L. R., & Lynam, D. R. (2009). Comparing two alternative models of general personality in the assessment of psychopathy: A test of the NEO PI-R and the MPQ. *Journal of Personality, 77*, 965–996.

*Gore, W. L., & Widiger, T. A. (2013). The DSM-5 dimensional trait model and five-factor models of general personality. *Journal of Abnormal Psychology, 122*, 816–821.

*Griffin, S. A., & Samuel, D. B. (2014). A closer look at the lower-order structure of the Personality Inventory for DSM-5: Comparison with the Five Factor Model. *Personality Disorders: Theory, Research, and Treatment, 5*, 406–412.

Gunderson, J. G. (2010). Revising the borderline diagnosis for DSM-V: An alternative proposal. *Journal of Personality Disorders, 24*, 694–708.

Gunderson, J. G. (2013). Seeking clarity for future revisions of the personality disorders in DSM-5. *Personality Disorders: Theory, Research, and Treatment, 4*, 368–376.

*Gudonis, L. C., Miller, D. J., Miller, J. D., & Lynam, D. R. (2008). Conceptualizing personality disorders from a general model of personality functioning: Antisocial personality disorder and the five-factor model. *Personality and Mental Health, 2*, 249–264.

Hare, R. D. (1991). *The Psychopathy Checklist-Revised*. Toronto, ON: Multi-Health Systems.

Hopwood, C. J., Thomas, K. M., Markon, K. E., Wright, A. G., & Krueger, R. F. (2012). DSM-5 personality traits and DSM-IV personality disorders. *Journal of Abnormal Psychology, 121*, 424–432.

Krueger, R. F., Derringer, J., Markon, K., Watson, D., & Skodol, A. (2012). Initial construction of a maladaptive personality trait model and inventory for DSM-5. *Psychological Medicine, 42*, 1879–1890.

*Lawton, E. M., Shields, A. J., & Oltmanns, T. F. (2011). Five-Factor Model personality disorder prototypes in a community sample: Self- and informant-reports predicting interview-based DSM diagnoses. *Personality Disorders: Theory, Research, and Treatment, 2*, 279–294.

Lilienfeld, S. O., Watts, A. L., & Smith, S. F. (2012). The DSM revision as a social psychological process: A commentary on Blashfield and Reynolds. *Journal of Personality Disorders, 26*, 830–834.

Livesley, J. (2012). Tradition versus empiricism in the current DSM-5 proposal for revising the classification of personality disorders. *Criminal Behaviour and Mental Health, 22*, 81–90.

Livesley, W. J., Jackson, D. N., & Schroeder, M. L. (1992). Factorial structure of traits delineating personality disorders in clinical and general population samples. *Journal of Abnormal Psychology, 101*, 432–440.

Lynam, D. R., Gaughan, E. T., Miller, J. D., Miller, D. J., Mullins-Sweatt, S., & Widiger, T. A. (2011). Assessing the basic traits associated with psychopathy: Development and validation of the Elemental Psychopathy Assessment. *Psychological Assessment, 23*, 108–124.

Lynam, D. R., & Widiger, T. A. (2001). Using the five-factor model to represent the DSM-IV personality disorders: An expert consensus approach. *Journal of Abnormal Psychology, 110*, 401–412.

Lynam, D. R., & Widiger, T. A. (2007). Using a general model of personality to understand sex differences in the personality disorders. *Journal of Personality Disorders, 21*, 583–602.

Maples, J. L., Carter, N. T., Few, L. R., Crego, C., Gore, W. L., Samuel, D. B., . . . Miller, J. D. (2015). Testing whether the DSM-5 personality disorder trait model can be measured with a reduced set of items: An item response theory investigation of the Personality Inventory for DSM-5. *Psychological Assessment, 27*, 1195–1210.

McCrae, R. R. (2008). A note on some measures of profile agreement. *Journal of Personality Assessment, 90*, 105–109.

*Miller, J. D., Bagby, R. M., & Pilkonis, P. A. (2005). A comparison of the validity of the five-factor model (FFM) personality disorder prototypes using FFM self-report and interview measures. *Psychological Assessment, 17*, 497–500.

Miller, J. D., Bagby, R. M., Pilkonis, P. A., Reynolds, S. K., & Lynam, D. R. (2005). A simplified technique for scoring the DSM-IV personality disorders with the five-factor model. *Assessment, 12*, 404–415.

*Miller, J. D., & Campbell, W. K (2008). Comparing clinical and social-personality conceptualizations of narcissism. *Journal of Personality, 76*, 449–476.

*Miller, J. D., Dir, A., Gentile, B., Wilson, L., Pryor, L. R., & Campbell, W. K. (2010). Searching for a vulnerable dark triad: Comparing factor 2 psychopathy, vulnerable narcissism, and borderline personality disorder. *Journal of Personality, 78*, 1529–1564.

Miller, J. D., Few, L. R., Lynam, D. R., & MacKillop, J. (2015). Pathological personality traits can capture DSM-IV personality disorder types. *Personality Disorders: Theory, Research, and Treatment, 6*, 32–40.

*Miller, J. D., Gaughan, E. T., & Pryor, L. R. (2008). The Levenson Self-Report Psychopathy Scale: An examination of the personality traits and disorders associated with the LSRP factors. *Assessment, 15*, 450–463.

*Miller, J. D., Gaughan, E. T., Pryor, L. R., & Kamen, C, & Campbell, W. K. (2009). Is research using the NPI relevant for understanding Narcissistic Personality Disorder? *Journal of Research in Personality, 43*, 482–488.

*Miller, J. D., Gentile, B., Wilson, L., & Campbell, W. K. (2013). Grandiose and vulnerable narcissism and the DSM-5 pathological personality trait model. *Journal of Personality Assessment, 95*, 284–290.

*Miller, J. D., & Lynam, D. R. (2008). Dependent personality disorder: Comparing an expert-generated and empirically derived Five-Factor Model personality disorder count. *Assessment, 15*, 4–15.

Miller, J. D., & Lynam, D. R. (2013). Missed opportunities in the DSM-5 section III personality disorder model. *Personality Disorders: Theory, Research, and Treatment, 4*, 365–366.

*Miller, J. D., Lynam, D. R., Pham-Scottez, A., De Clercq, B., Rolland, J. P., & De Fruyt, F., (2008). Using the Five-Factor Model of personality to score the DSM-IV personality disorders. *Annales Médico Psychologiques, 166*, 418–426.

*Miller, J., Lynam, D., Widiger, T., & Leukefeld, C. (2001). Personality disorders as extreme variants of common personality dimensions: Can the five factor model adequately represent psychopathy? *Journal of Personality, 69*, 253–276

*Miller, J. D., Maples, J., Pryor, L. R., Morse, J. Q., Yaggi, K., & Pilkonis, P. A. (2010). Using clinician-rated Five-Factor Model data to score the DSM-IV personality disorders. *Journal of Personality Assesment, 92*, 296–305.

Miller, J. D., Morse, J. Q., Nolf, K., Stepp, S. D., & Pilkonis, P. A. (2012). Can DSM-IV borderline personality disorder be diagnosed via dimensional personality traits: Implications for the DSM-5 personality disorder proposal. *Journal of Abnormal Psychology, 121*, 944–950.

Miller, J. D., Pilkonis, P. A., & Morse, J. Q. (2004). Five-factor model prototypes for personality disorders: The utility of self-reports and observer ratings. *Assessment, 11*, 127–138.

*Miller, J. D., Reynolds, S. K., & Pilkonis, P. A. (2004). The validity of the five-factor model prototypes for personality disorders in two clinical samples. *Psychological Assessment, 16*, 310–322.

Morey, L. C., Skodol, A. E., & Oldham, J. M. (2014). Clinician judgments of clinical utility : A comparison of DSM-IV-TR personality disorders and the alternative model for DSM-5 personality disorders. *Journal of Abnormal Psychology, 123*, 398–405.

Mullins-Sweatt, S. N., & Lengel, G. J. (2012). Clinical utility of the Five-Factor Model of personality disorder. *Journal of Personality, 80*, 1615–1639.

*Poy, R., Segarra, P., Esteller, À., López, R., & Moltó, J. (2014). FFM description of the triarchic conceptualization of psychopathy in men and women. *Psychological Assessment, 26*, 69–76.

Presnall, J. R. (2012). Disorders of personality: Clinical treatment from a five-factor perspective. In T. A. Widiger & P. T. Costa (Eds.), *Personality disorders and the Five-Factor Model of personality* (3rd ed., pp. 409–432). Washington, DC: APA.

*Rojas, S. L., & Widiger, T. A. (2014). Convergent and discriminant validity of the five factor form. *Assessment, 21*, 143–157.

Rottman, B., Ahn, W. K., Sanislow, C., & Kim, N. (2009). Can clinicians recognize DSM-IV personality disorders from five-factor model descriptions of patient cases? *American Journal of Psychiatry, 166*, 427–433.

*Samuel, D. B., Ansell, E. B., Hopwood, C. J., Morey, L. C., Markowitz, J. C., Skodol, A. E., & Grilo, C. M. (2010). The impact of NEO PI-R gender norms on the assessment of personality disorder profiles. *Psychological Assessment, 22*, 539–545.

*Samuel, D. B., Edmundson, M., & Widiger, T. A. (2011). Five factor model prototype matching scores: Convergence within alternative models. *Journal of Personality Disorders, 25*, 571–585.

Samuel, D. B., Hopwood, C. J., Krueger, R. F., Thomas, K. M., & Ruggero, C. J. (2013). Comparing methods for scoring personality disorder types using maladaptive traits in DSM-5. *Assessment, 20*, 353–361.

Samuel, D. B., Lynam, D. R., Widiger, T. A., & Ball, S. A. (2012). An expert consensus approach to relating the proposed DSM-5 types and traits. *Personality Disorders: Theory, Research, and Treatment, 3*, 1–16.

Samuel, D. B., & Widiger, T. A. (2004). Clinicians' personality descriptions of prototypic personality disorders. *Journal of Personality Disorders, 18*, 286–308.

Samuel, D. B., & Widiger, T. A. (2006). Clinicians" judgments of clinical utility: A comparison of the DSM-IV and five-factor models. *Journal of Abnormal Psychology, 115*, 298–308.

Samuel, D. B., & Widiger, T. A. (2008). A meta-analytic review of the relationships between the five-factor model and DSM-IV-TR personality disorders: A facet level analysis. *Clinical Psychology Review, 28*, 1326–1342.

Shedler, J., Beck, A., Fonagy, P., Gabbard, G.O., Gunderson, J., Kernberg, O., Michels, R., & Westen, D. (2010). Personality disorders in DSM-5. *American Journal of Psychiatry, 167*, 1026–1028.

Spitzer, R. L., First, M. B., Shedler, J., Westen, D., & Skodol, A. E. (2008). Clinical utility of five dimensional systems for personality diagnosis: A "consumer preference" study. *The Journal of Nervous and Mental Disease, 196*, 356–374.

Sprock, J. (2003). Dimensional versus categorical classification of prototypic and nonprototypic cases of personality disorder. *Journal of Clinical Psychology, 59*, 991–1014.

*Stepp, S., & Trull, T. J. (2007). Predictive validity of the five-factor model prototype scores for antisocial and borderline personality disorders. *Personality and Mental Health, 1*, 27–39.

*Tapscott, J. L., Vernon, P. A., & Veselka, L. (2012). A comparison of the construct validity of two alternative approaches to the assessment of psychopathy in the community. *Journal of Personality Assessment, 94*, 541–554.

*Thomas, K. M., Yalch, M. M., Krueger, R. F., Wright, A. G., Markon, K. E., & Hopwood, C. J. (2013). The convergent structure of DSM-5 personality trait facets and five-factor model trait domains. *Assessment, 20*, 308–311.

Trull, T.J., & Widiger, T.A. (1997). *Structured Interview for the Five-Factor Model of Personality (SIFFM): Professional manual*. Odessa, FL: PAR.

*Trull, T.J., Widiger, T.A, Lynam, D. R., & Costa, P. T. (2003). Borderline personality disorder from the perspective of general personality functioning. *Journal of Abnormal Psychology, 112*, 193–202.

*Van den Broeck, J., Rossi, G., De Clercq, B., Dierckx, E., & Bastiaansen, L. (2013). Validation of the FFM PD count technique for screening personality pathology in later middle-aged and older adults. *Aging & Mental Health, 17*, 180–188.

Warner, M. B., Morey, L. C., Finch, J. F., Gunderson, J. G., Skodol, A. E., Sanislow, C. A . . . Grilo, C. M. (2004). The longitudinal relationship of personality traits and disorders. *Journal of Abnormal Psychology, 113*, 217–227.

*Watson, D., Stasik, S. M., Ro, E., & Clark, L. A. (2013). Integrating normal and pathological personality relating the DSM-5 trait-dimensional model to general traits of personality. *Assessment, 20*, 312–326.

Widiger, T. A. (2013). A postmortem and future look at the personality disorders in DSM-5. *Personality Disorders: Theory, Research, and Treatment, 4*, 382–387.

Widiger, T. A., & Boyd, S. (2009). Personality disorder assessment instruments. In J. N. Butcher (Ed.), *Oxford handbook of personality assessment* (3rd ed., pp. 336–363). New York, NY: Oxford University Press.

Widiger, T. A., & Costa, P. T. Jr. (Eds.). (2013). *Personality disorders and the five-factor model of personality* (pp. 285–310). Washington, DC, US: American Psychological Association.

Widiger, T. A., & Lynam, D. R. (1998). Psychopathy and the five-factor model of personality. In T. Millon & E. Simonsen (Eds.), *Psychopathy: Antisocial, criminal, and violent behavior* (pp. 171–187). New York, NY: Guilford.

Widiger, T. A., & Trull, T. J. (1992). Personality and psychopathology: An application of the five-factor model. *Journal of Personality, 60*, 363–393.

Widiger, T. A., Trull, T. J., Clarkin, J. F., Sanderson, C. J., & Costa, P. T. (1994). A description of the DSM-III-R and DSM-IV personality disorders with the five-factor model of personality. In P. T. Costa, Jr., & T. A. Widiger (Eds.), *Personality disorders and the five-factor model of personality* (pp. 41–56). Washington, DC: APA.

Wright, A. G., Hopwood, C. J., & Zanarini, M. C. (2015). Associations between changes in normal personality traits and borderline personality disorder symptoms over 16 years. *Personality Disorders: Theory, Research, and Treatment, 6*, 1–11.

Zimmerman, M., Rothschild, L., & Chelminski, I. (2005). The prevalence of DSM-IV personality disorders in psychiatric outpatients. *American Journal of Psychiatry, 162*, 1911–1918.

Assessment Methods and Issues

4

Using Basic Personality Process Models to Inform the Personality Disorders

Core Momentary Stressor-Symptom Contingencies as Basic Etiology

WILLIAM FLEESON, R. MICHAEL FURR, MALEK MNEIMNE, AND ELIZABETH MAYFIELD ARNOLD ■

The modern scientific fields of personality and abnormal psychology share a common heritage in 19th-century psychoanalysis. Disagreement among its early members notwithstanding, the field was able to agree on two main points. First, that everyone is neurotic; and second, that the key undertaking in life is to overcome one's neurosis (Adler, 1988; Freud, 1959; Jung, 1964; Valliant & Perry, 1985). Both of these ideas have persisted to some degree throughout the years to shape the fields of personality and abnormal psychology; indeed, neuroticism and the treatment of disorders in which neuroticism is a central component remain highly researched topics. Though too untenable for most clinicians and scientists, owing primarily to a paucity of empirical support for its premises, a major strength of psychoanalytic theory is its comprehensiveness. Psychoanalytic theory includes hypotheses about structural, individual differences in the ways in which people think, feel, and act, and hypotheses about distal or developmental and proximal or momentary processes underlying those individual differences. The aim of this chapter is to provide such a comprehensive framework for understanding personality disorders (PDs) by drawing upon research on both the structure and processes of normal personality.

The purpose of this book is to explore the potential that research on normal personality has to inform research and knowledge about disordered personality.

Research on normal personality has made a great deal of progress in identifying the content of traits (Krueger, Skodol, Livesley, Shrout, & Huang, 2007; Saulsman & Page, 2004; Trull & Widiger, 2013; Wright et al., 2012). The content of traits includes both the identification of which traits exist and the structural relations among the traits (Costa & McCrae, 2006; Saucier, 2009; Wright, 2011). In recent years, this progress has been used to advance our understanding of PDs. As many chapters in this book attest, the content of normal personality dimensions can fruitfully inform the content of abnormal personality dimensions.

In agreement with Wright (2011), we argue that *process* as well as *content* could benefit from a similar advance. That is, we argue that models about the processes underlying normal personality traits may help facilitate mutually beneficial communication between personality and clinical psychologists. Process models are models that describe the mechanisms of traits and the etiology of traits. If the content of normal personality dimensions can be translated to abnormal personality, then the processes of those dimensions ought to translate as well. Ultimately, we will want to know not only the dimensions that underlie PDs but also how they work.

Incorporating the process models of normal personality may make the translation of normal personality to PDs more useful. Although assessment of personality structure can facilitate selection among empirically supported treatments, many clinicians focus largely on processes rather than on structure, because processes explain the onset and maintenance of symptomatology and their treatment constitutes the majority of patients' and clinicians' work. Thus, a translation that includes features of process may be especially valuable to clinicians. Adding process elements to the structural elements already in place may facilitate the adoption of a dimensional classification system of PDs.

Admittedly, there has been much less progress with regard to understanding the processes underlying normal personality (but see the Special Issue in *Journal of Research in Personality* on integrative models of personality; Fajkowska & DeYoung, 2015). However, whole trait theory (WTT; Fleeson, 2001, 2004, 2007, 2012), an empirically derived structural and process model of personality, may offer useful insights into personality pathology. We translate this to borderline personality disorder (BPD) with the core contingency model (Miskewicz et al., 2015).

The purpose of this chapter is to make four main points. The first point is that the translation of normal personality to PDs should include process models, not only structural content and associations. The process model we suggest leads to the second main point, which is that symptoms can be treated as distinct, momentary events rather than only as stable, enduring features of people. Each occurrence of a symptom can be taken as a short-lasting event of personal significance. Just like seizures are symptoms of epilepsy that unfold in real time, engaging in efforts to avoid abandonment and self-harm are symptoms of BPD that wax and wane in real time. We believe that much can be gained by treating PD symptoms in this manner, rather than thinking of them primarily as features of people that are always present. Third, etiology should concern not only the developmental or distal determinants of between-person differences in symptoms and disorders. Etiology should also concern the proximal mechanisms that lead to temporally bounded symptom occurrences (e.g., what in-the-moment, social-cognitive factors might drive momentary efforts to avoid abandonment and momentary self-harm?). Fourth, the core contingency model captures these ideas in a translation of normal personality models to models that are sensitive to the unique features of PDs.

DIMENSIONAL STRUCTURAL MODELS OF PERSONALITY

The premise of this book, that models of normal personality can inform models of PDs, is based upon a Galenic-Hippocratic sort of continuity between normal and abnormal personality. Using a dimensional model of PDs, individuals would be rated along several basic personality dimensions (Widiger, Trull, Hurt, Clarkin, & Frances, 1987). A specific configuration of dimensions, rather than arbitrary cut-points, would then be used to identify individuals with PDs.

Since the introduction of categorical and prototypical classification systems of psychopathology (American Psychological Association, 1952; World Health Organization, 1948), practitioners and researchers have noted problems with their applicability, including unreliability, a lack of discriminant validity, a high degree of comorbidity among disorders, and a high rate of "not-otherwise-specified" diagnoses, and have proposed alternative dimensional classification systems (Frances, 1982; Hines & Williams, 1975; Kelly, 1965; Wright, 2011). The task force for the *Diagnostic and Statistical Manual of Mental Disorders*, fifth edition (*DSM-5*) was cognizant of these problems and noted that "the typical patient meeting criteria for a specific personality disorder frequently also meets criteria for other personality disorders. Similarly, other specified or unspecified personality disorder is often the correct (but mostly uninformative) diagnosis, in the sense that patients do not tend to present with patterns of symptoms that correspond with one and only one personality disorder," but opted to retain the prototypical classification system "to preserve continuity with current clinical practice" (APA, 2013, p. 761).

A major impediment to the implementation of a dimensional classification system has been in deciding upon a basic structure of personality to adopt (Frances, 1993; Trull & Widiger, 2013; Widiger & Simonsen, 2005). Indeed, the text revision of the fourth edition of the *DSM* (*DSM-IV-TR*; APA, 2000) included in its appendix several structural models of personality, including the five-factor model (Big 5; neuroticism, extraversion, openness to experience, agreeableness, conscientiousness; Costa & McCrae, 2006), Cloninger's seven-factor model, Livesley's four-factor model, Clark and Watson's three-factor model, the two-factor interpersonal circumplex, and Millon's three-factor model. Although these personality models enjoy robust empirical support, they are largely descriptive or structural in nature and do not emphasize process accounts of trait-relevant behavior. Thus, although promising in their ability to accurately classify individuals with PDs, structural models of personality mainly provide half of the picture, or tell half of the story, of PDs.

WHOLE TRAIT THEORY

WTT is an empirically derived, integrated structural/descriptive and etiological/process model of normal personality. It emerged largely as a result of insights gained by the field's great endeavor to understand whether structural approaches to personality or social-cognitive approaches to behavior are more powerful in their predictions of behavior (Mischel, 1973; Fleeson, 2004). WTT tries to combine the insights of both perspectives into an integrated model of personality, one that is inclusive of both structural and process advances in personality psychology.

The Descriptive Side of Traits

WTT starts with the notion that traits are partly descriptive. For example, when we say that someone is extraverted, we are at least in part describing how that person acts. Although knowledge about the descriptive content of traits has advanced considerably, there has been less progress in developing one aspect of descriptive content: the patterns of behavior implicated by a trait. Importantly, this part of the content of traits is a part with a close connection to processes of traits.

When traits are used in this descriptive sense, the question arises as to what behaviors the traits are supposed to be describing. How much do people manifest their traits in their behavior? How much and how far do they deviate from their traits in their behavior?

Identifying what is described by trait terms requires discovering the traits people actually manifest as they live their lives. The discovery of the traits people are manifesting can be based on the concept of a personality state. A personality state is identical to a personality trait in every manner, except that it is manifested and assessed on a shorter time scale than traits (i.e., it is a momentary trait), much in the same way that state and trait affect and mood have been differentiated for nearly half a century (e.g., Spielberger, Gorsuch, & Lushene, 1970). Thus, a personality state is the personality a person manifests at the moment.

Examinations of personality states have typically required participants to carry a personal digital assistant (e.g., iPod) with them for 1 to 4 weeks and report on their recent (e.g., past 5 minutes to 3 hours) personality traits several times a day (Fleeson, 2004). For example, an item assessing extraversion may ask a participant to rate how talkative he or she was during the last 15 minutes. The question is, what personalities do people actually have at the moment, and how do these correspond to the personalities they report on traditional personality questionnaires?

One fundamental question is whether the state concept adequately represents the content of the Big 5. In a within-person, chain-p factor analysis, the factor analysis is conducted on variability across time within people. Every variable is centered within person on their mean, so that all differences between people are removed and only differences across time remain. All people are then chained together, so that the data set has cases equal to the number of participants times the number of reports completed by the average participant. The factor analytic results reveal which variables wax and wane together across time.

A pattern that has emerged in many of our studies is that state items factor into groups based on the Big 5. In fact, the Big 5 emerge so clearly in study after study that one could use the within-person factor analysis as a check on the quality of the data entry. The most common deviations are that a small number of variables (5% to 20%) cross-load onto another factor or load on the wrong factor altogether. Thus, results clearly indicate that these states do not fundamentally change the meaning of the Big 5 when instructions refer to "right now" rather than "in general."

Given that the states appear to reflect the same content as the Big 5 traits, the question arises as to what traits people are manifesting in their daily behavior, whether there are individual differences in them, and whether they relate to traits as assessed in traditional questionnaires. The central tendency of states is indicative of an individual's general or typical level of the corresponding trait. Central tendencies usually vary across the spectrum of each trait with a reasonably normal distribution (Fleeson & Gallagher, 2009). For example, some people typically manifest moderate introversion in their lives, other people typically manifest moderate extraversion in their lives, and most typically manifest something in between extraversion and introversion.

These individual differences in central tendencies are remarkably stable. If individual differences are calculated in one week and then are calculated for the same individuals in a subsequent week, the stabilities will be nearly perfect. Across studies, stability correlations range from .7 to .9 (Fleeson, 2012). Thus, these central tendencies represent personality variables, in that the way people typically act is consistent across time.

Furthermore, central tendencies correlate with scores from traditional questionnaires. Reporting a mega-analysis across 15 studies, Fleeson and Gallagher (2009) found that trait scores correlated with central tendencies at the .4 to .6 level. This is supportive evidence that trait scores describe the traits people typically manifest in their daily lives. Thus, trait ascriptions to individuals are indeed descriptive of the traits those individuals manifest in daily life, the states people manifest in their daily lives contain the same content that traits contain, and the traits people are manifesting are consistent and predictable from week to week. However, correlations of .4 to .6 suggest that the traits people report in traditional questionnaires do not describe the whole picture of what is happening on the ground as people actually express their trait content.

In addition to the central tendency, however, the next question is how frequently and how far people deviate from their central tendency. Under some circumstances, the extraverted, conscientious, open, emotionally stable, and disagreeable individual may very well act in introverted, unproductive, rigid, neurotic, and/or agreeable ways (e.g., Mischel & Peake, 1982). This behavioral variability indicates that people are not simply automatons; rather, people are flexible and discriminative.

To assess the extent to which people deviate from their central tendency, we have used the straightforward within-person standard deviation, which reflects the degree of cross-situational variability in a person's personality states. Each person has a standard deviation on each state, indicating how much the person's states varied across moments. Large standard deviations indicate high variability in the manifestation of a trait, whereas small standard deviations indicate low variability in the manifestation of a trait. The average of the standard deviations across all people is the typical individual's amount of variability. Surprisingly, the typical individual's amount of variability is very large (Fleeson, 2001). It is almost as much as the total amount that behavior varies across people. Moreover, within-person variation in personality states is about the same as the amount of within-person variation in affect, something that is commonly known to vary so much that it is hard to conceive of it as a trait. Finally, it is more than the amount of variability between individuals, meaning that individuals differ from themselves more than they differ from others.

Despite individuals' within-person variability in the manifestation of a trait, they also retain their average over time. As such, there are both large degrees of within-person variability and mean-level individual differences in the manifestation of a trait. Combining the high variability with the stable means suggests that density distributions of states are the best way to characterize trait manifestation. Density distributions plot frequencies of the manifestation of a particular trait over a short time span (e.g., a day, week) on the y-axis against each level of that trait on the x-axis (Fleeson & Jayawickreme, 2015). Over time, a participant's manifestations form a distribution, showing how many times that participant acted at each level of a trait.

As shown in Figure 4.1, the distributions are wide, reflecting the high degree of within-person variability in behavior. This leads to the result that distributions of people on even opposite sides of a trait dimension overlap considerably in the frequencies with which they enact each state level (Fleeson & Gallagher, 2009). Nonetheless, distributions differ between people, primarily in the central tendency of their distributions along the dimension. These differences in distribution central tendency are highly stable, and over time they reveal strong individual differences in personality traits. This finding that the patterns of behavior are represented as density distributions has implications for process models of traits.

Why So Much Change? The Explanation Side of Traits

The large amount of variability revealed in trait manifestation raises the question as to why people are changing their personality so much. People enact frequent and rapid change in the personality they are manifesting at any given moment. What explains this?

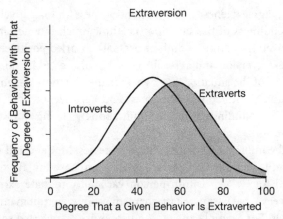

Figure 4.1. Statistically predicted distributions of extraversion states for two individuals, based on the empirical means and standard deviations of distributions. One individual scored 1 SD above the mean on an extraversion trait scale, and the other scored 1 SD below the mean on the extraversion trait scale.

SOURCE: Adapted with permission from Fleeson, W., & Gallagher, P. (2009). The implications of Big Five standing for the distribution of trait manifestation in behavior: Fifteen experience-sampling studies and a meta-analysis. *Journal of Personality and Social Psychology, 97,* 1097–1114. doi:10.1037/a0016786.

Traits are partially descriptions of how people act, and the descriptions of how people act appear to take the form of density distributions of states. If these are true, then explaining traits would mean explaining the density distributions of states. There are two main features of density distributions to be explained. The first feature is the central tendencies of people's distributions, and their explanation reflects the developmental or distal etiological origins of individual differences in traits. We call this distal etiology to emphasize that the causes are those that occurred in the distant past (e.g., childhood) or distant in the causal chain to symptoms (e.g., genes).

The second feature to be explained is the variability within a distribution, and this explanation reveals the mechanisms that produce trait manifestations. Explaining within-person variability involves trying to determine when and why individuals enact the states they enact at any given time. This could also be called the study of proximal etiology because it the study of the near in time causes of symptom occurrences.

Recent research has begun to explain density distributions. Consistent with the social/experimental tradition, WTT postulates that an individual's personality states in a given moment are caused by proximal, social-cognitive mechanisms (i.e., situational characteristics, perceptions, goals, attributions, expectations, etc.). In support of this principle, Fleeson (2007) found that situational characteristics accounted for within-person variability in state extraversion, neuroticism, agreeableness, and conscientiousness. Specifically, the anonymity of the situation (i.e., the number of, and familiarity with, others who were present) covaried

positively with agreeableness and conscientiousness and negatively with neuroticism; the friendliness of the situation (i.e., how much interaction was involved
and the perceived friendliness of others present) covaried positively and predominantly with extraversion and agreeableness, but also conscientiousness; and the
task orientation of the situation (i.e., whether the situation was imposed or not)
covaried positively with conscientiousness and negatively with extraversion and
neuroticism. These findings have been built upon by Huang and Ryan (2011) in a
workplace setting.

Assessing the influence of motivational processes, McCabe and Fleeson (2012)
found that people's momentary goals (e.g., trying to have fun, trying to stir things
up) accounted for 74% of within-person variability in state extraversion. This
means that a very large part of the mechanism producing trait manifestation is the
pursuit of goals. For example, the reason people are extraverted sometimes is because they are pursuing goals that need extraversion to be achieved. Furthermore,
half to three quarters of the between-person differences in states were predicted
by goals. This means that goals also explain the proximal etiology of traits. Recall
that traits are partially descriptions of individual differences in how people act;
thus, a major cause of traits is the goals people are pursuing.

Thus, variability in people's moment-to-moment manifestation of traits can
be explained by proximal situational and motivational factors and the extent to
which they react to those factors. Casting the descriptive side of traits as density
distributions of states facilitated these discoveries of proximal etiology, which revealed the purposive nature of trait-expressive behavior.

WHOLE TRAITS

An abiding tension in personality psychology has been whether traits should be
considered descriptions of the way people act or causal forces that explain the way
people act (Buss & Craik, 1983; DeYoung, 2015; Zuroff, 1986). Traits are descriptive when they are used to describe what a person is like and what can be expected
of him or her. Traits are causal explanations when they are used to give an account
of why a person acted or acts the way he or she did or does. There is a danger of
circularity if the same entity is used both to describe the behavior and to explain
it. Rather, the description of behavior and the explanation of the same behavior
must be two different entities.

Where does one look for compelling characterizations of traits as descriptions
or for compelling characterizations of the explanations for traits? The trait approach has achieved a compelling characterization of traits as descriptions. An
impressive body of research has demonstrated that the everyday adjectives used
to describe or label individuals (e.g., smart, funny, lazy, silly) can be divided
into five factors (i.e., the Big 5; Goldberg, 1992), that these factors predict trait-
relevant behavior at about the .5 level (Fleeson & Gallagher, 2009), are replicated
across cultures with different lexicons (Church, 2009; Saucier, 2009), occur in observer ratings of animals' personalities (e.g., Hirayoshi & Nakajima, 2009; King,
Weiss, & Farmer, 2005; Morris, Gale, & Duffy, 2002), and predict life outcomes at
about the .3 to .4 level, including job and school performance (Hogan & Holland,

2003; Noftle & Robins, 2007) and mortality (Roberts, Kuncel, Shiner, Caspi, & Goldberg, 2007). However, there has been limited research on the ability to explain why those behaviors occur (Fleeson & Jayawickreme, 2015; Hampson, 2012; but see Gray & McNaughton, 2000, for a neurobiological explanation of personality traits).

The social-cognitive approach to personality has provided excellent characterizations of explanations for why behaviors occur (e.g., Coifman, Berenson, Rafaeli, & Downey, 2012; Mischel, 1973; Mischel & Shoda, 1995; Morf & Rhodewalt, 2001). It explains variability in behavior as the result of proximal information processing mechanisms (e.g., expectancies, goals, elicited affects, behavioral scripts). However, this approach has been hampered by a lack of descriptive content to apply to. Although it acknowledges that behavior varies and explains behavioral variability in terms of proximal information processing mechanisms, there is little description of what behaviors differ.

The trait approach and the social-cognitive approach thus provide good places to look for descriptive and explanatory accounts of traits. Furthermore, each has a strength that the other lacks. Thus, they may fit well together. However, there was a bit of a problem, in that the two approaches had been at odds for decades (Fleeson, 2004). Whereas the trait tradition believed cross-situational stability of traits to be high and of primary importance in understanding and predicting behavior, the social-cognitive tradition believed cross-situational stability of traits to be low and unimportant in understanding and predicting behavior. The two approaches were the leading opponents in the person-situation debate and, as such, appeared to be promoting incompatible approaches to understanding personality.

WTT proposes that the incompatibility was only apparent. Rather, the two approaches should be brought together. WTT builds upon the strengths of both sides of the great divide, which can account for the others' weaknesses. The trait approach provides the description of how people act and the structure of that description. The social-cognitive approach provides the explanation of why people act that way. Thus, the descriptive and explanatory are brought together, but they are different entities. When the two parts are put together, they make whole traits that have both descriptive and explanatory sides within them (Fleeson, 2012; Fleeson & Jayawickreme, 2015; Fleeson & Jolley, 2006; see also Fournier, Moskowitz, & Zuroff, 2008; Read et al., 2010).

Thus, WTT proposes that traits consist of two parts, joined together in a cause-effect relationship. As shown in Figure 4.2, the explanatory part causes the descriptive part. Mechanism (or proximal etiology) and distal etiology together make up the explanatory part of traits. The set of proximal social-cognitive mechanisms that produce trait manifestations together constitute the explanatory side of traits. Density distributions of states make up the descriptive side of traits.

More specifically, the explanatory side consists of links between inputs, intermediates, and outputs. The inputs are things such as environmental events. The intermediates are things such as interpretations, expectations, goals, and other similar social-cognitive variables (see Mischel, 1973; Mischel & Shoda, 1995). The outputs are primarily the personality states or manifestations of the

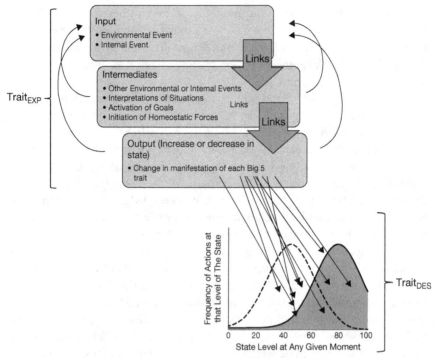

Figure 4.2. Whole trait theory. Trait$_{DES}$ = the descriptive part of traits; Trait$_{EXP}$ = the explanatory part of traits.
SOURCE: Adapted with permission from Fleeson, W., & Jayawickreme, E. (2015). Whole trait theory. *Journal of Research in Personality, 56*, 82–92.

personality traits. These variables are connected to each other by links. The links lead from the activation of one variable to the activation of another variable or to the personality state. The proximal etiology of personality states resides in the operation of these links and variables.

Where do individual differences in density distributions come from? Although the mechanisms involved in the proximal etiology are general to people, individuals will also differ in them. Specially, individuals will differ in the strengths of links between various nodes. Individuals may also differ in the readiness of certain nodes to be activated or to be linked to other nodes. In turn, those individual differences in links will ultimately result in individual differences in density distributions of states. In this way, WTT proposes that distal etiology has its effects on traits by producing these individual differences in links, ultimately producing individual differences in density distributions of states.

WHOLE TRAIT THEORY AND PERSONALITY DISORDERS

A purpose of this book is to consider the relevance of normal personality for advances in understanding PDs. In recent years, progress has been made along these lines (Saulsman & Page, 2004; Trull & Widiger, 2013; Wright, 2011). Most of that progress has concerned advances in normal personality describing the content and structure of personality dimensions, and the application of those dimensions to the PDs. In this chapter, we argue that not only do the content and structure of normal personality have implications for the understanding of PDs, but also that the process models, such as WTT, have important implications for PDs. In this section, we lay out the translation we have been developing for BPD (Miskewicz et al., 2014).

Three Conceptual Analogies

Much in the same way that WTT views personality traits as a distribution of momentary personality states that are brought about by proximal social-cognitive mechanisms (Fleeson, 2001, 2007), so too may PDs be conceptualized as a distribution of momentary symptoms that are brought about by proximal social-cognitive mechanisms. That is, PDs may be viewed as configurations of maladaptive traits that people manifest, the maladaptive traits may contain the same content as the corresponding symptoms that people manifest in their daily lives, and the symptoms that people manifest may be consistent and predictable from week to week, yet vary considerably as a function of proximal social-cognitive mechanisms. This proposal requires three conceptual analogies, as shown in Table 4.1. If these three analogies are conceptually and empirically viable, then the whole trait theory model of normal personality can be used to make advances in the understanding of PDs.

The first analogy is based on the state concept. Just as the trait the person is manifesting in the moment can be seen as a time-bound state, it is possible to see symptoms as occurring in time-bound moments. Each occurrence of a symptom is taken as a short-lasting event of personal significance. For example, a hollow sense of self occurring for a few hours is taken as a distinct event of significance to the individual feeling hollow. This approach recognizes that symptom expression is not constant; rather, there is variability in daily experiences—a person's anger, emptiness, or impulsivity flares (sometimes violently) and then subsides within minutes or hours.

Table 4.1 ANALOGIES TRANSLATING WHOLE TRAIT THEORY COMPONENTS INTO PERSONALITY DISORDER COMPONENTS

Normal Personality	Borderline Personality Disorder
Occurrences of states	Occurrences of symptoms
Traits as distributions of states	Disorders as distributions of symptoms
Mechanism or proximal etiology = causes of states	Mechanism or proximal etiology = causes of symptom occurrences

Second, just as the descriptive side of traits can be characterized as density distributions of such states across time, the descriptive side of disorders may be characterized as density distributions of symptom occurrences across time. Each distribution would depict frequencies of one symptom. The x-axis would indicate the degree of intensity of symptom experience. The y-axis would indicate the frequency of that level of symptom occurring. People would not be characterized by whether they have a given symptom or not, but rather by the frequencies with which they have the symptom at each level of intensity.

Alternatively, one distribution could be created for each disorder. The x-axis would depict the average level of all the symptom intensities at each moment, and the y-axis would depict the frequency of that level of symptoms. Such a distribution would show an individual's frequency of state borderline personality disorder levels. People would be characterized not by whether they have BPD or not, but by the frequencies with which they have BPD states at each level of intensity.

The third critical analogy is between the mechanism or proximal etiological factors that cause personality states and the mechanism or proximal etiological factors that cause symptom occurrences. A conceptual similarity in the etiology of personality states and symptoms implies that symptoms, like personality states, are instigated through "if-then" contingencies with proximal social-cognitive factors (i.e., situational characteristics, perceptions, goals, attributions, expectations, etc.). This contingency perspective implies further that symptom manifestation is not stable across situations and time and instead shows variability within people. The degree of within-person variability depends upon the presence of stressors: when a stressor is present, a relevant symptom is likely to occur; when a stressor is absent, a relevant symptom is unlikely to occur. Thus, a person's individual variability in symptom occurrences can be accounted for by proximal stressors encountered in everyday life.

Consistent with this proposal, several theories of psychopathology have postulated contingencies between proximal stressors and symptoms. For example, whereas the theory of rational-emotive behavior therapy hypothesizes that absolute goals (i.e., demands) primarily bring about psychopathology (Ellis & Dryden, 2007), the theory of cognitive therapy hypothesizes that erroneous perceptions (i.e., cognitive errors) primarily bring about psychopathology (Kovacs & Beck, 1978; Wenzel, Chapman, Newman, Beck, & Brown, 2006). Both theories are transdiagnostic in the sense that they postulate a proximal etiological mechanism for most psychopathology, including PDs, and both have received empirical support over the years, primarily through cross-sectional or treatment studies (e.g., David, Szentagotai, Lupu, & Cosman, 2008; Leichsenring & Leibing, 2003).

A General Model of Borderline Personality Disorder

We are developing a full translation of this model for BPD (see Miskewicz, 2014). In this model, BPD is partly a description of people focused on how they act. The description to be used is the density distributions of BPD symptoms. People are expected to manifest different levels of BPD symptoms at different times, and most people are expected to manifest a variety of levels of BPD symptoms. The frequencies with which a person manifests each level of a symptom represents a BPD-relevant density distribution for that person. Thus, people do differ in their BPD, but the differences between people are not characterized by whether they have the disorder or not. The differences between people are also not characterized by the level of BPD that people have. Rather, people will have distributions of symptoms, and differences between people in distributions will be highly stable. The best way to characterize individual differences in BPD, then, would be by individual differences in the distributions as wholes.

In this model, BPD is not only a description of people, BPD is also a constellation of latent mechanisms that drive behavior. This causal machinery of latent mechanisms is what produces the density distributions of symptoms of BPD. The causal machinery includes the mechanisms or proximal etiology that explains the occurrences of symptoms, and it is influenced by distal etiology.

In our model of BPD, based on extant theories describing BPD, the causal machinery is based on the notion of a "core contingency." The core contingency is a contingency between an instigating event or stressor and the occurrence of a stressor. When a stressor is present, a relevant BPD symptom is likely to occur; when a stressor is absent, a relevant BPD symptom is unlikely to occur. Just as in normal personality, the core contingency works through a series of inputs and intermediates via links, ultimately resulting in a BPD symptom. Individual differences reside in individual differences in the strength and existences of links.

We have put this together into a general model of BPD . The core of the general model is the core contingency. An elegant feature of this model is that it also allows the straightforward inclusion of distal etiology. This etiology can include factors such as genetics, traumatic events, personality traits, and upbringing that affect the core contingency.

Distal etiology is theorized to affect BPD by affecting the components of the core contingency. First, distal etiology may increase the frequency of triggering events, such as when trait neuroticism or clinical anxiety leads to negative interpretations of events (Mogg & Bradley, 1998; Salemink, van den Hout, & Kindt, 2010). Second, distal etiology may directly increase the frequency of symptoms, such as in the case of generally strengthened amygdala activity (Gray & McNaughton, 2000). Third, distal etiology may affect the strength of the contingency between triggering events and symptoms. In our model, this last effect is the core effect.

Immediate Questions Arising From This Model

Capitalizing on this translation raises immediate research questions. Some of these questions include the following:

1. How often do people experience symptoms?
2. Are symptoms constant or variable?

3. Do people at all points along the BPD spectrum experience symptoms?
4. Is there continuity with normal personality at the level of manifestation of the symptoms?
5. Do symptom occurrences factor?
6. Do different individuals have different structures of symptom occurrences?
7. Are symptoms caused by stressors?
8. Does the stressor-symptom contingency depend on BPD status?
9. Does the stressor-symptom contingency explain the heightened symptoms of those with BPD?

Thus, we believe this model is fertile for advances in understanding the PDs.

Initial Empirical Evidence in Support of the Translation

The conceptual similarities between PDs and traits have been recognized for some time; with some notable exceptions during the time of the great divide (Mischel, 1973), both PDs and personality traits have been considered stable across situations and time. Indeed, since their introduction, the *DSM* has defined PDs in terms of "a lifelong pattern" (p. 34, APA, 1952) or "an enduring pattern of inner experience and behavior that . . . is pervasive and inflexible . . . stable over time" (p. 645, APA, 2013).

A conceptual similarity between PD symptoms and personality states is less clear, however. As noted earlier, personality states are temporary and variable by definition, and this conceptualization is inherent in their measurement. On the other hand, the *DSM* has considered PD symptoms as doubly stable and pervasive; not only is stability of PD symptoms reflected in the wording of many of the individual diagnostic criteria (e.g., *chronic* feelings of emptiness and *persistently* unstable self-image for BPD), but the symptoms themselves are listed under a heading that indicates that they will tend to occur in terms of a stable pattern (e.g., APA, 2000, 2013).

Thus, it is important to test our model of PDs. Our lab has just completed a National Institute of Mental Health–supported, 5-year longitudinal investigation of the model. The goal was to obtain direct, in-the-moment accounts of BPD symptoms and relevant stressors. Based upon conceptualizations of BPD (e.g., APA, 2000; Linehan, 1993), we have focused on interpersonal and detached stressors, such as rejection, abandonment, isolation, and boredom, as possible triggers. Collecting data on symptoms and relevant stressors allows us to test hypotheses about the proximal situational antecedents of BPD symptoms or the core contingency. We have also collected data on participants' goals to test hypotheses about the proximal motivational antecedents of BPD symptoms.

We enrolled a total of 282 participants in the first wave, including 84 participants meeting *DSM-IV* criteria for BPD (APA, 2000). We utilized two sampling methods, one that targeted people with high BPD symptomatology and one that targeted people across the full range of BPD symptomatology. Approximately two thirds of the sample was recruited using the former method, and one third was recruited using the latter method. Whereas participants had to endorse seven items on the McLean Screening Instrument for BPD (MSI-BPD; Zanarini et al., 2003) for the former, there was no requirement on the MSI-BPD score for the latter.

Participants underwent several clinical interviews administered by trained clinicians with either a master's degree in social work or a PhD in clinical psychology. Subsequently, participants began a layered, experience sampling methodology (ESM), in which they reported upon their everyday experiences, including their symptoms, stressors, and affects, five times a day for 2 weeks, once daily for 2 weeks, once monthly for 6 months, once every 6 months, and once every 18 months. The items on the reports were the same but differed with regard to the timeframe. Thus, for example, on the immediate reports, participants described their experiences during the past 60 minutes, whereas on the 18-month reports, they described their experiences during the past 18 months. All symptoms were worded as closely as possible to the *DSM-IV* wording of the symptoms (e.g., "An interpersonal relationship of mine was unstable or intense In the last 60 minutese"), and each symptom was assessed using two items, except for self-harm, which was assessed using one item.

Paralleling the case for normal personality, a between-person factor-analytic study found that the self-reported symptoms collected using ESM showed a similar unidimensional structure as clinician-rated symptoms (Hawkins et al., 2014). Additional analyses from our lab using chain-p factor analysis also revealed a very similarone-factor within-person structure of the symptoms. These results suggest that the content and structure of the momentary symptoms are similar to the content and structure of the between-person symptoms.

Further paralleling normal personality, individuals differed in the central tendencies of their symptoms. These individual differences were stable, indicating that people differed reliably in their experience of daily symptoms, and that these differences indicate the severity of BPD in individuals' lives.

Nonetheless, momentary BPD symptom occurrences of difficulty controlling anger, relationship and identity instability, and feelings of emptiness were infrequent, nonpervasive, and showed abrupt increases and decreases over a short time span. That is, each person manifested different levels of BPD symptoms at different times. These findings build on the important findings of Trull and colleagues (Tragesser, Solhan, Schwartz-Mette, & Trull, 2007), who showed highly variable affect within BPD. They again parallel the case for normal personality and suggest that distributions of symptom occurrences may be the best way to conceive of individual differences in BPD.

Our general model proposes that BPD has both a descriptive side, describing the extent to which individuals experience BPD symptoms, and an explanatory side, consisting of the set of mechanisms that produce BPD symptoms in the moment. Studies conducted in our laboratory have found that BPD symptom occurrences are contingent upon BPD-relevant situational stressors (e.g., perceived rejection and abandonment; Miskewicz et al., 2015) and negative affect (Law, Fleeson, Arnold, & Furr, 2015). These findings provide support for the core contingency model and begin to detail the mechanisms involved in the proximal etiology of BPD. These findings also parallel findings from other labs investigating similar questions. For example, studies have found a contingency of psychotic and dissociative symptoms on negative affect (Kramer et al., 2013), a contingency of intense anger on rejection (Berenson, Downey, Rafaeli, Coifman, & Paquin, 2011), a contingency of negative interpersonal experiences on risky/impulsive behaviors (Coifman et al., 2012), a contingency of psychotic and dissociative symptoms on stress (Glaser, Van Os, Thewissen, & Myin-Germeys, 2010; Stiglmayr et al., 2008), and a contingency of antagonistic behavior on others' perceived antagonistic behavior (Sadikaj, Moskowitz, Russell, Zuroff, & Paris, 2013).

Such findings argue for the notion of PD symptoms as temporary occurrences or states. Moreover, findings that short-term changes in the manifestation of trait-relevant behavior were found to predict short-term changes in PD symptoms argue for a conceptual similarity between personality states and symptoms. Together, these several initial findings provide promising support for the notion that PD symptoms, like personality states, may be brought about by proximal social-cognitive factors.

CONCLUSIONS

As an integrated structural-process model of normal personality, WTT has much to offer to the study of PDs. We believe that viewing PDs as a configuration of momentary, transient personality symptoms that are brought about by social-cognitive processes provides a rich and compelling framework for understanding both the structure and etiology of PDs. To date, we have found some preliminary support for these hypotheses. Nonetheless, future research would do well to explore further the link between proximal cognitive factors (e.g., attributions, goals, perceptions), affect, and PD symptoms, as well as the link between normal personality states and PD symptoms.

ACKNOWLEDGMENTS

Research presented in this manuscript was supported by the National Institute of Mental Health of the National Institutes of Health under award number R01MH70571. The content is solely the responsibility of the authors and does not necessarily represent the official views of the National Institutes of Health.

REFERENCES

Adler, A. (1988). The child's inner life and a sense of community. *Individual Psychology: Journal of Adlerian Theory, Research & Practice, 44*, 417–423.

American Psychiatric Association. (1952). *Diagnostic and statistical manual of mental disorders* (1st ed.). Washington, DC: American Psychiatric Association Mental Hospital Service.

American Psychiatric Association. (2000). *Diagnostic and statistical manual of mental disorders* (4th ed., text revision). Washington, DC: American Psychiatric Publishing.

American Psychiatric Association. (2013). *Diagnostic and statistical manual of mental disorders* (5th ed.). Arlington, VA: American Psychiatric Publishing.

Berenson, K. R., Downey, G., Rafaeli, E., Coifman, K. G., & Paquin, N. L. (2011). The rejection-rage contingency in borderline personality disorder. *Journal of Abnormal Psychology, 120*(3), 681–690. doi:10.1037/a0023335.

Buss, D. M., & Craik, K. H. (1983). The act frequency approach to personality. *Psychological Review, 90*(2), 105–126. doi:10.1037/0033-295X.90.2.105

Church, A. (2009). Prospects for an integrated trait and cultural psychology. *European Journal of Personality, 23*, 153–182. doi:10.1002/per.700.

Coifman, K. G., Berenson, K. R., Rafaeli, E., & Downey, G. (2012). From negative to positive and back again: Polarized affective and relational experience in borderline personality disorder. *Journal of Abnormal Psychology, 121*(3), 668–679. doi:10.1037/a0028502.

Costa, P. T. J., & McCrae, R. R. (2006). *Trait and factor theories*. In J. C. Thomas, D. L. Segal, & M. Hersen (Eds.), *Comprehensive handbook of personality and psychopathology, Vol. 1: Personality and everyday functioning* (pp. 96–114). Hoboken, NJ: John Wiley & Sons.

David, D., Szentagotai, A., Lupu, V., & Cosman, D. (2008). Rational emotive behavior therapy, cognitive therapy, and medication in the treatment of major depressive disorder: A randomized clinical trial, posttreatment outcomes, and six-month follow-up. *Journal of Clinical Psychology, 64*, 728–746. doi: 10.1002/jclp.20487.

DeYoung, C. G. (2015). Cybernetic Big Five theory. *Journal of Research in Personality, 56*, 33–58. http://doi.org/10.1016/j.jrp.2014.07.004

Ellis, A., & Dryden, W. (2007). *The practice of rational emotive behavior therapy* (2nd ed.). New York, NY: Springer.

Fajkowska, M., & DeYoung, C. G. (2015). Introduction to the special issue on integrative theories of personality. *Journal of Research In Personality, 56*, 1–3. doi:10.1016/j.jrp.2015.04.001

Fleeson, W. (2001). Toward a structure- and process-integrated view of personality: Traits as density distributions of states. *Journal of Personality and Social Psychology, 80*, 1011–1027. doi:10.1037/0022-3514.80.6.1011.

Fleeson, W. (2004). Moving personality beyond the person-situation debate: The challenge and the opportunity of within-person variability. *Current Directions in Psychological Science, 13*, 83–87. doi:10.1111/j.0963-7214.2004.00280.x.

Fleeson, W. (2007). Situation-based contingencies underlying trait-content manifestation in behavior. *Journal of Personality, 75*, 825–862. doi:10.1111/j.1467-6494.2007.00458.x.

Fleeson, W. (2012). *Perspectives on the person: Rapid growth and opportunities for integration*. In K. Deaux & M. Snyder (Eds.), *The Oxford handbook of personality and social psychology* (pp. 33–63). New York, NY: Oxford University Press.

Fleeson, W., & Gallagher, P. (2009). The implications of Big Five standing for the distribution of trait manifestation in behavior: Fifteen experience-sampling studies and a meta- analysis. *Journal of Personality and Social Psychology, 97,* 1097–1114. doi:10.1037/a0016786.

Fleeson, W., & Jayawickreme, E. (2015). Whole trait theory. *Journal of Research in Personality, 56,* 82–92.

Fleeson, W., & Jolley, S. (2006). A proposed theory of the adult development of intraindividual variability in trait-manifesting behavior. In D. Mroczek & T. D. Little (Eds.). *Handbook of personality development* (pp. 41–59). Mahwah, NJ: LEA.

Fournier, M. A., Moskowitz, D. S., & Zuroff, D. C. (2008). Integrating dispositions, signatures, and the interpersonal domain. *Journal of Personality and Social Psychology, 94*(3), 531–545. doi:10.1037/0022-3514.94.3.531

Frances, A. J. (1982). Categorical and dimensional systems of personality diagnosis: A comparison. *Comprehensive Psychiatry, 23,* 516–527.

Frances, A. J. (1993). Dimensional diagnosis of personality—not whether, but when and which. *Psychological Inquiry, 4,* 110–111.

Freud, S. (1959). *Character and anal erotism.* In J. Strachey (Ed)., *The standard edition of the complete psychological works of Sigmund Freud* (pp. 167–175.). London, UK: Hogarth Press.

Glaser, J.-P., Van Os, J., Thewissen, V., & Myin-Germeys, I. (2010). Psychotic reactivity in borderline personality disorder. *Acta Psychiatrica Scandinavica, 121*(2), 125–134. doi:10.1111/j.1600-0447.2009.01427.x

Goldberg, L. R. (1992). The development of markers for the Big-Five factor structure. *Psychological Assessment, 4,* 26–42. doi:10.1037/1040-3590.4.1.26.

Gray, J. A., & McNaughton, N. (2000). *The neuropsychology of anxiety* (2nd ed.). New York, NY: Oxford University Press.

Hampson, S. E. (2012). Personality processes: Mechanisms by which personality traits "get outside the skin." *Annual Review of Psychology, 63,* 315–339. doi:10.1146/annurev-psych-120710-100419

Hawkins, A., Furr, R. M., Arnold, E. A., Law., M. K., Mneimne, M., & Fleeson, W. (2014) The structure of borderline personality disorder symptoms: A multi-method, multi-sample examination. *Personality Disorders: Theory, Research, and Treatment, 5,* 380–389.

Hine, F. R., & Williams, R. B. (1975). Dimensional diagnosis and the medical student's grasp of psychiatry. *Archives of General Psychiatry, 32,* 525–528.

Hirayoshi, S., & Nakajima, S. (2009). Analysis of personality-trait structure of dogs with personality-trait descriptors. *Japanese Journal of Animal Psychology, 59,* 57–75. doi:10.2502/janip.59.1.8.

Hogan, J., & Holland, B. (2003). Using theory to evaluate personality and job-performance relations: A socioanalytic perspective. *Journal of Applied Psychology, 88,* 100–112. doi:10.1037/0021-9010.88.1.100.

Huang, J. L., & Ryan, A. (2011). Beyond personality traits: A study of personality states and situational contingencies in customer service jobs. *Personnel Psychology, 64,* 451–488. doi:10.1111/j.1744-6570.2011.01216.x.

Jung, C. G. (1964). *Man and his symbols.* New York, NY: Anchor Books.

Kelly, G. A. (1965). *The role of classification in personality theory.* In M. M. Katz, J. O. Cole, & W. E. Barton (Eds.), *The role and methodology of classification in psychiatry and psychopathology* (pp. 155–164). Washington, DC: Government Printing Office.

King, J. E., Weiss, A., & Farmer, K. H. (2005). A chimpanzee (Pan troglodytes) analogue of cross-national generalization of personality structure: Zoological parks and an African sanctuary. *Journal of Personality*, *73*, 389–410. doi:10.1111/ j.1467-6494.2005.00313.x.

Kovacs, M., & Beck, A. T. (1978). Maladaptive cognitive structures in depression. *American Journal of Psychiatry*, *135*, 525–533.

Kramer, I., Simons, C. J. P., Wigman, J. T. W., Collip, D., Jacobs, N., Derom, C., . . .Wichers, M. (2013). Time-lagged moment-to-moment interplay between negative affect and paranoia: New insights in the affective pathway to psychosis. *Schizophrenia Bulletin*, *40*, 278–286. doi:10.1093/schbul/sbs194.

Krueger, R. F., Skodol, A. E., Livesley, W. J., Shrout, P. E., & Huang, Y. (2007). Synthesizing dimensional and categorical approaches to personality disorders: Refining the research agenda for DSM-V axis II. *International Journal of Methods in Psychiatric Research*, *16*, S65–S73. doi:10.1002/mpr.212.

Law, M. K., Fleeson, W., Arnold, E. M., & Furr, R. M. (2015). Using negative emotions to trace the experience of borderline personality pathology: Interconnected relationships revealed in an experience eampling study. *Journal of Personality Disorders*, *30*, 52–70. https://doi.org/10.1521/pedi_2015_29_180

Leichsenring, F., & Leibing, E. (2003). The effectiveness of psychodynamic therapy and cognitive behavior therapy in the treatment of personality disorders: A meta-analysis. *American Journal of Psychiatry*, *160*, 1223–1232.

Linehan, M. M. (1993). *Cognitive-behavioral treatment of borderline personality disorder*. New York, NY: Guilford Press.

McCabe, K. O., & Fleeson, W. (2012). What is extraversion for? Integrating trait and motivational perspectives and identifying the purpose of extraversion. *Psychological Science*, *23*, 1498–1505. doi:10.1177/0956797612444904.

Mischel, W. (1973). Towards a cognitive social learning reconceptualization of personality. *Psychological Review*, *80*, 252–283.

Mischel, W., & Peake, P. K. (1982). Analyzing the construction of consistency in personality. *Nebraska Symposium on Motivation*, *30*, 233–262.

Mischel, W., & Shoda, Y. (1995). A cognitive-affective system theory of personality: Reconceptualizing situations, dispositions, dynamics, and invariance in personality structure. *Psychological Review*, *102*, 246–268.

Miskewicz, K., Fleeson, W., Arnold, E. M., Law, M. K., Mneimne, M., & Furr, R. M. (2015). A contingency-oriented approach to understanding borderline personality disorder: Situational triggers and symptoms. *Journal of Personality Disorders*, *29*, 486–502.

Mogg, K., & Bradley, B. P. (1998). A cognitive-motivational analysis of anxiety. *Behaviour Research and Therapy*, *36*, 809–848.

Morf, C. C., & Rhodewalt, F. (2001). Unraveling the paradoxes of narcissism: A dynamic self- regulatory processing model. *Psychological Inquiry*, *12*, 177–196.

Morris, P. H., Gale, A., & Duffy, K. (2002). Can judges agree on the personality of horses? *Personality and Individual Differences*, *33*, 67–81. doi:10.1016/S0191-8869(01)00136-2.

Noftle, E. E., & Robins, R. (2007). Personality predictors of academic outcomes: Big Five correlates of GPA and SAT scores. *Journal of Personality and Social Psychology*, *93*, 116–130. doi:10.1037/0022-3514.93.1.116.

Read, S. J., Monroe, B. M., Brownstein, A. L., Yang, Y., Chopra, G., & Miller, L. C. (2010). A neural network model of the structure and dynamics of human personality. *Psychological Review*, *117*(1), 61–92. doi:10.1037/a0018131

Roberts, B. W., Kuncel, N. R., Shiner, R., Caspi, A., & Goldberg, L. R. (2007). The power of personality: The comparative validity of personality traits, socioeconomic status, and cognitive ability for predicting important life outcomes. *Perspectives on Psychological Science, 2*, 313–345. doi:10.1111/j.1745-6916.2007.00047.x.

Sadikaj, G., S. D., Russell, J. J., Zuroff, D. C., & Paris, J. (2013). Quarrelsome behavior in borderline personality disorder: Influence of behavioral and affective reactivity to perceptions of others. *Journal of Abnormal Psychology, 122*, 195–207. doi:10.1037/a0030871.

Salemink, E., van den Hout, M., & Kindt, M. (2010). How does cognitive bias modification affect anxiety? Mediation analyses and experimental data. *Behavioural and Cognitive Psychotherapy, 38*, 59–66. doi:10.1017/S1352465809990543.

Saucier, G. (2009). Recurrent personality dimensions in inclusive lexical studies: Indications for a big six structure. *Journal of Personality, 77*, 1577–1614. doi:10.1111/j.1467-6494.2009.00593.x.

Saulsman, L. M., & Page, A. C. (2004). The five-factor model and personality disorder empirical literature: A meta-analytic review. *Clinical Psychology Review, 23*, 1055–1085.

Spielberger, C. D., Gorsuch, R. L., & Lushene, R. E. (1970). *Manual for the state-trait anxiety inventory.* Palo Alto, CA: Consulting Psychologists Press.

Stiglmayr, C. E., Ebner-Priemer, U. W., Bretz, J., Behm, R., Mohse, M., Lammers, C.-H., . . . Bohus, M. (2008). Dissociative symptoms are positively related to stress in borderline personality disorder. *Acta Psychiatrica Scandinavica, 117*(2), 139–147.

Tragesser, S. L., Solhan, M., Schwartz-Mette, R., & Trull, T. J. (2007). The role of affective instability and impulsivity in predicting future BPD features. *Journal of Personality Disorders, 21*(6), 603–614. doi:10.1521/pedi.2007.21.6.603

Trull, T. J., & Widiger, T. A. (2013). Dimensional models of personality: The five-factor model and the DSM-5. *Dialogues in Clinical Neuroscience, 15*, 135–146.

Vaillant, G. E., & Perry, J. C. (1985). *Personality disorders.* In H. I. Kaplan & B. J. Sadock (Eds.), *Comprehensive textbook of psychiatry* (4th ed., pp. 958–986). Baltimore, MD: Williams & Wilkins.

Wenzel, A., Chapman, J. E., Newman, C. F., Beck, A. T., & Brown, G. K. (2006). Hypothesized mechanisms of change in cognitive therapy for borderline personality disorder. *Journal of Clinical Psychology, 62*, 503–516. doi:10.1002/jclp.20244.

Widiger, T. A., & Simonsen, E. (2005). Alternative dimensional models of personality disorder: Finding a common ground. *Journal of Personality Disorders, 19*, 110–130. doi: 10.1521/pedi.19.2.110.62628.

Widiger, T. A., Trull, T. J., Hurt, S. W., Clarkin, J., & Frances, A. (1987). A multidimensional scaling of the DSM-III personality disorders. *Archives of General Psychiatry, 44*, 557–563.

World Health Organization. (1948). *International classification of diseases* (6th ed.). Geneva, Switzerland: WHO Press.

Wright, A. G. C. (2011). Qualitative and quantitative distinctions in personality disorder. *Journal of Personality Assessment, 93*, 370–379. doi:10.1080/00223891.2011.577477.

Wright, A. G. C., Thomas, K. M., Hopwood, C. J., Markon, K. E., Pincus, A. L., & Krueger, R. F. (2012). The hierarchical structure of DSM-5 pathological personality traits. *Journal of Abnormal Psychology, 121*, 951–957. doi:10.1037/a0027669.

Zanarini, M. C., Vujanovic, A. A., Parachini, E. A., Boulanger, J. L., Frankenburg, F. R., & Hennen, J. (2003). A screening measure for BPD: The McLean Screening Instrument for Borderline Personality Disorder (MSI-BPD). *Journal of Personality Disorders, 17,* 568–573. doi:10.1521/pedi.17.6.568.25355

Zuroff, D. C. (1986). Was Gordon Allport a trait theorist? *Journal of Personality and Social Psychology, 51*(5), 993–1000. doi:10.1037/0022-3514.51.5.993

5

The Interpersonal Situation

Integrating Personality Assessment,
Case Formulation, and Intervention

CHRISTOPHER J. HOPWOOD, AARON L. PINCUS,
AND AIDAN G. C. WRIGHT ■

The official diagnostic system clinicians are currently asked to use to integrate their patients' personalities into a comprehensive clinical diagnosis employs a medical model that is empirically problematic and largely unhelpful for personality assessment, case formulation, treatment planning, and intervention. Trait-based (Widiger & Simonsen, 2005) and process-based (Eaton, South, & Krueger, 2009) alternatives address important limitations of the medical model. However, structure and process models, in isolation, fail to provide a full picture of human functioning (DeYoung, 2015; Fleeson, 2001; Pincus & Wright, 2011) and are particularly ill suited for clinical applications (Hopwood, Zimmermann, Pincus, & Krueger, 2015; Wright, 2011). Coupling evidence-based models of personality structure (Harkness, Reynolds, & Lilienfeld, 2014; Wright & Simms, 2014) with evidence-based models of the dynamic processes underlying psychopathology, personality, and clinical intervention (Ebner-Premier, Eid, Kleindienst, Stabenow, & Trull, 2009; Roche, Pincus, Rebar, Conroy, & Ram, 2014; Thomas, Hopwood, Woody, Ethier, & Sadler, 2014) offers the basis for a revolution in clinical assessment and psychiatric diagnosis (Hopwood et al., 2015; Krueger, 2013).

In this context, the *Diagnostic and Statistical Manual of Mental Disorders*, fifth edition (*DSM-5*; American Psychiatric Association, 2013) alternative PD model represents an historical effort to integrate clinical theories of pathological personality processes (found in Criterion A), with an empirically derived dimensional trait model (found in Criterion B). However, this system is not well integrated into a cohesive framework sufficiently buttressed by clinical theory and research. Despite offering an apparent conceptual, empirical, and clinical improvement over the categorical diagnoses of *DSM-5*, Section II (Krueger & Markon, 2014), the alternative model is nevertheless somewhat cumbersome and redundant, and it thus fails to provide a fully effective framework for making specific clinical formulations and predictions.

A more flexible and coherent conceptual model is needed to guide assessment, formulation, and intervention. Such a model should (a) cover the range of characteristics and difficulties that are likely to be of clinical interest; (b) conform to an evidence-based structure of individual differences; (c) afford a means for describing both what a person is like in general and the processes that lead to variability and change over time; (d) integrate diverse evidence-based models of psychopathology, personality, and intervention; (e) provide a framework for integrating multimethod assessment data, (f) be parsimonious and portable; and (g) connect assessment, formulation, and intervention. In the next section, we present the contemporary integrative interpersonal theory of personality (CIIT: Pincus, 2005; Pincus & Ansell, 2013) and the interpersonal paradigm of personality assessment (Wiggins, 2003) as a framework for connecting structure and process for the purpose of personality-based clinical practice.

CONTEMPORARY INTEGRATIVE INTERPERSONAL THEORY

CIIT provides an evidenced-based model of personality structure linked with dynamic social-cognitive, affective, and behavioral processes that offer a scientifically grounded framework to generate testable clinical hypotheses regarding diagnosis, formulation, and treatment (Anchin & Pincus, 2010; Pincus et al., 2014). In this section, we lay out specific assumptions in CIIT regarding personality structure and process.

Structural Assumptions

In the interpersonal paradigm, the organizational metaframework of agency and communion (Wiggins, 1991) provides scaffolding for defining and assessing the fundamental constructs of interpersonal functioning (Figure 5.1, top). The agency and communion metaframework gives rise to the interpersonal circumplex (IPC) model (Figure 5.1, bottom). This metaframework, and its empirically validated derivations of the IPC, are a "key conceptual map" (Kiesler, 1996, p. 172) for an interpersonal description of personality structures and personality processes.

Interpersonal theory (Wiggins & Trapnell, 1996) and research (Ansell & Pincus, 2004) conclude that all domains of the five-factor model of personality traits have agentic and communal implications. However, whereas trait systems have traditionally emphasized that traits are amalgams of multiple levels of psychological functioning, including motives, cognition, and behaviors, the IPC system draws meaningful distinctions between these levels even as it organizes them with the

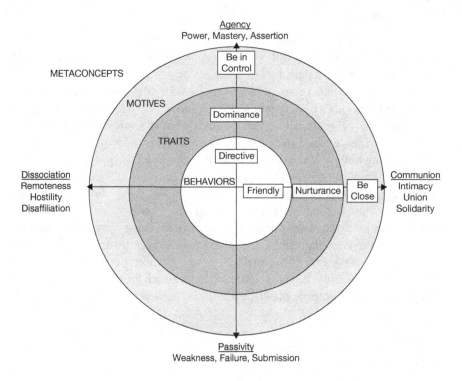

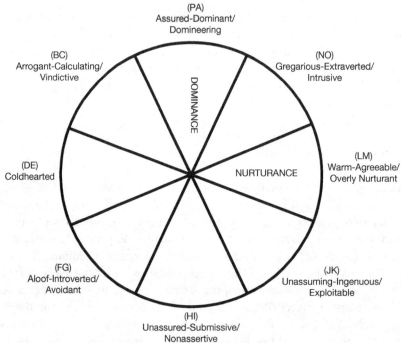

Figure 5.1. (*Top*) Agency and communion metaframework; (*bottom*) interpersonal circumplex.

SOURCE: From Pincus et al., (2014). Multimethod assessment of interpersonal dynamics. In C. J. Hopwood & R. F. Bornstein (Eds.), *Multimethod clinical assessment* (p. 52). New York, NY: Guilford. Reprinted with permission from Guilford Press

same structural model. These distinctions are depicted in the top of Figure 5.1 in which motives, traits, and behaviors represent different aspects of interpersonal functioning (Locke, 2010). The system also extends trait models in that interpersonal assessment focuses on both dispositions at multiple levels of functioning *and* dynamic patterns of functioning across time and situations (Pincus et al., 2014). From the CIIT perspective, aspects of interpersonal situations, including a person's particular level of warmth or dominance at any given moment, are dynamically linked experiential elements with established connections to basic traits such as neuroticism, extraversion, agreeableness, and conscientiousness (e.g., Johnson, Miller, Lynam, & South, 2012). Thus, trait assessments can be used to make predictions about particular behavioral patterns in interpersonal situations.

One interesting behavioral pattern directly involves the structure of the IPC. Recent research suggests that, although dominance and warmth as measured by IPC instruments are generally orthogonal in the population, they can correlate within individuals (e.g., Fournier et al., 2008, 2009; Roche, Pincus, Hyde, Conroy, & Ram, 2013; Roche et al., 2014). Within-person covariance might occur if a person is able to be warm when in charge but is cold when someone else takes the lead. Deviations from orthogonality can also occur in perception, such as when an individual thinks that others are only warm when they are being submissive, such that a show of assertiveness in another is taken as cold or hostile. Such patterns are likely to interfere with interpersonal functioning and thus have important clinical implications.

Process Assumptions

The core assumption of the interpersonal perspective is that the most important expressions of personality and psychopathology occur in phenomena involving more than one person. Sullivan (1953a, 1953b) suggested that individuals live in communal existence with the social environment and express integrating tendencies which bring people together in the mutual pursuit of satisfactions (generally a large class of biologically grounded needs), security (i.e., anxiety-free functioning), and self-esteem. A potential misinterpretation of the term "interpersonal" is to assume it refers to a limited class of phenomena that can be observed only in the immediate interaction between two proximal people. In contrast, in CIIT interpersonal functioning is assumed to occur not only between people but also inside people's minds via the capacity for mental representation of self and others (e.g., Blatt, Auerbach, & Levy, 1997; Lukowitsky & Pincus, 2011). *Interpersonal situations* occur in perceptions of contemporaneous events, memories of past experiences, dreams, and fantasies or expectations of future experiences. Both proximal and internal interpersonal situations continuously influence an individual's learned relational strategies, regulatory functioning, and self-concept.

Interpersonal processes involve interpersonal patterns of perceiving, interpreting, feeling, and behaving over time. These patterns are socially reinforced through various transactional influences impacting self and others throughout development as they resolve, negotiate, or exacerbate the unfolding interpersonal situations that make up human life. Interpersonal behaviors probabilistically invite or evoke delimited classes of responses from the other in a continual, dynamic transactional process. Thus, reciprocal interpersonal patterns are the consistent agentic and communal behavioral responses to the perceived agentic and communal characteristics of others in an interpersonal situation (Pincus et al., 2010).

The IPC provides conceptual anchors and a lexicon to systematically describe reciprocal interpersonal patterns. The most basic of these patterns is referred to as interpersonal *complementarity* (Carson, 1969; Kiesler, 1983). Interpersonal complementarity occurs when the agentic and communal needs of both persons are met in the interpersonal situation, leading to stability and likely recurrence of the pattern. Complementarity is defined via the IPC based on the social exchange of status (agency) and love (communion) as reflected in oppositeness for the vertical dimension (i.e., dominance pulls for submission; submission pulls for dominance) and sameness for the horizontal dimension (friendliness pulls for friendliness; hostility pulls for hostility). Although complementarity is neither the only reciprocal interpersonal pattern that can be described by the IPC nor a proposed universal law of interaction, empirical studies consistently find support for its probabilistic predictions (Sadler, Ethier, & Woody, 2010). This research suggests that complementarity should be considered a common baseline for the reciprocal influence of interpersonal behavior associated with healthy socialization; and deviations from complementary interpersonal patterns are more likely to disrupt interpersonal relations or be self-destructive or costly. Chronic deviations from complementarity across relationships may be indicative of pathological personality functioning (Hopwood et al., 2013; Roche, Pincus, Conroy, Hyde, & Ram, 2013).

Consistent with object relations (Fairbairn, 1952) or social-cognitive (Shoda, Mischel, & Wright, 1994) personality process models, CIIT proposes that mediating internal psychological features (e.g., self–other schemas, motives and needs embedded in these schemas, and emerging emotional experiences) influence the likelihood of complementary interpersonal patterns. Chronic deviations from normative social processes suggest impairments in (1) recognizing the consensual understanding of interpersonal situations, (2) adaptively communicating one's own interpersonal needs and motives, and (3) comprehending the needs of others and the intent of their interpersonal behavior. In such cases, the individual may react chaotically or rigidly pull for responses that complement his or her own interpersonal behavior but have significant difficulty replying with responses complementary to others' behavior. This reduces the likelihood that the agentic and communal needs of both persons will be satisfied in the interpersonal situation (Hopwood et al., 2013; Horowitz et al., 2006; Pincus & Hopwood, 2012). Psychopathology is understood in terms of these kinds of disturbances (Pincus & Wright, 2011).

THE INTERPERSONAL SITUATION

Pincus and Ansell (2003) summarized Sullivan's concept of the *interpersonal situation* as "the experience of a pattern of relating self with other associated with varying levels of anxiety (or security) in which learning takes place that influences the development of self-concept and social behavior" (p. 210). From the perspective of CIIT, the interpersonal situation is the key human experience where social learning occurs, and over the life span, it promotes personality organization, development, and adjustment (Pincus & Ansell, 2013). Interactions with others develop into increasingly complex patterns of interpersonal experience that are encoded in memory via age-appropriate social learning from infancy throughout the life span. According to Sullivan, interpersonal learning of self-concept and social behavior is based on an anxiety gradient associated with interpersonal situations, which ranges from rewarding (highly secure, esteem promoting) through various degrees of anxiety (insecurity, low self-esteem). The interpersonal situation underlies the genesis, development, maintenance, and mutability of personality and psychopathology through the continuous patterning and repatterning of interpersonal experience in an effort to increase security and self-esteem while avoiding anxiety. Over time, developmental experiences give rise to mental representations of self and others (what Sullivan termed "personifications") as well as to enduring patterns of adaptive or disturbed interpersonal relating. Individual variation in learning occurs due to the interaction between the developing person's level of cognitive maturation and the facilitative or toxic characteristics of the interpersonal situations encountered. In both proximal interactions and mental representation, the affective valence associated with an interpersonal situation is a function of one's ability to satisfy basic motives for interpersonal security and self-esteem. When needs for security and self-esteem are met, the interaction is pleasant and the behavior is reinforced; when these needs are frustrated, it is unpleasant, prompting dysregulation and distress and a need to cope and adapt.

In Figure 5.2, we present a model that builds upon the IPC to account for the structure of interpersonal situations (revised from Hopwood et al., 2013). Both self and other are depicted and both include their own self and affect systems (it is important to recall that the other may either be a proximal individual or a mental representation). The *self system* is organized by underlying agentic and communal interpersonal motives (Grosse-Holtforth, Thomas, & Caspar, 2010; Horowitz et al., 2006) that lead to behavioral styles, aversions, problems, and capabilities via social learning. Identity, self-concept, and self-worth vary according to the degree to which interpersonal motives are satisfied. The *affect system*, which is structured by affective arousal and valence (Posner, Russell, & Peterson, 2005), has a highly sensitive and dynamic relationship with the self system that is indicated by the bidirectional arrows between the interpersonal and affective circles within the self and the other. For instance, emotional experiences provide critical feedback regarding motive satisfaction that can color and intensify or dull interpersonal

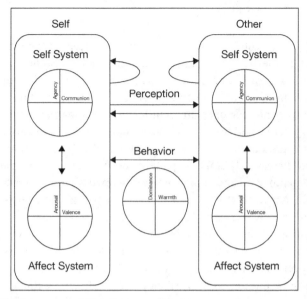

Figure 5.2. The interpersonal situation.
SOURCE: Reprinted from Hopwood, C. J., Wright, A. G. C., Ansell, E. B., & Pincus, A. L. (2013). The interpersonal core of personality pathology. *Journal of Personality Disorders, 27*, 270–295. Copyright 2017 Christopher J. Hopwood, Aaron L. Pincus, and Aidan G. C. Wright.

behavior. In turn, interpersonal behavior modulates affective experiences via the achievement of interpersonal goals.

The *interpersonal field* encapsulates the relationship between the self and other. Each person's independent perceptions of self (curved arrows) and other (unidirectional arrows) are represented as inputs, perceived in terms of their agentic and communal behaviors and impacts. The specific behaviors enacted within the field (which are simultaneously output and input) are indicated by the bidirectional arrow between self and other. Overall, the integration of structure and process of the interpersonal field is best captured by the entirety of the interpersonal situation as indicated by the box outlining the figure. Within the interpersonal field, perceptual processes moderate the functioning of the self system, affect system, and behavior.

Personality Pathology as Dysregulation and Distortion in Interpersonal Situations

In CIIT, personality pathology is defined as the severity of *dysregulation* and *distortion* in interpersonal situations (Pincus, 2005, 2011). The severity of personality pathology is characterized by pervasiveness and intensity of *dysregulation* and *distortion*, whereas the style of PD is characterized by consistent relational *patterns of dysregulation and distortion*, that is, input–intermediary–output chains, encompassing perception, interpretation, motivation, affect, and behavior in the interpersonal situation (Hopwood et al., 2013; Pincus & Hopwood, 2012; Wright, 2014).

DYSREGULATION

The failure to achieve security and self-esteem in interpersonal situations causes dysregulation in the self (e.g., ego threat), affect (e.g., anger), and the interpersonal field (e.g., hostility) (Pincus, 2005; Pincus et al., 2010; see Figure 5.3). *Self-regulation* involves the ability to effectively manage one's social cognition and self-concept, or how one thinks about oneself in relation to others in interpersonal situations (Sullivan, 1953b). *Affect regulation* involves the ability to modulate one's inner emotional states and affective expression (Gratz & Roemer, 2004), or how one feels in interpersonal situations. *Field regulation* involves modulating the processes by which one relates to others in interpersonal transactions, or how one behaves and impacts others' behavior in interpersonal situations (Wiggins & Trobst, 1999). One way to organize these concepts is that self, affective, and field regulation domains correspond to how one thinks about oneself and others, feels about oneself and others, and behaves in interpersonal situations.

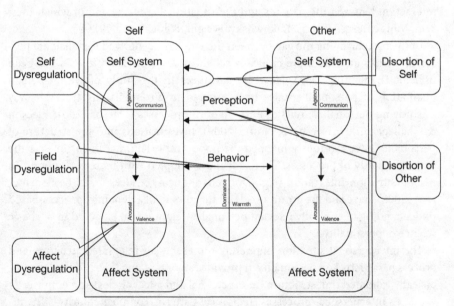

Figure 5.3. Personality pathology as dysregulation and distortion in the interpersonal situation.
SOURCE: Adapted from Hopwood, C. J., Wright, A. G. C., Ansell, E. B., & Pincus, A. L. (2013). The interpersonal core of personality pathology. *Journal of Personality Disorders, 27*, 270–295. Copyright 2017 Christopher J. Hopwood, Aaron L. Pincus, and Aidan G. C. Wright.

DISTORTION

Sullivan (1953b) proposed the concept of "parataxic distortion" to describe the potentially biasing influence of internal subjective interpersonal situations on observable interpersonal behavior. Distortions are thought to occur when one's mental representation of an interpersonal situation does not match an objective interpretation of the situation, instead fitting the contours of an alternative, internal, and psychologically impactful or conflictual situation. In this sense, maladaptive interpersonal behavior can oftentimes be understood as a logical response to a misperception, deeply rooted in an individual's social learning history.

The Interpersonal Situation as an Integrative Framework for Personality Assessment

Traditional conceptualizations of personality traits have emphasized stability and cross-situational generality, and thus research has prioritized studying the structure of between-person differences (Fleeson, 2012). In contrast, theories of personality pathology rooted in clinical practice often describe dysfunction in terms of dynamic within-person processes (Beck, Freeman, & Davis, 2004; Clarkin, Yeomans, & Kernberg, 2006; Kohut, 1977; Pincus, 2005). The dynamic processes that form the focus of clinical description and intervention generally involve an interaction between the patients and the situational contexts within which their symptoms emerge (Pincus, Lukowitsky, Wright, & Eichler, 2009).

In the past, bridging the gap between the empirically derived dimensional personality traits and the more clinically salient processes related to PDs has been difficult (Benjamin, 1993). However, advances in the study of within-person fluctuation of personality states have ushered in an empirically tractable way of studying personality traits as ensembles of processes (Fleeson, 2001; Fleeson & Ghallager, 2009; Fleeson & Noftle, 2009). Investigations into the structure of personality have rigorously mapped the important orienting dimensions for the empirical study of processes. These advances, coupled with increased interest in person-situation integration (e.g., Donnellan, Lucas, & Fleeson, 2009; Fournier et al., 2008), have laid the groundwork for the pursuit of a dynamic, process-based understanding of clinically relevant personality features that is rooted in the basic science of personality.

The interpersonal situation inherently represents an integrated structure and process perspective on personality. It provides an organizing theory, as well as empirically validated trait structure (interpersonal and affect circles) and empirically validated interpersonal processes (reciprocal patterns/complementarity). The interpersonal situation specifies the important inputs, mediators, and outputs of interest in process-based formulations (e.g., Wang et al., 2014) and provides a systematic lexicon to organize structural and dynamic constructs (e.g., Lukowitsky & Pincus, 2011) that is based in personality science.

Thus, the key concepts of CIIT provide scaffolding for an evidence-based approach to conceptualizing and treating clinically relevant aspects of personality.

Within this lens, individual differences in personality and symptoms are based on the same empirically supported structure such that personality pathology is considered a distortion or disturbance of normal interpersonal functioning. CIIT allows clinicians to identify and organize the salient interpersonal data regarding patients' typical ways of seeing themselves and others, patients' typical ways of reacting and relating to others in the moment, and patients' maladaptive interpersonal patterns emerging over time both in the consulting room (e.g., Thomas et al., 2014; Tracey, Bludworth, & Glidden-Tracey, 2012) and across the natural settings of daily life (e.g., Roche et al., 2014; Sadikaj, Moskowitz, Russell, Zuroff, & Paris, 2013; Wright, Hopwood, & Simms, 2015).

PERSONALITY DIAGNOSIS AND THE INTERPERSONAL SITUATION — THE CASE OF DAVID

In the remainder of this chapter we demonstrate the value of using the interpersonal situation to organize clinical formulations by describing "David," a 26-year-old Latino man who presented for a personality assessment after contemplating suicide. David was married to "Jenna," and they had a 2-year-old daughter. Three weeks prior to moving back to their mutual hometown to be closer to their parents, David became so distressed that he left his phone and keys at the house and walked for several miles. He made his way to some train tracks, where he sat, feeling "dazed." For several hours he considered throwing himself in front of a moving train, before ultimately returning home. Although he did not seek medical help at the time, his wife insisted on a psychological assessment. David presented 3 weeks after moving into an apartment in his hometown, 6 weeks after the incident.

David appeared motivated despite having been referred by Jenna. Although he reported occasional suicidal ideation, current risk was judged to be low. The *Personality Assessment Inventory* (Morey, 1991) was used to assess general features of personality and psychopathology. Validity scales were all within normal limits. His only significant elevations (i.e., $T > 70$) were on the suicidal ideation and stress scales. Depression, his next highest elevation, was 61T. The overall pattern of scores suggested passivity and isolation.

Interpersonal Assessment: Across Levels, Across Interactions, Within Interactions

Interpersonal theory has long emphasized the systematic assessment of clinical characteristics across levels of personality functioning, situations, and time (Kiesler, 1996; Leary, 1957). Likewise, the interpersonal situation as represented in Figure 5.2 is meant to be highly flexible so as to serve and connect a range of clinical functions. The model can be simplified in the form of the IPC, or elaborated to account for different levels of interpersonal functioning or time. Contemporary interpersonal assessment enables the elaboration of the interpersonal situation across three levels of functioning: interpersonal dynamics that occur across levels of interpersonal functioning within the person, patterns of interaction across situations, and patterns of interaction within situations (Pincus et al., 2014).

To better understand and integrate different *levels of interpersonal functioning* (Leary, 1957), David agreed to complete a battery of IPC questionnaires (Figure 5.4), including the *Inventory of Interpersonal Problems-Short Circumplex* (IIP-SC; Horowitz et al., 1988; Soldz et al., 1995), the *Circumplex Scales of Interpersonal Values* (CSIV; Locke, 2000), the *Personality Assessment Inventory* Interpersonal trait scales (Morey, 1991), and the *Interpersonal Sensitivities Circumplex* (ISC; Hopwood et al., 2011). Jenna also rated him on the IIP-SC.

David and Jenna also agreed to rate interpersonal situations every day (Table 5.1) for 2 weeks to assess *patterns of interaction across interpersonal situations.* David rated 29 total interactions across a variety of relationships, 10 of which were focused on interactions with Jenna. Jenna also rated 10 interactions with David. They both rated five variables for each interaction: self warmth, self dominance, other warmth, other dominance, and positive versus negative affective valence for self on a 1–7 scale.

Finally, *patterns within therapy sessions* were assessed by trained coders who rated the clinician's and David's warmth and dominance during the first, second, and third sessions using a computer-based momentary interpersonal coding system (Table 5.2) (Lizdek et al., 2012; Sadler et al., 2009) that records a data point for each dimension every half second. These data can be used to examine moment-to-moment interactions that occur within a particular interpersonal situation, including therapy sessions (Thomas et al., 2014; Tracey et al., 2012). At the conclusion of session 4, David was trained to use the procedure by the clinician, which included observation and practice. David then coded 5 minutes and 50 seconds of an interaction during session 2 (Table 5.3). In the following section, we integrate these assessments using the interpersonal situation to develop a clinically useful formulation of David's personality and difficulties.

Field Dysregulation

When asked to describe the events leading up to his suicidal gesture, David reported being stressed by being a parent and husband. He felt like a failure because he had been unemployed and wasn't doing enough to help Jenna. David described playing online video games as his "only release," but Jenna criticized him for playing video games while she was taking care of their son, cleaning the house, and so on. He basically agreed with her, but this criticism set off an avalanche of self-blame and hopelessness. The day of his gesture, David said he "just couldn't take it, and didn't know what to do." David's tendency to withdraw conflicted with his desire to be close to his son and to his wife, to be helpful and connected, and to do the "right thing." He resented Jenna for her criticism and wanted her to be more gentle but also readily sympathized with her position. David wanted to be able to be there for Jenna when she needed him but also to find ways to take a break when things got too stressful, and he wanted to figure out what was making that difficult. David and the clinician agreed that one goal of the assessment would be to answer the question: *How can I manage closeness and distance?*

Questionnaire data indicated that David's predominant interpersonal trait and problem disposition was to be cold and submissive, whereas he was most sensitive to others' closeness (Figure 5.4). Jenna rated him as relatively cold and submissive (Table 5.1), which was consistent with the average of the trained coders' momentary ratings (Table 5.2). In the initial three clinical sessions, David exhibited below-average warmth, which was highly discrepant (Cohen's d > 2.0) from the clinician's behavior in these same sessions. These data converged in suggesting that David's characteristic interpersonal style is to be cold and detached, with limited flexibility around that set point.

However, this portrait belies appreciable complexity. First, while David did report being too cold on the IIP-SC, he also reported problems being too warm

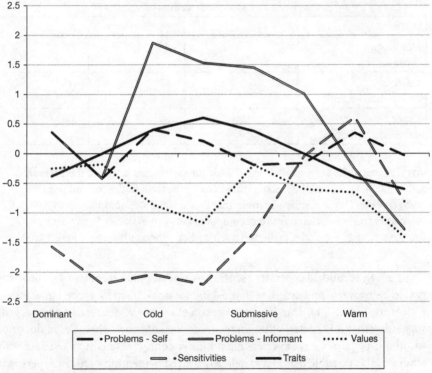

Figure 5.4. Interpersonal assessment of David's internal dynamics.
NOTE: The x-axis indicates variability around the eight octants of the interpersonal circumplex. Y-axis indicates standard scores on IPC measures. To provide a common metric for comparing measurement surfaces, norms for all instruments are from college student samples, with the exception of the Personality Assessment Inventory (PAI), which was normed using a community sample. Trait estimates from the PAI are unlike other data in that the interpersonal profile is based on single scores for warmth and dominance, rather than eight octant scores (the other data points are inferred from these vectors).

Table 5.1 RESULTS OF REPEATED ASSESSMENTS OF INTERPERSONAL SITUATIONS
FROM DAVID AND JENNA

	David's Report of Interactions Across 2 Weeks (k = 29)	David's Report of Interactions With Jenna (k = 10)	Jenna's Report of Interactions With David (k = 10)
MEAN (SD)			
David warmth	4.55 (1.52)	5.10 (1.20)	3.30 (1.25)
David dominance	4.41 (1.59)	5.10 (1.37)	2.60 (1.26)
Other warmth	5.10 (1.35)	5.40 (1.17)	4.20 (1.32)
Other dominance	3.86 (1.48)	3.70 (1.63)	3.50 (1.51)
Self positive vs. negative affect	4.62 (1.54)	4.90 (1.45)	3.44 (1.26)
CROSS-CORRELATIONS			
Warm complementarity	.78	.84	.90
Dominance complementarity	−.43	−.43	.06
David dominance-warmth	.62	.42	−.48
Other dominance-warmth	.34	.20	.00

NOTE: All variables were rated on a 1–7 scale for each interaction and then averaged across interactions, with high scores indicated by the term in the column (e.g., high scores on David dominance mean that David was more dominant than submissive). Cross-correlations were computed between variables (e.g., warm complementarity = correlation between self and other warmth across interactions).

(Figure 5.4). Second, in contrast to scores on dispositional IPC measures, David reported being warm and assertive in most interactions, including when interacting with Jenna (Table 5.1). Thus, across assessment methods, discrepancies emerged, suggesting that it is possible that there are important times when David does not withdraw. Perhaps he is experiencing an inner conflict related to closeness with others, or it is possible that David held a distorted perception of his interpersonal patterns. We discuss each of these possibilities more later.

We also examined David's unique interpersonal structure (i.e., the within-person correlations between warmth and dominance across time) in both the interactions and momentary coded data (Tables 5.1 and 5.2). In the interaction-level data, David reported that when he is dominant, he is also warm, whereas when he is submissive, he is cold. Observers' momentary ratings revealed an opposite pattern, as did Jenna's report of their mutual interactions. Overall, these complex patterns suggest that (a) David's withdrawal is connected to dominance

Table 5.2 MOMENTARY DYNAMICS ACROSS SESSIONS

	Session 1	Session 2	Session 3
MEAN (SD)			
David warmth	−163 (86)	−76 (57)	−23 (57)
David dominance	118 (251)	−13 (262)	25 (262)
Clinician warmth	94 (45)	117 (30)	88 (36)
Clinician dominance	−74 (270)	89 (225)	−20 (266)
CROSS-CORRELATIONS			
Warm complementarity	.25	−.14	−.05
Dominance complementarity	−.96	−.93	−.94
David dominance-warmth	−.76	−.67	−.55
Clinician dominance-warmth	.25	.55	−.09

NOTE: Momentary scores range from −1000 to 1000. All correlations were computed after covarying time. The average correlations among the time series of individual raters for both dimensions across sessions was .73.

Table 5.3 MOMENTARY ASPECTS OF A CLIP FROM SESSION 2 FROM OBSERVER AND PATIENT PERSPECTIVES

	Trained Observer	Patient
MEAN (SD)		
David warmth	−139 (49)	−391 (483)
David dominance	187 (189)	78 (445)
Clinician warmth	129 (13)	−38 (495)
Clinician dominance	13 (177)	−350 (510)
CROSS-CORRELATIONS		
Warm complementarity	−.06	.25
Dominance complementarity	−.95	−.76
David dominance-warmth	−.61	−.36
Clinician dominance-warmth	.01	.23

NOTE: Momentary scores range from −1,000 to 1,000. All correlations were computed after covarying time.

and submission in interpersonal situations and (b) his perception of his own behavior is likely distorted in important ways that relate to his withdrawal.

SELF-DYSREGULATION

David reported valuing being both cold-dominant and submissive in relationships
(Figure 5.4). As with his self-reported problems, the existence of two nonadjacent
elevations in the dispositional values profile could reflect an internal conflict between his desire to put himself first and his desire to comply with the wishes of
others. Remarkably, his general interpersonal style, cold-submissive withdrawal,
was his least valued interpersonal orientation (Figure 5.4). This pattern, in which
David views himself as being the way he least values, suggests self-loathing and an
experience of failure in interpersonal situations, in that the person he would like
to be and the person he is are very different from one another. These patterns be-
tray inner conflicts with regard to identity and self-worth, and raise the possibility
that interpersonal withdrawal serves a defensive function, helping him regulate
these inner conflicts.

David related a story that occurred while he was being trained for a new job in
a factory. One element of the training required him to hear a subtle signal which
he could not hear because of tinnitus. However, he hesitated to tell his manager
about his disability, creating some confusion. When a coworker explained the situation, David's manager was understanding and in fact expressed relief, saying
"I thought you were just dumb!" David became quite anxious and self-critical in
response to this half-joke, and his self-critical rumination became so severe that
evening that he called in sick the next day. He reported an inner monologue as
follows: "Of course it would be OK, it is not my fault, but why did I need someone
else to stand up for me? I am just weak and worthless." He reported often feeling
in a similar position with respect to his wife, whom he perceived as more effective at parenting, managing their finances, and keeping the house organized, and
whom he experienced as critical and demanding. David and the assessor agreed
that a second question was: *How can I assert myself effectively?*

In talking further with David, it became clear that inner conflicts related to
self-worth and value typically preceded withdrawal. Within the interpersonal situation, then, the detached behavior that is most commonly observed by others
seems to be connected to an inner identity of worthlessness and incompetence.
Others' criticism is presumed implicitly, to some degree independent of the proximal others' reaction in interpersonal fields, and it connects easily with his inner
critic. The connection between dysregulation in the self-system and interpersonal withdrawal raises questions about the developmental origins of this pattern,
the role of parataxic distortion, and his affective experience of this interpersonal
sequence.

AFFECT DYSREGULATION

As described earlier, David reported limited distress in general across self-report
instruments. His IIP-SC elevation was in the normal range, suggesting average
levels of interpersonal distress. The affective valence of his interaction ratings was

also quite positive, in that they were consistently above the midpoint of the scale and significantly higher than Jenna's affect ratings (Table 5.1).

In discussing the interaction ratings, David was struck by how well things actually seemed to be going for him. He emphasized that things only go bad once in a while; generally his interactions are good. If anything, he felt he was even more warm and assertive, and felt better, when interacting with Jenna. He understood the discrepancy between his ratings and Jenna's in terms of her dissatisfaction, which he attributed to his incompetence. "She's unhappy with me, it is not so much that I am unhappy," he said. This stance was in contrast to some of the things that he said earlier about the inner experiences precipitating his suicidal gesture. When asked about this discrepancy, David said that things were bad then but had gotten better now that he had moved home. However, Jenna was not reporting significant changes in his behavior, casting some doubt on his report. It would appear that David was somewhat closed off to his negative emotions.

An interesting clue about David's affect system emerged in his ratings of his interaction with the clinician (Table 5.3). The scene that David coded for momentary behavior involves David telling the therapist about the time that his colleague told his boss about David's hearing difficulty. This scene picks up following the clinician asking him to describe a situation in which he had a difficult time asserting himself. Although there was not significant evidence of distortion in David's ratings, the time series data from David's momentary assessment were substantially more variable than those of the coders. The clinician identified areas of David's time series where there were intense shifts in their warmth levels and inquired with David about his experience of those moments. In one instance, he rated both the clinician and himself as increasing sharply on warmth. It was after the clinician said, "That really does sound intense" about David's inner experience of his colleague talking to his boss. When asked, he said, "I really felt that you understood what I was saying, and I guess that felt good." In another instance, the clinician's time series had a sharp downward spike on affiliation, during a time when David was saying how embarrassed he felt. When asked about this, David reported that "I just felt like I was being so annoying, you must have been bored."

Further probing made it clear that David's emotional experiences were, in fact, quite intense. However, he disavowed them immediately and automatically. Following a discussion of these experiences, David and the clinician agreed that these are the kinds of experiences he was withdrawing from the day of his suicide gesture, and that this pattern is similar to what happens routinely with Jenna. It is not Jenna that he was withdrawing from, but when interpersonal situations lead to affective disruption, her presence in those situations blocks his most trusted defensive patterns. To get away from the feelings, he has to remove himself from the situation, which means moving away from her. David agreed that this pattern would be difficult for her to see, as it was for the clinician to see given his report of limited distress on the questionnaires. David also acknowledged that he often did not see it so clearly himself.

DISTORTION

Assessment data consistently suggested the importance of distortion in understanding David's problems in living. To start with, Jenna reported that he has significantly more problems than he himself reported on the IIP-SC. This difference was corroborated in mean values in the interaction ratings, in which Jenna rated David's warmth, David's dominance, her own warmth, and affective valence all significantly ($p < .05$) lower than did David (effect sizes ranged from .96 to 1.91). Every direct comparison indicated that Jenna was significantly less satisfied than David in their interactions than he reported, consistent with the possibility that he was not fully aware of the extent of his interpersonal difficulties.

A more nuanced difference in their perceptions involved within-person correlations between David's dominance and warmth across situations (Table 5.1). As discussed earlier, correlations between David's self-reported dominance and warmth scores were .62 in general and .42 in interactions with Jenna. He saw himself as vacillating somewhat between a position of warm dominance in which he feels effective and connected (correlations with positive affect in his data were .87 for warmth and .56 for dominance) to a position in which he is withdrawn, self-critical, and hopeless. In contrast, Jenna saw David's dominance and warmth as strongly negatively correlated (–.48). From her perspective, he vacillates between asserting himself in a manner that is hostile and cold to withdrawing via compliance and ingratiation.

However, when David coded his own session, his correlations between his dominance and warmth were similar to observers. Specifically, dominance and warmth were correlated negatively, as the coders and Jenna had reported (albeit his ratings had a smaller correlation than the observer ratings). After the task, David described feeling "blown away" by how differently he looks on the outside than he feels on the inside. He said: "When I see myself talk, I just want to turn the other way; I'm so negative even when I don't think I'm being that way. No wonder Jenna doesn't think I care enough." This highlights the utility of engaging a patient in the task of perspective taking, which is aided by concrete and readily accessible assessment data. Further, it shows that David has the capacity for accurately encoding his own behavior, even though this becomes derailed in affectively charged situations in the real world.

As is often the case in collaborative interpersonal assessment (Finn, 2007; Hopwood, 2010), this "perception test" had actually served as a powerful intervention, providing David with insights regarding how he comes across to others. That proved to be an important moment for David, because it helped him understand Jenna's experience of him and how different it is from how he feels. During the times when he feels warm and dominant on the inside (self system: effective and caring husband), he actually comes across as cold and brooding (field system: aloof and self-centered). Although his affect and self systems are highly sensitive to interpersonal dynamics, as indicated by his experience of significant variability over time, his behavior is relatively flat due to his characteristic avoidance of negative emotions, making him seem unaffected. It was likely very difficult for Jenna (or David) to know when or why he was upset. Likewise, his perceptions of others' behavior are colored by his expectation of judgment and criticism, and his perceptions of his own behavior. These distortions had been supporting a pattern, rooted in development, which had become a core theme in David's interpersonal dysfunction.

Formulation

The goal of personality assessment is to conceptualize all aspects of patient functioning into a coherent and parsimonious formulation that answers specific referral questions. An initial subgoal involves characterizing the individual's general configuration of personality traits that indicate areas of dysfunction in interpersonal situations, as shown by the black symbols in Figure 5.5. David's affective experience is constrained to low arousal and low valence. His interpersonal

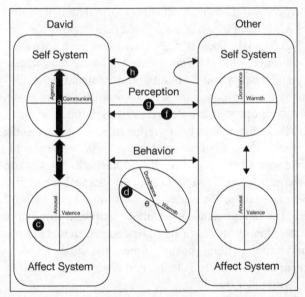

Figure 5.5. Areas of interpersonal dysfunction implied by David's *DSM-5* Section III diagnosis.

NOTE: Bolded circles and arrows indicate particular areas of dysfunction, which include (in counterclockwise order starting at the top left): (a) conflicts regarding agency and self-worth; (b) a tight connection between his sense of self and his affects; (c) predominantly negative, low arousal affects; (d) cold, submissive behavior; (e) conflation between warmth and dominance in self and others (as indicated by the oval shaped circle, as opposed to a black arrow or circle); (f) others' misperception of him; (g) misperception of others; and (h) misperception of self.

SOURCE: Adapted from Hopwood, C. J., Wright, A .G. C., Ansell, E. B., & Pincus, A. L. (2013). The interpersonal core of personality pathology. *Journal of Personality Disorders*, *27*, 270–295. Copyright 2017 Christopher J. Hopwood, Aaron L. Pincus, and Aidan G. C. Wright.

behavior is withdrawn, and there is an inverse correlation between dominance and warmth in his behavior (at least as experienced by others). He has identity conflicts related to power versus weakness that are strongly connected to his affects, although this connection is only partially in David's awareness. Finally, he has significantly distorted perceptions of both his own behaviors and others' perceptions of him. Likewise, others routinely fail to recognize his inner turmoil and thus misattribute the reasons for his withdrawal.

Although this rough portrait is useful in distinguishing David from other patients, in general, it fails to establish a connection between David's personality and his marital difficulties and suicidal behavior or to specify interventions that are likely to be effective. Understanding how these features play out in interpersonal situations helps establish those connections. The key task of the assessor is to *develop a formulation about when and how maladaptive patterns emerge.*

Interpersonal situations can be reconfigured as successive stages in order to understand how processes, such as the inner phenomena that lead David to withdraw, play out over time (Pincus & Hopwood, 2012). Such a model can be used to integrate interpersonal assessment data into a formulation of cyclical maladaptive patterns (see Anchin & Pincus, 2010; Luborsky, 1977; Strupp & Binder, 1984), as depicted in Figure 5.6. In the first stage, David sustains his sense of security with grandiose fantasies in which he finds himself in heroic roles such as "videogame grand champion," "employee of the month," and "husband of the year" (represented in the figure as a warm-dominant self-image, with parentheses indicating his inner experience as opposed to outer behavior), admired and entrusted by those around him (these inner objects are represented by the parenthesized warm-submissive other). The configuration of mental representations in stage 1 likely provides David with a sense of self-worth and shields him against deep feelings of failure and incompetence. However, it is highly fragile because it depends upon unreasonable expectations. In reality, David is not a hero; he is a "regular guy." Yet because of the unreasonable expectations that stem from an inner world in which David sees himself as a hero, he experiences his actual behavior with a deep and automatic sense of falling short. At times, his actual behavior was less than it could be because of the dysregulation and distortion involved in bridging his inner fantasy with outer reality.

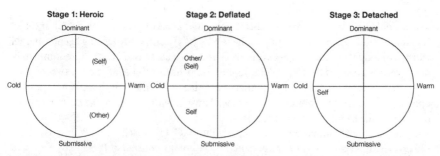

Figure 5.6. Formulation of David's core maladaptive pattern within interpersonal situations.

This gives way to a second stage in which David feels deflated and hopeless. He sees himself as incompetent (submissive self-image) and disconnected (cold self-image). Hostile and unforgiving internal objects (e.g., in the form of internal self-criticism) as indicated by his parenthesized self in Figure 5.6 reinforce feelings of shame and worthlessness. These hostile critics, a powerful and automatic element of David's inner experience for as long as he could remember, likely reflected internalized messages from his developmental environment (Benjamin, 1993). This configuration sets the stage for parataxic distortion, such that David's behavior complements the inner self-critics but leads to strained interactions with proximal others in the interpersonal field (as was exhibited in his story about feeling incompetent at work due to hearing difficulties). For instance, during this stage David may come across to others as brooding and self-defeating (cold submissive) even when others are supportive and autonomy granting (warm submissive). This leads proximal others (e.g., Jenna or his boss) to become confused or frustrated and ultimately express genuine disappointment (i.e., become cold and dominant, as indicated in Figure 5.6), providing further fuel for self-criticism.

When confirmation of David's most intense insecurity in stage 2 leads to a level of self and affect dysregulation that is unbearable, he detaches himself from the stressful situations, creating a negative reinforcement loop that sustains the maladaptive pattern. In many situations, he could use minor withdrawals, such as ignoring the other person and retreating to inner fantasy, going for a walk, or playing video games. His suicidal gesture could be understood in this context as a more extreme behavior that was nevertheless the output of a generalizable interpersonal process, similar in function to withdrawal from his family to play video games.

Intervention

By depicting core areas of David's dysfunction and the dynamics of a cyclical maladaptive pattern, this formulation leads to specific transtheoretical and transdiagnostic treatment recommendations. It can be helpful to connect specific strategies to particular aspects of the interpersonal situation, in order to integrate interventions and demarcate areas for specific assessments of change. Next, we describe several treatment recommendations designed to affect certain aspects of David's interpersonal situations, as depicted in Figure 5.7.

HOW CAN I MANAGE CLOSENESS AND DISTANCE?

Three strategies were recommended for helping David manage closeness and distance (Figure 5.7). First, David agreed to a behavioral plan in which he would engage in five concrete behaviors per week involving closeness to his wife. These behaviors would be monitored in weekly meetings with the clinician, and follow-up data would be collected from David and Jenna regarding the reduction in his withdrawal behavior. Second, the clinician was consistently warm during the sessions, in order to increase David's warmth (see Tracey, 2002) in the therapeutic

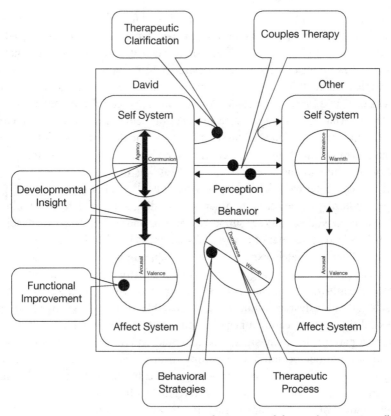

Figure 5.7. Connecting treatment strategies to distortion and dysregulation in David's interpersonal situations.
SOURCE: Adapted from Hopwood, C. J., Wright, A. G. C., Ansell, E. B., & Pincus, A. L. (2013). The interpersonal core of personality pathology. *Journal of Personality Disorders, 27*, 270–295. Copyright 2017 Christopher J. Hopwood, Aaron L. Pincus, and Aidan G. C. Wright.

relationship and model how to stay connected during moments of inner turmoil. Table 5.2 shows both the stability of the clinician's warmth and the increasing levels of David's warmth during the early stages of their interactions. Finally, couples therapy was recommended to improve communication and address problematic relational patterns directly via clarifying perceptual disconnections between David and Jenna. In particular, it would be important for David to help Jenna understand that his withdrawal was in response to intense and painful inner feelings, and for them to develop strategies for communicating during those moments of intensity that do not leave him feeling overwhelmed and her feeling abandoned.

How Can I Assert Myself More Effectively?
David agreed to a behavior plan in which he practiced asserting himself in increasingly anxiety-provoking situations. Improvement was assessed based on his behavior and experience of each situation, as well as overall changes in IPC

follow-along measures. In addition to increasing the frequency of effective self-assertion, it was hoped that this practice might have the additional benefit of helping David integrate his unrealistic aspirations with a more realistic sense of his strengths and how they might help him achieve his goals. This would, in turn, reduce his experience of failure and disrupt his cyclical maladaptive pattern in general. A better understanding of the developmental origins of agentic conflicts would further facilitate insight, which could contribute to improved regulation in David's self system and a loosened connection between identity disruption and dysregulated affect. Insight could be developed in a psychotherapy focused upon connecting here-and-now interaction patterns with developmental experiences, and which also leveraged aspects of the interpersonal process itself (e.g., Anchin & Pincus, 2010; Hill & Knox, 2009). Specifically, by occupying a warm and submissive position in the therapeutic interaction, the clinician would invite David to be warm and dominant, and by maintaining a clear distinction between warmth and dominance, the clinician could model a more normative interpersonal stance than characterized by David's behavior in which assertion is usually done in a brooding, negativistic manner, and compliance is conflated with connection.

SUMMARY

Contemporary psychiatric diagnosis is mostly disconnected from clinical practice because it does not provide the kind of information clinicians need to help their patients. Organizing clinical data in terms of the structure and processes of personality provides a framework that connects assessment to individual lives and specific interventions (Krueger, 2013; Millon, 1969; Sullivan, 1954). The interpersonal situation offers a system that can build upon *DSM-5* assessment, buttressed by the clinically rich principles of CIIT, decades of empirical research, and a suite of clinically sensitive assessment tools, to provide a powerful framework for personality assessment.

By integrating personality *structure* and *process*, CIIT and the interpersonal situation satisfy all of the requirements of a useful system for conceptualizing cases laid out at the beginning of this chapter. The interpersonal situation (Figure 5.2) covers the range of characteristics and difficulties that are likely to be of clinical interest in most cases. The elements of the interpersonal situation conform to an evidence-based structure of individual differences (i.e., the interpersonal and affective circles, which themselves can be connected to general trait models). The interpersonal situation affords a means for describing what a person is like in general, variability around these general characteristics, and specific contextualized dynamic patterns. It can integrate diverse evidence-based models of psychopathology, personality, and intervention, exemplified by the use of techniques from a variety of orientations in the case demonstration. It provides a framework for integrating multimethod assessment data (Hopwood & Bornstein, 2014), as shown in the case earlier in which informant, self-report, performance, and observational methods were used to provide a comprehensive portrait of David's interpersonal situations. Perhaps most important, the case demonstrated how the interpersonal situation can connect assessment, formulation, and intervention.

An ongoing challenge in CIIT and personality assessment in general has to do with portability. Although interpersonal assessment is highly elegant and parsimonious, day-to-day clinicians do not have the resources to conduct some elements of the assessment described in this chapter. Furthermore, only the most simplistic analyses are presented here; but in fact intensive repeated measures in particular open the clinician and researcher to an array of powerful analytic techniques which have the advantage of making more use of these kinds of data, with the disadvantage of being intimidating and difficult to automate for the practicing clinician. Our hope is that, with advancing technology, such techniques will become increasingly viable, and it will become routine to assess patients over time and across different levels of personality, time, and informant (Roche et al., 2014). To successfully accomplish this, researchers and clinicians will need a model for integrating these various sources of information. The interpersonal situation provides an evidence-based model that is well suited to that purpose.

ACKNOWLEDGMENTS

We thank the editors of this book as well as Emily Dowgwillo, Sindes Dawood, Steve Finn, Alytia Levendosky, Kate Thomas, and Leila Wu for helpful comments on a previous draft of this paper.

REFERENCES

American Psychiatric Association. (2013). *Diagnostic and statistical manual of mental disorders* (5th ed.) (*DSM-5*). Washington, DC: Authors.

Anchin, J. C., & Pincus, A. L. (2010). Evidence–based Interpersonal psychotherapy with personality disorders: Theory, components, and strategies. In J. J. Magnavita (Ed.), *Evidence–based treatment of personality dysfunction: Principles, methods, and processes* (pp. 113–166). Washington, DC: American Psychological Association.

Ansell, E. B., & Pincus, A. L. (2004). Interpersonal perceptions of the five-factor model of personality: An examination using the structural summary method for circumplex data. *Multivariate Behavioral Research, 39*, 167–201.

Beck, A. T., Freeman, A., & Davis, D. D. (2004). *Cognitive therapy of personality disorders* (2nd ed.). New York, NY: Guilford.

Benjamin, L. S. (1993). Every psychopathology is a gift of love. *Psychotherapy Research, 3*, 1–24.

Blatt, S. J., Auerbach, J. S., & Levy, K. N. (1997). Mental representations in personality development, psychopathology, and the therapeutic process. *Review of General Psychology, 1*, 351–374.

Carson, R. C. (1969). *Interaction concepts of personality*. Chicago, IL: Aldine.

Clarkin, J. F., Yeomans, F., & Kernberg, O. F. (2006). *Psychotherapy of borderline personality: Focusing on object relations*. Washington, DC: American Psychiatric Publishing.

DeYoung, C. G. (2015). Cybernetic Big Five theory. *Journal of Research in Personality, 56*, 33–58.

Donnellan, M. B., Lucas, R. E., & Fleeson, W. (2009). Personality and assessment at age 40: Introduction to the legacy of the past person-situation debate and emerging directions of future person-situation integration. *Journal of Research in Personality, 43*, 117–119.

Eaton, N. R., South, S. C., & Krueger, R. F. (2009). The Cognitive-Affective Processing System (CAPS) approach to personality and the concept of personality disorder: Integrating clinical and social-cognitive research. *Journal of Research in Personality, 43*, 208–217.

Ebner-Priemer, U. W., Eid, M., Kleindienst, N., Stabenow, S., & Trull, T. J. (2009). Analytic strategies for understanding affective (in)stability and other dynamic processes in psychopathology. *Journal of Abnormal Psychology, 2009*, 195–202.

Fairbairn, W. R. (1952). *Psychoanalytic studies of the personality*. London, UK: Tavistock.

Fleeson, W. (2001). Towards a structure- and process-integrated view of personality: Traits as density distributions of states. *Journal of Personality and Social Psychology, 80*, 1011–1027.

Fleeson, W. (2012). Perspectives on the person: Rapid growth and opportunities for integration. In K. Deaux and M. Snyder (Eds.), *The Oxford handbook of personality and social psychology*. Oxford, UK: Oxford University Press.

Fleeson, W., & Gallagher, P. (2009). The implications of big-five standing for the distribution of trait manifestation in behavior: Fifteen experience-sampling studies and a meta-analysis. *Journal of Personality and Social Psychology, 97*, 1097–1114.

Fleeson, W., & Noftle, E. E. (2009). In favor of the synthetic resolution to the person-situation debate. *Journal of Research in Personality, 43*, 150–154.

Fournier, M. A., Moskowitz, D. S., & Zuroff, D. C. (2008). Integrating dispositions, signatures, and the interpersonal domain. *Journal of Personality and Social Psychology, 94*, 531–545.

Fournier, M., Moskowitz, D. S., & Zuroff, D. (2009). The interpersonal signature. *Journal of Research in Personality, 43*, 155–162.

Gratz, K. L., & Roemer, L. (2004). Multidimensional assessment of emotion regulation and dysregulation: Development, factor structure, and initial validation of the Difficulties in Emotion Regulation Scale. *Journal of Psychopathology and Behavioral Assessment, 36*, 41–54.

Harkness, A. R., Reynolds, S. M., & Lilienfeld, S. O. (2014). A review of systems for psychology and psychiatry: Adaptive systems, Personality Psychopathology-Five (PSY-5), and DSM-5. *Journal of Personality Assessment, 96*, 121–139.

Hill, C. E., & Knox, S. (2009). Processing the therapeutic relationship. *Psychotherapy Research, 19*, 13–29.

Hopwood, C. J. (2010). An interpersonal perspective on the personality assessment process. *Journal of Personality Assessment, 92*, 471–479.

Hopwood, C. J. (2011). Personality traits in the DSM-5. *Journal of Personality Assessment, 93*, 398–405.

Hopwood, C. J., Ansell, E. B., Pincus, A. L., Wright, A. G. C., Lukowitsky, M. R., & Roche, M. J. (2011). The circumplex structure of interpersonal sensitivities. *Journal of Personality, 79,* 708–740.

Hopwood, C. J., & Bornstein, R. F. (2014). *Multimethod clinical assessment.* New York, NY: Guilford.

Hopwood, C. J., Wright, A. G. C., Ansell, E. B., & Pincus, A. L. (2013). The interpersonal core of personality pathology. *Journal of Personality Disorders, 27,* 270–295.

Hopwood, C. J., Zimmermann, J., Pincus, A. L., & Krueger, R. F. (2015). Connecting personality structure and dynamics: Towards a more evidence based and clinically useful diagnostic scheme. *Journal of Personality Disorders, 29*(4), 431–448.

Horowitz, L. M., Rosenberg, S. E., Baer, B. A., Ureno, G., & Villasenor, V. S. (1988). Inventory of Interpersonal Problems: Psychometric properties and clinical applications. *Journal of Consulting and Clinical Psychology, 56,* 885–892.

Horowitz, L. M., Wilson, K. R., Turan, B., Zolotsev, P., Constantino, M. J., & Henderson, L. (2006). How interpersonal motives clarify the meaning of interpersonal behavior: A revised circumplex model. *Personality and Social Psychology Review, 10,* 67–86.

Johnson, J. A., Miller, M. L., Lynam, D. R., & South, S. C. (2012). Five-factor model facets differentially predict in-the-moment affect and cognitions. *Journal of Research in Personality, 46,* 752–759.

Kiesler, D. J. (1983). The 1982 interpersonal circle: A taxonomy for complementarity in human transactions. *Psychological Review, 90,* 185–214.

Kiesler, D. J. (1996). *Contemporary interpersonal theory and research: Personality, psychopathology, and psychotherapy.* New York, NY: John Wiley & Sons.

Kohut, H. (1977). *The restoration of the self.* New York, NY: International Universities Press.

Krueger, R. F. (2013). Personality disorders: The vanguard of the post DSM-5 era. *Personality Disorders: Theory, Research, and Treatment.*

Krueger, R. F., & Markon, K. E. (2014). The role of the DSM-5 personality trait model in moving toward a quantitative and empirically based approach to classifying personality and psychopathology. *Annual Review of Clinical Psychology, 10,* 477–501.

Leary, T. (1957). *Interpersonal diagnosis of personality.* New York, NY: Ronald Press.

Lizdek, I., Sadler, P., Woody, E., Ethier, N., & Malet, G. (2012). Capturing the stream of behavior: A computer joystick method for coding interpersonal behavior continuously over time. *Social Sciences Computer Review, 30,* 513–521.

Locke, K. D. (2000). Circumplex scales of interpersonal values: Reliability, validity, and applicability to interpersonal problems and personality disorders. *Journal of Personality Assessment, 75,* 249–267.

Luborsky, L. (1977). Measuring a pervasive psychic structure in psychotherapy: The core conflictual relationship theme. In N. Freedman and S. S. Grand (Eds.), *Communicative structures and psychic structures* (pp. 367–395). New York, NY: Plenum Press.

Lukowitsky, M. R., & Pincus, A. L. (2011). The pantheoretical nature of mental representations and their ability to predict interpersonal adjustment in a nonclinical sample. *Psychoanalytic Psychology, 28,* 48–74.

Millon, T. (1969). *Modern psychopathology: A biosocial approach to maladaptive learning and functioning.* Philadelphia, PA: W.B. Saunders.

Morey, L. C. (1991). *Personality assessment inventory professional manual.* Odessa, FL: Psychological Assessment Resources.

Pincus, A. L. (2005). A contemporary integrative interpersonal theory of personality disorders. In M. Lenzenweger & J. Clarkin (Eds.), *Major theories of personality disorder* (2nd ed., pp. 282–331). New York, NY: Guilford.

Pincus, A. L., & Ansell, E. B. (2003). Interpersonal theory of personality. In T. Millon & M. Lerner (Eds.), *Comprehensive handbook of psychology Vol. 5: Personality and social psychology* (pp. 209–229). Hoboken, NJ: Wiley.

Pincus, A. L., & Ansell, E. B. (2013). Interpersonal theory of personality. In J. Suls & H. Tennen (Eds.), *Handbook of psychology, vol. 5, Personality and social psychology* (2nd ed., pp. 141–159). Hoboken, NJ: Wiley.

Pincus, A. L., & Hopwood, C. J. (2012). A contemporary interpersonal model of personality pathology and personality disorder. In T. A. Widiger (Ed.), *Oxford handbook of personality disorders* (pp. 372–398). Oxford, UK: Oxford University Press.

Pincus, A. L., Lukowitsky, M. R., & Wright, A. G. C. (2010). The interpersonal nexus of personality and psychopathology. In T. Millon, R. Kreuger, & E. Simonsen (Eds.), *Contemporary directions in psychopathology: Scientific foundations for DSM-V and ICD-11* (pp. 523–552). New York, NY: Guilford.

Pincus, A. L., Lukowitsky, M. R., Wright, A. G. C., & Eichler, W. C. (2009). The interpersonal nexus of persons, situations, and psychopathology. *Journal of Research in Personality, 43,* 264–265.

Pincus, A. L., Sadler, P., Woody, E., Roche, M. J., Thomas, K. M., & Wright, A. G. C. (2014). Assessing interpersonal dynamics. In C. J. Hopwood & R. F. Bornstein (Eds.), *Multimethod clinical assessment* (pp. 51–91). New York, NY: Guilford Press.

Pincus, A. L., & Wright, A. G. C. (2011). Interpersonal diagnosis of psychopathology. In L. M. Horowitz & S. Strack (Eds.). *Handbook of interpersonal psychology* (pp. 359–381). Hoboken, NJ: Wiley.

Posner, J., Russell, J. A., & Peterson, B. S. (2005). The circumplex model of affect: An integrative approach to affective neuroscience, cognitive development, and psychopathology. *Development and Psychopathology, 17,* 715–734.

Roche, M. J., Pincus, A. L., Conroy, D. E., Hyde, A. L., & Ram, N. (2013). Pathological narcissism and interpersonal behavior in daily life. *Personality Disorders: Theory, Research, and Treatment, 4,* 315–323.

Roche, M. J., Pincus, A. L., Hyde, A. L., Conroy, D. E., & Ram, N. (2013). Within-person co-variation of agentic and communal perceptions: Implications for interpersonal theory and assessment. *Journal of Research in Personality, 47,* 445–552.

Roche, M. J., Pincus, A. L., Rebar, A. L., Conroy, D. E., & Ram, N. (2014). Enriching psychological assessment using a person-specific analysis of interpersonal processes in daily life. *Assessment, 21,* 515–528.

Sadikaj, G., Moskowitz, D. S., Russell, J. J., Zuroff, D. C., & Paris, J. (2013). Quarrelsome behavior in borderline personality disorder: Influence of behavioral and affective reactivity to perceptions of others. *Journal of Abnormal Psychology, 122,* 195–207.

Sadler, P., Ethier, N., Gunn, G. R., Duong, D., & Woody, E. (2009). Are we on the same wavelength? Interpersonal complementarity as shared cyclical patterns during interactions. *Journal of Personality and Social Psychology, 97,* 1005–1020.

Shoda, Y., Mischel, W., & Wright, J. C. (1994). Intraindividual stability in the organization and patterning of behavior: Incorporating psychological situations into the ideographic analysis of personality. *Journal of Personality and Social Psychology, 67,* 674–687.

Soldz, S., Budman, S., Demby, A., & Merry, J. (1995). A short form of the Inventory of Interpersonal Problems Circumplex scales. *Assessment, 2,* 53–63.

Strupp, H. S., & Binder, J. L. (1984). *Psychotherapy in a new key: A guide to time-limited dynamic psychotherapy.* New York, NY: Basic Books.

Sullivan, H. S. (1953a). *Conceptions of modern psychiatry.* New York, NY: Norton.

Sullivan, H. S. (1953b). *The interpersonal theory of psychiatry.* New York, NY: Norton.

Sullivan, H. S. (1954). *The psychiatric interview.* New York, NY: Norton.

Thomas, K. M., Hopwood, C. J., Woody, E., Ethier, N., & Sadler P. (2014). Interpersonal processes in psychotherapy: A reanalysis of the Gloria films. *Journal of Counseling Psychology, 61, 1–14.*

Tracey, T. J., Bludworth, J., & Glidden-Tracey, C. E. (2012). Are there parallel processes in psychotherapy supervision? An empirical examination. *Psychotherapy, 49,* 330–343.

Tracey, T. J. G. (2002). Stages of counseling and therapy: An examination of complementarity and the working alliance. In G. S. Tryon (Ed.), *Counseling based on process research: Applying what we know* (pp. 265–297). Boston, MA: Allyn & Bacon.

Wang, S., Roche, M. J., Pincus, A. L., Conroy, D. E., Rebar, A. L., & Ram, N. (2014). Interpersonal dependency and emotion in everyday life. *Journal of Research in Personality, 53,* 5–12.

Widiger, T. A., & Simonsen, E. (2005). Alternative dimensional models of personality disorder: Finding a common ground. *Journal of Personality Disorders, 19,* 110–30.

Wiggins, J. S. (1991). Agency and communion as conceptual coordinates for the understanding and measurement of interpersonal behavior. In D. Cicchetti & W. M. Grove (Eds.), *Thinking clearly about psychology: Essays in honor of Paul E. Meehl, Vol. 2: Personality and psychopathology* (pp. 89–113). Minneapolis: University of Minnesota Press.

Wiggins, J. S. (2003). *Paradigms of personality assessment.* New York, NY: Guilford.

Wiggins, J. S., & Trapnell, P. D. (1996). A dyadic-interactional perspective on the five-factor model. In J. S. Wiggins (Ed.), *The five-factor model of personality: Theoretical perspectives* (pp. 88–162). New York, NY: Guilford.

Wiggins, J. S., & Trobst, K. K. (1999). The fields of interpersonal behavior. In L. Pervin & O. P. John (Eds.), *Handbook of personality: Theory and research* (2nd ed., pp. 653–670). New York, NY: Guilford.

Wright, A. G. C. (2011). Qualitative and quantitative distinctions in personality disorder. *Journal of Personality Assessment, 93,* 370–379.

Wright, A. G. C. (2014). Integrating trait and process based conceptualizations of pathological narcissism in the DSM-5 era. In A. Besser (Ed.), *Handbook of psychology of narcissism: Diverse perspectives* (pp. 153–174). Hauppauge, NY: Nova Science Publishers.

Wright, A. G. C., Hopwood, C. J., & Simms, L. J. (2015). Daily interpersonal and affective dynamics in personality disorder. *Journal of Personality Disorders, 29,* 503–525.

Wright, A. G. C., & Simms, L. J. (2014). On the structure of personality disorder traits: Conjoint analyses of the CAT-PD, PID-5, and NEO-PI-3 trait models. *Personality Disorders: Theory, Research, and Treatment, 5*, 43–54.

Wright, A. G. C., Thomas, K. M., Hopwood, C. J., Markon, K. E., Pincus, A. L., & Krueger, R. F. (2012). The hierarchical structure of DSM-5 pathological personality traits. *Journal of Abnormal Psychology, 121*, 951–957.

Zimmermann, J., Benecke, C., Bender, D. S., Skodol, A. E., Schauenburg, H., Cierpka, M., & Leising, D. (2014). Assessing DSM-5 level of personality functioning from videotaped clinical interviews: A pilot study with untrained and clinically inexperienced students. *Journal of Personality Assessment, 96*, 397–409.

6

Personality Dysfunction and Trait Extremity

Conceptually, but Not Empirically Distinct?

LEE ANNA CLARK, ELIZABETH J. DALY, STEPHANIE LAREW,
HALLIE NUZUM, THOMAS KINGSBURY, JAIME L. SHAPIRO,
XIA ALLEN, AND EUNYOE RO ■

Despite their many well-documented problems (e.g., see Widiger & Simonsen, 2005), the personality disorder (PD) criteria in the main text (Section II) of the *Diagnostic and Statistical Manual of Mental Disorders*, fifth edition (*DSM-5-II*; APA, 2013; hereafter "PD-II") are identical to those in *DSM-IV* (American Psychiatric Association [APA], 1994). The PD-II diagnostic types are considered "qualitatively distinct clinical syndromes" and are defined conceptually as personality traits that "deviate markedly from the expectations of the individual's culture" and "are manifested in at least two of the following areas: cognition, affectivity, interpersonal functioning, or impulse control." Personality traits, in turn, are defined as "enduring patterns of perceiving, relating to, and thinking about the environment and oneself that are exhibited in a wide range of social and personal contexts" or, for short, "enduring patterns of inner experience and behavior" (APA, 2013, p. 645).

Criterion A of each of the 10 PD-II diagnostic types first describes a characteristic pattern and then lists seven-to-nine specific indicators of the pattern, some minimum number of which must be exhibited for a diagnosis. For some PD-II types, however, two distinct patterns comprise Criterion A, and there is no clear mandate to ensure that indicators of both are present. For example, the Criterion A description of schizotypal PD is "social and interpersonal deficits marked by acute discomfort with, and reduced capacity for, close relationships as well as by cognitive or perceptual distortions and eccentricities of behavior" (APA, 2013, p. 655). Of the nine specific indicators, only two (arguably three) specifically represent social or interpersonal deficits, but standard procedure is to make the diagnosis as long as the minimum of five indicators is present, regardless of whether *any* indicator of social or interpersonal deficits is manifested. Further, there is not always a clear correspondence between the Criterion A pattern description and its purported specific indicators. For example, the Criterion A description for borderline personality disorder (BPD) is "instability of interpersonal relationships, self-image, and affects, and marked impulsivity" (APA, 2013, p. 663), but it is unclear how "chronic feelings of emptiness" reflects this pattern. Thus, although the PD-II types are *conceptualized* in terms of traits, they typically are *diagnosed* via specific indicators that relate inconsistently to the defining trait patterns.

ALTERNATIVE MODEL OF PERSONALITY DISORDER

In contrast, the alternative model of PD in *DSM-5*, Section III ("Emerging Models and Measures"), hereafter PD-III, defines PD as "moderate or greater impairment in personality (self/interpersonal) functioning"[1] and "one or more pathological personality traits" (APA, 2013, p. 761). Moreover, PD-III diagnosis is directly aligned with this definition. Specifically, PD-III provides descriptors for rating impairment level in four areas of personality functioning (identity and self-direction for self functioning, and intimacy and empathy for interpersonal functioning) on a 5-point scale. Unlike the implied normal-pathological dichotomy of PD-II, these five impairment levels are understood to represent a continuous distribution of functioning from 0 (no impairment) to 4 (extreme impairment).

For assessing personality traits, PD-III provides definitions of 25 trait facets, organized in five trait domains—Negative Affectivity, Detachment, Antagonism, Disinhibition, and Psychoticism—all of which are also understood to represent continuous distributions ranging from low to high levels. Although PD-III offers no specific guidance for assessing trait elevation, it does provide a set of self-report, other-report, and clinician-rating scales for this purpose (e.g., Krueger, Derringer, Markon, Watson, & Skodol, 2012; Markon, Quilty, Bagby, & Krueger, 2013) that use a 4-point (0–3) scale with ratings of two or higher considered pathological.

Much has been made of the fact that PD-III distinguishes personality dysfunction and traits conceptually (e.g., Livesley, 2012; Wakefield, 2013), based on the argument that trait extremity per se is not necessarily pathological (Livesley & Jang, 2005). However, there has been limited discussion of the fact that PD-III Criterion B requires not one or more *extreme* traits, but "one or more *pathological* traits" (APA, 2013, p. 761). Nonetheless, given that every trait researched to date has been shown to be continuously distributed in the population, "pathological traits" presumably doesn't mean that the traits themselves are pathological (because, if that were the case, then it would be possible for an individual to exhibit a normal level of a pathological trait, which is nonsensical). Rather, what is meant by "pathological traits" is that the person's trait *level* or *expression* is pathological. However, the term *expression* is conceptually problematic, because the phrase *pathological trait expression* is confounded with personality-functioning impairment. Thus, more neutral terms such as *level, elevation,* or *extremity* are preferable, although their use then requires empirical determination of one or more cut points for designating a given trait level as pathological (see Finn, 1982, for a discussion of the pitfalls of using single, fixed cut points for this determination and for clinical decision making).

A further difficulty with the current PD-III model is that there is clear *descriptive* overlap between PD-III personality impairment and "pathological traits." To give but two examples: (1) Criterion A identity impairment is reflected in Criterion B trait-domain Negative Affectivity, specifically its emotional-lability facet, and (2) Criterion A impaired intimacy is reflected in Criterion B trait-domain Detachment, particularly its intimacy-avoidance facet (see Table 6.1 for details). This overlap also raises measurement issues: Shared content increases scale intercorrelations and confounds efforts to investigate the distinction between trait extremity and personality impairment. Thus, although distinguishing trait extremity and personality impairment is attractive conceptually, it is difficult empirically, and would be impossible if they are linked inherently. If distinguishing trait extremity and personality impairment is simply empirically difficult, then there is much measure-development work to do, whereas if their linkage is inherent, that is, if trait extremity is *intrinsically* pathological, then separate assessment of personality dysfunction and traits would be neither necessary nor desirable. It is possible that the only way to adjudicate these issues is to attempt their separate assessment and either succeed or fail in the effort.

Measuring Personality Functioning and Traits

Considering self-report, trait measurement has a long history, and there are many well-established measures with strong psychometric properties. In contrast, assessment of personality dysfunction is a relatively new enterprise. To address this issue, the field's inclination likely will be to develop personality-functioning measures that minimize content overlap with established trait measures. However, it also is worth attempting to modify existing—or to develop new—trait measures to reflect trait extremity more purely, without the "contamination" of personality dysfunction.

Turning to clinician ratings, there are few established measures of either personality dysfunction or traits, which represents an opportunity to try to distinguish severity of personality functioning impairment from trait levels through new scale-development projects. Before embarking on any measure-modification or development projects, however, we need to understand better how personality functioning and traits are interrelated. To this end, Clark and Ro (2014) analyzed interrelations among multiple self-report measures of personality dysfunction and traits, along with other measures typically included in the concept of functioning.

They first examined interrelations among the functioning measures and replicated the three dimensions reported by Ro and Clark (2013) of poor versus good social/interpersonal functioning, self-pathology versus well-being/life

Table 6.1 CONTENT OVERLAP OF PERSONALITY DYSFUNCTION AND TRAIT DEFINITIONS WITH EXAMPLES IN LEVEL OF PERSONALITY FUNCTIONING SCALE DESCRIPTORS

Personality Functioning Domain and Definition	Trait Domain/Facet and Definition	Level of Personality Functioning Scale
Identity • Capacity for, and ability to regulate, a range of emotional experience	Emotional lability (NA) • Instability of emotional experiences and mood • Emotions that are easily aroused, intense, and/or out-of-proportion to events and circumstances	1- Strong emotions may be distressing, associated with a restriction in range of emotional experience. 3- Emotions may be rapidly shifting or a chronic, unwavering feeling of despair.
Self-direction • Pursuit of coherent and meaningful short-term and life goals • Utilization of constructive and pro-social internal standards of behavior	Impulsivity (DIS) • Acting on a momentary basis without a plan or consideration of outcomes • Difficulty establishing and following plans.	3- Has difficulty establishing and/or achieving personal goals. 4- Has poor differentiation of thoughts from actions, so goal-setting ability is severely compromised, with unrealistic or incoherent goals.
Empathy • Comprehension and appreciation of others' experiences and motivations • Understanding the effects of one's own behavior on others	Callousness (ANT) • Lack of concern for the feelings or problems of others • Lack of guilt or remorse about the negative or harmful effects of one's actions on others	2- Is generally unaware of or unconcerned about the effect of own behavior on others; or has an unrealistic appraisal of own effect.
Intimacy • Depth and duration of connection with others; • Desire and capacity for closeness.	Intimacy avoidance (DET) • Avoidance of close or romantic relationships, interpersonal attachments, and intimate sexual relationships.	4- Desire for affiliation is limited because of profound disinterest or expectation of harm. Engagement with others is detached, disorganized, or consistently negative.

NOTE: NA = negative affectivity; DIS = disinhibition; ANT = antagonism; DET = detachment.

satisfaction, and basic functioning (e.g., self-care, mobility, poor health/environ-ment). They then factored the trait measures and found a hierarchical structure which, at the five-factor level, reflected four of the familiar "Big Five" factors—neuroticism/negative affectivity (N/NA), (low) sociability, disinhibition, and (dis)agreeableness—plus a fifth factor they termed "rigid goal engagement." This factor reflected obsessive-compulsive (OC) traits and can be identified as the dimen-sion that in the ICD-11 (World Health Organization, 2018) section on personality disorders is termed "anankastia" (i.e., the noun form of *anankastic*, the British adjective for describing OCPD traits). Finally, when all functioning and trait measures were co-factored, a hierarchical structure again emerged which, at the five-factor level, included two factors that blended personality and functioning—*internalizing* (N/NA converged with the self-pathology vs. well-being/life satis-faction factor) and *externalizing* (social/interpersonal dysfunction was joined by traits low sociability and disagreeableness), whereas the last three factors reflected either just personality traits (disinhibition and rigid goal engagement/anankastia, respectively) or just functioning (basic functioning).

Thus, the analyses indicated that personality dysfunction overlapped with some, but not all, trait dimensions. Specifically, more behavioral traits—disinhibition and rigid goal engagement/anankastia—were largely independent of personality functioning, whereas affective and interpersonal personality traits—N/NA, (low) sociability, and antagonism–agreeableness—were intertwined with personality dysfunction, with the traditional functioning domain of quality-of-life/satisfac-tion forming the opposite end of the broad N/NA–self-pathology factor.

OVERVIEW

In this chapter, we report on a second study with, again, an extensive self-report battery of personality functioning, trait, and other functioning measures, par-tially overlapping with that of the first study. In addition, we used a single semistructured interview to rate both the PD-II and PD-III criteria. We examine how, and how well, personality functioning and trait measures separately (via raw correlations) and jointly (via multiple regressions) predict dimensional ratings of the PD-II types—specifically, aggregated criterion ratings—which blend personality functioning and traits. As predictors, we used a set of traits that were hypothesized a priori (specifically, in 2011 by the first author [LAC][2], before trait-facet assignments were made for the PD-III types) to relate to each of the PD-II types' criteria (shown in Table 6.4). For example, the avoidant PD cri-terion "views self as socially inept, personally unappealing, or inferior to others" (APA, 1994, p. 665) was mapped to depressivity ("feelings of inferior self-worth," APA, 2013, p. 779), whereas the narcissistic PD criterion "has a grandiose sense of self-importance" (APA, 1994, p. 661) was mapped to grandiosity ("believing that one is superior to others and deserves special treatment . . . feelings of enti-tlement"; APA, 2013, p. 780). All trait facets that mapped to any criterion were included as predictors for a given PD type. We detail our analytic strategy at the end of the Method section.

METHOD

The study method and sample from which this subset was drawn were described in Clark et al. (2015). We refer readers there for more detailed descriptions.

Participants and Procedure

Participants were 164 "high-risk" community adults and 135 psychiatric outpatients. The community adults were screened for two or more positive responses (the recommended cut-point) on the Iowa Personality Disorder Screen (IPDS), which has good sensitivity and specificity in identifying PD (Langbehn et al., 1999). Unless otherwise noted, all reported analyses are based on these 299 participants.

Patients were referred primarily from a community mental health center and by local practitioners; a small minority were recruited using listservs, newsletters, and mass emails sent to University of Notre Dame staff, faculty, and graduate students, as well as by word of mouth, as long as we could verify current mental health patient status. Hereafter, we call these the "high-risk" and "patient" subsamples.

DEMOGRAPHICS

Mean age was 48.0 years (SD = 12.4; range = 18–84); most (60%) participants were female; 27% were racial/ethnic minorities, of which most (70%) were Black/African American. A minority (35%) was employed and 26% were on disability; 51% had an annual family income below $20,000, and only 22% over $50,000. Approximately one third of participants each were married or living with a partner (38.5%), divorced/separated or widowed (34.5%), or single/never married (27%). The subsamples differed significantly in sex, age, racial/ethnic composition, employment status, income level, and relationship status, but not average educational level. Briefly, the patient subsample had proportionately fewer women, was older and more racially diverse, was more likely to be on disability (vs. employed), had lower average income, and was more likely to be single/never married, whereas the high-risk subsample was more likely to be married or living with a partner.

PROCEDURE

Participants came to our research facility and gave written informed consent before beginning the study. Most completed the questionnaires alone on a computer; the rest were assisted by a team member. Participation required ~6 hours; interviews were interspersed with computer sections to maintain interest and reduce fatigue. All procedures were approved by the University of Notre Dame Institutional Review Board.

Self-Report Measures

PERSONALITY FUNCTIONING
We used three measures that had developed relatively recently at the time of data collection (2012-early 2014) to assess personality functioning. We standardized all scales to put them on the same metric and then averaged the self- and interpersonal-pathology scales from each measure, respectively, to derive overall measures of self and interpersonal pathology.

GENERAL ASSESSMENT OF PERSONALITY DISORDER
For the General Assessment of Personality Disorder (GAPD; Livesley, 2010), we used a 15-item self-pathology ($\alpha = .92$) and an 11-item interpersonal-pathology scale ($\alpha = .90$) derived from the GAPD via replicated factor analysis. Respondents rate items considering how they "usually are, think, feel, believe, or act" using a 5-point Likert-type scale (very unlike me—very like me).

MEASURE OF DISORDERED PERSONALITY FUNCTIONING
For the Measure of Disordered Personality Functioning (MDPF; Parker et al., 2004), Parker's non-coping (self) and non-cooperativeness (interpersonal) factors were assessed with 11-item ($\alpha = .88$) and 12-item ($\alpha = .88$) scales, respectively. The MDPF uses a 4-point Likert-type format (definitely false—definitely true) and a general time frame.

SEVERITY INDICES OF PERSONALITY PROBLEMS–SHORT FORM
For the Severity Indices of Personality Problems–Short Form (SIPP; Verheul et al., 2008), we used two scales—Identity (9 items, $\alpha = .89$) and Relationships (11 items, $\alpha = .85$)—developed via replicated factor analysis to assess self and interpersonal functioning, respectively. The SIPP uses a 4-point Likert scale (fully agree—fully disagree) with a past-3-months time frame.

PERSONALITY TRAITS
The Personality Inventory for *DSM-5* (PID-5; Krueger et al., 2012) has 220 items rated using a 4-point scale from 0 (very false or often false) to 3 (very true or often true). It assesses 25 trait facets organized in five domains and was developed in conjunction with the PD-III model. Mean $\alpha = .85$ (range = .71 [callousness] to .95 [cognitive-and-perceptual dysregulation]).

Interview-Based Measures

We administered the *Structured Interview for DSM-IV Personality (SIDP-IV*; Pfohl, Blum, & Zimmerman, 1997) and from it both scored the 10 PD-II diagnoses and PD-III Criteria A (personality impairment) and B (pathological personality traits). The PD-II criteria were scored on a 4-point Likert-type scale (0 = no to minimal evidence of the criterion to 3 = prominent personality feature). Criterion scores were aggregated to yield a dimensional score for each PD-II diagnosis.

Following standard administration and earlier described scoring of the SIDP, the interviewer also provided ratings of the PD-III Criterion A and Criterion B. To rate PD-III Criterion A, we used the PD-III Levels of Personality Functioning Scale (LPFS), which details five impairment levels (0 = little or no impairment to 4 = extreme impairment) for the PD-III components of self-pathology (identity and self-direction) and interpersonal pathology (empathy and intimacy). These then were aggregated to yield self-pathology, interpersonal pathology, and overall personality-dysfunction scores. To rate PD-III Criterion B, we used the Clinicians' Rating Form (CRF) which uses a 4-point scale (0 = not at all like the person to 3 = extremely like the person) to rate all 25 PD-III trait facets.

Data-Analytic Strategy

We first examined the zero-order correlations between dimensional ratings of each PD-II type with their hypothesized PD-III traits and with personality dysfunction—both overall and for self- and interpersonal pathology separately—using both interview and self-report measures, respectively. We then conducted a series of multiple regression analyses to predict each PD-II type from its hypothesized PD-III traits and personality dysfunction. For each type, we first entered all hypothesized traits and then used backward regression until only traits with significant ($p < .05$) beta weights remained. Next, we did the same with self- and interpersonal dysfunction. Finally, we performed two sets of hierarchical multiple regressions, first entering self- and/or interpersonal dysfunction (depending on what was significant in the backward regressions), followed by the significant trait set for each PD-II type and then vice versa, to determine the relative predictive power of traits versus personality dysfunction in predicting the PD-II types.

RESULTS

Reliability and Convergent/Discriminant Validity

PD-III RATINGS
We first examined the interrater reliabilities ($N = 28$) for the LPFS and CRF (PD-III Criterion A and B, respectively), shown in the first numerical column of Table 6.2. The mean intraclass coefficient (ICC) for the four PD-III Criterion A ratings was .72 (range = .67 [empathy] to .76 [self-direction]), whereas that for the facets was .67 (range = .35 [eccentricity] to .91 [separation insecurity]).[3] The quality of these ratings is highly encouraging, especially given that they were made based on information gathered with an interview designed for the PD-II-type diagnoses.

Table 6.2 INTERRATER RELIABILITIES AND CONVERGENT
VALIDITY OF DIMENSIONAL RATINGS

Measure	ICC	Convergent *r*s
PERSONALITY FUNCTIONING		
Overall (Four Components' Mean)	.83	.48
Self-pathology (Components' Mean)	.77	.50
Identity	.71	
Self-direction	.76	
Interpersonal dysfunction (Components' Mean)	.77	.43
Empathy	.67	
Intimacy	.73	
TRAIT FACETS		
Negative Affectivity		
Emotional lability	.85	.55
Anxiousness	.64	.35
Separation insecurity	.91	.44
Submissiveness	.48	.36
Hostility	.78	.52
Perseveration	.55	.25
Detachment		
Withdrawal	.76	.59
Intimacy avoidance	.63	.42
Anhedonia	.57	.47
Depressivity	.72	.54
Restricted affectivity	.49	.27
Suspiciousness	.66	.42
Antagonism		
Manipulativeness	.80	.44
Deceitfulness	.61	.42
Grandiosity	.73	.32
Attention seeking	.84	.51
Callousness	.59	.34
Disinhibition		
Irresponsibility	.85	.39
Impulsivity	.82	.49
Distractibility	.44	.29
Risk taking	.68	.22

Table 6.2 CONTINUED

Measure	ICC	Convergent *rs*
Psychosis		
Unusual beliefs and experiences	.57	.37
Eccentricity	.35	.13
Cognitive and perceptual dysregulation	.65	.24
Trait Mean	**.69**	**.40**

NOTE: Rigid perfectionism omitted due to errors in the ratings.

ICC = intraclass correlation coefficient (N = 28 pairs of interviews); convergent r = interviewer–self-report correlations.

As measures are developed specifically to assess the PD-III constructs, interrater reliability may be expected to improve.

We then examined the convergent/discriminant correlations between the interview-based and self-report ratings of personality functioning and traits; the convergent validities are shown in the last column of Table 6.2. The personality functioning measures, both individually and when aggregated, showed a good convergent/discriminant pattern (i.e., correlated most strongly with their counterpart and significantly less with the other domain); the aggregated convergent/discriminant correlations averaged .57 and .33, respectively.

For the 25 facets, average convergence (mean r = .40; range = .13 [eccentricity] to .59 [withdrawal]) was considerably higher than the average discriminant correlation (mean r = .13); 68% of the convergent correlations were the highest for both sets of ratings. In another 20%, the convergent correlation was the highest for one of the two paired measures (e.g., CRF anhedonia correlated most strongly with PID-5 anhedonia [r = .47], but PID-5 anhedonia correlated slightly stronger [r = .50] with CRF depressivity). Thus, only three facets—anxiousness, eccentricity, and cognitive-and-perceptual aberration—did not converge either way, suggesting that these three PID-5 scales may benefit from modification to reflect the facet definition more closely and/or that the facet definitions themselves need refinement.

PD-II TYPE DIAGNOSES
We next examined the interrater reliabilities and internal consistencies of the 10 PD-II-type diagnoses. The ICCs (shown in the first numerical column of Table 6.3) were quite strong: M = .87, range = .73 (OCPD) to .96 (avoidant PD). We then calculated Cronbach's alpha for the set of traits hypothesized to correspond to each of the 10 PD-II types, both without Criterion A (i.e., traits only), and then adding the Criterion A ratings (LPFS) or aggregated self-report scale score (shown in the middle portion of Table 6.3). Internal consistencies

Table 6.3 RELIABILITIES OF DIMENSIONAL RATINGS OF INTERVIEW- AND SELF-REPORT SCALE-BASED PERSONALITY DISORDER TYPES

Construct (No. of Traits)	PD-II ICC	PD-III Alpha				PD-III Mean Interitem Correlation			
		CRF		PID-5		CRF		PID-5	
		B	A+B	B	A+B	B	A+B	B	A+B
Antisocial PD[a] (7)	.83	.85	.86	.86	.86	.45	.47	.47	.47
Avoidant PD (4)	.96	.77	.81	.74	.84	.46	.52	.42	.57
Borderline PD (7)	.86	.75	.80	.74	.89	.30	.36	.29	.54
Narcissistic PD (4)	.94	.76	.78	.71	.78	.44	.47	.38	.47
Obsessive-Compulsive PD (4)	.73	.41	.57	.58	.71	.15	.25	.26	.38
Schizotypal PD (7)	.85	.75	.80	.80	.85	.30	.36	.36	.45
Dependent PD (4)	.90	.75	.79	.78	.83	.43	.48	.47	.55
Histrionic PD (2)	.92	.37	.58	.79	.88	.23	.41	.65	.79
Paranoid PD (4)	.85	.68	.78	.73	.81	.35	.47	.40	.52
Schizoid PD (4)	.89	.75	.78	.71	.81	.43	.47	.38	.52
Mean	**.87**	**.68**	**.76**	**.74**	**.83**	**.35**	**.43**	**.41**	**.53**

NOTE: [a]Adult criteria. Conduct disorder criteria α = .96. PD types common to PD-II-III listed first, then PD-III-only PDs; in alphabetical order, respectively.

PD-II-III = *DSM-5*, Section II–III personality disorder types, respectively; CRF = Clinician's Rating Form; PID-5 = Personality Inventory for *DSM-5* (Krueger et al., 2013); ICC = intraclass coefficient (N = 28 pairs of interviews); PD = personality disorder.

for the self-report scales were higher than for the interview-based ratings for both the traits alone (i.e., Criterion B; means = .74 and .68, respectively) and with Criterion A included (means = .83 and .76, respectively), which might be expected given that the self-report scores already were reliable aggregates of multiple items. Including Criterion A increased internal consistency substantially (average alpha increased from .68 to .76 for the interview-based ratings and from .74 to .83 for the self-report scales), indicating that the traits shared considerable common variance with personality dysfunction.

Because some of the alpha coefficients were rather low (e.g., .37 and .41 for interview-based HPD and OCPD, respectively) and because the number of traits hypothesized to map to the PD-II types ranged from 2 to 7, we also examined the average interitem correlations (AICs). None of the values was below Clark and Watson's (1995) recommended range of .15 to .50, indicating that the low alpha values derived, at least in part, from the small number of traits mapped to certain PD-II types. Interestingly, one of the interview-based sets of ratings, and seven (35%) of the self-report scale sets exceeded the recommended maximum. Indeed, even the average AIC—averaged across both the self-reported traits and the personality pathology measures was .53 (see the last column of Table 6.3). These results again underscore the overlap between PD-III Criterion A and B, especially when assessed via self-report measures.

Relations of PD-III Traits and Personality Dysfunction to PD-II-Type Dimensions

ZERO-ORDER CORRELATIONS

The first and third numeric columns in Table 6.4 present the zero-order correlations of each PD-II type's dimensional ratings with its hypothesized traits and with self- and interpersonal dysfunction, for interview-rated and self-reported measures, respectively. The first and third numeric columns in the left and right halves of Table 6.5 present the averages of the trait and self-and-interpersonal dysfunction correlations, respectively, for each PD-II type for interview-rated and self-reported measures, respectively. In both tables, the six PD types common to Sections II and III are listed first, followed by the Section-II-only types, alphabetized within each subgroup. The average trait correlations were generally somewhat higher than those for personality dysfunction, and the interview-based correlations were higher than those for self-report: For traits and personality dysfunction, respectively, interview-based mean rs = .58 and .43, and self-report mean rs = .38 and .29.

Correlations between the trait ratings and the PD-II-type diagnoses can be interpreted similarly to each other across methods, because both the interview-based and self-report measures were derived directly from the PD-III trait-facet definitions. Specifically, the interviewers rated the trait facets based on their definitions, and the self-raters completed the PID-5, which was designed to reflect these same definitions. Of course, the targets for both sets of raters were the interviewers' PD-II diagnostic ratings, so interviewers had the advantage of using the same material to rate the PD-II diagnoses and PD-III traits, whereas the self-raters completed the PID-5 scales and we examined their relations with the interviewers' PD-II-type ratings. Thus, it is not surprising that the interview-based correlations are higher. Nonetheless, the moderate to moderately strong correlations of the self-report scales with the corresponding PD-II-type ratings provide evidence of the PID-5 scales' convergent validity with interview-based ratings.

In contrast, the meaning of the personality dysfunction–PD-II correlations is somewhat different for the interview-based ratings versus self-report scales, because the measures used by the two sets of raters were rather different. Interviewers rated personality dysfunction using the PD-III definitions and their elaboration in the LPFS, whereas self-raters responded to personality-functioning scales that had been developed prior to *DSM-5*'s publication. Moreover, again, interviewers used the same material to make both PD-II and PD-III ratings.

Facet	CRF (Interview)			PID-5 (Self-report)		
	r	R	Sig. Beta	r	R	Sig. Beta
SIDP-IV ANTISOCIAL PD						
Irresponsibility	.78		1.41	.44		1.70
Deceitfulness	.70		.53	.40		—
Impulsivity	.70		.72	.44		—
Manipulativeness	.65		.60	.34		—
Callousness	.60		—	.39		—
Risk taking	.54		.69	.43		1.68
Hostility	.43		.39	.26		—
Self-dysfunction	.45		—	.21		—
Interpersonal-dysfunction	.42		—	.29		.51
Adj. R: Final Model		.87			.53	
SIDP-IV AVOIDANT PD						
Withdrawal	.60		1.69	.49		1.73
Anxiousness	.60		1.53	.37		—
Depressivity	.53		.85	.44		—
Intimacy avoidance	.35		—	.19		—
Self-dysfunction	.40		—	.51		1.66
Interpersonal-dysfunction	.28		—	.47		—
Adj. R: Final Model		.72			.56	
SIDP-IV BORDERLINE PD						
Emotional lability	.70		1.61	.57		1.60
Impulsivity	.59		1.43	.47		1.29
Hostility	.52		.52	.45		—
Depressivity	.50		.47	.53		—
Separation insecurity	.47		.43	.46		—
Suspiciousness	.39		—	.45		—
Cognitive and perceptual dysregulation	.37		.39	.47		—
Self-dysfunction	.69		1.00	.57		1.39
Interpersonal-dysfunction	.49		—	.39		—
Adj. R: Final Model		.86			.65	

Table 6.4 CONTINUED

Facet	CRF (Interview)			PID-5 (Self-report)		
	r	R	Sig. Beta	r	R	Sig. Beta
SIDP-IV NARCISSISTIC PD						
Grandiosity	.78		2.60	.40		1.34
Manipulativeness	.58		1.07	.35		1.53
Attention seeking	.55		.78	.42		—
Callousness	.54		—	.22		—
Self-dysfunction	.39		—	.07		—
Interpersonal-dysfunction	.52		.73	.15		.49
Adj. R: Final Model		.86			.47	
SIDP-IV OBSESSIVE-COMPULSIVE PD						
Perseveration	.66		2.05	.22		—
Rigid perfectionism	.58		1.34	.41		2.09
Intimacy avoidance	.09		—	.12		—
Restricted affectivity	−.03		—	.15		—
Self-dysfunction	.21		—	.07		—
Interpersonal-dysfunction	.24		—	.11		—
Adj. R: Final Model		.72			.41	
SIDP-IV SCHIZOTYPAL PD						
Unusual beliefs and experiences	.66		1.22	.42		1.38
Cognitive and perceptual dysregulation	.60		.95	.30		—
Eccentricity	.57		.85	.23		—
Suspiciousness	.53		.43	.29		—
Withdrawal	.46		.48	.36		—
Intimacy avoidance	.42		.33	.35		.67
Restricted affectivity	.24		—	.19		—
Self-dysfunction	.50		—	.26		—
Interpersonal-dysfunction	.54		—	.38		.71
Adj. R: Final Model		.81			.52	

(*continued*)

Table 6.4 CONTINUED

Facet	CRF (Interview)			PID-5 (Self-report)		
	r	R	Sig. Beta	r	R	Sig. Beta
SIDP-IV DEPENDENT PD						
Separation Insecurity	.76		2.20	.44		1.12[a]
Submissiveness	.68		1.83	.36		.90[a]
Anxiousness	.38		—	.42		—
Depressivity	.37		—	.37		.—
Self-dysfunction	.45		—	.41		.69[a]
Interpersonal-dysfunction	.25		—	.09		—[a]
Adj. R: Final Model		**.82**			**.52**	
SIDP-IV HISTRIONIC PD						
Attention seeking	.79		2.84	.51		1.85
Emotional lability	.40		.68	.29		.74
Self-dysfunction	.28		—	.14		—
Interpersonal-dysfunction	.28		—	-.03		—
Adj. R: Final Model		**.82**			**.54**	
SIDP-IV PARANOID PD						
Suspiciousness	.78		2.19	.53		2.14
Hostility	.54		.52	.36		—
Withdrawal	.39		.33	.31		—
Unusual beliefs and experiences	.42		—	.23		—
Self-dysfunction	.53		.46	.27		—
Interpersonal-dysfunction	.58		—	.46		1.07
Adj. R: Final Model		**.81**			**.54**	
SIDP-IV SCHIZOID PD						
Withdrawal	.70		1.11	.47		.80
Intimacy avoidance	.64		.61	.46		.96
Restricted affectivity	.55		1.33	.28		—
Anhedonia	.48		—	.26		—
Self-dysfunction	.32		—	.21		—
Interpersonal-dysfunction	.50		.38	.44		.45
Adj. R: Final Model		**.81**			**.54**	

NOTE: Beta weights are from the final equation.

[a]Including interpersonal dysfunction, beta weights are 1.07, .74, 1.08, −.61, respectively.

CRF = Clinicians' Rating Form; PID-5 = Personality Inventory for *DSM-5* (Krueger et al., 2012); Sig. = significant; r = correlation; R = multiple correlation; — = nonsignificant; Adj. = adjusted; Dysfx = dysfunction.

Table 6.5 Summary of Zero-Order Correlations and Multiple Regressions Predicting Dimensional Ratings of *DSM-5*, Section II Personality Disorders PD-III Traits and Self- and Interpersonal Dysfunction

Personality Disorder	Clinicians' Rating Form							Personality Inventory for DSM-5						
	Traits		PDys		ΔR^2		Final R	Traits		PDys		ΔR^2		Final R
	Mean r	R^a	Mean r	R^a	+PDys	+Traits		Mean r	R^a	Mean r	R^a	+PDys	+Traits	
Antisocial	.64	.87	.44	.47	.00	.54	.87	.39	.52	.25	.29	.01	.20	.53
Avoidant	.53	.72	.34	.40	.00	.36	.72	.38	.53	.49	.55	.04	.02	.56
Borderline	.51	.85	.60	.69	.02	.27	.86	.49	.65	.49	.57	.01	.10	.65
Narcissistic	.62	.85	.46	.53	.02	.46	.86	.35	.46	.11	.14	.01	.20	.47
Obsessive-compulsive	.36	.72	.22	.23	.00	.47	.72	.23	.41	.09	.10	.00	.15	.41
Schizotypal	.51	.81	.52	.56	.00	.34	.81	.31	.51	.32	.38	.01	.13	.52
Dependent	.57	.82	.36	.45^b	.00	.47	.82	.40	.51	.26	.41^c	.01	.07	.51^d
Histrionic	.63	.82	.28	.28	.00	.60	.82	.41	.54	.09^e	.18	.01	.27	.54
Paranoid	.56	.80	.56	.60	.00	.38	.81	.37	.54	.37	.46	.04	.12	.57
Schizoid	.60	.81	.41	.50	.01	.41	.81	.37	.54	.33	.44	.01	.10	.54
Mean	**.58**	**.81**	**.43**	**.48**	**.004**	**.43**	**.82**	**.38**	**.52**	**.29**	**.36**	**.015**	**.14**	**.53**

NOTE: ^a For hypothesized traits or self/interpersonal dysfunction, respectively, remaining at $p < .05$ using backward regression. See text for details. ^b $R = .46$ including interpersonal dysfunction with a negative beta weight. ^c $R = .45$ including interpersonal dysfunction with a negative beta weight. ^d $R = .52$ including interpersonal dysfunction with a negative beta weight. ^e Of absolute values; interpersonal dysfunction correlation is negative.

PD = personality disorder; PDys = personality dysfunction; ΔR^2 = R^2 change after adding significant self/interpersonal dysfunction or hypothesized traits to the other, respectively; mean r = average of zero-order correlations, for all hypothesized traits or self-and-interpersonal dysfunction, respectively; R = multiple R; based on adjusted R^2s.

Thus, the interview-based correlations more or less directly indicate the degree to which PD-III personality functioning is inherent in the PD-II types' criteria. For example, the interview-based results suggest that personality dysfunction is an important aspect of PD-II-BPD (mean $r = .60$), but it is much less important in PD-II-OCPD (mean $r = .22$). Interestingly, these findings are consistent with those of Sharp et al. (2015), who found, using bifactor analysis, that BPD criteria loaded strongly on a general PD factor (mean $= .64$), whereas OCPD criteria did not (mean $= .27$).

For the self-report scales, however, the correlations reflect the extent to which the personality-functioning *scales' content* overlaps with that of the PD-II-types' criteria, rather than directly tapping the PD-III personality-functioning definitions. As mentioned, this is because these scales were developed prior to PD-III's development. However, the PD-III personality-functioning definitions may have been influenced by the personality-functioning scales' content, because the authors of two of the three measures (GAPD and SIPP) were original members of the *DSM-5* Personality and Personality Disorders Work Group (P&PDWG). Moreover, the results are reasonably parallel across methods. For example, as with the interview-based ratings, the personality-functioning scales correlated moderately strongly with ratings of PD-II-BPD criteria (mean $r = .49$), but minimally with ratings of PD-II-OCPD (mean $r = .09$). Moreover, the interview-self-report convergent correlations (see Table 6.2) were similar for self- and interpersonal pathology (mean $rs = .50, .43$, respectively) versus traits (mean $rs = .40$). Finally, the mean correlational pattern of the PD-II types across methods (i.e., correlating respective Table 6.5 columns) was actually higher for personality pathology than for traits ($rs = .63$ vs. 42, respectively). Thus, although the meaning of the correlations may be different conceptually, the values were comparable empirically.

Interestingly, the average predictive power was not significantly higher for the six PD types common to Sections II and III (i.e., antisocial, avoidant, borderline, narcissistic, OC, and schizotypal PD) compared to those that are only in Section II (i.e., paranoid, schizoid, histrionic, and dependent PDs). For traits, the mean values were .60 and .58, respectively, whereas for overall personality dysfunction, self-dysfunction, and interpersonal dysfunction, they were, respectively, .47, .43, and .42 versus .44, .40, and .41. Thus, from the perspective of personality functioning and traits, there is no reason for some PD-II types to have been included and others excluded in PD-III.

MULTIPLE REGRESSIONS PREDICTING PD-II-TYPE DIMENSIONS FROM PD-III PERSONALITY DYSFUNCTION AND TRAITS

The second and fourth columns of Table 6.4 present the beta weights for the final regression equations predicting dimensional ratings of each PD-II type from its significant hypothesized traits plus personality dysfunction, for the interview ratings and self-report scales, respectively. The final adjusted multiple Rs also are provided. Several aspects of these results are noteworthy. First, more of the hypothesized traits were significant predictors for the interview-based ratings (77%) than the self-reports (38%), perhaps because the trait intercorrelations were somewhat stronger among the self-report scales than interview-based ratings (mean rs= .34 vs. .22). Second, personality dysfunction was more likely to contribute to predicting the PD-II types for self-report than interviews (eight vs. four PD-II types). This may be because interviewers based their ratings on a single interview and/or because members of the P&PDWG developed the definitions for both PD-III Criteria A and B, whereas the trait and personality-functioning scales were distinct measures developed by different researchers. Third, when personality dysfunction did contribute to the equation, only self- or interpersonal dysfunction was a significant predictor, never both.[4]

Summaries of the steps that led to these final equations are shown in Table 6.5. Specifically, the second and fourth columns (for each half: the interviews and self-reports, respectively) give the multiple Rs for the hypothesized traits and personality pathology, respectively. The fifth and sixth columns in each half of the table give the change in R^2 when personality dysfunction was added to traits and vice versa, and the last columns give the final adjusted multiple Rs (as mentioned, also shown in Table 6.4). Again, several aspects of the results are noteworthy.

First, for the clinician ratings, traits strongly predicted the PD-II diagnoses; average multiple R = .81 (range= .72 [OCPD] to .87 antisocial PD [ASPD]). The mean ICC for the PD-II types was .87, so these results suggest that the PD-III trait ratings predicted almost all of the reliable variance of the PD-II types. Using self-reports, traits' predictive power was moderately strong, averaging .53 (range= .41 [OCPD] to .65 [ASPD]), again indicating good convergent validity of self-reports with interview-based ratings. The second striking finding is that when both traits and personality dysfunction were entered into the equations, the traits always significantly incremented the predictive power over personality dysfunction (the sixth columns in each of the left and right halves of Table 6.5), again more strongly for the interview-based than the self-report measures (mean ΔR^2= .43 and .14, respectively). In contrast, personality dysfunction provided little to no additional predictive power over traits for either interview ratings or self-report scales (mean ΔR^2= .004 and .015; maximums= .02 and .04, respectively), although even these small increments were significant in three cases for the interviews and all but one case in self-reports.

Third, overall predictive power was notably higher for the interview-based ratings versus self-report measures (mean rs = .82 vs. .53), clearly a method-based difference but, again, the results generally indicate good convergent validity of self-report with interview-based ratings of the PD-II types. Finally, there was again no difference in the overall predictive power for the six PD types common to Sections II and III versus those that are only in Section II (mean rs both = .82 for the interview-based ratings and .53 and .54 for the self-reports).

COMPARING A PRIORI HYPOTHESIZED TRAITS AND TRAITS COMPRISING THE PD-III TYPES IN PREDICTING PD-II TYPE DIMENSIONS

The traits used to predict the PD-II types in the preceding sections were based on a priori hypotheses and are similar, but not identical, to the traits comprising the six PD-III types (except for ASPD and OCPD, for which they are identical). To determine whether the a priori hypotheses or the "official" PD-III traits better predicted ratings of the PD-II types, we reran the analyses starting with the traits comprising the PD-III types for the four PD types with a nonidentical trait set (i.e., avoidant, borderline, narcissistic, and schizotypal PDs). In all cases, the hypothesized trait set yielded either the same model after nonsignificant traits were eliminated or a higher multiple *R*, although in most cases the difference was small, never exceeding .02. Of course, these trait sets are hardly independent, as the hypotheses were finalized by a member of the *DSM-5* P&PDWG with its input. Also, in one case (NPD), manipulativeness was hypothesized and contributed to predicting PD-II NPD, but it was deliberately omitted by the *DSM-5* P&PDWG because its inclusion increased comorbidity with ASPD, whereas here we examined only predictive validity.

STRUCTURAL PLACEMENT OF PERSONALITY DYSFUNCTION

Another way to examine relations between the PD-II types and PD-III personality dysfunction is through broad structural analyses. To this end, we ran two principal-axis factor analyses with varimax rotation, one using interview-based ratings and the other self-reports.

INTERVIEW-BASED RATINGS OF PD-II TYPES

For the interview-based analyses, we factored the 10 PD-II-types' dimensional scores with the ratings of PD-III self- and interpersonal dysfunction. We extracted three factors, as indicated by parallel analysis. The results (see Table 6.6), reflect

Table 6.6 PRINCIPAL-AXIS FACTOR ANALYSIS OF THE PD-II TYPES SCORED
DIMENSIONALLY AND PD-III SELF- AND INTERPERSONAL DYSFUNCTION

Measure	Psychoticism	Externalizing	Internalizing
Schizoid PD	**.73**	−.12	.04
Schizotypal PD	**.70**	.23	.13
Interpersonal Dysfunction	**.68**	**.41**	.26
Paranoid PD	**.61**	.25	.23
Obsessive-compulsive PD	.21	.17	.13
Narcissistic PD	.30	**.71**	−.06
Histrionic PD	−.06	**.70**	.12
Antisocial PD	.20	**.56**	.17
Dependent PD	.02	.15	**.64**
Self Dysfunction	.27	**.52**	**.59**
Borderline PD	**.50**	**.39**	**.59**
Avoidant PD	.34	−.25	**.54**

NOTES: Self and Interpersonal Dysfunction (shown in italics) comprise Criterion A of the PD-III General Diagnostic Criteria. All loadings > .35 are in bold.

PD = personality disorder; II, III = Sections II and III, respectively, of the *Diagnostic and Statistical Manual of Mental Disorders* (5th ed.).

the traditional *DSM* PD-category cluster structure with two exceptions: BPD split across all three clusters, loading most strongly on the third factor, and OCPD did not load on any dimension (although when a fourth factor was extracted, it was the sole marker). These findings again are consistent with those of Sharp et al. (2015), whose results suggest that the BPD criteria lie at the core of personality pathology, whereas those of OCPD are more peripheral.

Despite the parallelism with the traditional *DSM* PD cluster structure, we labeled these factors psychoticism, externalizing, and internalizing, terms used very commonly in the psychopathology-structure literature (e.g., Bagby et al., 2014; Caspi et al., 2014), to facilitate linking the PD and broader psychopathology literatures. Interestingly, interpersonal dysfunction split across the psychoticism and externalizing factors, loading most strongly on the former, whereas self-dysfunction split across the externalizing and internalizing factors, loading slightly more strongly on the latter. This pattern indicates that these two aspects of personality functioning may have somewhat different relations to personality pathology and, by extension, may relate differently to psychopathology in general. One interpretation of the fact that interpersonal dysfunction does not load on the internalizing factor is that internalizing psychopathology may have a less deleterious effect on interpersonal relations. By the same token, however, it is puzzling that psychoticism was not strongly related to self pathology, because it seems reasonable that being high on psychoticism would have a disruptive influence on one's identity and self-direction. This finding needs further investigation.

STRUCTURE OF PD-III PERSONALITY DYSFUNCTION AND TRAITS

To examine structural relations between PD-III personality dysfunction and traits, we ran two principal-axis factor analyses with varimax rotation, one using the interview-based ratings and the other the self-report scales, each including the 25 PID-5 facet scales and measures of self- and interpersonal dysfunction. In both cases, we extracted four factors, based on the results of parallel analyses. The results are shown in Table 6.7. Although there were a number of cross-loadings, clear N/NA, antagonism + disinhibition, detachment, and psychoticism factors emerged in both analyses, and the facets' primary loadings showed the same pattern for all but four facets.

In each of these four cases, the facet loaded most strongly on the N/NA factor in the self-report analysis (range = .61–.72, except suspiciousness, for which its N/NA loading, although still its highest, was only .38), but it did not load on this factor in the interview-based analysis. Instead, in the interview-based analysis, (1) distractibility had no strong loading on any factor; and (2) suspiciousness loaded most strongly on the detachment and psychoticism factors (.44 and .48, respectively); whereas (3) perseveration loaded moderately strongly on psychoticism (.49 and .46 in the self-report and interview-based analyses, respectively) and (4) anhedonia loaded moderately strongly on detachment (.48 and .59, respectively), the difference being that these were primary loadings in the interview-based analysis and secondary loadings in the self-report analysis. This pattern emerged, in part, because the N/NA factor was considerably larger in the

Table 6.7 PRINCIPAL-AXIS FACTOR ANALYSIS OF THE PD-III FACET SCALES AND MEASURES OF SELF- AND INTERPERSONAL DYSFUNCTION USING INTERVIEW RATINGS AND SELF-REPORT SCALES

Measure	N/NA		Antagonism		Detachment		Psychoticism	
	SR	INT	SR	INT	SR	INT	SR	INT
Depressivity	**.82**	**.67**	.01	.04	**.35**	**.37**	.09	.00
Self dysfunction	*.83*	*.63*	*.05*	*.37*	*.41*	*.38*	*.14*	*.31*
Anxiousness	**.77**	**.63**	−.03	−.01	.10	.34	.29	.23
Distractibility*	**.72***	.30	.08	.33	.13	.10	.20	.21
Emotional lability	**.66**	**.53**	.10	.26	.12	.07	**.39**	.26
Separation insecurity	**.64**	**.67**	.19	.10	−.06	.03	.24	.12
Submissiveness	**.46**	**.54**	.17	−.08	−.17	−.06	−.01	.04
Suspiciousness*	.38	.14	.30	.21	.30	**.44**	.31	**.48**
Deceitfulness	.13	−.01	**.78**	**.84**	.19	.05	.14	.05
Manipulativeness	.00	.02	**.73**	**.78**	.04	.00	.17	.11
Risk taking	.01	−.02	**.69**	**.55**	−.06	.07	.00	.10
Callousness	.08	−.05	**.68**	**.70**	**.43**	.19	.11	.23
Attention seeking	.11	−.03	**.64**	**.48**	−.31	−.22	.26	.33
Impulsivity	.42	.27	**.60**	**.69**	.04	−.04	.17	.01
Grandiosity	−.06	−.16	**.56**	**.46**	.06	.02	**.46**	**.52**
Irresponsibility	**.46**	.22	**.53**	**.71**	.23	.06	.03	.01
Hostility	**.37**	.17	**.39**	**.42**	.33	.27	**.40**	.34
Anhedonia*	**.67***	.32	−.11	.12	**.48**	**.59**	−.02	.08
Interpersonal dysfunction	*.22*	*.24*	*.22*	*.40*	*.82*	*.57*	*.08*	*.42*
Withdrawal	.26	.25	−.11	−.15	**.77**	**.73**	.17	.07
Restricted affectivity	−.09	−.12	.19	.04	**.54**	**.44**	.16	.04
Intimacy avoidance	.12	.09	−.02	−.01	**.52**	**.75**	.13	.06
Perseveration*	**.61***	.32	.16	.06	.08	−.06	**.49**	**.46**
Rigid perfectionism	**.40**	.12	.30	.22	.26	.25	**.63**	**.51**
Cognitive and perceptive dysregulation	.17	.22	.06	−.09	.14	−.03	**.62**	**.43**
Unusual beliefs and experiences	.24	.23	.25	.19	.15	.28	**.60**	**.46**
Eccentricity	**.38**	.02	.29	.23	.28	.31	**.49**	**.44**

NOTE: Loadings ≥ .35 are in bold. Results for personality (self and interpersonal) dysfunction are in italics.

*Facets and loading that showed a different pattern between self- and interview raters.

N/NA = Neuroticism/Negative Affectivity; SR = self-report; INT = interview-based ratings.

self-report than the interview-based analysis, perhaps because internal distress is more salient to individuals experiencing it than to observers whose information derives largely from an interview.

Turning to the personality-dysfunction measures, in both analyses, self-dysfunction loaded strongly (.63–.83) on the N/NA factor and had a moderately strong loading (.38–.41) on the detachment factor. However, in the interview-based analysis, it also loaded moderately strongly (.37) on the antagonism/disinhibition factor. Interpersonal pathology, on the other hand, showed a somewhat different loading pattern in the two analyses. It marked the detachment factor in both analyses, but quite strongly (.82) and *only* that factor in the self-report analysis, whereas in the interview-based analysis, the loading was more moderate (.57) and the scale also loaded moderately strongly (.40–.42) on the antagonism and psychoticism factors. These results suggest that, in relation to traits, self-dysfunction is rated similarly by both self- and interview raters, except that self-raters link self-dysfunction more strongly with N/NA-factor traits, and only interviewers link self-dysfunction with antagonism. In contrast, interpersonal dysfunction is linked with traits differently by the two types of raters: Self-raters link interpersonal dysfunction only with detachment-factor traits, whereas interview raters link it broadly with all traits except N/NA-factor traits.

THE IMPORTANCE OF SEVERITY
Over the past two decades, multiple researchers (e.g., Caspi et al., 2014; Clark, Watson, & Reynolds, 1995; Tyrer, 2005; Tyrer et al., 2011) have noted that severity is a very important—but not well-defined or understood—dimension of psychopathology. An important question relevant to the issue of severity is the degree to which trait extremity and personality dysfunction are related *in general*, that is, not in relation to specific traits or trait factors, but overall. Our data allow us to examine this question by computing aggregate measures of trait extremity across all 25 PD-III facets. We did so, separately for self- and interview raters, and first tested whether such an aggregated measure could be interpreted as a metric of overall trait extremity/severity by computing internal consistency indices for the 25 facets in both the self-reports (α = .92; AIC = .32) and interview-based (α = .86; AIC = .20) ratings. These high values confirmed the interpretability of a composite index.

We then correlated these aggregates with self- and interview-based measures of self- and interpersonal dysfunction. It is clear from the results (see Table 6.8) that, using current measures, trait extremity and personality dysfunction are strongly overlapping constructs (*r*s = .76 and .80 for self-report and interview-ratings, respectively), with their overlap indexing "severity," broadly speaking. Indeed, the correlations are sufficiently strong that they largely explain why there was little to no increment in predicting PD-II types by personality dysfunction, above and beyond traits. Moreover, it also is clear that self-dysfunction is the stronger component in the correlation of personality dysfunction with trait extremity, at least for the self-ratings. Importantly, this is the case even though the within-method part-whole correlations of self- and interpersonal dysfunction with overall personality dysfunction are virtually the same (i.e., .90 vs. .88 and .92 vs. .93).

Table 6.8 CORRELATIONS AMONG OVERALL TRAIT EXTREMITY AND PERSONALITY DYSFUNCTION—OVERALL, SELF, AND INTERPERSONAL, FOR SELF-REPORT AND INTERVIEW-BASED MEASURES

Measure	Trait Extremity		Personality Dysfunction		Self Dysfunction		Interpersonal Dysfunction
	SR	INT	SR	INT	SR	INT	SR
INT Trait extremity	*.57*						
SR Personality dysfunction	.76	.56					
INT Personality dysfunction	.43	.80	*.48*				
SR Self dysfunction	.77	.51	.90	.44			
INT Self dysfunction	.44	.76	.48	.92	*.50*		
SR Interpersonal dysfunction	.58	.50	.88	.42	.60	.34	
INT Interpersonal dysfunction	.36	.72	.42	.93	.32	.72	*.43*

NOTE: Boxed correlations are between traits and personality dysfunction (overall and separately for self and interpersonal domains). Within-method correlations are in bold. Cross-method convergent correlations are in *underlined italics*.

SR = self-report; INT = interview based.

The cross-method difference in the nature of the personality dysfunction ratings noted earlier (i.e., based directly on PD-III for the interview-based ratings only) is supported in these analyses, in that the cross-method trait-extremity correlation (.57), for which both sets of ratings were based on the PD-III facets, was stronger than any of the other cross-method correlations (*r*s ranged from .43 to .50; although the only statistically significant difference among the four correlations was .57 vs. .43). In any case, the strong correlations between PD-III Criteria A and B for both types of measures represent a very strong measurement challenge to any theory-based distinction between them.

DISCUSSION

Meta-analyses (Samuel & Widiger, 2008; Saulsman & Page, 2004) have shown that normal-range personality-trait measures relate systematically to PD-II types.

Moreover, dimensional interview-based measures of PD-II-types and trait profiles show a clear convergent/discriminant pattern (e.g., Miller, Reynolds, & Pilkonis, 2004; Miller, Bagby, & Pilkonis, 2005; Samuel, Connolly, & Ball, 2012), with convergence averaging ~.40-.50. Our results were similar (mean r = .53, range = .41-.65) using the PID-5, which was designed to assess the 25 PD-III facets' more extreme high ends. Although critics have countered that this convergence level is too low to consider traits as a replacement for traditional diagnoses, it is comparable to that obtained between structured and unstructured clinical interviews (mean r = .42, range= .32-.51; Miller, Few, & Widiger, 2012).

Further, we obtained considerably stronger convergence (mean R = .81, range = .72-.87) using an interview-based trait measure. This value is slightly higher than the convergence between two interview-based measures (.77; Miller et al., 2012). The "too low" values reported previously thus seemingly reflect method variance, rather than any inadequacy of traits per se to assess PD. Interestingly, all 10 PD-II types were equally well predicted, thus mitigating concerns that four PD-II types are not represented in PD-III. Although they are not specifically depicted, they are easily diagnosed using two or three PD-III traits in the presence of self- and/or interpersonal dysfunction.

Given (1) the infamous problems with the PD-II types, (2) clear evidence that traits not only can capture the personality pathology they represent but can do so in a way that is clinically useful (e.g., Bach, Markon, Simonsen, & Krueger, 2015; Clark et al., 2015; Glover, Crego, & Widiger, 2012), and (3) over a 6- to 10-year follow-up, "a system that integrates normal and pathological traits generally showed the largest validity coefficients in predicting a host of important clinical outcomes" (p. 1705), we contend that it is time to focus PD research on advancing our understanding entirely from a dimensional perspective, particularly that of its core components, personality dysfunction and extreme traits.

"Borderline" Personality Disorder

There is no question that BPD captures the vast majority of current clinical and research attention on PD. Our results, along with those of Sharp et al. (2015), offer some reasons for why that may be. First, when we factor analyzed interview-based ratings of the PD-II types plus personality dysfunction, BPD ratings split across all three factors. Indeed, the PD-II BPD criteria reflect not only all three major PD factors—"transient stress-related paranoid ideation or severe dissociative symptoms" taps psychoticism, "impulsivity in at least two areas that are potentially self-damaging" reflects externalizing, and "affective instability due to a marked reactivity of mood" taps internalizing—but also both self-dysfunction ("identity disturbance: markedly and persistently unstable self-image or sense of self") and interpersonal dysfunction ("a pattern of unstable and intense interpersonal relationships") (APA, 2013, p. 663). We investigated this further by correlating interviewers' ratings of overall personality dysfunction and mean trait extremity with the PD-II type ratings and found that BPD had the strongest correlation in each case, correlating .64 with overall personality dysfunction and .71 with mean trait extremity (vs. the next highest values of .61 and .53, respectively.)

It also is noteworthy that the PD-II BPD criteria do not reflect a clear set of traits, but rather a mix of traits (e.g., impulsivity), symptoms (e.g., chronic feelings of emptiness), specific behaviors (e.g., recurrent suicidal behavior), and personality dysfunction (e.g., identity disturbance). This is in contrast to other PD types, such as paranoid or avoidant PD, in which one or a few traits predominate (respectively, suspiciousness and anxiousness + detachment). Thus, BPD most likely garners the most clinical and research attention not because it is a particular syndrome, but because it is essentially a synonym for complex, severe PD. Recognition of this fact and acknowledgment that complex, severe PD is heterogeneous, reflecting diverse trait combinations, will facilitate research into both etiology and treatment.

Limitations

Our study has several limitations: (1) We used a single PD interview, and given the generally low agreement among PD interviews (median kappa = .35; Clark, Livesley, & Morey, 1997), our results need replication with another interview. (2) Our self-report personality-dysfunction measures were developed prior to PD-III and do not specifically provide for its subdomains. However, post-hoc analyses indicated that four of the six scales we used to create the self- and interpersonal-dysfunction indices correlated most strongly with the four interview-based subdomain scores compared to other functioning measures in our battery, ranging from .31 (MDPF Non-cooperativeness with Empathy) to .47 (GAPD Self-pathology with Identity), indicating the possibility of developing at least somewhat distinct self-report scales for the four subdomains. (3) Three PD-III facets—anxiousness, eccentricity, and cognitive-and-perceptual aberration—did not converge between the interview-based ratings and self-report scales, and five others showed less than optimal convergence. Thus, these facets may benefit from further clarification and improved measurement in multiple modalities.

SUMMARY, CONCLUSIONS, AND FUTURE DIRECTIONS

Taken together, our findings indicate clearly that personality dysfunction and trait extremity are strongly interrelated in existing measures of these constructs. Moreover, even though personality dysfunction is not an explicit construct in PD-II-types' conceptualization, both interview-based and self-ratings of personality dysfunction correlated moderately strongly with PD-II-type diagnoses (mean rs = .46 and .32, respectively, for overall personality dysfunction). Further, using interview-based trait ratings, our analyses indicate even stronger relations between PD-II types and personality traits, to the point that they account for virtually all their reliable variance (mean R = .81), whereas measures of personality dysfunction had little to no additional predictive power (mean R = .004).

Personality dysfunction is a relatively new research domain, however, so the extent to which a strong interrelation with traits is inherent in these constructs versus a measurement-based artifact remains unknown. That is, there is content overlap in the definitions and descriptions of existing personality-dysfunction and trait measures, and we do not know how strongly these constructs would relate if measures were developed based on nonoverlapping definitions. Nor do we know whether it even is possible to define these constructs without overlapping content. If these constructs are inherently intertwined, there may be no, or only a few, ways in which personality dysfunction can be manifested independently of trait expression. Thus, we have much to learn regarding the conceptualization and measurement of personality dysfunction. Determining whether trait measures can be developed that are—at least in terms of their content—distinct from personality dysfunction and vice versa is a primary future research task.

NOTES

1. Thus, we use the terms "personality impairment" and "personality dysfunction" interchangeably.
2. Members of the P&PDWG contributed to these predictions, but LAC takes full responsibility for selection and (mis)predictions of the final set.
3. The ICC for rigid perfectionism is not provided due to errors in the rating data.
4. With one exception: When interpersonal dysfunction was included with a negative beta weight predicting Dependent PD in self-report.

REFERENCES

American Psychiatric Association. (1994). *Diagnostic and statistical manual* (4th ed.). Arlington, VA: Author.

American Psychiatric Association. (2013). *Diagnostic and statistical manual* (5th ed.). Arlington, VA: Author.

Bach, B., Markon, K., Simonsen, E., & Krueger, R. F. (2015). Clinical utility of the *DSM-5* alternative model of personality disorders: Six cases from practice. *Journal of Psychiatric Practice, 21*(1), 3–25. doi:10.1097/01.pra.0000460618.02805.ef

Bagby, R. M., Sellbom, M., Ayearst, L. E., Chmielewski, M. S., Anderson, J. L., & Quilty, L. C. (2014). Exploring the hierarchical structure of the MMPI-2-RF personality psychopathology five in psychiatric patient and university student samples. *Journal of Personality Assessment, 96*(2), 166–172. doi:10.1080/00223891.2013.825623

Caspi, A., Houts, R. M., Belsky, D. W., Goldman-Mellor, S., Harrington, H., Israel, S., . . . Moffitt, T. E. (2014). The p factor: One general psychopathology factor in the structure of psychiatric disorders? *Clinical Psychological Science, 2*(2), 119–137. doi:10.1177/2167702613497473

Clark, L. A., Livesley, W. J., & Morey, L. (1997). Personality disorder assessment: The challenge of construct validity. *Journal of Personality Disorders, 11*, 205–231.

Clark, L. A., & Ro, E. (2014). Three-pronged assessment and diagnosis of personality disorder and its consequences: Personality functioning, pathological traits, and psychosocial disability. *Personality Disorder: Theory, Research, & Treatment, 5*(1), 55–69. doi:10.1037/per0000063

Clark, L. A., Vanderbleek, E., Shapiro, J., Nuzum, H., Allen, X., Daly, E., . . . Ro, E. (2015). The brave new world of personality disorder-trait specified: Effects of additional definitions on prevalence and comorbidity. *Psychopathology Review, 2*(1), 52–82. doi:10.5127/pr.00

Clark, L. A., & Watson, D. B. (1995). Constructing validity: Basic issues in objective scale development. *Psychological Assessment, 7*, 309–319.

Clark, L. A., Watson, D., & Reynolds, S. K. (1995). Diagnosis and classification in psychopathology: Challenges to the current system and future directions. *Annual Review of Psychology, 46*, 121–153. doi:10.1146/annurev.psych.46.1.121

Finn, S. E. (1982). Base rates, utilities, and DSM-III: Shortcomings of fixed-rule systems of psychodiagnosis. *Journal of Abnormal Psychology, 91*(4), 294–302. doi:10.1037/0021-843X.91.4.294

Glover, N. G., Crego, C., & Widiger, T. A. (2012). The clinical utility of the five-factor model of personality disorder. *Personality Disorders: Theory, Research, and Treatment, 3*(2), 176–184. doi:10.1037/a0024030

Krueger, R. F., Derringer, J., Markon K. E., Watson D., & Skodol, A. E. (2012). Initial construction of a maladaptive personality trait model and inventory for DSM-5. *Psychological Medicine, 42*(9), 1879–1890. doi:10.1017/S0033291711002674

Langbehn, D. R., Pfohl, B. M., Reynolds, S., Clark, L. A., Battaglia, M., Cadoret, R., . . . Links, P. (1999). The Iowa Personality Disorder Screen: Development and preliminary validation of a brief screening interview for non-antisocial *DSM* personality diagnoses. *Journal of Personality Disorders, 13*, 75–89.

Livesley, J. (2010). *General assessment of personality disorder.* Port Huron, MI: Sigma Assessment Systems.

Livesley, J. (2012). Tradition versus empiricism in the current *DSM-5* proposal for revising the classification of personality disorders. *Criminal Behaviour and Mental Health, 22*(2), 81–90. doi:10.1002/cbm.1826

Livesley, W. J., & Jang, K. L. (2005). Differentiating normal, abnormal, and disordered personality. *European Journal of Personality, 19*(4), 257–268. doi:10.1002/per.559

Markon, K. E., Quilty, L. C., Bagby, R. M., & Krueger, R. F. (2013). The development and psychometric properties of an informant-report form of the personality inventory for DSM-5 (PID-5). *Assessment, 20*(3), 370–383. doi:10.1177/1073191113486513

Miller, J. D., Bagby, R. M., & Pilkonis, P. A. (2005). A comparison of the validity of the five-factor model (FFM) personality disorder prototypes using FFM self-report and interview measures. *Psychological Assessment, 17*(4), 497–500. doi:10.1037/1040-3590.17.4.497

Miller, J. D., Few, L. R., & Widiger, T. A. (2012). Assessment of personality disorders and related traits: Bridging *DSM-IV-TR* and *DSM-5.* *The Oxford handbook of personality disorders* (pp. 108–140). New York, NY: Oxford University Press. doi:10.1093/oxfordhb/9780199735013.013.0006

Miller, J. D., Reynolds, S. K., & Pilkonis, P. A. (2004). The validity of the five-factor model prototypes for personality disorder in two clinical samples. *Psychological Assessment*, *16*(3), 310–322. doi:10.1037/1040-3590.16.3.310

Parker, G., Hadzi-Pavlovic, D., Both, L., Kumar, S., Wilhelm, K., & Olley, A. (2004). Measuring disordered personality functioning: To love and to work reprised. *Acta Psychiatrica Scandinavica*, *110*, 230–239.

Pfohl, B. M., Blum, N., & Zimmerman, M. (1997). *Structured Interview for DSM-IV Personality (SIDP-IV)*. Washington, DC: American Psychiatric Association.

Ro, E., & Clark, L. A. (2013). Interrelation between psychosocial functioning and adaptive- and maladaptive-range personality traits. *Journal of Abnormal Psychology*, *122*(3), 822–835. doi:10.1037/a0033620

Samuel, D. B., Connolly, A. J., & Ball, S. A. (2012). The convergent and concurrent validity of trait-based prototype assessment of personality disorder categories in homeless persons. *Assessment*, *19*(3), 287–298. doi:10.1177/1073191112444461

Samuel, D. B., & Widiger, T. A. (2008). A meta-analytic review of the relationships between the five-factor model and DSM-IV-TR personality disorders: A facet level analysis. *Clinical Psychology Review*, *28*(8), 1326–1342. doi:10.1016/j.cpr.2008.07.002

Saulsman, L. M., & Page, A. C. (2004). The five-factor model and personality disorder empirical literature: A meta-analytic review. *Clinical Psychology Review*, *23*, 1055–1085. doi:10.1016/j.cpr.2002.09.001

Sharp, C., Wright, A. G. C., Fowler, C., Frueh, C., Oldham, J., & Clark, L. A. (2015). The structure of personality pathology: Both general ("g") and specific (s's) factors? *Journal of Abnormal Psychology*, *124*(2), 387–398. doi:10.1037/abn0000033

Verheul, R., Andrea, H., Berghout, C. C., Dolan, C., Busschbach, J. J. V., van der Kroft, P. J. A., . . . Fonagy, P. (2008). Severity Indices of Personality Problems (SIPP-118): Development, factor structure, reliability, and validity. *Psychological Assessment*, *20*, 23–34. doi:10.1037/1040-3590.20.1.23

Tyrer, P. (2005). The problem of severity in the classification of personality disorder. *Journal of Personality Disorders*, *19*(3), 309–314. doi:10.1521/pedi.2005.19.3.309

Tyrer, P., Crawford, M., Mulder, R., Blashfield, R., Farnam, A., Fossati, A., . . . Reed, G. M. (2011). The rationale for the reclassification of personality disorder in the 11th revision of the international classification of diseases (ICD-11). *Personality and Mental Health*, *5*(4), 246–259. doi:10.1002/pmh.190

Wakefield, J. C. (2013). *DSM-5* and the general definition of personality disorder. *Clinical Social Work Journal*, *41*(2), 168–183. doi:10.1007/s10615-012-0402-5

Widiger, T. A., & Simonsen, E. (2005). Alternative dimensional models of personality disorder: Finding a common ground. *Journal of Personality Disorders*, *19*(2), 110–130. doi:10.1521/pedi.19.2.110.62628

World Health Organization (2018). International Classification of Diseases. Available athttps://icd.who.int.

Development Across the Life Course

7

The Principles of Personality Trait Development and Their Relation to Psychopathology

BRENT W. ROBERTS AND RODICA I. DAMIAN ■

A recent review of prospective research (Bleidorn, Hopwood, & Lucas, 2018) showed that life experiences are associated with change in personality traits, and that different life experiences are differentially related to personality trait domains. Specifically, the most robust findings across the review were that transitioning to the first romantic relationship increased Extraversion and decreased Neuroticism (e.g., Neyer & Lehnart, 2007; Wagner, Becker, Lüdtke, & Trautwein, 2015), and that transitioning from high school to college/work increased Agreeableness, Conscientiousness, Openness, and decreased Neuroticism (e.g., Bleidorn, 2012; Lüdtke, Roberts, Trautwein, & Nagy, 2011). Furthermore, studies have found that life experiences are associated with personality change in middle- (van Aken, Denissen, Branje, Dubas, & Goossens, 2006) and old-adulthood (Mottus, Johnson, & Deary, 2012).

For the longest time, the field of personality development was caught in pot holes of its own making. The field wallowed between two extreme trenches (Roberts & Caspi, 2001). In one trench were the essentialists who thought, even if they did not say so openly, that personality traits were functionally fixed and unchanging. The perspective that traits were fixed and unchanging was most often manifest in the way they were used, which typically was as predictors of outcomes, not outcomes themselves. In the other trench were the situationists who held the perspective that there was nothing of substance to the idea of traits (Lewis, 2001). There was no need to think about how personality traits developed if they were not consequential constructs in the first place. These two perspectives became adversarial positions, reducing the dialogue from something constructive to something overly simplistic (Roberts, 2009).

Somewhere along the way, things changed, not entirely because people changed their minds, but because, despite these extreme positions, a critical mass of data

emerged to trump the ideological debates. Though in the mid-20th century longitudinal research was rare, the turn of the century saw a huge influx of new longitudinal studies. Along with the critical mass of data came a clearer sense for how
personality traits developed. Based on this data edifice, we began to extrapolate certain principles of development (Roberts & Wood, 2006). In this chapter, we seek to
re-examine the principles of development outlined in what we describe as the neo-
socioanalytic theory of personality development (Roberts & Nickel, 2017; Roberts,
Wood, & Caspi, 2008). In some cases, dozens of new studies have emerged to confirm, disconfirm, or qualify the principles as original stated. In other cases, the principles still await further testing. After reviewing the evidence for and against the
principles, we will consider their relevance to the interface between personality and
clinical psychology.

PRINCIPLES OF PERSONALITY TRAIT DEVELOPMENT

Cumulative Continuity

The cumulative continuity principle posits that personality traits increase in rank-
order consistency throughout the life span, peaking between the ages of 50 and
60, and even then not being quite fixed (Roberts & DelVecchio, 2000). The cumulative continuity principle was derived from the results of a meta-analysis of
the rank-order consistency of personality traits, which cataloged the aggregate
patterns of continuity across 152 longitudinal studies (Roberts & DelVecchio,
2000). When organized by age, personality consistency shows a clear increase.
Test-retest correlations (unadjusted for measurement error) increased from 0.41
in childhood to 0.55 at age 30, and then reached a plateau around 0.70 between
ages 50 and 70. The pattern of increasing consistency held true for all of the Big
Five categories of traits as well as for men and women.

Several factors are thought to contribute to the stabilization of personality
over time. First, longitudinal data on twins suggest that much of the stability in
adult personality is attributable to genetic factors (e.g., McGue et al., 1993). To
the extent that genetic factors might increase in their effect with age, they might
also be partially responsible for the increase in personality consistency, thought
the best evidence to date for personality shows no increase in heritability and
a role for both consistent genetic factors and consistent environmental factors
playing a role in adult personality consistency (Briley & Tucker-Drob, 2014). It is
also possible that niche-building processes promote continuity. Niche building
encompasses at least three different processes whereby people (a) create,
(b) seek out, or (c) are selected into environments that are correlated with their
traits. Once in a trait-correlated environment, the environment may support the
persistence of personality traits and diminish the press to change (see the niche-
picking principle below). Also, normative-developmental changes in personality may contribute to increasing personality continuity across the life course.
Traits associated with the domains of Agreeableness, Conscientiousness, and

Emotional Stability not only increase with age (see the maturity principle), they are also positively correlated with increased personality consistency. That is, people who are interpersonally effective, planful, decisive, and considerate show more rank-order consistency over time (e.g., Roberts et al., 2001). Although there is no conclusive explanation for this finding, one possibility is that agreeable, conscientious, and emotionally stable people are better equipped to deal with developmental challenges across the life course. They have more personal capital in the form of increased resilience that allows them to master more efficiently the life challenges that they face and to recuperate more quickly from aversive and disappointing life events that they encounter. In contrast, their more brittle counterparts may be more susceptible to the influence of their environment. The robust finding that some people are more prone to change than others calls for research that systematically tests reasons for it.

Reviewing the ongoing support for the cumulative continuity principle was made quite easy by the fact that Ferguson (2010) replicated the original meta-analysis with a second meta-analysis of studies that had been published in the intervening decade. Once again, it was found that personality trait consistency increased with age and that these patterns were not affected by gender. Moreover, Ferguson (2010) found that clinical patient populations demonstrated the same levels of personality consistency over time and the increases in consistency with age. Therefore, it appears that the cumulative continuity principle is one of the most robust, replicable, and consistently supported patterns of personality development. The evidentiary value for the cumulative continuity principle borders on that from the behavior genetics literature for the heritability of psychological constructs, which is described as the "first law" of behavior genetics; that is, all phenotypes are heritable. In this case, it appears that the first law of personality development should be that at a population level, rank-order consistency increases with age.

Maturity Principle

The second principle of personality development is that people become more psychologically mature with age, if maturity is defined as becoming more socially adapted. And, specifically, if being socially adapted is reflected in changes that increase a person's ability to negotiate social relationships and challenges more effectively. Psychological theories proposed two different interpretations of maturation: the humanistic and the social adaptation interpretations (Hogan & Roberts, 2004). The humanistic interpretation proposes that people mature over time by becoming more self-actualized, that is, less defensive and rigid and more creative and open to feelings. The data do not support this developmental progression; instead, after young adulthood, people actually exhibit declines on traits related to openness to experience (Roberts, Walton, & Viechtbauer, 2006; Small et al., 2003). The social adaption or functional interpretation equates maturity with the capacity to become a productive and involved contributor to society. According to this interpretation, people should become better at planning, more deliberate, and decisive, but also more considerate and charitable. This latter definition of psychological maturation aligns more closely with what we observe in the data, that is, higher levels of conscientiousness, emotional stability, and agreeableness over time. These three traits are conspicuous because they are predictive of greater levels of effectiveness and functioning in the domains of love, work, and health (Roberts et al., 2007).

A meta-analysis of the mean-level changes in personality traits over time solidified empirical support for the maturity principle (Roberts, Walton, & Viechtbauer, 2006). This study found that most people become more agreeable, conscientious, and emotionally stable over their life span. In particular, increases in emotional stability occurred from adolescence to middle age. Conscientiousness appears to begin a systematic increase in young adulthood and then shows increases even into old age. Changes in agreeableness were less clear, but they tended to show small increases across adulthood. Interestingly, the meta-analysis also showed robust increases in a facet of extraversion, described as social dominance. Social dominance reflects higher levels of assertiveness, self-confidence, and dominance and showed marked increases in young adulthood. Similar to the findings for rank-order consistency, there were no clear gender differences in these patterns.

The increase in social dominance invites the question of whether it should be folded into a definition of psychological maturity. There has been little discussion of this topic to date. An argument for the inclusion of social dominance in the maturity principle would have to rest on evidence that social dominance is an unambiguous marker of better social functioning. On the one hand, the relation of these types of traits to leadership emergence (Anderson, John, Keltner, & Kring, 2001) and the conceptual overlap with emotional stability (e.g., self-confidence) would argue for its inclusion. On the other hand, the extent to which the manifestations also include aggressiveness would argue against its inclusion on the definition of maturity. Whether to include social dominance in the definition of maturity remains one of the issues that need empirical work in the near future.

Both cross-sectional and longitudinal research since 2006 has shown support for the argument that people generally increase in agreeableness, conscientiousness, and emotional stability. Numerous cross-sectional aging studies have now shown, across cohorts, that older people are more agreeable, conscientious, and emotionally stable (Donnellan & Lucas, 2008). The longitudinal evidence in support of the maturity principle is impressive because it encompasses data from multiple, independent research teams, and multiple longitudinal studies from a variety of countries. For example, a longitudinal study of Iowans found increases in measures of constraint, a form of conscientiousness and marked decreases in measures of neuroticism in the transition to young adulthood (Donnellan, Conger, & Burzette, 2007). Remarkably similar findings have been reported for longitudinal studies from Minnesota (Johnson, Hicks, McGue, & Iacono, 2007), Germany (Lüdtke, Roberts, Trautwein, & Nagy, 2011), Finland (Joseffsson et al., 2013), and Italy (Vecchione, Alessandri, Barbaranelli, & Caprara, 2012). More recently, a study on a large US sample (N = 1,795) tracked across 50 years (Damian, Spengler, Sutu, & Roberts, in press) showed large changes in the maturational direction (i.e., increased agreeabless, conscientiousness, and emotional stability) across the lifespan. Like the cumulative continuity principle, the maturity principle has relatively strong support.

Several limitations in the database limit the generalizability of the maturity principle. First and foremost, most of the longitudinal studies tracked changes in self-reports only. Where observer ratings were conducted, they tend to confirm the self-reported changes (e.g., Donnellan et al., 2007). Nonetheless, very few studies have tracked changes in personality using multiple methods. Second, the age periods when maturity can and does occur may vary from culture to culture. For example, countries in which normative expectations for role transitions are shifted earlier in the life course show evidence for an accelerated pattern of personality trait maturation (Bleidorn et al., 2013). Third, because of an idiosyncrasy of the assessment of the Big Five, little evidence has accumulated testing the idea that the social dominance facet of extraversion increases with age. There has been a rash of large panel longitudinal studies published in the last decade that all inadvertently used abbreviated measures of the Big Five. For better or worse, these measures do not assess the social dominance aspect of extraversion and instead focus on the social vitality, or gregariousness aspect of extraversion. Gregariousness tends to show no change or decreases with age. Thus, the one riddle plaguing the maturity principle, whether to include social dominance in the definition, remains without enough data to solve.

Social Investment

The social investment principle is an attempt to explain why the maturity principle exists. Specifically it posits that personality trait change in young adulthood occurs because of investments in conventional social roles, which bring with them experiences and expectations for being nurturing, responsible, and emotionally stable (Roberts, Wood, & Smith, 2005). In other words, the personalities of young adults change as they commit to adult social roles (Lodi-Smith & Roberts, 2007). This seems to be a normative process (Helson, Kwan, John, & Jones, 2002), because across most societies, people commit themselves to the adult roles found in the social structures of family, work, and community.

One mechanism via which personality change may occur as a result of social roles that people adopt in the transition toward adulthood is that social roles contain expectations that are widely held by most age groups in society (Wood & Roberts, 2006). Therefore, people anticipate changes in behavior that will be needed as they enter new roles, such as taking their first career-related job or becoming a parent for the first time (Roberts & Wood, 2006). Moreover, others will promote and reward these changes because they share the expectations with the role participant. Finally, new roles come with explicit experiences, rewards, and punishments that lead to changes in thoughts, feelings, and behaviors, which translate into personality change over time.

Indeed, longitudinal data support these ideas by having shown that changes in social investment correlate with changes in personality traits. For example,

Lehnart and colleagues (2010) found that young adults who became increasingly socially invested in romantic relationships over time experienced simultaneous increases in emotional stability and self-esteem. In a study of age differences in personality traits across 62 countries, people who adopted adult roles earlier showed an accelerated form of personality development consistent with the social investment principle (Bleidorn et al., 2013). Furthermore, a 2-year longitudinal study of students from Finland showed that initiating a career or job for the first time was linked to increases in conscientiousness (Leikas & Salmela-Aro, 2015).

More important, a number of studies have shown that participating in activities that are counternormative is associated with either arrested development or negative trends in personality change that actually contradict the normative changes found for the majority of the population. These findings are critical for the viability of the social investment principle, as it relies in part on the inference that social experience, rather than genetics, is the driving force for personality trait change. If the results had only shown that normative experiences (e.g., starting a new job) were associated with positive change (e.g., increases in conscientiousness), then it would be possible that a third variable, such as a gene, was the hidden cause of personality development. However, the finding that people can buck the general trends in personality change in young adulthood bolsters the inference that social experience is the causal force. Supporting this idea, there is now a strong set of longitudinal studies showing that "deinvestment" is associated with a lack of increases and sometimes decreases in traits like neuroticism and conscientiousness. For example, participating in counterproductive work behaviors, like stealing, arriving at work drunk, or fighting with one's coworkers and supervisors was associated with decreases in emotional stability over time (Roberts, Walton, Bogg, & Caspi, 2006). Similarly, continuing to abuse alcohol in young adulthood is associated with a lack of change in conscientiousness-related traits such as impulsiveness, which typically decreases during this age period (Littlefield, Sher, & Steinley, 2010).

Two findings from recent research pose a challenge to the social investment principle. First, one study showed that longitudinal changes in the psychological investment in work were associated with increases in conscientiousness; this finding would putatively support the basic premise of the social investment principle (Hudson, Roberts, & Lodi-Smith, 2012). However, the relation between changes in investment to work and changes in personality did not differ by age group. That is to say, older individuals who showed increases in social investment at work showed similar levels of increases in conscientiousness, as did younger individuals. Although this is only one study, and although it was partially supportive of the social investment principle, the findings are relevant to the age specificity of the principle. It may be that there is nothing particular about young adulthood and that relevant experiences can lead to consonant personality trait changes at any age. If so, it would be incumbent to show that the preponderance of factors associated with the social investment principle occur in young adulthood—an empirical finding yet to be demonstrated.

The second finding that poses a problem for the social investment principle is the lack of personality change associated with becoming a parent. Unlike other normative transitions, becoming a parent is not associated with the requisite increases in agreeableness, conscientiousness, or emotional stability that are the basis of the social investment principle. In fact, if anything, becoming a parent is associated with no change or slightly negative changes (e.g., Galdiolo & Roskam, 2014). Two possibilities arise as a result of these findings. First, it may be that the relevant change happens well in advance of the acquisition of the role of parenting. Perhaps people who have children have planned far in advance to have children and have done the appropriate work on their identity before embarking on that path. The second possibility highlights the importance of getting the definition of social investment right and correctly identifying the causal mechanism. For example, the cause of personality trait change may not be the acquisition of the role or even commitment to the role, but the sense of mastery over the role that comes with successfully fulfilling the obligations of the role. Future research should attempt to tease these factors apart in researching just what aspect of experience is associated with normative changes in personality traits in young adulthood.

Corresponsive Principle

The corresponsive principle is the least well understood of the personality development principles originally put forward. This, we suspect, is largely the result of it having been poorly articulated combined with the fact that there needs to be a second complementary principle, which we will come to in a moment. First, the definition of the corresponsive principle is that people enter specific environments and have specific experiences because of their personality traits, and then, in turn, those experiences change their personality traits. The qualifier in this case is that the change imparted by those corresponsive experiences is to enhance the traits that got the person into his or her current situation in the first place. To exemplify, the corresponsive principle predicts that if a person chooses a job, such as management, because she is extraverted, then the experience of being a manager will make her even more extraverted than before. The idea is nothing more or less than the idea of a reciprocal relationship, which is a hallmark of self-efficacy theory, for example.

The corresponsive principle links two mutually supportive life-course dynamics: "social selection," wherein people select environments that are correlated with their personality traits, and "social influence," wherein environmental experiences affect personality functioning. According to longitudinal data, the traits that "select" people into specific experiences are the traits that are most "influenced" in response to those experiences (e.g., the personality trait of dominance selects people into jobs that involve resource power, and employment in such jobs further increases dominance). That is, life experiences do not impinge themselves on people in a random fashion causing widespread personality transformations; rather, the traits that people already possess are changed (i.e., deepened and elaborated) by trait-correlated experiences that they create. This is not to propose that all experiences are corresponsive, just that a noticeable proportion of them appear to be.

The corresponsive principle emerged out of and was tested by testing a wide swath of personality traits along with an equally wide array of outcomes. For example, the life goals students pursued in college were predictable from their standing on the Big Five. Students who were more agreeable wanted more children; students who were less open wanted a successful career (Roberts & Robins, 2000). In turn, pursuing family goals was associated with increases in agreeableness, and pursuing career goals was associated with decreases in openness (Roberts, O'Donnell, & Robins, 2004). Similar patterns emerged in examinations of personality and college climate (Roberts & Robins, 2004), personality and work experiences (Roberts, Caspi, & Moffitt, 2003), and personality traits and life events (Lüdtke et al., 2011).

Subsequent research by a different set of researchers has produced a set of findings supporting the original argument that personality and experiential factors are corresponsive. In one case, the relation between goal and personality change was tested within a genetically informed model (Bleidorn et al., 2010). The longitudinal study confirmed the corresponsive relation between traits and goals, such that agentic goals were associated with extraversion, but also showed that the corresponsive relation was both genetic and environmental in origin. Similar findings have shown corresponsive relations between personality and psychopathology (Klimstra et al, 2010), and between neuroticism and negative life events (Jeronimus, Riese, Sanderman, & Ormel, 2014).

Despite the supportive findings, conceptual and empirical issues have proven to be a challenge to testing the corresponsive principle. First, although the pattern across multiple measures appears to the naked eye (e.g., when examining covariance matrices, for example), it is difficult to obtain point estimate or to conduct a statistical test on the pattern of corresponsive instances. The best we have done so far is to count the number of significant predictions for selection and socialization effects, correlate the column of predictive correlations and change correlations, or just point out that the percentage of corresponding relations is greater than chance. None of these approaches is necessarily satisfactory. It would be beneficial if future research could derive a more rigorous way of testing whether corresponsive relations exist.

Second, the conceptual confusion that has emerged from attempts to understand the corresponsive principle necessitates both a clearer definition and possibly another principle of development. Specifically, the original idea was to capture the nature of the change relationships that emerged in longitudinal studies of personality trait development. We have attempted to be clearer earlier about that aspect of the definition. Also, we should note that the original statement of corresponsive principle was coupled with the acknowledgment that many associations between personality traits and life experiences were noncorresponsive. For example, in the case of life events (Lüdtke et al., 2011), we find that people who are more neurotic tend to have more difficulties in their sex lives, their sleeping and eating habits, and their finances. These factors, in turn, predict increases in neuroticism (e.g., corresponsiveness). However, the noncorresponsive associations for openness are fascinating because of their complementarity. People who are more open tended to have more problems with sex lives, their sleeping and eating habits, and their finances. Although these did not, in turn, affect changes in openness, they did contribute to increases in neuroticism. So, at least in this study, people who were more open inadvertently made themselves more neurotic by being open. Thus, not only are many patterns noncorrespForesive, but also quite interesting in their patterning.

The most common confusion is for researchers to consider the corresponsive principle as an indication that people become more consistent over time because of the social environments they select into—that is, to not change. In hindsight, it seems a reasonable confusion. Many researchers implicitly assume that the main effect of personality is to create social situations that "reinforce" one's personality. In this case, the term *reinforce* is being used to mean that one's personality is not changed so much as maintained because of the environment that one creates.

It might be constructive in this context to identify a new principle, albeit one with little or no empirical basis, but one nonetheless that deserves our attention. We would describe this as the niche-picking principle. Through their personality traits, people create social environments and paths in their lives that help maintain their current trait levels. Thus, this type of person-environment transaction should lead to greater consistency because of the selection effects of personality traits. This idea has, to our knowledge, only been tested twice. In particular, students who were more extraverted and disagreeable fit into the college climate better than other students at a highly competitive university. In turn, higher levels of fit were associated with greater levels of continuity and less absolute levels of change (Roberts & Robins, 2004). This finding was partially replicated in a second longitudinal study of another set of college students at a second, highly competitive university (Harms, Roberts, & Winter, 2006). Nonetheless, the overarching idea of niche picking, despite its appeal, has not been tested well or rigorously in longitudinal research. We propose the niche-picking principle as a complement to the corresponsive principle in the hopes that it might help clarify the corresponsive principle and provide an impetus to test the niche-picking principle.

Plasticity Principle

The plasticity principle posits that personality traits can and do change at any age. Supporting this idea, numerous studies have shown that personality change may occur at previously unimagined ages and evidence for this principle appears to be strong. Of course, the life course pattern of increasing continuity would argue against plasticity (Roberts & DelVecchio, 2000). But, as was found at the time, the levels of consistency, which peak in middle age, are far from unified. Also, test-retest continuity is not an optimal indicator of change. For example, it is still quite possible for traits to go up or down even in the case of perfect test-retest stability (Block, 1971). Alternatively, mean-level changes or individual differences in change are better indices of plasticity. Individual differences in change are especially strong indicators of plasticity, because by their very nature they show that people change differently from one another over time even if the general trend is up or down (Roberts & Mroczek, 2008). If we found no changes for these two indices, then we would have good evidence against plasticity.

In terms of mean-level changes, there is now robust evidence that personality traits change throughout the life course. It has been found repeatedly that young adulthood is the primary age in which mean-level change in personality occurs and mostly for the better (Donnellan et al., 2007; Johnson et al., 2007; Josefsson et al., 2013; Vecchione et al., 2012). Nonetheless, studies also show evidence for mean-level personality trait change in middle age (Allemand, Gomez, & Jackson, 2010) and old age (Kandler, Kornadt, Hagemeyer, & Neyer, 2015; Wortman, Lucas, & Donnellan, 2012). However, in many cases the change in old age is not for the better.

Research on individual differences in personality trait change also supports the plasticity principle. Many studies have found associations between life experiences such as relationship factors (Lehnart, Neyer, & Eccles, 2010), stressful live events (Jeronimus, Riese, Sanderman, & Ormel, 2014; Laceulle, Nederhof, Karreman, Ormel, & van Aken, 2012), and work experiences (Le, Donnellan, & Conger, 2014) with individual differences in personality trait change in adolescence and young adulthood. Yet more convincing is the fact that similar findings have been reported for middle age (van Aken, Denissen, Branje, Dubas, & Goossens, 2006) and old age (Mottus, Johnson, & Deary, 2012). Moreover, there are now a number of studies showing that personality traits change in old age and are associated with experiential factors. For instance, a recent study showed that increases in perceived social support among older adults (age 60–90) were positively related to changes in conscientiousness (Hill et al., 2014). Another study showed that being more engaged in old age was positively associated with changes in conscientiousness and agreeableness (Lodi-Smith & Roberts, 2012). Although it is also the case that some studies find less plasticity for specific traits in middle and old age (Allemand et al., 2010), the preponderance of findings would support the argument that personality traits remain plastic throughout the life course.

Supporting previous research, and bringing new evidence for the plasticity principle, a more recent paper (Damian, Spengler, Sutu, & Roberts, in press) showed, in a large longitudinal US sample that was tracked across 50 years, that the mean-level change in personality traits over 50 years was, on average, slightly over a half of a standard deviation. Furthermore, changes in personality traits such as agreeableness, conscientiousness, and emotional stability (i.e., the traits that showed most change in previous work) were around 1 to 1.5 standard deviations which are both (a) larger than change across shorter periods of time (e.g., 10 years, where effects were about a quarter to a third of a standard deviation), and (b) consistent with estimates of cumulative change across the lifespan extrapolated from meta-analytic findings (Roberts et al., 2006), and which follow the plasticity model, whereby change continues and cumulates across the lifespan.

Moreover, this study also showed evidence for individual differences in change across the lifespan, which also supports the plasticity principle.

The most relevant question that arises in relation to the plasticity principle is why it exists at all. Why would humans remain capable of change at the level of personality traits even in old age? One possibility is that it is simply a vestige of the learning system that exists in childhood and young adulthood that never got turned off. That is to say, it is most likely quite adaptive for humans to learn to adapt their personality, at least in part, to the prevailing demands of their social environment. The continued plasticity in old age may have no functional significance because it may simply be a leftover system from an age period when it was critical for survival. On the other hand, it is easy to see how being capable of change at any age might still be adaptive. People who increased on conscientiousness also increased their self-perceived health and health behaviors across the life course (Takahashi, Edmonds, Jackson, & Roberts, 2013). The changes in health that resulted from changes in personality might very well improve a wide variety of outcomes for people in old age as much as for those who change when they are young. Nonetheless, the functional significance of personality plasticity merits further attention in future research.

Role Continuity and Identity Development Principles

Two principles have received little or no empirical attention and are thus difficult to evaluate. The role continuity principle posits that consistent roles rather than consistent environments are the cause of continuity in personality over time. Though this is an intriguing idea, no test for it has been developed so far. In addition, there are some contradictory findings. For instance, Neyer and Lehnart (2007) found that staying in a relationship longer was related to more personality trait change, which goes against the role continuity principle that would have suggested more consistency.

The identity development principle proposes that with age, the process of developing, committing to, and maintaining an identity leads to greater personality consistency (Roberts & Caspi, 2003). Identity development is thought to facilitate personality consistency by providing clear reference points for making life decisions. Strong identities serve as a filter for life experiences and lead individuals to interpret new events in ways that are consistent with their identities. Likewise, to the extent that a person's identity becomes known to others in the form of a reputation, it leads others to treat the person in ways that are consistent with his or her personality (Roberts & Wood, 2006). To date, there is only one study that has examined the relation of identity structure to personality continuity; the results indicate that that self-concept clarity is unrelated to personality consistency (Lodi-Smith, Spain, Cologgi, & Roberts, 2017). Thus what little research there is does not support the identity development principle. Nonetheless, more research is necessary to evaluate both the role continuity and identity development principles.

IMPLICATIONS FOR THE INTERFACE BETWEEN CLINICAL AND PERSONALITY PSYCHOLOGY

The principles of personality development provide a set of clear implications and questions for the burgeoning literature linking normal personality traits to the study of psychopathology. We will highlight several ideas that we believe are the most important. The first idea has to do with using the maturity principle to understand the typical life course patterns of psychopathology (Durbin & Hicks, 2014). Like personality traits, psychopathology changes with age. Prototypically, psychopathology goes in the opposite direction of personality traits, such that people decrease or "burn out" of their various forms of psychopathology (Blonigen, 2010). One interpretation of this pattern is that people overcome their various forms of psychopathology, in part, because of changes in personality traits. This idea is predicated on the assumption that personality traits and psychopathology are different constructs, such that personality traits cause psychopathology or make people vulnerable to psychopathology. For example, children who are more anxious may be more likely to develop depression because of the vulnerability their personality trait of neuroticism burdens them with. If, however, one considers the spectrum models, where personality traits and psychopathology represent different levels of the same construct, the putative association between changes in personality and changes in psychopathology takes on a different character. For example, it may be that personality maturation comes about because people overcome their pathologies, which are more common in adolescence and young adulthood. Teasing apart these alternative views on the maturity principle and the normative trends in psychopathology will take some creative longitudinal research. At the very least, it would be constructive to conduct longitudinal research in which both psychopathology and normal personality traits are assessed together over time. This would allow one to test whether apparent gains in personality are in fact simply losses in psychopathology.

A second issue that arises from examining the principles of personality development is how one should think of personality disorders. The entire system of dividing psychopathology between Axis I and Axis II disorders was predicated on the notion that personality disorders were difficult, if not impossible to treat. Although we would not diminish the significance of trying to modify, if not eliminate a personality disorder like borderline personality disorder or antisocial personality disorder, the personality trait development literature does hold out some hope for change. If personality traits continue to develop well into adulthood, then it would be reasonable to assume that similar syndromes, like personality disorders, would also change with age and may also be amenable to intervention. Of course, intervening to change characteristics like personality disorders or personality traits may take a different approach (e.g., Magidson et al., 2014) than what is typically employed to treat problems like depression and anxiety. Nonetheless, the recent research showing that typical clinical interventions also result in personality trait change (Roberts, Luo, Briley, Chow, Su, & Hill, 2017), should open the door to thinking about personality disorders as syndromes that can be changed.

A final thought can be derived from the social investment principle. From our naïve vantage point, it appears quite common to treat mental health issues from a medical model framework. In this type of framework, issues like depression are considered diseases and, most important, diseases that are best treated with medication or in a hospital context where the person is taken out of his or her normal, day-to-day experience so that the disease can be isolated and treated. To the extent that the social investment principle is correct, normative, positive trait development happens at the interface between the person and his or her social milieu. Most important, positive development occurs when people are capable of handling their social challenges with confidence. It is, of course, common for people to experience depression and other issues when they find themselves unable to handle normal life tasks. And, in some circumstances, taking people out of their normal flow may be necessary to reboot their life. On the other hand, focusing more concretely on successful integration into one's social life and handling normative social tasks, something akin to a vocational rehabilitation approach, may offer a more efficacious route to treatment that leverages the insights gleaned from research on normal personality development.

REFERENCES

Allemand, M., Gomez, V., & Jackson, J. J. (2010). Personality trait development in midlife: Exploring the impact of psychological turning points. *European Journal of Ageing*, *7*(3), 147–155.

Anderson, C., John, O. P., Keltner, D., & Kring, A. M. (2001). Who attains social status? Effects of personality and physical attractiveness in social groups. *Journal of Personality and Social Psychology*, *81*(1), 116.

Bleidorn, W. (2012). Hitting the road to adulthood: Short-term personality development during a major life transition. *Personality and Social Psychology Bulletin*, *38*(12), 1594–1608.

Bleidorn, W., Hopwood, C. J., & Lucas, R. E. (2018). Life events and personality trait change. *Journal of Personality*, *86*, 83–96.

Bleidorn, W., Klimstra, T. A., Denissen, J. J., Rentfrow, P. J., Potter, J., & Gosling, S. D. (2013). Personality maturation around the world: A cross-cultural examination of social-investment theory. *Psychological Science*, *24*(12), 2530–2540.

Bleidorn, W., Kandler, C., Hülsheger, U. R., Riemann, R., Angleitner, A., & Spinath, F. M. (2010). Nature and nurture of the interplay between personality traits and major life goals. *Journal of Personality and Social Psychology*, *99*(2), 366.

Block, J. (1971). *Lives through time*. Berkeley, CA: Bancroft.

Blonigen, D. M. (2010). Explaining the relationship between age and crime: Contributions from the developmental literature on personality. *Clinical Psychology Review, 30*(1), 89–100.

Briley, D. A., & Tucker-Drob, E. M. (2014). Genetic and environmental continuity in personality development: A meta-analysis. *Psychological Bulletin, 140*(5), 1303.

Damian, R. I., Spengler, M., Sutu, A., & Roberts, B. W. (in press). Sixteen going on sixty-six: A longitudinal study of personality stability and change across 50 years. *Journal of Personality and Social Psychology*.

Donnellan, M. B., Conger, R. D., & Burzette, R. G. (2007). Personality development from late adolescence to young adulthood: Differential stability, normative maturity, and evidence for the maturity-stability hypothesis. *Journal of personality, 75*(2), 237–264.

Donnellan, M. B., & Lucas, R. E. (2008). Age differences in the Big Five across the life span: evidence from two national samples. *Psychology and Aging, 23*(3), 558.

Durbin, C. E., & Hicks, B. M. (2014). Personality and psychopathology: A stagnant field in need of development. *European Journal of Personality, 28*(4), 362–386.

Ferguson, C. J. (2010). A meta-analysis of normal and disordered personality across the life span. *Journal of Personality and Social Psychology, 98*(4), 659.

Galdiolo, S., & Roskam, I. (2014). Development of personality traits in response to child-birth: A longitudinal dyadic perspective. *Personality and Individual Differences, 69*, 223–230.

Harms, P. D., Roberts, B. W., & Winter, D. (2006). Becoming the Harvard man: Person-environment fit, personality development, and academic success. *Personality and Social Psychology Bulletin, 32*(7), 851–865.

Helson, R., Kwan, V. S., John, O. P., & Jones, C. (2002). The growing evidence for per-sonality change in adulthood: Findings from research with personality inventories. *Journal of Research in Personality, 36*(4), 287–306.

Hill, P. L., Payne, B. R., Roberts, B. W., & Stine-Morrow, E. A. L. (2014). Perceived so-cial support predicts increased conscientiousness during older adulthood. *Journal of Gerontology: Psychological Sciences, 69*, 543–547.

Hogan, R., & Roberts, B.W. (2004). A socioanalytic model of maturity. *Journal of Career Assessment, 12*, 207–217.

Hudson, N. W., Roberts, B. W., & Lodi-Smith, J. (2012). Personality trait development and social investment at work. *Journal of Research in Personality, 46*, 334–344.

Jeronimus, B. F., Riese, H., Sanderman, R., & Ormel, J. (2014). Mutual reinforcement be-tween neuroticism and life experiences: A five-wave, 16-year study to test reciprocal causation. *Journal of Personality and Social Psychology,107*(4), 751.

Johnson, W., Hicks, B. M., McGue, M., & Iacono, W. G. (2007). Most of the girls are alright, but some aren't: Personality trajectory groups from ages 14 to 24 and some associations with outcomes. *Journal of Personality and Social Psychology, 93*(2), 266.

Josefsson, K., Jokela, M., Cloninger, C. R., Hintsanen, M., Salo, J., Hintsa, T., . . . Keltikangas-Järvinen, L. (2013). Maturity and change in personality: developmental trends of temperament and character in adulthood. *Development and Psychopathology, 25*(3), 713–727.

Kandler, C., Kornadt, A. E., Hagemeyer, B., & Neyer, F. J. (2015). Patterns and sources of personality development in old age. *Journal of Personality and Social Psychology, 109*(1), 175–191.

Klimstra, T. A., Akse, J., Hale III, W. W., Raaijmakers, Q. A., & Meeus, W. H. (2010). Longitudinal associations between personality traits and problem behavior symptoms in adolescence. *Journal of Research in Personality, 44*(2), 273–284.

Laceulle, O. M., Nederhof, E., Karreman, A., Ormel, J., & Aken, M. A. G. (2012). Stressful events and temperament change during early and middle adolescence: The TRAILS study. *European Journal of Personality, 26*(3), 276–284.

Le, K., Donnellan, M. B., & Conger, R. (2014). Personality development at work: Workplace conditions, personality changes, and the corresponsive principle. *Journal of Personality, 82*(1), 44–56.

Lehnart, J., Neyer, F. J., & Eccles, J. (2010). Long-term effects of social investment: The case of partnering in young adulthood. *Journal of Personality,78*(2), 639–670.

Leikas, S., & Salmela-Aro, K. (2015). Personality trait changes among young Finns: The role of life events and transitions. *Journal of Personality, 83*(1), 117–126.

Lewis, M. (2001). Issues in the study of personality development. *Psychological Inquiry, 12*, 67–83.

Littlefield, A. K., Sher, K. J., & Steinley, D. (2010). Developmental trajectories of impulsivity and their association with alcohol use and related outcomes during emerging and young adulthood I. *Alcoholism: Clinical and Experimental Research, 34*(8), 1409–1416.

Lodi-Smith, J. L., & Roberts, B. W. (2007). Social investment and personality: A meta-analytic analysis of the relationship of personality traits to investment in work, family, religion, and volunteerism. *Personality and Social Psychology Review, 11*, 68–86.

Lodi-Smith, J. L., & Roberts, B. W. (2012). Concurrent and prospective relationships between social engagement and personality traits in older adulthood. *Psychology and Aging, 27*(3), 720.

Lodi-Smith, J., Spain, S. M., Cologgi, K., & Roberts, B. W. (2017). Development of identity clarity and content in adulthood. *Journal of Personality and Social Psychology, 112*(5), 755.

Lüdtke, O., Roberts, B. W., Trautwein, U., & Nagy, G. (2011). A random walk down university avenue: Life paths, life events, and personality trait change at the transition to university life. *Journal of Personality and Social Psychology, 101*(3), 620.

Magidson, J. F., Roberts, B. W., Collado-Rodriguez, A., & Lejuez, C. W. (2014). Theory-driven intervention for changing personality: Expectancy value theory, behavioral activation, and conscientiousness. *Developmental Psychology, 50*(5), 1442–1450.

McGue, M., Bacon, S., & Lykken, D. T. (1993). Personality stability and change in early adulthood: A behavioral genetic analysis. *Developmental Psychology, 29*(1), 96.

Mottus, R., Johnson, W., & Deary, I. J. (2012). Personality traits in old age: Measurement and rank-order stability and some mean-level change. *Psychology and Aging, 27*(1), 243.

Neyer, F. J., & Lehnart, J. (2007). Relationships matter in personality development: Evidence from an 8-year longitudinal study across young adulthood. *Journal of Personality, 75*(3), 535–568.

Roberts, B. W. (2009). Back to the future: Personality and assessment and personality development. *Journal of Research in Personality, 43*, 137–145.

Roberts, B. W., & Caspi, A. (2001). Personality development and the person-situation debate: It's déjà vu all over again. *Psychological Inquiry, 12*, 104–109.

Roberts, B. W., & Caspi, A. (2003). The cumulative continuity model of personality development: Striking a balance between continuity and change in personality traits across the life course. In R. M. Staudinger & U. Lindenberger (Eds.), *Understanding human development: Lifespan psychology in exchange with other disciplines* (pp. 183–214). Dordrecht, the Netherlands: Kluwer Academic.

Roberts, B. W., Caspi, A., & Moffitt, T. (2001). The kids are alright: Growth and stability in personality development from adolescence to adulthood. *Journal of Personality and Social Psychology, 81*, 670–683.

Roberts, B. W., Caspi, A., & Moffitt, T. E. (2003). Work experiences and personality development in young adulthood. *Journal of Personality and Social Psychology, 84*(3), 582.

Roberts, B. W., & DelVecchio, W. F. (2000). The rank-order consistency of personality from childhood to old age: A quantitative review of longitudinal studies. *Psychological Bulletin, 126*, 3–25.

Roberts, B. W., Kuncel, N., Shiner, R., N., Caspi, A., & Goldberg, L. R. (2007). The power of personality: The comparative validity of personality traits, socio-economic status, and cognitive ability for predicting important life outcomes. *Perspectives in Psychological Science, 2*, 313–345.

Roberts, B. W., & Nickel, L. (2017). A critical evaluation of the Neo-Socioanalytic Model of personality. In J. Specht (Ed.), *Personality Development Across the Life Span* (Chapter 11). Elsevier.

Roberts, B. W., Luo, J., Briley, D. A., Chow, P. I., Su, R., & Hill, P. L. (2017, January 5). A systematic review of personality trait change through intervention. *Psychological Bulletin.*

Roberts, B. W., O'Donnell, M., & Robins, R. W. (2004). Goal and personality trait development in emerging adulthood. *Journal of Personality and Social Psychology, 87*(4), 541.

Roberts, B. W., & Robins, R. W. (2000). Broad dispositions, broad aspirations: The intersection of the Big Five dimensions and major life goals. *Personality and Social Psychology Bulletin, 26*, 1284–1296.

Roberts, B. W., & Robins, R. W. (2004). A longitudinal study of person-environment fit and personality development. *Journal of Personality, 72*, 89–110.

Roberts, B. W., Walton, K., Bogg, T., & Caspi, A. (2006). De-investment in work and non- normative personality trait change in young adulthood. *European Journal of Personality, 20*(6), 461–474.

Roberts, B. W., Walton, K. E., & Viechtbauer, W. (2006). Patterns of mean-level change in personality traits across the life course: A meta-analysis of longitudinal studies. *Psychological Bulletin, 132*(1), 1.

Roberts, B. W., & Wood, D. (2006). Personality development in the context of the NEO-socioanalytic model of personality. In D. Mroczek & T. Little (Eds.), *Handbook of personality development* (pp. 11–39). Mahwah, NJ: Lawrance Erlbaum.

Roberts, B. W., Wood, D., & Caspi, A. (2008). The development of personality traits in adulthood. In O. P. John, R. W. Robins, & L. A. Pervin (Eds.), *Handbook of personality: Theory and research* (3rd ed., pp. 375–398). New York, NY: Guilford.

Roberts, B. W., Wood, D., & Smith, J. L. (2005). Evaluating five factor theory and social investment perspectives on personality trait development. *Journal of Research in Personality, 39*(1), 166–184.

Takahashi, Y., Edmonds, G. E., Jackson, J. J., & Roberts, B. W. (2013). Longitudinal correlated changes in conscientiousness, preventative health-related behaviors, and self-perceived physical health. *Journal of Personality, 81*, 417–427.

Small, B. J., Hertzog, C., Hultsch, D. F., & Dixon, R. A. (2003). Stability and change in adult personality over 6 years: Findings from the Victoria Longitudinal Study. *The Journals of Gerontology Series B: Psychological Sciences and Social Sciences, 58*(3), P166–P176.

Van Aken, M. A., Denissen, J. J., Branje, S. J., Dubas, J. S., & Goossens, L. (2006). Midlife concerns and short-term personality change in middle adulthood. *European Journal of Personality, 20*(6), 497–513.

Vecchione, M., Alessandri, G., Barbaranelli, C., & Caprara, G. (2012). Gender differences in the Big Five personality development: A longitudinal investigation from late adolescence to emerging adulthood. *Personality and Individual Differences, 53*(6), 740–746.

Wagner, J., Becker, M., Lüdtke, O., & Trautwein, U. (2015). The first partnership experience and personality development: A propensity score matching study in young adulthood. *Social Psychological and Personality Science, 6*(4), 455–463.

Wood, D., & Roberts, B. W. (2006). The effect of age and role information on expectations for Big Five personality traits. *Personality and Social Psychology Bulletin, 32*(11), 1482–1496.

Wortman, J., Lucas, R. E., & Donnellan, M. B. (2012). Stability and change in the Big Five personality domains: Evidence from a longitudinal study of Australians. *Psychology and Aging, 27*(4), 867.

8

Advances in Child Personality Research and Relevance for Personality Pathology

JENNIFER L. TACKETT, KATHLEEN W. REARDON, KATHRIN HERZHOFF, AND SHAUNA C. KUSHNER ■

Dispositional differences in characteristic patterns of thinking, feeling, and behaving hold great import for predicting consequential outcomes across the life span. Such dispositions are evident from very early in life, with infants showing differences in preference for novelty and toddlers ranging from highly active and exuberant to quiet and calm. Developmental changes occur rapidly in early life, with substantial growth occurring across childhood and adolescence in diverse domains (e.g., physiological, neurological, emotional, and social). These rapid changes create a fascinating dynamic system of intrapersonal development, yet they also pose unique challenges to researchers interested in examining personality traits in younger populations, particularly from a longitudinal perspective or with an interest in linking early dispositional traits to those commonly investigated in research on adults.

The goals of this chapter are to review the current state of research on defining and organizing normal-range personality traits in youth, the even newer body of work defining and organizing maladaptive personality traits in youth, evidence for the hierarchical organization of both normal-range and maladaptive early personality traits, and the implications of this work, highlighting important future directions for the field. Throughout this chapter, we seek to provide direct comparisons to work on younger populations with existing research on adults, in order to facilitate an integrative life-span perspective of personality and personality pathology.

PERSONALITY TRAITS IN EARLY LIFE

Personality Versus Temperament

Much existing work examining individual differences in youth has focused on temperament traits, rather than personality traits, although such constructs are highly overlapping, at least at a theoretical level (Shiner et al., 2012; Tackett, Kushner, Mervielde, & De Fruyt, 2013). Temperament is traditionally conceptualized as having a biological basis, reflecting behavioral tendencies that are emotional or reactive in nature, and emerging very early in life (Rothbart, 2007; Shiner 1998). Personality is traditionally used to describe broad tendencies to think, feel, and behave in consistent ways, and it is sometimes considered to be more inclusive than temperament (Shiner & Caspi, 2003). Although initially conceptualized as distinct domains, there is evidence to suggest that personality and temperament may be more similar than different (De Pauw & Mervielde, 2010; McCrae et al., 2000). Specifically, personality and temperament both show moderate genetic influence (Bouchard & Loehlin, 2001), and they both capture normative variations in positive and negative emotionality (Rothbart, Ahadi, & Evans, 2000; Watson 2000), motivation, and regulatory tendencies (Caspi, Roberts, & Shiner, 2005; Shiner & Caspi, 2003).

Among adults, investigations of personality often focus on a five-factor model (FFM; McCrae & Costa, 2008) or "the Big Five" (John & Srivastava, 1999), which includes Extraversion, Neuroticism, Conscientiousness, Agreeableness, and Openness to Experience. The FFM has been praised as a useful taxonomy for synthesizing a disjointed literature about personality structure, including taxonomic discrepancies across development (De Pauw & Mervielde, 2010). Three-factor models—which typically include Extraversion/Positive Emotionality, Neuroticism/Negative Emotionality, and Conscientiousness/Constraint—have also received a good deal of theoretical and empirical support in adults, and both overlap with, and are hierarchically related to, the FFM (John & Srivistava, 1999; Markon, Krueger, & Watson, 2005). Three-factor models also show a high degree of overlap with Rothbart's model of child temperament, which includes Surgency, Negative Affectivity, and Effortful Control (Rothbart, Ahadi, Hershey, & Fisher, 2001).

Upon review of common temperament and personality models, three higher order traits appear to be most generalizable across models and across development: two traits indexing affectivity/emotionality (i.e., Extraversion/Surgency and Neuroticism/Negative Emotionality) and one trait indexing self-control, or differences in reactivity and regulation (Conscientiousness/Effortful Control; Watson, Clark, & Harkness, 1994). With regard to the affective traits, Surgency shows conceptual overlap with Extraversion, whereas Negative Affectivity shows conceptual overlap with Neuroticism. In both children and adults, the Extraversion/Surgency domain shows important similarities to the conceptualizations of approach motivation and reward sensitivity, and it shows meaningful connections to risk behavior and certain types of externalizing psychopathology (Shiner & Caspi,

2003; Tackett, 2006). In children, the Negative Affectivity/Neuroticism domain also includes aspects of Disagreeableness (Tackett et al., 2012), which distinguishes childhood manifestations of this dimension from most conceptualizations of Neuroticism in adults. Further support for cross-developmental consistency of these "superfactors" comes from longitudinal research showing the stability of Positive and Negative Emotionality from ages 3 to 7 years (Durbin, Hayden, Klein, & Olino, 2007; Durbin, Klein, Hayden, Buckley, & Moerk, 2005).

Consistencies have also emerged for the third, broader, disinhibitory construct. This domain encompasses Constraint, Effortful Control, and Conscientiousness, as well as (potentially) elements of Agreeableness (Caspi, Roberts, & Shiner, 2005). Overlap between Agreeableness and Conscientiousness observed in temperament models may reflect a single trait in early childhood, which becomes differentiated later in development (John, Naumann, & Soto, 2008; Tackett et al., 2012); however, empirical evidence for this hypothesis is somewhat mixed, with some studies indicating that Effortful Control may not capture variations in Agreeableness but primarily reflects Conscientiousness content (Tackett, Kushner et al., 2013).

Despite evidence for cross-developmental consistency, several important developmental differences have emerged in childhood temperament and personality models (Caspi et al., 2005; Tackett et al., 2012). For example, Agreeableness does not consistently emerge as a higher order trait in younger ages, which is evident from its absence in temperament models. Affiliativeness, which is a somewhat analogous temperament construct, emerges in adolescence and adulthood models (Evans & Rothbart, 2007). It is also notable that Agreeableness in childhood often reflects different content than Agreeableness in adulthood, including greater coverage of agreeable compliance and antagonism in children than in adults (De Pauw & Mervielde, 2010; Tackett, Krueger, Iacono, & McGue, 2008). Additionally, the Big Five trait of Openness to Experience has been somewhat inconsistent in childhood conceptualizations of individual differences. Some researchers posit that it does not exist in childhood (Eder, 1990), but others have found it in very young age groups (De Pauw, Mervielde, & Van Leeuwen, 2009). Often, similar constructs like curiosity, imagination, and intellect are measured in children (Gjerde & Cardilla, 2009; Halverson et al., 2003; Herzhoff & Tackett, 2012), whereas some elements of Openness to Experience like cultural interests and aesthetic appreciation are only included in adult measures.

There are some content differences in other traits as well. The trait of Extraversion has a highly salient activity component in children, which becomes much less influential in adulthood. Neuroticism has a fearful/inhibited component in younger ages, which manifests differently across age. Neuroticism in childhood can be divided into lower order traits of fearful or anxious distress and anger/irritability (Caspi et al., 2005). It seems that the anger/irritability component becomes more closely related to the trait of Agreeableness in older children, which emphasizes that the two lower order traits have different developmental trajectories, and that there is valuable information to be gained through considering development and examining these traits separately (Shiner & Caspi, 2003). Overall, it is important to take developmental stage into account because there is mounting evidence that individual differences show a great deal of heterotypic continuity; that is, traits may manifest in different ways across different developmental periods.

Additional evidence for age-related differences is apparent in mean-level changes in traits across development. Specifically, Soto and colleagues (2011) showed the following age-related trends: Conscientiousness and Agreeableness decreased in late childhood into adolescence but increased into emerging adulthood; Neuroticism peaked in midadolescence for females, but not for males; both Extraversion and Openness to Experience decreased across childhood and adolescence, although only Openness to Experience increased into emerging adulthood. These age-related differences point to periods in the life span that may have special relevance for the development of dispositional traits.

One of the questions facing the study of child personality research is how best to conceptualize dispositional traits in youth. Given the prominent influence of the FFM on the adult personality literature, initial research on child personality tended to impose this five-factor structure on youth individual differences in a developmentally "top-down" manner (Halverson, Kohnstamm, & Martin, 1994). The top-down development of adult personality measures for use in children typically involves the adaptation of adult instruments (e.g., rewording items to capture youth-specific experiences; Goldberg, 2001; John, Donahue, & Kentle, 1991; Soto et al., 2011; Tackett, Krueger et al., 2008). Unsurprisingly, the factor structures of such instruments generally resemble their adult counterparts (e.g., Allik, Laidra, Realo, & Pullmann, 2004; McCrae et al., 2002; Parker & Stumpf, 1998); however, important age differences have emerged. Child personality measures have also been developed following a complementary "bottom-up" approach. For example, Halverson and colleagues (2003) developed the Inventory of Child Individual Differences (ICID) using free-language descriptions of children collected in eight countries. The structure of the ICID items corresponds to five factors that are roughly analogous to the Big Five (Extraversion, Neuroticism, Conscientiousness, Agreeableness, and Openness/Intellect), providing important support for top-down theoretical extensions of the adult Big Five model to youth. The Hierarchical Personality Inventory for Children (HiPIC; Mervielde & De Fruyt, 1999) is another measure developed using a bottom-up approach. It was again developed using parental free-language descriptions of children (Kohnstamm, Halverson, Mervielde, & Havill, 1998), and it assesses five higher order traits resembling the FFM. The emergence of similar traits in top-down and bottom-up measures is indicative that certain traits show consistency across development, although some important differences have emerged.

Content differences have also emerged between measures developed following a bottom-up approach and adult-based Big Five measures (e.g., the Big Five Inventory [BFI]; John et al., 1991). For example, when Agreeableness emerges from the bottom-up approach, it often includes facets that are roughly analogous to the "easy–difficult" temperament dimension (e.g., compliance and dominance; De Fruyt, Mervielde, Hoekstra, & Rolland, 2000; De Fruyt, Mervielde, & Van Leeuwen, 2002). Accordingly, bottom-up approaches may capture features of child Agreeableness that may not be as salient for adults. Similarly, when Openness to

Experience emerges from the bottom-up approach, it often places a heavier emphasis on intellect than is seen in adults, in addition to capturing aspects of creativity and curiosity (De Fruyt et al., 2002; Herzhoff & Tackett, 2012). Ultimately, content differences in traits assessed using bottom-up measures compared to traits measured in adulthood underscore the limitations of relying only on adult-based measures for work in younger age groups (Tackett et al., 2012).

Joint examinations of personality and temperament may provide a more comprehensive depiction of individual differences in youth, and the specific ways in which these models overlap can be complex. In service of this question, De Pauw and colleagues (2009) examined the joint factor structure of the HiPIC and three measures of temperament: the Emotionality, Activity, and Sociability (EAS) Temperament Survey (Buss & Plomin 1984), the Behavioral Styles Questionnaire (BSQ; McDevitt & Carey 1978), and the Child Behavior Questionnaire—short form (CBQ; Putnam & Rothbart 2006). Results of these analyses yielded a six-factor solution composed of Sociability, Activity, Conscientiousness, Disagreeableness, Emotionality, and Sensitivity. This structure did not deviate substantially from the Big Five traits, but it highlighted an ongoing question around whether dispositional activity (typically subsumed under Extraversion/Surgency) reflects an additional higher order trait in children (Soto & John, 2014). Along these lines, Tackett, Kushner and colleagues (2013) examined temperamental correlates of the HiPIC (Mervielde & De Fruyt, 1999) and the ICID-S (Deal, Halverson, Martin, Victor, & Baker, 2007). They hypothesized that, in accordance with the findings and interpretation from De Pauw and colleagues (2009), there would be both shared and nonoverlapping variance between personality and temperament measures. Specifically, the most isomorphic overlap was found for Conscientiousness and Effortful Control, whereas temperamental Negative Affectivity reflected both Neuroticism and Agreeableness, and temperamental Surgency reflected Neuroticism and Extraversion (Tackett, Kushner et al., 2013). Overall, the pattern of prediction across the two personality measures was similar, which implies that empirically derived child personality measures are more similar to one another than to temperament measures, but also that there is important convergence across the domains of childhood personality and temperament. Taken together, this prior work indicates that these measures do in fact capture both overlapping and nonoverlapping variance, and that temperament and personality are not totally distinct or redundant, but complementary to one another.

Personality Pathology Traits in Early Life

In contrast to personality and temperament traits, which capture normative variance in individual differences, personality pathology traits capture abnormal or maladaptive variance in those tendencies (e.g., Samuel, Simms, Clark, Livesley, & Widiger, 2010; Samuel & Widiger, 2008). Individuals high in personality pathology traits often lack insight into their behavior and have greater difficulty flexibly adapting their behavior in appropriate and helpful ways (APA, 2013; Tackett, Kushner et al., 2014). Despite such distinctions between adaptive and maladaptive traits, the FFM of personality has been conceptualized as adequately describing the higher order structure of both normative and maladaptive traits in adults (Clark, 2007); however, research on pathological personality traits in early life has severely lagged behind that in adulthood. Researchers have only recently begun to agree that pathological traits do emerge early in life and are as reliably measured and as temporally stable as pathological personality traits in adulthood (Cicchetti & Crick, 2009; Ferguson, 2010; Tackett, Balsis, Oltmanns, & Krueger, 2009).

Similar to evidence in adults, researchers frequently find a four-factor structure of pathological personality traits in early life (Widiger, De Clercq, & De Fruyt, 2009), with recent advances supporting a potential fifth factor (Tackett, Silberschmidt, Krueger, & Sponheim, 2008; Verbeke & De Clercq, 2014; see Figure 8.1). The four most commonly identified traits across development are Introversion, Emotional Instability, Compulsivity, and Disagreeableness, which are measured by the Dimensional Personality Symptom Item Pool (DIPSI; De Clercq, De Fruyt, Van Leeuwen, & Mervielde, 2006). More recently, the DIPSI has been adapted to encompass a fifth Oddity/Peculiarity trait (Verbeke & De Clercq, 2014). Introversion is characterized by extremely low Extraversion and is also positively associated with Neuroticism. Emotional Instability is characterized by Anxious and Depressive Traits as well as traits assessing overly dependent behavior and is positively associated with Neuroticism. Compulsivity is characterized by extremely high Conscientiousness and is positively associated with both normative Conscientiousness and Neuroticism. Disagreeableness is characterized both by extremely low Agreeableness and low Conscientiousness, with some elements of high Extraversion (e.g., activity) as well. Specifically, the low Agreeableness aspects of Disagreeableness include Dominance-Egocentrism and Irritable-Aggressive Traits, the high Extraversion aspects include Hyperexpressive and Hyperactive Traits, and the low Conscientiousness aspects include Distraction and Disorderliness. Finally, Oddity is characterized by Daydreaming, Extreme Fantasy, Odd Thoughts and Behavior, and Oversensitivity to Feelings. It is associated with high Neuroticism and low Agreeableness more strongly than with its

TEMPERAMENT	Negative Emotionality	Surgency	Effortful Control		
PERSONALITY	Neuroticism	Extraversion	Conscientiousness	Agreeableness	Openness-to-Experience
PD TRAITS	Emotional Instability	Introversion (reversed)	Compulsivity	Disagreeableness (reversed)	Oddity

Figure 8.1. The map of temperament, personality, and personality disorder (PD) traits in youth.

supposed counterpart, Openness to Experience, and it is highly correlated with broadband dimensions of psychopathology.

Dimensional approaches to personality pathology traits have been proposed as a useful framework that is applicable across development (De Clercq & De Fruyt, 2012), allowing comparison and contrast of these traits across early life and adulthood. Generally speaking, pathological traits show substantial consistency across development. Specifically, pathological personality traits in early life seem to be as stable as they are in later life (e.g., Johnson et al., 2000). Early pathological traits and adult personality pathology traits follow similar maturation pathways, such that mean levels of early personality pathology traits decrease across age, an effect that is less pronounced among individuals with higher mean levels (De Clercq, Van Leeuwen, Van Den Noortgate, De Bolle, & De Fruyt, 2009). Also similar to adults, early internalizing personality pathology traits characterized by paranoid, shy, and withdrawn traits seem to be the least flexible (De Clercq et al., 2009).

Important differences also exist between personality pathology traits in early life and adulthood. At the facet level, manifestations of certain traits are necessarily different across developmental stages, a distinction which is often reflected in measures of personality pathology traits across the life span. For example, Intimacy Avoidance is a lower order facet of the adult personality pathology measure, the Personality Inventory for DSM-5 (PID-5; Krueger, Derringer, Markon, Watson, & Skodol, 2012), but it is not represented in the DIPSI given its irrelevance at an earlier age (De Clercq et al., 2014). Similarly, whereas identity disturbance is a central feature of borderline personality disorder (APA, 2013), identity is typically not considered to be fully developed in childhood, and therefore it is not covered by measures of early personality pathology traits (De Clercq, De Fruyt, & Widiger, 2009). Furthermore, Disagreeableness in early life seems to be broader than in later life as evidenced by its inclusion of content spanning low Agreeableness, high Extraversion, and low Conscientiousness (De Clercq et al., 2006). Traits that were not theoretically included as part of the Disagreeableness construct in adults (Hyperexpressive and Hyperactive Traits, Impulsivity, and Risk-Taking) were found to load on the Disagreeableness factor among youth (De Clercq et al., 2006). Finally, evidence for psychoticism in early life may be a stronger marker of general dysfunction than in adulthood (De Clercq et al., 2014). Taken together, important differences in personality pathology traits exist between early life and adulthood, underscoring the importance of using developmentally appropriate approaches to measuring pathological personality traits at any age.

Four core components have been proposed as crucial elements of a developmental conceptualization of personality pathology: (1) traits, (2) emotions, (3) interpersonal relationships, and (4) identity (Tackett, Herzhoff, Balsis, Cooper, 2014). Similarly, Shiner (2009) leveraged McAdams and Pals's (2006) framework for understanding the processes by which personality pathology traits develop in early life. This framework includes three domains: (1) the dispositional signature includes personality traits that affect how people behave across situations and time, (2) the characteristic adaptations affect how people behave in more specific situations or at specific times, and (3) personal narratives affects how people make sense of their behaviors over time. What follows is a brief summary of each core component proposed by Tackett, Herzhoff, and colleagues that highlights similarities with McAdam and Pals's (2006) domains and Shiner's (2009) conceptual analysis.

First, normative personality traits, which would fall under McAdams and Pals's dispositional signatures domain, differentiate between Clusters of personality pathology (Tackett, Herzhoff et al., 2014). In general, Cluster A, which is characterized by odd behaviors, has been associated with high Openness to Experience, low Extraversion, and low Agreeableness; Cluster B, which is characterized by dramatic, emotional, or erratic behavior, has been associated with low Agreeableness and Conscientiousness, as well as high Neuroticism; Cluster C, which is characterized by anxious or fearful behavior, has been associated with low Extraversion, high Neuroticism, and low Openness to Experience (De Clercq & De Fruyt, 2003). In addition to normative personality traits, callous-unemotional (CU) traits have also been identified as a key component in personality pathology (e.g., psychopathy; Barry et al., 2000; Salekin & Frick, 2005). In adolescence, CU traits have been associated with both normative (Latzman, Lilienfeld, Latzman, & Clark, 2013) and maladaptive traits (Decuyper, De Caluwé, De Clercq, & De Fruyt, 2014).

Second, disturbances in emotions, which would be included in McAdam and Pals's characteristic adaptations domain, have also been identified as an important component of early personality pathology (Tackett, Herzhoff et al., 2014). Emotion regulation is the ability to effectively modulate the timing, duration, and intensity of one's emotions, and disturbances in emotion regulation have been hypothesized to be associated with all personality pathology clusters. Cluster A personality pathology has been conceptualized as being associated with a lack of emotional responses, Cluster B with dysregulated emotions, and Cluster C with overregulated emotions (Shiner & Tackett, 2014). Most empirical research, however, has focused specifically on borderline personality pathology (a Cluster B pathology). Related to emotion dysregulation, Shiner (2009) also pointed to coping strategies, such as engagement versus disengagement as more situational and time-specific aspects (i.e., characteristic adaptations), that can help explain how children might develop personality pathology.

Third, disturbances in interpersonal relationships have been conceptualized as a core distinguishing factor between normal personality traits and personality pathology (Livesley & Jang, 2000; Verheul et al., 2008), with most empirical research focusing on the role of attachment and social cognition in personality pathology. Attachment has been conceptualized as a mental representation of an infant's relationship with their caregiver serving as a template for the interpersonal relationships later in life (Shiner & Tackett, 2014). Borderline personality pathology is notably characterized by disrupted attachment, including greater insecure attachment that is characterized by abandonment fears (Westen, Nakash, Thomas, & Bradley, 2006). Along with attachment, social cognition has also been found to be relevant for disturbances in interpersonal relationships that are characteristic of personality pathology, with (1) emotion recognition, (2) theory of mind (also known as mentalizing), and (3) trust being the most relevant (Sharp, 2012).

Fourth, disturbances in identity are the final core component as identified by Tackett, Herzhoff, and colleagues (2014), with most empirical research focusing on identity issues in borderline personality pathology, although they seem to be relevant to a wide range of personality pathology. Within Shiner's (2009) proposed framework, identity disturbance fits into the personal narratives domain and affects how people make sense of their behaviors over time. In this domain, Shiner described two explanatory mechanisms for the early development of personality pathology: (1) the child's ability to incorporate negative experiences into his or her personal narrative and (2) the child's ability to tell a coherent narrative that makes sense of his or her behavior across situations and time. Taken together, pathological personality traits play an important role in the development of personality pathology, but there is a need to supplement them with additional domains to adequately distinguish pathological traits from normative traits and to more comprehensively capture the complexities of personality pathology.

THE STRUCTURE OF PERSONALITY TRAITS IN EARLY LIFE

A relevant issue for the consideration of taxonomy is delineating the overarching structural relations among both normal-range and pathological personality traits (see Figure 8.2). Specifically, the examination of hierarchical structure can be highly informative in understanding differences between trait models, including distinctions between temperament and personality, as well as distinctions between child and adult personality (Markon et al., 2005; Tackett et al., 2012). Furthermore, differences in trait content across the life span may be extended by an understanding of how trait covariation differs across age groups. Next, we review recent focused examinations of hierarchical trait structure for both normal-range and pathological personality traits in youth.

Hierarchical Structure of Personality in Children

Research with both adult (Markon et al., 2005) and child (Martel, Nigg, & Lucas, 2008; Tackett, Krueger et al., 2008) samples has found that different models of individual differences are hierarchically related, which facilitates the synthesis of information across studies and models. In childhood, researchers observed a two-factor solution (Martel et al., 2008) consisting of an avoidance component (consisting of low resiliency, Negative Emotionality, Neuroticism, Conscientiousness, and Effortful Control) and an approach component (consisting of Extraversion and low reactive control). Another investigation found a similar two-factor solution in childhood consisting of Openness to Experience/Extraversion and Agreeableness/

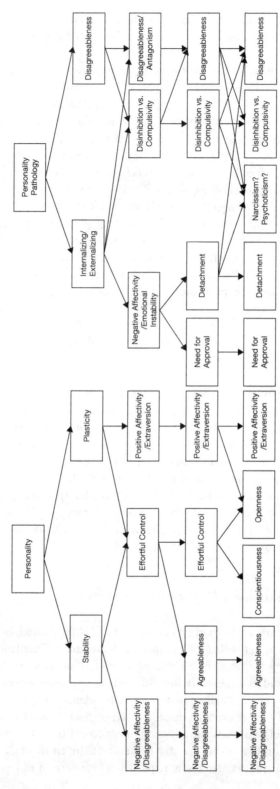

Figure 8.2. Hierarchical structure of normative personality versus personality pathology in childhood.

Neuroticism (Tackett et al., 2012). These two models are also consistent with the structure found in adults, specifically Digman's (1997) conceptualization of two superordinate factors, labeled Alpha (Agreeableness, Conscientiousness, and Neuroticism reversed) and Beta (Extraversion and Openness to Experience; see also De Young, 2006). Similar to interpretations in adults, this two-factor structure in children is often interpreted as reflecting a "bottom-up" system (stimulus response and reward-seeking tendencies; reactive control) and a "top-down" system (cognitive or effortful control; Martel et al., 2008). Slobodskaya and Kuznetsova (2013) examined the relationship of these two hypothesized "superfactors" (Digman, 1997; De Young, 2006) and they found evidence that high reward sensitivity (similar to behavioral activation) and low punishment sensitivity (similar to behavioral inhibition) were related to low Alpha and high Beta, and that low reward sensitivity and high punishment sensitivity were related to high Alpha and low Beta.

At the third level of personality hierarchy (i.e., three-factor structures), studies found components resembling Positive Emotionality/Extraversion, Negative Emotionality/Neuroticism, and Conscientiousness/Constraint (Martel et al., 2008; Tackett et al., 2012). This is largely consistent with the three-factor structure found in temperament measures (Rothbart et al., 2001), as well as with established patterns in children and adults (Markon et al., 2005; Tackett, Krueger et al., 2008). At the fourth level of the hierarchy, childhood traits generally resemble the FFM without Openness, such that Constraint/Effortful Control is represented by differentiable Agreeableness and Conscientiousness traits (Martel et al., 2008; Tackett, Krueger et al., 2008; Tackett et al., 2012). At the fifth level, a largely analogous FFM trait structure emerges, with notable content differences for younger populations, as described previously.

This general hierarchical structure of personality was found to be relatively consistent across child age groups and countries (Tackett et al., 2012). Across all age groups, spanning from ages 3 to 14 years, the authors found robust replication for two superfactors consisting of Extraversion/Openness to Experience (e.g., approach) and Agreeableness/Neuroticism (e.g., avoidance). Some structural differences across ages emerged as well. For example, in younger ages (age groups encompassing individuals aged 3–8 years), Tackett and colleagues (2012) found that Agreeableness shows substantial influence from aspects of Conscientiousness in an "agreeable compliance" factor that is distinct from adult manifestations of Agreeableness (DePauw & Mervielde, 2010; Tackett, Krueger et al., 2008). However, in older children, there was a much cleaner split between Conscientiousness and Agreeableness, which is also consistent with a broader, higher order disconstraint factor containing both elements of Conscientiousness and Agreeableness, and potentially differentiating across child development. For most age groups (ages 3–11 years), a "typical" Neuroticism trait did emerge, but Agreeableness largely reflected antagonistic aspects of Neuroticism, even at the five-factor level of the hierarchy (Tackett et al., 2012). In contrast, in older children (ages 12–14 years), a more adult-typical Agreeableness was found, but Neuroticism continued to reflect high loadings of antagonism, rather than the sad or anxious elements more typically defining Neuroticism in adults (Tackett et al., 2012).

There are some important similarities and differences across hierarchical personality structures derived in adults and those in children. One important similarity found across all models is the evidence for two higher order traits, which seem to index broadly defined neurobiological systems (Markon, 2009). These two systems can also be described as motivational, encompassing approach/ avoidance and regulatory abilities (disinhibition versus constraint; Read et al., 2010). Generally, Tackett and colleagues (2012) found more similarities than differences when comparing their structure to adult models (Markon et al., 2005). The FFM was represented at lower levels of their hierarchy in both children and adults, although the psychological space covered by these trait names may be slightly discrepant. For example, Conscientiousness and Intellect, an important facet of Openness to Experience, are more highly correlated in children than in adults (Goldberg, 2001; Tackett et al., 2012). It is important to note that in Tackett and colleagues' investigation (2012), Disagreeableness and Negative Emotionality covaried at multiple levels of the hierarchy, which implies that this combined cluster of antagonistic traits may be especially important for children, relative to adults. For example, Evans and Rothbart (2009) found that Agreeableness was related to Extraversion rather than to Neuroticism and Conscientiousness in their adult temperament model.

"Pure" Neuroticism was not consistently found at the lower levels of the hierarchy in children in the same way that it is in adults (e.g., emphasizing sadness and anxiety). This may at least partly reflect the difficulty in measuring internal aspects of Neuroticism in children (Tackett, 2010; Tackett et al., 2012). Another important difference in children when compared to adults is antagonism, which seems to be much more important for children. Adult-typical manifestations of Agreeableness and Neuroticism are hard to find at higher levels of the hierarchy, but a combined Agreeableness/Neuroticism trait emerges and remains salient across childhood and early adolescence (Tackett et al., 2012; Tackett, Krueger et al., 2008). This higher order trait may be similar to the concept of "difficult temperament," which has a rich history as a highly behaviorally relevant and salient early individual difference (Tackett, 2006). A final difference that is salient to the structure of personality traits in children is the issue of activity. In a six-factor model, activity is treated as a separate construct (De Pauw & Mervielde, 2010), but in other models, it is treated as a subcomponent of Extraversion (Caspi et al., 2005). In other investigations, this domain did not emerge (Martel et al., 2008; Tackett et al., 2012; Tackett, Krueger et al., 2008). It is not yet clear how activity should best be classified, a question that has important implications given that activity ratings are normatively much higher for children than for adults (Tackett et al., 2012). As in adults, a hierarchical structure of normative individual differences is an important and informative way to synthesize contributions from various fields, and although there are clearly important similarities across the life span, the differences between hierarchical structures in adults and children help to illuminate the unique content and covariation of individual differences in childhood.

Hierarchical Structure of Pathological Personality Traits in Early Life

Interest in the hierarchical structure of pathological personality traits has grown since Markon and colleagues' (2005) formative research on the joint structure of abnormal and normal personality traits. As in other domains of personality research, investigations of the pathological trait hierarchy have largely focused on adult samples (Kushner, Quilty, Tackett, & Bagby, 2011; Wright et al., 2012). Among adults, the pathological trait hierarchy has been studied in student samples (De Fruyt et al., 2013; Wright et al., 2012), in clinical samples (Bagby et al., 2014; Kushner et al., 2011), and in community samples of older adults (Van den Broeck et al., 2014). Overall, these studies showed moderate convergence across the first through fourth levels of the hierarchy. Specifically, most studies observed broad internalizing/externalizing dimensions at the second level of the hierarchy (Achenbach & Edelbrock, 1978; Krueger, 1999). At the third level, most studies observed dimensions that correspond to maladaptive variants of the "Big Three" model of temperament (i.e., negative emotionality, positive emotionality, and disinhibition; Clark & Watson, 2008); however, Bagby and colleagues observed a factor representing psychoticism at the third level, in addition to factors representing internalizing and externalizing psychopathology. At the fourth level, most studies observed dimensions that correspond to prominent four-factor models of personality psychopathology (i.e., emotional dysregulation, dissocial behavior, inhibitedness, and compulsivity; Livesley, Jang, & Vernon, 1998; Livesley & Jackson, 2009; Widiger & Simonsen, 2005), also reflecting maladaptive variants of the FFM with the exclusion of Openness to Experience. At the fifth level, the components derived by Wright and colleagues (2012) are consistent with investigations observing a fifth factor labeled psychoticism (e.g., Harkness & McNulty, 1994; Tackett, Silberschmidt et al., 2008). These five factors are consistent with the five broad trait domains listed in the alternative *DSM-5* model for PDs: Detachment, Negative Affectivity, Disinhibition, Antagonism, and Psychoticism (American Psychiatric Association, 2013). It is notable that Kushner and colleagues (2011) did not have adequate content coverage to observe a fifth factor reflecting psychotic or peculiarity items, but identified a fifth factor that was characterized by insecure attachment, narcissism, and submissiveness, which resembled Clark, Livesley, Schroeder, and Irish's (1996) Need for Approval factor, and was labeled accordingly.

More recently, research on pathological trait hierarchies has been extended to youth samples (De Clercq et al., 2014; Kushner, Tackett, & De Clercq, 2013). Within an adolescent community sample, Kushner et al. examined the joint structure of two measures of youth personality pathology: the DIPSI (De Clercq, De Fruyt, & Mervielde, 2003) and the youth version of the Schedule for Nonadaptive and Adaptive Personality (SNAP-Y; Linde, Stringer, Simms, & Clark, 2013). These measures were developed following two approaches to measuring youth dispositional traits. Specifically, the DIPSI was developed using maladaptive variants of parents' free description of their children (i.e., a bottom-up instrument), whereas the SNAP-Y was adapted from a pre-existing measure of adult PD traits (i.e., a top-down instrument). Across all levels of the hierarchy, components were composed of both SNAP-Y and DIPSI scales, suggesting substantial overlap (at the higher order level, at least) in the content covered by these top-down and bottom-up measures. Further, the resulting hierarchy components are analogous to higher order dimensions observed in previous research on adults (Kushner et al., 2011; Wright et al., 2012), although notable discrepancies also emerged. For example, Kushner et al. (2013) observed that facets measuring aspects of aggression loaded more highly on Disagreeableness than on Emotional Instability, suggesting that aggressive and nonaggressive negative affect are more strongly linked among youth than adults. This is consistent with research on the structure of normative personality traits in childhood, which appears to indicate a stronger connection between Antagonism and Neuroticism among youth than has been observed in adults (Tackett et al., 2012). In addition, a distinct higher order trait reflecting detachment (i.e., pathological introversion) emerged at the fourth level in the adolescent sample, whereas it typically emerges at the third level in adult samples. Among adolescents, detachment emerged alongside need for approval at the fourth level (Kushner et al., 2013). Like Kushner and colleagues (2011), measures used by Kushner and colleagues (2013) included only limited content coverage of psychotic or peculiarity items, which may account for the absence of a psychoticism factor in the adolescent pathological trait hierarchy. Overall, these findings raise questions about the extent to which differences in the adolescent pathological hierarchy versus that observed in adults reflect measurement challenges in younger age groups versus true developmental phenomena.

Evaluation of the content and structure for a fifth factor in the pathological trait hierarchy for youth represents an important task for elucidating manifestations of personality pathology in youth. Along these lines, researchers have examined the suitability of the Psychoticism construct in younger populations. Using the PID-5 (Krueger et al., 2012)—an adult-based instrument that includes items on eccentricity, perceptual dysregulation, and unusual beliefs—De Clercq and colleagues (2014) recovered a psychoticism factor in Flemish adolescents; however, this factor showed inconsistencies with adult samples. Specifically, Psychoticism was more strongly correlated with Detachment, Negative Affectivity, Disinhibition, and Antagonism than typically observed in adult samples. The authors raise two possible interpretations: (1) Psychoticism reflects general dysfunction in youth, or (2) Psychoticism, as characterized by the PID-5, is a developmentally inappropriate construct. Verbeke and De Clercq (2014) subsequently extended this work by examining the placement of oddity items within the hierarchical structure of the DIPSI. Their results provide support for the emergence of an Oddity factor at the five-factor level, which accounted for unique variance in youth psychopathology above the effects of other pathological trait dimensions.

Together, the existing research shows important areas of overlap and distinction between the youth and adult pathological trait hierarchies. Convergence between adolescent and adult hierarchies supports the hypothesis that pathological traits emerge prior to adulthood and show structural stability (De Bolle et al., 2009), whereas divergence may point to developmental differences in the manifestations of personality pathology. The reviewed literature also underscores the importance of considering test construction procedures and item content coverage in future studies of personality pathology in childhood and adolescence. The structure of personality pathology in preadolescent youth has yet to be investigated. Research on the emergence and course of pathological personality traits in childhood is particularly needed. Such work will be instrumental for identifying critical periods in the development and treatment of personality pathology.

IMPLICATIONS AND FUTURE DIRECTIONS

In this chapter, we reviewed the current state of research on normative and maladaptive personality in childhood and adolescence, particularly highlighting discrepancies and overlap with what is known about analogous phenomena in adults. Specifically, we reviewed historical distinctions between temperament and child personality traits, noting increasing consensus in the field that such dispositional frameworks highly overlap with one another, and with popular personality models in adulthood. Similarly, subsequent attempts at the empirical classification and description of youth pathological personality traits demonstrate substantial convergence with adult-based models. We then reviewed parallel work on normal-range and maladaptive personality in youth that has focused on hierarchical trait structure. Such approaches complement and extend basic descriptive research by emphasizing connections between levels of trait hierarchy, as well as patterns of trait covariation. Again, such studies have demonstrated substantial convergence in both normal and pathological personality trait covariation and hierarchy across the life span.

Nonetheless, the infrequent—yet critical—use of empirically based bottom-up assessment approaches in youth underscores highly relevant differences from work with adults that may be missed if the field relied exclusively on adult-based measures and theory when examining personality at younger ages. Some examples have emerged across studies, such as the high covariation between Neuroticism and Agreeableness in childhood. Evidence for this covariation emerges from early models of temperament, which position antagonistic content in the higher order trait domain of Negative Emotionality, but also from empirically based measures of child personality, which typically show high loading of antagonistic content on trait Agreeableness as well. Furthermore, examination of the structural hierarchy of normal-range and pathological personality traits similarly shows substantial overlap between Neuroticism and Agreeableness in youth, relative to analogous examinations in adults. Both traits are, of course, highly relevant for the emergence and development of personality pathology across the life span, highlighting the relevance of this discrepancy (even in a broader context of developmental convergence).

Another developmentally relevant aspect of the work reviewed here relates to the identification of "the fifth factor" in youth dispositional trait models. Parallel inconsistencies have emerged for Openness to Experience in normative models and for Psychoticism/Oddity in pathological models. The fifth factor has proven challenging in adult research as well (e.g., Gore & Widiger, 2013; Tackett, Silberschmidt et al., 2008). Openness to Experience is not well represented in most temperament models, and the content for child personality measures tends to be heavily weighted by intellect (Herzhoff & Tackett, 2012; Tackett et al., 2012). Indeed, hierarchical examinations demonstrate developmental differences for both normal-range Openness to Experience (which covaries more highly with Conscientiousness than it does in adults; Tackett et al., 2012) and pathological Oddity (which demonstrates more diffuse pathological associations than it does in adults; Verbeke & De Clercq, 2014). Thus, this domain requires further elucidation in younger populations, particularly in attempts to better understand the early emergence of pathological personality and its development over time.

Another pressing issue for researchers and practitioners concerns the assessment of early dispositional traits. Among younger populations, reliable self-reports may not be easily obtained. In instances where youth self-report is available (e.g., in adolescence), it is almost always combined with reports from other informants or sources of information. Thus, attempts to measure child personality and personality pathology highlight issues of informant biases (e.g., strengths and weakness of parent informants; Tackett, 2010), informant discrepancies (De Los Reyes & Kazdin, 2005; Tackett, Herzhoff, Reardon, Smack, & Kushner, 2013), developmental limitations and complexities, and the difficulty in assessing variance that is highly relevant for developing personality pathology (e.g., more internalized aspects of trait Neuroticism). Child clinicians and researchers have long grappled with measurement challenges such as these, but many are not unique to younger populations, positioning developmental researchers as potentially offering greater insight and innovation to personality pathology measurement across the life span.

REFERENCES

Achenbach, T. M., & Edelbrock, C. S. (1978). The classification of child psychopathology: A review and analysis of empirical efforts. *Psychological Bulletin, 85,* 1275–1301. doi:10.1037/0033-2909.85.6.1275

Allik, J., Laidra, K., Realo, A., & Pullmann, H. (2004). Personality development from 12 to 18 years of age: Changes in mean levels and structure of traits. *European Journal of Personality, 18,* 445–462. doi:10.1002/per.524

American Psychiatric Association. (2013). *Diagnostic and statistical manual of mental disorders: DSM-5.* (5th ed.). Arlington, VA: American Psychiatric Association.

Bagby, R. M., Sellbom, M., Ayearst, L. E., Chmielewski, M. S., Anderson, J. L., & Quilty, L. C. (2014). Exploring the hierarchical structure of the MMPI-2-RF personality psychopathology five in psychiatric patient and university student samples. *Journal of Personality Assessment, 96,* 166–172. doi:10.1080/00223891.2013.825623

Barry, C. T., Frick, P. J., DeShazo, T. M., McCoy, M. G., Ellis, M., & Loney, B. R. (2000). The importance of callous-unemotional traits for extending the concept of psychopathy to children. *Journal of Abnormal Psychology, 109,* 335–340. doi:10.1037/0021-843X.109.2.335

Bouchard Jr, T. J., & Loehlin, J. C. (2001). Genes, evolution, and personality. *Behavior Genetics, 31,* 243–273. doi:10.1023/A:1012294324713

Buss, A. H., & Plomin, R. (1984). *Temperament: Early developing personality traits.* Hillsdale, NJ: Erlbaum.

Caspi, A., Roberts, B. W., & Shiner, R. L. (2005). Personality development: Stability and change. *Annual Review of Psychology, 56,* 453–484. doi:10.1146/annurev.psych.55.090902.141913

Cicchetti, D., & Crick, N. R. (2009). Precursors and diverse pathways to personality disorder in children and adolescents. *Development and Psychopathology, 21,* 683–685. doi:http://dx.doi.org/10.1017/S0954579409000388

Clark, L. A. (2007). Assessment and diagnosis of personality disorder: Perennial issues and an emerging reconceptualization. *Annual Review of Psychology, 58,* 227–257. doi:10.1146/annurev.psych.57.102904.190200

Clark, L. A., Livesley, W. J., Schroeder, M. L., & Irish, S. L. (1996). Convergence of two systems for assessing specific traits of personality disorder. *Psychological Assessment, 8,* 294–303. doi:10.1037/1040-3590.8.3.294

Clark, L. A., & Watson, D. (2008). *Temperament: An organizing paradigm for trait psychology.* New York, NY: Guilford Press.

De Bolle, M., De Clercq, B., Van Leeuwen, K., Decuyper, M., Rosseel, Y., & De Fruyt, F. (2009). Personality and psychopathology in Flemish referred children: Five perspectives on continuity. *Child Psychiatry and Human Development, 40,* 269–285. doi:10.1007/s10578-009-0125-1

De Clercq, B., & De Fruyt, F. (2003). Personality disorder symptoms in adolescence: A Five-Factor Model perspective. *Journal of Personality Disorders, 17,* 269–292. doi:10.1521/pedi.17.4.269.23972

De Clercq, B., & De Fruyt, F. (2012). A Five-Factor Model framework for understanding childhood personality disorder antecedents. *Journal of Personality, 80,* 1533–1563. doi:10.1111/j.1467-6494.2012.00778.x

De Clercq, B., De Fruyt, F., De Bolle, M., Van Hiel, A., Markon, K. E., & Krueger, R. F. (2014). The hierarchical structure and construct validity of the PID-5 trait measure in adolescence. *Journal of Personality, 82,* 158–169. doi:10.1111/jopy.12042

De Clercq, B. J., De Fruyt, F., & Mervielde, I. (2003). *Construction of the Dimensional Personality Symptom Item Pool (DIPSI).* Ghent, Belgium: Ghent University.

De Clercq, B., De Fruyt, F., Van Leeuwen, K., & Mervielde, I. (2006). The structure of maladaptive personality traits in childhood: A step toward an integrative developmental perspective for DSM-V. *Journal of Abnormal Psychology, 115,* 639–657. doi:10.1037/0021-843X.115.4.639

De Clercq, B., De Fruyt, F., & Widiger, T. A. (2009). Integrating a developmental perspective in dimensional models of personality disorders. *Clinical Psychology Review, 29,* 154–162. doi:10.1016/j.cpr.2008.12.002

De Clercq, B., Van Leeuwen, K., Van den Noortgate, W., De Bolle, M., & De Fruyt, F. (2009). Childhood personality pathology: Dimensional stability and change.

Development and Psychopathology, 21, 853–869. doi:http://dx.doi.org/10.1017/S0954579409000467

De Fruyt, F., De Clercq, B., De Bolle, M., Wille, B., Markon, K., & Krueger, R. F. (2013). General and maladaptive traits in a five-factor framework for DSM-5 in a university student sample. *Assessment, 20,* 295–307. doi:10.1177/1073191113475808

De Fruyt, F., Mervielde, I., Hoekstra, H. A., & Rolland, J. P. (2000). Assessing adolescents" personality with the NEO PI-R. *Assessment, 7,* 329–345. doi:10.1177/107319110000700403

De Fruyt, F., Mervielde, I., & Van Leeuwen, K. (2002). The consistency of personality type classification across samples and five-factor measures. *European Journal of Personality, 16,* S57–S72. doi:10.1002/per.444

De Los Reyes, A., & Kazdin, A. E. (2005). Informant discrepancies in the assessment of childhood psychopathology: A critical review, theoretical framework, and recommendations for further study. *Psychological Bulletin, 131,* 483–509. doi:10.1037/0033-2909.131.4.483

De Pauw, S. S., & Mervielde, I. (2010). Temperament, personality and developmental psychopathology: A review based on the conceptual dimensions underlying childhood traits. *Child Psychiatry and Human Development, 41,* 313–329. doi:10.1007/s10578-009-0171-8

De Pauw, S. S., Mervielde, I., & Van Leeuwen, K. G. (2009). How are traits related to problem behaviors in preschoolers? Similarities and contrasts between temperament and personality. *Journal of Abnormal Child Psychology, 37,* 309–325. doi:10.1007/s10802-008-9290-0

Deal, J. E., Halverson, C. F., Martin, R. P., Victor, J., & Baker, S. (2007). The Inventory of Children's Individual Differences: Development and validation of a short version. *Journal of Personality Assessment, 89,* 162–166. doi:10.1080/00223890701468550

Decuyper, M., De Caluwé, E., De Clercq, B., & De Fruyt, F. (2014). Callous-unemotional traits in youth from a DSM-5 trait perspective. *Journal of Personality Disorders, 28,* 334–357. doi:10.1521/pedi_2013_27_120

DeYoung, C. G. (2006). Higher-order factors of the Big Five in a multi-informant sample. *Journal of Personality and Social Psychology, 91,* 1138–1151. doi:10.1037/0022-3514.91.6.1138

Digman, J. M. (1997). Higher-order factors of the Big Five. *Journal of Personality and Social Psychology, 71,* 1246–1256. doi:10.1037/0022-3514.73.6.1246

Durbin, C. E., Hayden, E. P., Klein, D. N., & Olino, T. M. (2007). Stability of laboratory-assessed temperamental emotionality traits from ages 3 to 7. *Emotion, 7,* 388–399. doi:10.1037/1528-3542.7.2.388

Durbin, C. E., Klein, D. N., Hayden, E. P., Buckley, M. E., & Moerk, K. C. (2005). Temperamental emotionality in preschoolers and parental mood disorders. *Journal of Abnormal Psychology, 114,* 28–37. doi:10.1037/0021-843X.114.1.28

Eder, R. A. (1990). Uncovering young children's psychological selves: Individual and developmental differences. *Child Development, 61,* 849–863. doi:10.1037/0021-843X.114.1.28

Evans, D. E., & Rothbart, M. K. (2007). Developing a model for adult temperament. *Journal of Research in Personality, 41,* 868–888. doi:10.1016/j.jrp.2006.11.002

Evans, D. E., & Rothbart, M. K. (2009). A two-factor model of temperament. *Personality and Individual Differences, 47,* 565–570. doi:10.1016/j.paid.2009.05.010

Ferguson, C. J. (2010). A meta-analysis of normal and disordered personality across the life span. *Journal of Personality and Social Psychology, 98,* 659–667. doi:10.1037/a0018770

Gjerde, P. F., & Cardilla, K. (2009). Developmental implications of openness to experience in preschool children: Gender differences in young adulthood. *Developmental Psychology, 45,* 1455–1464. doi:10.1037/a0016714

Goldberg, L. R. (2001). Analyses of Digman's child-personality data: Derivation of Big-Five factor scores from each of six samples. *Journal of Personality, 69,* 709–743. doi:10.1111/1467-6494.695161

Gore, W. L., & Widiger, T. A. (2013). The DSM-5 dimensional trait model and Five-Factor Models of general personality. *Journal of Abnormal Psychology, 122,* 816–821. doi:10.1037/a0032822

Halverson, C. F., Havill, V. L., Deal, J., Baker, S. S. R., Victor, J. B., Pavlopoulos, V., ... Wen, L. (2003). Personality structure as derived from parental ratings of free descriptions of children: The Inventory of Child Individual Differences. *Journal of Personality, 71,* 995–1026. doi:10.1111/1467-6494.7106005

Halverson, C. F., Kohnstamm, G. A., & Martin, R. P. (Eds.). (1994). *The developing structure of temperament and personality from infancy to adulthood.* Hillsdale, NJ: Lawrence Erlbaum.

Harkness, A. R., & McNulty, J. L. (1994). The Personality Psychopathology Five (Psy-5): Issues from the pages of a diagnostic manual instead of a dictionary. In S. Strack & M. Lorr (Eds.), *Differentiating normal and abnormal personality* (pp. 291–315). New York, NY: Springer.

Herzhoff, K., & Tackett, J. L. (2012). Establishing construct validity for Openness-to-Experience in middle childhood: Contributions from personality and temperament. *Journal of Research in Personality, 46,* 286–294. doi:10.1016/j.jrp.2012.02.007

John, O. P., Donahue, E. M., & Kentle, R. L. (1991). *The Big Five Inventory—Versions 4a and 54.* Berkeley: University of California.

John, O. P., Naumann, L. P., & Soto, C. J. (2008). Paradigm shift to the integrative Big Five trait taxonomy. In O. P. John, R. W. Robins, & L. A. Pervin (Eds.), *Handbook of personality: Theory and research* (3rd ed., pp. 114–158). New York, NY: Guilford Press.

John, O. P., & Srivastava, S. (1999). The Big Five trait taxonomy: History, measurement, and theoretical perspectives. In L. A. Pervin & O. P. John (Eds.), *Handbook of personality* (pp. 102–138). New York, NY: Guilford Press.

Johnson, J. G., Cohen, P., Kasen, S., Skodol, A. E., Hamagami, F., & Brook, J. S. (2000). Age-related change in personality disorder trait levels between early adolescence and adulthood: A community-based longitudinal investigation. *Acta Psychiatrica Scandinavica, 102,* 265–275. doi:10.1034/j.1600-0447.2000.102004265.x

Kohnstamm, G. A., Halverson Jr, C. F., Mervielde, I., & Havill, V. L. (1998). Analyzing parental free descriptions of child personality. In G. A. Kohnstamm, C. F. Halverson Jr, I. Mervielde, & V. L. Havill, V. L. (Eds.), *Parental descriptions of child personality: Developmental antecedents of the Big Five?* (pp. 1–19). Hillsdale, NJ: Lawrence Erlbaum.

Krueger, R. F. (1999). The structure of common mental disorders. *Archives of General Psychiatry, 56,* 921–926. doi:10.1001/archpsyc.56.10.921.

Krueger, R. F., Derringer, J., Markon, K. E., Watson, D., & Skodol, A. E. (2012). Initial construction of a maladaptive personality trait model and inventory for DSM-5. *Psychological Medicine, 42*, 1879–1890. doi:10.1017/S0033291711002674

Kushner, S. C., Quilty, L. C., Tackett, J. L., & Bagby, R. M. (2011). The hierarchical structure of the Dimensional Assessment of Personality Pathology (DAPP-BQ). *Journal of Personality Disorders, 25*, 504–516. doi:10.1521/pedi.2011.25.4.504

Kushner, S. C., Tackett, J. L., & De Clercq, B. J. (2013). The joint hierarchical structure of adolescent personality pathology: Converging evidence from two approaches to measurement. *Journal of the Canadian Academy of Child and Adolescent Psychiatry, 22*, 199–205.

Latzman, R. D., Lilienfeld, S. O., Latzman, N. E., & Clark, L. A. (2013). Exploring callous and unemotional traits in youth via general personality traits: An eye toward DSM-5. *Personality Disorders: Theory, Research, and Treatment, 4*, 191–202. doi:10.1037/a0000001

Linde, J. A., Stringer, D. M., Simms, L. J., & Clark, L. A. (2013). The Schedule for Nonadaptive and Adaptive Personality-Youth Version (SNAP-Y): Psychometric properties and initial validation. *Assessment, 20*, 387–404. doi:10.1177/1073191113489847

Livesley, W. J., & Jackson, D. N. (2009). *Manual for the dimensional assessment of personality pathology—Basic questionnaire.* Port Huron, MI: Sigma Press.

Livesley, W. J., & Jang, K. L. (2000). Toward an empirically based classification of personality disorder. *Journal of Personality Disorders, 14*, 137–151. doi:10.1521/pedi.2000.14.2.137

Livesley, W. J., Jang, K. L., & Vernon, P. A. (1998). Phenotypic and genetic structure of traits delineating personality disorder. *Archives of General Psychiatry, 55*, 941–948. doi:10.1001/archpsyc.55.10.941

Markon, K. E. (2009). Hierarchies in the structure of personality traits. *Social and Personality Psychology Compass, 3*, 812–826. doi:10.1111/j.1751-9004.2009.00213.x

Markon, K. E., Krueger, R. F., & Watson, D. (2005). Delineating the structure of normal and abnormal personality: An integrative hierarchical approach. *Journal of Personality and Social Psychology, 88*, 139–157. doi:10.1037/0022-3514.88.1.139

Martel, M. M., Nigg, J. T., & Lucas, R. E. (2008). Trait mechanisms in youth with and without attention-deficit/hyperactivity disorder. *Journal of Research in Personality, 42*, 895–913. doi:10.1016/j.jrp.2007.12.004

McAdams, D. P., & Pals, J. L. (2006). A new Big Five: Fundamental principles for an integrative science of personality. *American Psychologist, 61*, 204–217. doi:10.1037/0003-066X.61.3.204

McCrae, R. R., Costa, P. T., Ostendorf, F., Angleitner, A., Hrebickova, M., Avia, M. D., . . . & Sanchez-Bernardos, M. L. (2000). Nature over nurture: Temperament, personality and life span development. *Journal of Personality and Social Psychology, 78*, 173–186. doi:10.1037/0022-3514.78.1.173

McCrae, R. R., Costa, P. T., Jr., Terracciano, A., Parker, W. D., Mills, C. J., De Fruyt, F., & Mervielde, I. (2002). Personality trait development from age 12 to age 18: Longitudinal, cross-sectional and cross-cultural analyses. *Journal of Personality and Social Psychology, 83*, 1456–1468. doi:10.1037/0022-3514.83.6.1456

McDevitt, S. C., & Carey, W. B. (1978). Measurement of temperament in 3-7 year old children. *Journal of Child Psychology and Psychiatry, and Allied Disciplines, 19*, 245–253. doi:10.1111/j.1469-7610.1978.tb00467.x

Mervielde, I., & De Fruyt, F. (1999). Construction of the Hierarchichal Personality Inventory for Children (HIPIC). In I. Mervielde, I. Deary, F. De Fruyt, & F. Ostendorf (Eds.), *Personality psychology in Europe: Proceedings of the Eighth European Conference on Personality Psychology* (pp. 107–127). Tillburg, Germany: Tillburg University Press.

Parker, W. D., & Stumpf, H. (1998). A validation of the five-factor model of personality in academically talented youth across observers and instruments. *Personality and Individual Differences, 25*, 1005–1025. doi:10.1016/S0191-8869(98)00016-6

Putnam, S. P., & Rothbart, M. K. (2006). Development of short and very short forms of the Children's Behavior Questionnaire. *Journal of Personality Assessment, 87*, 102–112. doi:10.1207/s15327752jpa8701_09

Read, S. J., Monroe, B. M., Brownstein, A. L., Yang, Y., Chopra, G., & Miller, L. C. (2010). A neural network model of the structure and dynamics of human personality. *Psychological Review, 117*, 61–92. doi:10.1037/a0018131

Rothbart, M. K. (2007). Temperament, development, and personality. *Current Directions in Psychological Science, 16*, 207–212. doi:10.1111/j.1467-8721.2007.00505.x

Rothbart, M. K., Ahadi, S. A., & Evans, D. E. (2000). Temperament and personality: Origins and outcomes. *Journal of Personality and Social Psychology, 78*, 122–135. doi:10.1037/0022-3514.78.1.122

Rothbart, M. K., Ahadi, S. A., Hershey, K. L., & Fisher, P. (2001). Investigations of temperament at three to seven years: The Children's Behavior Questionnaire. *Child Development, 72*, 1394–1408. doi:10.1111/1467-8624.00355

Salekin, R. T., & Frick, P. J. (2005). Psychopathy in children and adolescents: The need for a developmental perspective. *Journal of Abnormal Child Psychology, 33*, 403–409. doi:10.1007/s10802-005-5722-2

Samuel, D. B., Simms, L. J., Clark, L. A., Livesley, W. J., & Widiger, T. A. (2010). An item response theory integration of normal and abnormal personality scales. *Personality Disorders: Theory, Research, and Treatment, 1*, 5–21. doi:10.1037/a0018136

Samuel, D. B., & Widiger, T. A. (2008). A meta-analytic review of the relationships between the five-factor model and DSM-IV-TR personality disorders: A facet level analysis. *Clinical Psychology Review, 28*, 1326–1342. doi:10.1016/j.cpr.2008.07.002

Sharp, C. (2012). The developmental building blocks of psychopathic traits: Revisiting the role for theory of mind. Presentation at the 1st World Conference on Personality, Stellenbosch, South Africa.

Shiner, R. L. (1998). How shall we speak of children's personalities in middle childhood? A preliminary taxonomy. *Psychological Bulletin, 124*, 308–332. doi:10.1037/0033-2909.124.3.308

Shiner, R. L. (2009). The development of personality disorders: Perspectives from normal personality development in childhood and adolescence. *Development and Psychopathology, 21*, 715–734. doi:http://dx.doi.org/10.1017/S0954579409000406

Shiner, R. L., Buss, K. A., McClowry, S. G., Putnam, S. P., Saudino, K. J., & Zentner, M. (2012). What is temperament now? Assessing progress in temperament research on the twenty-fifth anniversary of Goldsmith et al. *Child Development Perspectives, 6*, 436–444. doi:10.1111/j.1750-8606.2012.00254.x

Shiner, R. L., & Caspi, A. (2003). Personality differences in childhood and adolescence: Measurement, development, and consequences. *Journal of Child Psychology and Psychiatry, 44*, 2–32. doi:10.1111/1469-7610.00101

Shiner, R., & Tackett, J. L. (2014). Personality and personality disorders. In E. Mash & R. Barkley (Eds.), *Child psychopathology* (3rd ed., 848–896). New York, NY: Guilford.

Slobodskaya, H. R., & Kuznetsova, V. B. (2013). The role of reinforcement sensitivity in the development of childhood personality. *International Journal of Behavioral Development, 37*, 248–256. doi:10.1177/0165025413475895

Soto, C. J., & John, O. P. (2014). Traits in transition: The structure of parent-reported personality traits from early childhood to early adulthood. *Journal of Personality, 82*, 182–199. doi:10.1111/jopy.12044

Soto, C. J., John, O. P., Gosling, S. D., & Potter, J. (2011). Age differences in personality traits from 10 to 65: Big-Five domains and facets in a large cross-sectional sample. *Journal of Personality and Social Psychology, 100*, 330–348. doi:10.1037/a0021717

Tackett, J. L. (2006). Evaluating models of the personality-psychopathology relationship in children and adolescents. *Clinical Psychology Review, 26*, 584–599. doi:10.1016/j.cpr.2006.04.003

Tackett, J. L. (2010). Measurement and assessment of child and adolescent personality pathology: Introduction to the special issue. *Journal of Psychopathology and Behavioral Assessment, 32*, 436–466. doi:10.1007/s10862-010-9205-6

Tackett, J. L., Balsis, S., Oltmanns, T. F., & Krueger, R. F. (2009). A unifying perspective on personality pathology across the life span: Developmental considerations for the fifth edition of the *Diagnostic and Statistical Manual of Mental Disorders. Development and Psychopathology, 21*, 687–713. doi:http://dx.doi.org/10.1017/S095457940900039X

Tackett, J. L., Herzhoff, K., Balsis, S., & Cooper, L. (2014). Toward a unifying perspective on personality pathology across the lifespan. In D. Cicchetti (Ed.), *Developmental psychopathology* (3rd ed., pp. 1–40). New York, NY: Wiley.

Tackett, J. L., Herzhoff, K., Reardon, K. W., Smack, A. J., & Kushner, S. C. (2013). The relevance of informant discrepancies for the assessment of adolescent personality pathology. *Clinical Psychology: Science and Practice, 20*, 378–392. doi:10.1111/cpsp.12048

Tackett, J. L., Krueger, R. F., Iacono, W. G., & McGue, M. (2008). Personality in middle childhood: A hierarchical structure and longitudinal connections with personality in late adolescence. *Journal of Research in Personality, 42*, 1456–1462. doi:10.1016/j.jrp.2008.06.005

Tackett, J. L., Kushner, S. C., De Fruyt, F., & Mervielde, I. (2013). Delineating personality traits in childhood and adolescence: Associations across measures, temperament, and behavioral problems. *Assessment, 20*, 738–751. doi:10.1177/1073191113509686

Tackett, J. L., Kushner, S. C., Josephs, R. A., Harden, K. P., Page-Gould, E., & Tucker-Drob, E. (2014). Cortisol reactivity and recovery in the context of adolescent personality disorder. *Journal of Personality Disorders, 28*, 25–39. doi:10.1521/pedi.2014.28.1.25

Tackett, J. L., Lahey, B. B., van Hulle, C., Waldman, I., Krueger, R. F., & Rathouz, P. J. (2013). Common genetic influences on negative emotionality and a general psychopathology factor in childhood and adolescence. *Journal of Abnormal Psychology, 122*, 1142–1153. doi:10.1037/a0034151

Tackett, J. L., Silberschmidt, A., Krueger, R. F., & Sponheim, S. (2008). A dimensional model of personality disorder: Incorporating Cluster A characteristics. *Journal of Abnormal Psychology, 117*, 454–459. doi:10.1037/0021-843X.117.2.454

Tackett, J. L., Slobodskaya, H. R., Mar, R. A., Deal, J., Halverson, C. F., Baker, S. R., . . . Besevegis, E. (2012). The hierarchical structure of childhood personality in five countries: Continuity from early childhood to early adolescence. *Journal of Personality, 80,* 847–879. doi:10.1111/j.1467-6494.2011.00748.x

Van den Broeck, J., Bastiaansen, L., Rossi, G., Dierckx, E., De Clercq, B., & Hofmans, J. (2014). Hierarchical structure of maladaptive personality traits in older adults: Joint factor analysis of the PID-5 and the DAPP-BQ. *Journal of Personality Disorders, 28,* 198–211. doi:10.1521/pedi_2013_27_114

Verbeke, L., & De Clercq, B. (2014). Integrating oddity traits in a dimensional model for personality pathology precursors. *Journal of Abnormal Psychology, 123,* 598–612. doi:10.1037/a0037166

Verheul, R., Helene, A., Berghout, C. C., Dolan, C., Busschbach, J. J. V., van der Kroft, P. J. A., . . . Fonagy, P. (2008). Severity Indices of Personality Problems (SIPP-118): Development, factor structure, reliability, and validity. *Psychological Assessment, 20,* 23–34. doi:10.1037/1040-3590.20.1.23

Watson, D. (2000). *Mood and temperament.* New York, NY: Guilford

Watson, D., Clark, L. A., & Harkness, A. R. (1994). Structures of personality and their relevance to psychopathology. *Journal of Abnormal Psychology, 103,* 18–31. doi:10.1037/0021-843X.103.1.18

Westen, D., Nakash, O., Thomas, C., & Bradley, R. (2006). Clinical assessment of attachment patterns and personality disorder in adolescents and adults. *Journal of Consulting and Clinical Psychology, 74,* 1065–1085. doi:10.1037/0022-006X.74.6.1065

Widiger, T. A., De Clercq, B., & De Fruyt, F. (2009). Childhood antecedents of personality disorder: An alternative perspective. *Development and Psychopathology, 21,* 771–791. doi:http://dx.doi.org/10.1017/S095457940900042X

Widiger, T. A., & Simonsen, E. (2005). Alternative dimensional models of personality disorder: Finding a common ground. *Journal of Personality Disorders, 19,* 110–130. doi:10.1521/pedi.19.2.110.62628

Wright, A. G. C., Thomas, K. M., Hopwood, C. J., Markon, K. E., Pincus, A. L., & Krueger, R. F. (2012). The hierarchical structure of DSM-5 pathological personality traits. *Journal of Abnormal Psychology, 121,* 951–957. doi:10.1037/a0027669

9

The Prevalence, Stability, and Impact of Personality Pathology in Later Life

Preliminary Findings From the SPAN Study

THOMAS F. OLTMANNS AND STEVE BALSIS ■

Relatively little information is available regarding the trajectory of personality pathology from middle adulthood into later life. Some empirical studies have shed light on the onset and stability of personality disorders, but they have focused primarily on childhood and adolescence through young adulthood (Cohen, 2008; Morey et al., 2007; Skodol, 2008). The purpose of this chapter is to outline important issues and questions that should be addressed by studies concerned with personality pathology in older adults. We will also review briefly some important findings from the St. Louis Personality and Aging Network (SPAN) Study, a prospective investigation of personality and health that is being conducted with a representative community sample of 1,630 older adults (Oltmanns, Rodrigues, Weinstein, & Gleason, 2014).

Personality disorders represent an important mental health problem for older adults, and there is a serious need for more information in this area (Oltmanns & Balsis, 2011). This population presents a number of interesting opportunities and advantages in comparison to the study of personality pathology among adolescents and young adults. One is that general personality traits have been shown to be relatively more stable in older individuals. Several reviews of normal personality development have concluded that there is substantial evidence for a gradual *increase* in stability from late adolescence through the adult years, with "strong stability" being achieved after the age of 50 (e.g., Costa, McCrae, & Siegler, 1999; Shiner, 2005). Another important consideration with regard to older adults is that they are also entering a period in their lives when the frequency of transitions and health problems will increase. The best time to study personality and personality disorders may be during periods of significant transition because the enduring behavioral and affective expressions that define the individual and distinguish individuals from one another will be exaggerated at such times (Caspi & Moffitt, 1993; Cervone & Mischel, 2002).

Our review will focus primarily on evidence regarding personality disorders as they are defined in Section I of the *Diagnostic and Statistical Manual of Mental Disorders*, fifth edition (*DSM-5*). Of course, the *DSM-5* workgroup on personality disorders also developed an alternative dimensional model of personality pathology. Where appropriate, we will comment on dimensional models and normal-range personality traits, such as neuroticism and agreeableness, as they relate to the assessment of personality pathology in later life.

PREVIOUS STUDIES REGARDING PREVALENCE

Personality disorders are relatively common in the general population and even more frequent among clinical samples (usually people seeking treatment for other mental health problems such as depression and substance use disorders). Standard epidemiological studies tell us how many people exhibit enough symptoms of personality disorders to be considered above the arbitrary threshold required for a diagnosis. A more accurate description of the prevalence of personality pathology, however, requires evidence regarding the distribution of scores on a particular personality scale or the distribution of people who exhibit specific numbers of features of personality disorder categories.

Although the exercise is somewhat artificial, it's useful to consider briefly how many people exhibit enough symptoms of personality disorders to be considered above the *DSM-5* threshold and warrant official diagnosis. Most of the evidence on this topic is based on the use of semistructured diagnostic interviews to identify *DSM*-based personality disorders (defined by the admittedly arbitrary thresholds established in that manual). Several reviews based on data from adult participants of all ages place the median prevalence for *any type* of *DSM-IV* personality disorder at approximately 10% to 14% (Lenzenweger, 2008; Torgersen, 2009), including those who exhibit mixed features and would be considered examples of personality disorder not otherwise specified (PDNOS). Of course, the specific figures vary from study to study, depending on ways in which samples are identified as well as the assessment instruments used to identify cases.

The specific features of some types of personality disorder seem to increase in frequency as people get older (e.g., schizoid personality disorder). Other types of personality disorder decrease in frequency (e.g., antisocial and borderline personality disorder) (Engels, Duijsens, Haringsma, & van Putten, 2003; Grant et al., 2008). The latter phenomenon is sometimes described as "burnout" and implies recovery by a person who formerly exhibited symptoms of the disorder. Conclusions regarding burnout of personality disorders are based on several kinds of evidence. One type of evidence comes from follow-up studies of patients who have received treatment for personality disorders, almost always as young adults. The Collaborative Longitudinal Personality Disorders Study (CLPS) is one example of this type of study. Shea et al. (2009) followed a portion of this sample, approximately 200 patients treated for borderline personality disorder, over a period of 6 years and reported similar levels of improvement for younger patients as for older patients (though the upper age limit for participation in that study was 45). Other studies that followed treated patients were reviewed by Paris (2003). A large proportion of those patients do, in fact, show significant improvement in their condition over a period of several months. The results must be interpreted with caution, however, because the original samples all included people who were sufficiently disturbed to seek treatment, and their improvement could reflect something as simple as regression to the mean (i.e., they enter treatment at the peak of their distress and would naturally decrease without treatment).

Evidence regarding the prevalence of specific personality disorders in later life comes from *cross-sectional* comparisons of younger and older people, using *DSM*-based thresholds to decide whether or not each person qualifies for a specific personality disorder diagnosis. Unfortunately, relatively little evidence has been collected in longitudinal studies. Rather, developmental inferences are drawn on the basis of cross-sectional comparisons between younger and older participants. The evidence is not overwhelming, but several studies indicate that Cluster A disorders (paranoid and schizoid personality disorder) and Cluster C disorders (obsessive-compulsive personality disorder) are more prevalent among older people than younger people (Abrams & Horowitz, 1996). In contrast, Cluster B disorders—especially borderline personality disorder and antisocial personality disorders—are less prevalent among older people than younger people (e.g., Samuels et al., 2002). This pattern is interesting, but considerable caution must be exercised in drawing conclusions about patterns of change on the basis of this evidence. Cross-sectional studies necessarily compare people from different cohorts who grew up in different eras as well as people from age groups who are currently living in different contexts. Differences in the extent of social isolation or dependence might reflect variation in life circumstances for younger and older adults rather than true developmental changes in the prevalence of specific personality problems.

An important study, known as the National Psychiatric Morbidity Survey (Singleton, Lee, & Melzer, 2001), reported on the prevalence of psychiatric disorders in the United Kingdom. A representative sample of 8,888 adults between the ages of 16 and 74 completed initial interviews regarding symptoms of various mental disorders. Data from this study have served as the basis for interesting papers regarding comparisons between younger and older participants as well as the potential impact of transitions, such as retirement, on mental health. Evidence suggests, for example, that men experience a somewhat dramatic decline in disorders related to anxiety and depression around the age of 65, perhaps in conjunction with retirement. Women showed a peak in prevalence rates around age 50 and then showed a more gradual decline in anxiety and depression over the next 25 years (Melzer, Buxton, & Villamil, 2004).

The NPMS data set has also been used to provide estimates regarding differences in the frequency of personality disorder symptoms among people who are at various points of the life span (Coid, Yang, Tyrer, Roberts, & Ullrich, 2006; Ullrich & Coid, 2009). The personality disorder measure used during the initial interview phase was the questionnaire for the Structured Clinical Interview for DSM-IV Personality Disorders (First, Gibbon, Spitzer, Williams, & Benjamin, 1997). In a second phase of assessment, 626 participants were selected to complete a semistructured clinical interview for symptoms of psychosis and personality disorders. Prevalence rates for any personality disorder decreased across age groups: 16–34 (11.4%); 35–54 (12.3%); and 55–74 (7.4%). More detailed age comparisons regarding the prevalence of specific symptoms for each disorder, as identified in the full sample using the self-report questionnaire (not interview), were subsequently reported. Comparisons across age groups indicated increased frequency across age groups for symptoms of schizoid and obsessive-compulsive personality disorder. Conversely, the data indicated a decreased frequency across age groups for all of the other forms of personality disorder.

The tentative evidence that has been reported suggests that the prevalence of certain features of personality pathology may change over the life span. Several conceptual and methodological challenges temper our enthusiasm regarding these findings (Oltmanns & Balsis, 2011). As if the situation were not already sufficiently complex, two additional issues are also important and move us farther beyond the question of how many people "have" a personality disorder and whether that number changes as a function of age. One important topic involves how we set diagnostic thresholds. It seems reasonable to consider the possibility that, defined in terms of impact on subjective distress and social adjustment, the threshold for a specific personality disorder should vary as a function of age.

The second issue concerns age-related changes in the expression of specific symptoms of personality disorder. For example, cross-sectional comparisons of younger and older patients being treated for borderline personality disorder suggest that older patients are less likely to experience problems related to impulsivity and suicidal behavior, but symptoms related to emotional distress (depression, anxiety, and difficulty controlling anger) were more consistent across age groups (Stepp & Pilkonis, 2008). As in most other studies, the upper age limit in the Stepp and Pilkonis (2008) study was 50. A 10-year follow-up evaluation of almost 300 borderline personality disorder patients, recruited during inpatient treatment between the ages of 18 and 35, found that marked improvement in some types of symptoms was frequently accompanied by persistent problems in other areas (Zanarini et al., 2007). Major improvements were most often seen in self-mutilation and suicidal behavior. Problems managing anger, dysphoria, and interpersonal difficulties related to fears of abandonment and dependency were the most consistent symptoms of borderline personality disorder. This study suggests important issues that should be explored systematically with middle-aged and older adults.

DESIGN OF THE SPAN STUDY

The SPAN Study (St. Louis Personality and Aging Network) was designed to answer important questions about the prevalence and impact of personality pathology in later life (Oltmanns & Gleason, 2011). The first phase of this prospective cohort study focused on the identification and recruitment of participants and completion of baseline assessments. In the following section, we will describe methods used to recruit 1,630 participants and 1,484 informants from the community for a prospective study on the impact of personality disorders in midlife. Then we will report descriptive data and prevalence rates for personality disorders in our sample at baseline, as assessed by an interviewer, the participant (self-report questionnaire), and an informant identified by the participant.

Participants were recruited from the city of St. Louis and its surrounding suburban areas. With the city and adjacent county (suburbs) combined, 30% of the population is African American, and 60% is Caucasian, though only 2% is Hispanic. Approximately 7% of people living in the St. Louis area are between the ages of 55 and 64 (the age of our sample at baseline).

Potential participants were offered $60 to come to the lab for a 3-hour assessment. Details regarding our protocol for contacting, recruiting, and testing our sample of participants have been reported elsewhere (Oltmanns et al., 2014). The final baseline sample included 1,630 participants (55% female) living in the St. Louis area (40% within the city limits and 60% in the adjoining county). All participants were between the ages of 55 and 64 when they entered the study (mean = 59.6, SD = 2.7 years). With regard to race and ethnic background, 65% were Caucasian, 33% were African American, and 2% were from other groups (e.g., Asian, American Indian). Thirty people described themselves as Hispanic or Latino (just under the expected 2%). Within certain methodological constraints (e.g., limiting the sample to people who could speak and read English and people with an address and phone number so that they could be followed over time), we did everything possible to recruit a representative sample of people living in St. Louis. Our participants represented a wide range of educational and income levels. Our sample, as a whole, had slightly higher incomes than the median household income in St. Louis, which was $55,500 in 2008 according to the US Census.

Two thirds (66%) of our participants were employed either part time or full time when they came in for their baseline assessment; 9% were unemployed due to disability, and a further 4% were seeking employment. Thirty-three percent of the participants had retired from at least one profession, but some of those had subsequently taken other employment. When asked to describe their current marital status, 48% of the participants said that they were currently married, 28% divorced, 2% separated, 7% widowed, and 15% were single. We also asked participants about their marital history: among the 794 participants who had ever been divorced, 73% had been divorced only once, 21% had been divorced twice, and 6% had been divorced three to five times.

PREVALENCE OF PERSONALITY PATHOLOGY

Personality disorders were assessed using three sources of information: the semistructured diagnostic interview (the SIDP-IV; administered to all 1,630 participants), a self-report questionnaire (the MAPP; 1,608 participants), and the same questionnaire via informant-report (I-MAPP; 1,447 participants). We first discuss the prevalence of personality disorders identified by the clinical interview, and then we turn to comparisons among the three sources of data for the 1,437 participants who provided us with sufficient data to examine prevalence from all three perspectives.

According to the SIDP, 134 participants (8.2%) met criteria for at least one personality disorder, and an additional 30 participants (1.8%) qualified for a diagnosis of PDNOS. We defined PDNOS as the presence of 10 or more miscellaneous criteria across all of the personality disorders without meeting the specific threshold for a diagnosis of any one personality disorder. In Table 9.1, we present the number of males and females in the sample who qualified for each personality disorder, as well as the number who fell one criterion short. Note that these numbers are not mutually exclusive because a small number of participants (16) qualified for two or three personality disorders. None qualified for more than three personality disorders. The most frequently observed types were avoidant personality disorder (2.5%) and obsessive-compulsive personality disorder (OCPD;

Table 9.1 NUMBER OF PARTICIPANTS MEETING DIAGNOSTIC CRITERIA (AND FALLING ONE CRITERION SHORT OF A DIAGNOSIS) FOR EACH TYPE OF PERSONALITY DISORDER BASED ON THE DIAGNOSTIC INTERVIEW (SIDP-IV)

	% of Sample Meeting Criteria			% of Sample Falling One Criterion Short (Subthreshold)		
	Male ($n = 740$)	Female ($n = 890$)	Total ($n = 1,630$)	Male ($n = 740$)	Female ($n = 890$)	Total ($n = 1,630$)
Paranoid	6 (0.8%)	7 (0.8%)	13 (0.8%)	6 (0.8%)	12 (1.3%)	18 (1.1%)
Schizoid	10 (1.4%)	1 (0.1%)	11 (0.7%)	11 (1.5%)	9 (1.0%)	20 (1.2%)
Schizotypal	0	1 (0.1%)	1 (0.1%)	1 (0.1%)	0	1 (0.1%)
Antisocial	9 (1.2%)	0	9 (0.6%)	7 (0.9%)	1 (0.1%)	8 (0.5%)
Borderline	3 (0.4%)	4 (0.4%)	7 (0.4%)	2 (0.3%)	2 (0.2%)	4 (0.2%)
Histrionic	1 (0.1%)	2 (0.2%)	3 (0.2%)	2 (0.3%)	3 (0.3%)	5 (0.3%)
Narcissistic	17 (2.3%)	3 (0.3%)	20 (1.2%)	10 (1.4%)	3 (0.3%)	13 (0.8%)
Avoidant	13 (1.8%)	28 (3.1%)	41 (2.5%)	8 (1.1%)	9 (1.0%)	17 (1.0%)
Dependent	1 (0.1%)	1 (0.1%)	2 (0.1%)	3 (0.1%)	3 (0.3%)	6 (0.4%)
Obsessive-compulsive	28 (3.8%)	19 (2.1%)	47 (2.9%)	33 (2.9%)	27 (3.0%)	60 (3.7%)

2.9%). Another 3.7% of the participants fell only one criterion short of qualifying for a diagnosis of OCPD. The least frequently observed types were schizotypal personality disorder (0.1%), dependent personality disorder (0.1%), and histrionic personality disorder (0.2%).

Our next aim was to compare the diagnostic properties of the SIDP interview with the self-report and informant-report MAPP. Table 9.2 presents the correlations between each of these three measures for every specific personality disorder. Correlations were low to moderate, indicating that the SIDP, self-MAPP, and informant-MAPP identify some of the same symptoms, but they also provide unique information about individuals. The highest correlations were observed between the SIDP and the self-MAPP, and the lowest between the SIDP and the informant-MAPP. Avoidant personality disorder and borderline personality disorder showed the highest levels of concordance among the three sources of personality assessment (average correlations of .39 and .35, respectively).

Another way of reporting the prevalence of different personality disorder types is to examine the specific numbers of symptoms (diagnostic criteria) that were exhibited by participants (see Figure 9.1) according to each source of information. For the purposes of this comparison, we looked at the number of endorsed criteria for each personality disorder based on the SIDP as compared with the self-MAPP and informant-MAPP. Criteria were considered to have been endorsed if one of the top two rating points was assigned to a given criterion on any of the questionnaires. For the SIDP, this means that the interviewer deemed the trait to be "present" or "strongly present" in the participant, and for the MAPP the participant or informant said the target person was "often" or "always" like this. With the notable exception of avoidant personality disorder, we found that the informant MAPP was more liberal than the SIDP or the self-MAPP; informants endorsed the presence of more symptoms across nine personality disorder types. For schizoid and schizotypal personality disorder, the self-MAPP was also less conservative than the SIDP interview.

COMMENTS ON PREVALENCE

The participants in this study are generally representative of middle-aged adults living in the St. Louis area. Our data regarding education, income, and other demographic variables can be compared to those for the St. Louis community using publicly available census data for the city (population 257,000 16 years and over) and its suburbs (population of St. Louis county 793,000 16 years and over) between 2007 and 2011. Mean levels of education for our participants were somewhat higher than expected for the population of St. Louis. For example, only 3% of our participants had less than a high school education, while the comparable figures were 8% in the suburbs and 18% in the city. This is most likely a result of excluding potential participants who were unable to read, which was necessary in order to be sure that questionnaires were completed in a meaningful way.

Table 9.2 Correlations Between Sources of Personality Assessment for Each of the 10 Personality Disorders

	PND	SZD	SZT	ATS	BDL	HST	NAR	AVD	DEP	OCD	Average
SIDP-MAPP	.43	.35	.36	.28	.43	.34	.34	.61	.43	.35	.39
SIDP-IMAPP	.20	.22	.17	.21	.35	.20	.25	.29	.20	.19	.23
MAPP-IMAPP	.28	.24	.22	.22	.26	.22	.13	.28	.25	.19	.23
Average	.30	.27	.25	.24	.35	.25	.24	.39	.23	.24	.28

NOTE: All correlations significant at *p* < .01. These analyses are based on the 1,437 participants who provided sufficient data on the self-MAPP and informant-MAPP (i.e., no more than two questions per personality disorder were omitted).

Figure 9.1. The number of criteria endorsed according to each source of personality assessment.

Number of Criteria	Paranoid			Schizoid			Schizotypal			Antisocial			Borderline		
	Self	Inf	SIDP	Self	Inf	SIDP	Self	Inf	SIDP	Self	Inf	SIDP	Self	Inf	SIDP
0	1065	884	1234	653	684	1171	1093	952	1253	1193	1069	1385	1155	994	1235
1	242	285	139	459	405	137	228	289	149	200	239	34	225	289	142
2	79	146	34	211	186	48	69	112	24	34	79	8	35	77	39
3	31	69	17	74	95	14	26	44	9	7	31	6	10	36	11
4	11	35	11	29	44	7	13	28	1	2	15	1	7	19	4
5	6	11	2	10	15	1	5	8	1	0	4	1	4	12	3
6	3	6	0	0	7	2	2	2	0	0	0	2	0	7	2
7	0	1	0	1	1	0	0	2	0	1	0	0	1	3	1
8	n/a*	n/a	n/a	n/a	n/a	n/a	0	0	0	n/a	n/a	n/a	0	0	0
9	n/a	n/a	n/a	n/a	n/a	n/a	1	0	0	n/a	n/a	n/a	0	0	0

NOTE: These data represent the 1,437 participants who provided sufficient data on the self-MAPP and informant-MAPP (i.e., no more than two questions per personality disorder were omitted). Shaded areas indicate presence of enough symptoms to meet the *DSM-IV* threshold for the disorder. n/a (not applicable) indicates that the *DSM-IV* definition for this disorder doesn't include this many features.

Number of Criteria	Histrionic Self	Histrionic Inf	Histrionic SIDP	Narcissistic Self	Narcissistic Inf	Narcissistic SIDP	Avoidant Self	Avoidant Inf	Avoidant SIDP	Dependent Self	Dependent Inf	Dependent SIDP	Obs-Comp Self	Obs-Comp Inf	Obs-Comp SIDP
0	1065	884	1244	1010	801	1183	1195	1133	1207	1273	1158	1307	646	282	851
1	242	285	135	312	342	156	149	165	135	132	175	94	393	451	322
2	79	146	31	73	145	52	45	69	40	18	54	25	224	331	170
3	31	69	19	28	70	20	21	45	17	6	25	5	94	195	51
4	11	35	5	9	31	11	17	20	18	6	14	5	50	92	28
5	6	11	3	2	28	11	7	4	10	2	9	0	16	51	11
6	3	6	0	2	10	2	1	1	7	0	1	1	14	23	3
7	0	1	0	0	6	1	2	0	3	0	0	0	0	10	1
8	0	0	0	1	4	1	2	n/a	n/a	0	1	0	0	2	0
9	n/a	n/a	n/a	0	0	0	n/a	n/a	n/a	n/a	n/a	n/a	n/a	n/a	n/a

Figure 9.1. Continued

Because we examined three different perspectives on personality pathology (self, informant, and interviewer), our data provide unique insights regarding the prevalence of personality pathology in a representative sample of middle-aged community residents. If we focus exclusively on data provided from the semistructured interview and adopt a *DSM-IV* categorical approach to the diagnosis of personality disorders, the prevalence rates found in our sample using the SIDP-IV (10%) match fairly closely the rates that have been reported in previous community studies (Lenzenweger, Lane, Loranger, & Kessler, 2007; Trull, Jahng, Tomko, Wood, & Sher, 2010). However, while 7% of our participants met criteria for exactly one type of personality disorder, only 1% met criteria for two or three disorders. The latter percentage is much lower than has been reported previously, especially in clinical samples, where rates of comorbidity are surely inflated. The supposed high rate of comorbidity has been one of the most important criticisms of the current *DSM-IV* system for diagnosing personality disorders (Zimmerman, 2011). Our data suggest that the problem of comorbidity may be somewhat exaggerated. We also found that only 2% of the people in our sample qualified for a diagnosis of PDNOS, despite the common usage of this diagnosis in practice settings (Verheul & Widiger, 2004).

The most common personality disorder types in our sample were avoidant and obsessive-compulsive. That finding is consistent with other community studies and was expected given the age of our sample. Evidence regarding the prevalence of specific personality disorders in later life comes from cross-sectional comparisons of younger and older people, using *DSM-IV* thresholds to decide whether or not each person qualifies for a specific personality disorder diagnosis. The evidence is not overwhelming, but several studies indicate that Cluster A disorders (paranoid and schizoid personality disorder) and Cluster C disorders (obsessive-compulsive personality disorder) are more prevalent among older people than younger people (Oltmanns & Balsis, 2011). We did find that Cluster C disorders were quite common in our sample, but we also found relatively low rates of Cluster A disorders (e.g., paranoid and schizoid personality disorders).

Our interview-based prevalence rates for borderline personality disorder (0.4%) and antisocial personality disorder (0.6%) were quite low compared to many previous reports for adults of all ages. For example, Trull's (2010) reanalysis of NESARC data found prevalence rates for antisocial personality disorder of 5.7% for men and 1.9% for women, and they also found rates for borderline personality disorder of 2.4% for men and 3.0% for women. The relatively low rates of borderline personality disorder and antisocial personality disorders in our data were expected because these specific types of personality pathology are known to decrease in frequency over the life span (Paris, 2003; Shea et al., 2009).

Viewed from a dimensional perspective, however, our data on symptoms indicate that substantial numbers of people exhibit at least some symptoms of personality pathology (Table 9.3). It has not been established that the arbitrary diagnostic thresholds listed in *DSM-IV* are, in fact, valid for this age group (or perhaps for any other). Our analyses do not hinge on the identification of specific cases, narrowly defined. As this prospective study unfolds over time, we will

Table 9.3 The Variance Explained by Normal and Maladaptive Personality on a Series of Health and Social Outcomes

	Total % of Variance Explained by Normal and Maladaptive Personality Combined	% of Variance Explained by Normal-Range Traits	% of Variance Explained by Maladaptive Variants	% Shared Variance	N
PHYSICAL HEALTH/HEALTH BEHAVIOR					
Heart disease*	7	<1	5	<1	1,395[a]
Diabetes*	8	3	5	<1	1,395[a]
Cancer*	5	<1	4	<1	1,395[a]
Arthritis*	4	<1	3	<1	1,395[a]
Obesity (BMI)	10	3	4	3	909[a]
Smoking	6	1	4	1	1,286[c]
Alcohol consumption	4	1	3	<1	1,291[c]
SUBJECTIVE HEALTH (HSI)					
General health perceptions	27	6	10	11	1,276[b]
Physical functioning	20	3	10	7	1,233[b]
Pain	18	3	7	8	1,270[b]
Energy/fatigue	34	9	4	21	1,245[b]
Sleep problems	21	5	8	8	617[d]
MENTAL HEALTH (LIFETIME DIAGNOSIS)					
Major depression*	13	5	3	5	1,395[a]
Alcohol dependence	10	1	6	3	1,396[a]

(continued)

Table 9.3 CONTINUED

	Total % of Variance Explained by Normal and Maladaptive Personality Combined	% of Variance Explained by Normal-Range Traits	% of Variance Explained by Maladaptive Variants	% Shared Variance	N
Stressful Experiences					
Major events (ongoing) LTE-Q	11	2	5	4	1,125[c]
Trauma (past) TLEQ	22	3	14	5	614[d]
Social integration					
Social activity level	44	3	11	29	1,281[b]
Social support	28	4	11	13	616[d]
Loneliness (UCLA scale)	47	6	12	29	883[a]
Social network size	20	5	8	7	618[d]
Volunteering	10	3	4	3	1,384[a]

NOTE: *Binary variables analyzed using logistic regression, pseudo R-squared estimated by McFadden method.

[a]SOURCE: Baseline assessment.

[b]SOURCE: Baseline assessment and first follow-up assessment.

[c]SOURCE: First follow-up assessment.

[d]SOURCE: Fifth follow-up assessment.

evaluate the extent to which various combinations and levels of symptoms are associated with social impairment and other forms of disturbance in these people's lives. This is, of course, exactly the kind of evidence that will be needed to establish the validity of these diagnostic constructs (Kendell, 2002). Our findings up to the present time indicate that symptoms of borderline personality disorder seem to be most important in predicting various kinds of problems, including problems that involve physical health (Powers & Oltmanns, 2012), other mental disorders (Agrawal, Narayanan, & Oltmanns, 2013; Galione & Oltmanns, 2013), marital relationships (Weinstein, Gleason, & Oltmanns, 2012), and the onset of stressful life events (Gleason, Powers, & Oltmanns, 2012). This is perhaps somewhat surprising in light of the fact that relatively few people in the study showed enough symptoms of borderline personality disorder to meet a full diagnosis for that disorder, suggesting that these effects must hold for people who exhibit subthreshold levels of symptoms.

The pattern of correlations among different sources of information—interview, self, and informant—provide further confirmation that different assessment methods provide complementary data that are not redundant. The correlations are all statistically significant, suggesting a modest level of agreement with regard to the expression of various kinds of personality pathology. They also indicate, however, that none of these sources provides an image that is necessarily superior to the others. Some proponents of self-report measures have argued that, to whatever extent informants disagree with the self, it is because they are wrong. We would point out that there is now considerable reason to believe that, in certain circumstances and especially with regard to certain kinds of personality traits, informants may know us better than we know ourselves (Vazire & Carlson, 2011). Informants seem to provide particularly useful information with regard to observable, evaluative traits such as those that are characteristic of the more dramatic personality disorders, including borderline personality disorder and antisocial personality disorder (Carlson, Vazire, & Oltmanns, 2013). To whatever extent prevalence estimates are based exclusively on the use of self-report questionnaires or diagnostic interviews, the evidence is almost surely incomplete.

The SIDP semistructured diagnostic interview was fairly consistently the most conservative measure in comparison to self- and informant reports (see Table 9.3). For most disorders and across all levels of severity, informants identified more people who exhibited characteristics of personality pathology. This could mean that informants are overreporting, but it also might suggest that they are more accurate. Another article from our research group used item response theory analyses to examine the psychometric properties of item endorsements by self and others for narcissistic personality disorder and found that informants reported higher raw scores relative to selves at lower levels of pathology (Cooper, Balsis, & Oltmanns, 2012). The discrepancy between self- and informant reports increased with the narcissistic personality disorder (NPD) scale. Informants also reported NPD features that participants themselves often did not. The suggestion seems to be that informants are more sensitive to low levels of personality pathology.

CONNECTING PERSONALITY DISORDERS
TO REAL-LIFE OUTCOMES

Substantial evidence suggests that personality disorders are extremely important in terms of their impact on people's lives. They disrupt interpersonal relationships (Whisman, Tolejko, & Chatav, 2007), interfere with the treatment of other types of mental disorder (Fournier et al., 2008), and contribute to a variety of physical health problems (Frankenburg & Zanarini, 2004). Nevertheless, personality disorders are controversial topics, in large part because of fundamental issues regarding their measurement. Findings from the baseline phase of our study indicate that, in a representative community sample of middle-aged participants, symptoms of personality disorders are evident in varying numbers depending on the source of information that is considered. The validity of these different measurement procedures and the utility of specific diagnostic thresholds will continue to be an important topic of investigation as this prospective study unfolds and further information is collected regarding the health and social adjustment of our participants.

In Phase I of the SPAN Study, we used the *MAPP* questionnaire (Oltmanns & Turkheimer, 2006) and the SIDP-IV interview to measure personality pathology. Items in the *MAPP* and the SIDP-IV correspond to the diagnostic criteria for each type of personality disorder listed in *DSM-IV*. Many are straightforward examples of maladaptive personality traits. Consider, for example, items associated with borderline personality disorder. They include (1) impulsivity in at least two areas that are potentially self-damaging, (2) affective instability, and (3) inappropriate, intense anger. Empirical studies that have compared the *DSM-IV* definition of borderline personality disorder with trait-based definitions of borderline personality disorder find that they are actually quite similar (Hopwood, Thomas, Markon, Wright, & Krueger, 2012; Mullins-Sweatt, Bernstein, & Widiger, 2012).

Findings from Phase I of the SPAN study indicate that personality pathology accounts for additional variance in health behaviors, subjective ratings of health, the presence of specific diseases, the frequency of stressful life events, and levels of social integration that are not explained by normal-range five-factor model (FFM) measures (e.g., the *NEO-PI-R*). The proportion of variance explained by personality variables is substantial. And for almost every outcome variable, measures of maladaptive variants account for more variance than measures of normal-range personality traits (Gleason et al., 2014). Several things are clear from these findings, including the need to assess personality broadly, across multiple measurement models, using different forms of reporting. The need is clear in terms of the unique predictive validity of each method, but also because evidence suggests that the mechanisms responsible for the personality–health relationship differ across reporting method (Lodi-Smith et al., 2010).

We have published several papers from this study since it was launched in 2007. Here we highlight briefly findings from a few of those papers, that is, those that are most directly related to physical health and stressful life events. Using cross-sectional data from our baseline assessment, one paper reported that features of borderline, antisocial, and schizoid personality disorders showed a negative association with self-perception of health, even after controlling for objective health indicators (Powers & Oltmanns, 2013b). Another paper extended these analyses to include follow-up data. Features of personality pathology predicted worse physical functioning (e.g., fatigue, pain) and increased health care utilization at 6-month follow-up (Powers & Oltmanns, 2012). A third paper on this topic reported that the relation between features of borderline personality disorder and medical disorders (e.g., diabetes) was mediated by obesity (Powers & Oltmanns, 2013a).

Other papers from our lab have been concerned with personality and stressful life events, which clearly have an impact on health (Miller, Chen, & Parker, 2011). One paper examined the link between personality at baseline and major life events measured 6 months later (Gleason et al., 2012). A telephone interview was employed if the participant reported any events on the self-report questionnaire. This process is extremely important because of problems with the validity of checklists for identifying major life events (Harkness & Monroe, 2016). Neuroticism and symptoms of borderline personality disorder predicted increased report of negative life events, using interviewer-adjusted reports of negative life events. Additional papers on this topic have reported that features of borderline personality disorder predict dependent (but not independent) life events (Conway, Boudreaux, & Oltmanns, in press; Powers, Gleason, & Oltmanns, 2013).

ANALYZING CHANGE

We have also examined changes in personality between Time 1 and Time 2 (2.5 years) using simple difference scores for 836 participants (Cooper, Balsis, & Oltmanns, 2014). We did find evidence of change in personality over time for both normal and maladaptive personality traits. Consistent with self-report data in this literature, trends point to maturing of personality with age, but informants report the opposite pattern of development. In other words, informants indicate that personality declines in a less "mature" manner, and maladaptive traits intensify.

Normal personality traits and personality disorder symptoms were assessed via self- and informant report at two time points approximately 2.5 years apart ($M = 2.59$, $SD = .20$). To be included in these analyses, SPAN participants were required to have Time 1 and Time 2 data for one standard measure of personality disorders, the Structured Interview for DSM-IV Personality (SIDP-IV; Pfohl, Blum, & Zimmerman, 1997), as well as Time 1 and Time 2 self- and informant-reported data for the MAPP and the Revised NEO Personality Inventory (NEO PI-R; Costa & McCrae, 1992).

As revealed by the results of our repeated measures t-tests, participants' total SIDP-IV scores decreased significantly over time, $t(835) = -10.72$, $p < .001$, by a mean of 3.14 response option points. Furthermore, 8 of the 10 scores for individual personality disorder types decreased significantly over time. Only schizoid personality disorder, which trended toward a significant increase over time, $t(835) = 1.65$, $p = .10$, and schizotypal personality disorder, which was nonsignificant (i.e., stable over time), did not decrease over time. This finding in part confirmed our first hypothesis—that personality disorder symptoms measured by a standard semistructured interview would decrease over time for many types of disorder.

The MAPP total score revealed a significant interaction effect, $F(1, 1092) = 7.59$, $p < .01$, such that self-reports decreased and informant reports slightly increased over time. We also found significant interactions for 5 of the 10 individual personality disorder types: antisocial, borderline, histrionic, avoidant, and dependent. For four of the five significant interactions (all but histrionic), self-reports slightly decreased and informant reports slightly increased or remained stable over time. For the histrionic personality disorder type, both selves and informants reported a decrease over time. The remaining five interactions were nonsignificant. The MAPP total score interaction confirmed our first hypothesis, that some self-reported personality disorder types would decrease with time, but disconfirmed our second hypothesis, that informant-reported personality disorder types would also decrease over time.

Four of the five personality domains from the NEO-PI-R (neuroticism, extraversion, agreeableness, and conscientiousness) showed a significant interaction effect. For neuroticism, selves reported a decrease and informants reported a slight increase over time, $F(1, 1098) = 22.65$, $p < .001$; for extraversion, selves reported a slight increase and informants reported a decrease over time, $F(1, 1098) = 19.30$, $p < .001$; for agreeableness, selves reported an increase and informants reported a decrease over time, $F(1, 1098) = 21.05$, $p < .001$; and for conscientiousness, selves reported an increase and informants reported a decrease over time, $F(1, 1098) = 48.51$, $p < .001$. Only the openness factor did not have a significant interaction effect. These results parallel the MAPP findings in that selves reported that they were getting "better" (i.e., more emotionally stable, agreeable, and conscientious) over time, while informants reported that the selves were getting "worse" (i.e., less extraverted, conscientious, and agreeable) over time.

The purpose of these analyses was to examine the longitudinal course of personality disorder dimensions and personality traits in community-dwelling adults from the perspectives of selves and their self-selected informants. This paper was the first to examine symptoms of personality disorders longitudinally in a community–based sample of adults nearing later life, and it was also the first to study personality disorders longitudinally in adulthood from the perspective of informants. A review of the literature led us to hypothesize that selves would report a decrease in personality disorder symptoms and an increase in positive personality traits over time. Lacking any precedent to suggest otherwise, we assumed that informant-reported personality disorder symptoms would follow the same trend. For informant-reported levels of normal-range personality traits, two previous studies with young adults led us to expect that informants might report a general worsening of personality traits over time. Consistent with our hypothesis as well as previous longitudinal research, selves often reported mean-level decreases in personality disorder features over time. This trend was consistent across the

SIDP-IV and MAPP data. Informant-reported data, however, often trended toward an increase of personality disorder symptoms and prototype scores over time. The informant-reported trajectories offer a different perspective than the common conclusion that mean levels of personality disorder features tend to decrease over time.

For normal personality traits, our self-reported results parallel the findings of Roberts, Walton, and Viechtbauer (2006), with mean-levels of emotional stability (the converse of neuroticism), agreeableness, and conscientiousness all increasing slightly over time. From the informants' perspective, however, extraversion, agreeableness, and conscientiousness each decreased over time. Similar to the personality disorder symptoms, therefore, the mean-level trajectory of many normal personality traits depends on which source (self or informant) one asks. The FFM results were also noteworthy because selves generally reported improvements in normal personality, similar to their reported improvements in personality disorder symptoms, while informants reported the opposite trends for both normal personality traits and personality disorder symptoms.

Our results lend some support to the general conclusion reached by Samuel et al. (2011) that the mean level of stability and change for personality disorders depends in part on the method of assessment used (i.e., diagnostic interview versus self-report questionnaire). In Samuel et al., their self-report personality disorder questionnaire was more stable than their diagnostic interview-based assessment. In our analyses, 8 of the 10 personality disorders as assessed via the SIDP-IV significantly decreased over time, whereas only 5 of the 10 personality disorders assessed via the self-report MAPP significantly decreased over time. Therefore, our self-report measure yielded a greater number of stable personality disorder dimensions than our diagnostic interview. Our results extend the findings of Samuel et al. (2011) by showing that the stability of features of personality disorders also depends on the source that one employs. Specifically, while selves often reported mean-level decreases in personality disorder symptoms over time, informants often reported increases in personality disorder symptoms over time.

Although we found many significant changes and interactions over time, the effect sizes for the interactions were very small—on the order of .01 (partial eta squared). On the MAPP, for example, the overall self-reported decrease of personality disorder traits over time was about three points on a scale that ranges from 0 to 320. This corresponds to less than one *DSM-5* personality disorder diagnostic criterion decrease per 3 years. On the SIDP-IV, the total score decreased 3.14 response option points over about 2.5 years, which corresponds to about one diagnostic criterion every 3 years. Compared to (Lenzenweger, Johnson, & Willett, 2004), who estimated that the personality disorders decrease at a mean-level rate of about 1.4 diagnostic criteria per year, the current study's change is relatively small. We believe that the ages of the participants could be a determining factor in the rate of change of personality disorder symptoms. The findings from Lenzenweger et al. were from a sample of college-aged adults. It is possible that our lower rate of change reflects a general solidification of personality in older adulthood (Roberts & DelVecchio, 2000) relative to younger adulthood. Personality disorder dimensions, along with personality traits, may change less over time in older adulthood relative to younger adults.

From a developmental psychopathology standpoint, the beginning of later life is not without its challenges. As stated earlier in the chapter, individuals in this phase of their lives are faced with many difficult transitions, including declines in physical health and mental capacities, and changing social roles (e.g., retirement, the "empty nest," and grandparenthood); they begin to face their own mortality, as well as the deaths of their parents and friends. We also know that, as individuals age, self-reported personality disorder symptoms are likely to remit (based on average profiles); self-reported normal-range personality traits generally improve; and self-reported positive affect increases, while negative affect decreases (Mroczek & Kolarz, 1998). From the perspective of selves, therefore, it seems that most adults handle the transition to later life well. For those who do not, however, these new life challenges may lead to the onset or exacerbation of psychopathology.

One interpretation of our data is that informant reports might be more likely than self-reports to identify those people who do experience an increase in various kinds of personality problems during this stage of the life span. In a previous analysis of data from this project, we reported that informants tend to report features of narcissistic personality disorder at lower levels of the latent trait of narcissism than selves are able or willing to report (Cooper, Balsis, & Oltmanns, 2012). The same pattern holds features of borderline personality pathology (Balsis, Loehle-Conger, Busch, Ungredda, & Oltmanns, 2018). Perhaps enhanced sensitivity to absolute levels of maladaptive personality traits would also translate into an improved ability to detect and report *changes* in traits that are associated with social impairment. Informants who are well acquainted with the participant might be quicker than the self to report the appearance or exacerbation of various negative personality characteristics. Most of the people in our large sample of middle-aged adults probably did not experience substantial changes in personality over this 2.5-year follow-up. Some probably did show positive changes, while others showed negative changes. Our overall pattern of changes in mean scores may indicate that informant reports are more likely than self-reports to identify those people whose personality problems did increase over time.

Why would informants be more likely than the self to detect and report negative personality changes? We don't know. From the perspective of social cognition, this pattern provides one more intriguing example of actor observer asymmetries in interpersonal perception (Malle, Knobe, & Nelson, 2007). The self and others are continuously engaged in the observation of a participant's interpersonal behaviors. Some of those events are interpreted as reflecting meaningful dispositions, and some are not. The literature on social cognition suggests that there are important differences between the self and others in terms of complex processes that govern inferences regarding the person's intentions, motives, and beliefs as well as the consistency with which changes in behavior might be expected to be maintained.

From the perspective of contemporary personality theory, our findings extend the consideration of self-other knowledge asymmetries, that is, who knows what about a person? Vazire (2010) found that internal states are better predicted by self-reports while ego-involved traits such as intelligence are better predicted by informant reports. Perhaps certain personality disorder features are more accurately assessed via self-reports, while others are more accurately assessed via informant reports (Cundiff, Smith, & Frandsen, 2012; Smith et al., 2008; Vazire & Carlson, 2011). Future research is needed to determine which source is more accurate in assessing which features of personality disorders. Perhaps "accuracy," though, is not as important as the ability of each source to predict outcomes, such as health and functional impairment. Most likely, self-reports are a better predictor for some variables, whereas informant reports are a better predictor for other variables (Oltmanns & Turkheimer, 2006).

One important limitation of the present findings is, in fact, that we were only able to consider personality data collected at two points in time. If we had three or more assessments, we would be able to use multilevel models to test whether personality pathology improves or deteriorates and whether this change occurs linearly or quadratically. In addition, these models would allow us to explore whether trajectories vary systematically between persons. As our longitudinal study progresses over time, we will take advantage of these more sophisticated analytic procedures.

CONCLUSIONS

Substantial evidence suggests that personality disorders are extremely important in terms of their impact on people's lives. They disrupt interpersonal relationships (Whisman et al., 2007), interfere with the treatment of other types of mental disorder (Fournier et al., 2008), and contribute to a variety of physical health problems (Frankenburg & Zanarini, 2008). Nevertheless, personality disorders are controversial topics, in large part because of fundamental issues regarding their measurement. Findings from the baseline phase of our study indicate that, in a representative community sample of middle-aged participants, symptoms of personality disorders are evident in varying numbers depending on the source of information that is considered.

For example, whereas previous research has suggested that personality disorder dimensions and personality traits generally improve over time, our results from the current study both supported and questioned this conclusion. With self-reported data, we observed the mean-level personality disorder decreases and personality trait increases that were consistent with previous research. With informant-reported data, however, the results often revealed a trend in the opposite direction, with personality disorder dimensions increasing and positive personality traits decreasing. In short, selves and informants sometimes provide contradictory perspectives on the trajectory of personality disorder symptoms and normal personality traits. Although there were interesting trends among the trajectories over time, the magnitude of the mean-level changes was small. The findings presented here probably raise more questions than they answer. Should we rely on selves or informants when analyzing personality disorder dimensions and personality traits? Which perspective is more useful in predicting outcomes? Why do the two perspectives reveal different trends? Is our current understanding about personality disorder change limited by reliance on self-reported data? Do these findings replicate in other age groups? We hope that this research promotes inquiry into these important questions.

REFERENCES

Abrams, R. C., & Horowitz, S. V. (1996). Personality disorders after age 50. In E. Rosowsky (Ed.), *Personality disorders in older adults* (271–281). Mahwah, NJ: Lawrence Erlbaum.

Agrawal, A., Narayanan, G., & Oltmanns, T. F. (2013). Personality pathology and alcohol dependence at midlife in a community sample. *Personality Disorders—Theory Research and Treatment, 4*(1), 55–61. doi:10.1037/a0030224

Balsis, S., Loehle-Conger, E., Busch, A. J., Ungredda, T., & Oltmanns, T. F. (2018). Self and informant report across the borderline personality disorder spectrum. *Personality Disorders: Theory, Research, and Treatment, 9*(5), 429–436.

Carlson, E. N., Vazire, S., & Oltmanns, T. F. (2013). Self-other knowledge asymmetries in personality pathology. *Journal of Personality, 81*(2), 155–170. doi:10.1111/j.1467-6494.2012.00794.x

Caspi, A., & Moffitt, T. E. (1993). When do individual differences matter? A paradoxial theory of personality coherence. *Psychological Inquiry, 4*, 247–271.

Cervone, D., & Mischel, W. (2002). Personality science. *Advances in Personality Science*, 1–26.

Cohen, P. (2008). Child development and personality disorder. *Psychiatric Clinics of North America, 31*(3), 477–493. doi:10.1016/j.psc.2008.03.005

Coid, J., Yang, M., Tyrer, P., Roberts, A., & Ullrich, S. (2006). Prevalence and correlates of personality disorder in Great Britain. *British Journal of Psychiatry, 188*, 423–431. doi:10.1192/bjp.188.5.423

Conway, C. C., Boudreaux, M., & Oltmanns, T. F. (in press). Dynamic associations between borderline personality disorder and stressful life events over five years in older adults. *Personality Disorders: Theory, Research, and Treatment.*

Cooper, L. D., Balsis, S., & Oltmanns, T. F. (2012). Self- and informant-reported perspectives on symptoms of narcissistic personality disorder. *Personality Disorders—Theory, Research, and Treatment, 3*(2), 140–154. doi:10.1037/A0026576

Cooper, L. D., Balsis, S., & Oltmanns, T. F. (2014). A longitudinal analysis of personality disorder dimensions and personality traits in a community sample of older adults: Perspectives from selves and informants. *Journal of Personality Disorders, 28*(1), 151–165.

Costa, P. T., Jr., & McCrae, R. R. (1992). *Professional manual: Revised NEO Personaltiy Inventory and NEO Five-Factor Inventory.* Odessa, FL: PAR, Inc.

Costa, P. T., Jr., McCrae, R. R., & Siegler, I. C. (1999). Continuity and change over the adult life cycle: Personality and personality disorders. In C. R. Cloninger (Ed.), *Personality and psychopathology* (pp. 129–154). Washington, DC: American Psychiatric Press.

Cundiff, J. M., Smith, T. W., & Frandsen, C. A. (2012). Incremental validity of spouse ratings versus self-reports of personality as predictors of marital quality and behavior during marital conflict. *Psychological Assessment, 24*(3), 676–684. doi:10.1037/a0026637

Engels, G. I., Duijsens, I. J., Haringsma, R., & van Putten, C. M. (2003). Personality disorders in the elderly compared to four younger age groups: A cross-sectional study of community residents and mental health patients. *Journal of Personality Disorders, 17*(5), 447–459. doi:10.1521/pedi.17.5.447.22971

First, M. B., Gibbon, M., Spitzer, R. L., Williams, J. B. W., & Benjamin, L. S. (1997). *Structured Clinical Interview for DSM-IV Axis II Personality Disorders (SCID-II)*. Washington, DC: American Psychiatric Press.

Fournier, J. C., DeRubeis, R. J., Shelton, R. C., Gallop, R., Amsterdam, J. D., & Hollon, S. D. (2008). Antidepressant medications v. cognitive therapy in people with depression with or without personality disorder. *British Journal of Psychiatry, 192*(2), 124–129. doi:10.1192/bjp.bp.107.037234

Frankenburg, F. R., & Zanarini, M. C. (2004). The association between borderline personality disorder and chronic medical illnesses, poor health-related lifestyle choices, and costly forms of health care utilization. *Journal of Clinical Psychiatry, 65*(12), 1660–1665.

Galione, J. N., & Oltmanns, T. F. (2013). The relationship between borderline personality disorder and major depression in later life: Acute versus temperamental symptoms. *American Journal of Geriatric Psychiatry, 21*(8), 747–756. doi:10.1016/j.jagp.2013.01.026

Gleason, M. E. J., Powers, A. D., & Oltmanns, T. F. (2012). The enduring impact of borderline personality pathology: Risk for threatening life events in later middle-age. *Journal of Abnormal Psychology, 121*(2), 447–457. doi:10.1037/A0025564

Grant, B. F., Chou, S. P., Goldstein, R. B., Huang, B., Stinson, F. S., Saha, T. D., . . . Ruan, W. J. (2008). Prevalence, correlates, disability, and comorbidity of DSM-IV borderline personality disorder: Results from the Wave 2 National Epidemiologic Survey on Alcohol and Related Conditions. *Journal of Clinical Psychiatry, 69*(4), 533–545.

Harkness, K. L., & Monroe, S. M. (2016). The assessment and measurement of adult life stress: Basic premises, operational principles, and design requirements. *Journal of Abnormal Psychology, 125*(5), 727–745.

Hopwood, C. J., Thomas, K. M., Markon, K. E., Wright, A. G. C., & Krueger, R. F. (2012). DSM-5 personality traits and DSM-IV personality disorders. *Journal of Abnormal Psychology, 121*(2), 424–432. doi:10.1037/A0026656

Kendell, R. E. (2002). The distinction between personality disorder and mental illness. *British Journal of Psychiatry, 180*, 110–115. doi:10.1192/bjp.180.2.110

Lenzenweger, M. F. (2008). Epidemiology of personality disorders. *Psychiatric Clinics of North America, 31*(3), 395–403. doi:10.1016/j.psc.2008.03.003

Lenzenweger, M. F., Johnson, M. D., & Willett, J. B. (2004). Individual growth curve analysis illuminates stability and change in personality disorder features—The longitudinal study of personality disorders. *Archives of General Psychiatry, 61*(10), 1015–1024. doi:10.1001/archpsyc.61.10.1015

Lenzenweger, M. F., Lane, M. C., Loranger, A. W., & Kessler, R. C. (2007). DSM-IV personality disorders in the National Comorbidity Survey Replication. *Biological Psychiatry, 62*(6), 553–564. doi:10.1016/j.biopsych.2006.09.019

Lodi-Smith, J., Jackson, J., Bogg, T., Walton, K., Wood, D., Harms, P., & Roberts, B. W. (2010). Mechanisms of health: Education and health-related behaviours partially mediate the relationship between conscientiousness and self-reported physical health. *Psychology & Health, 25*(3), 305–319. doi:Pii 909137670 10.1080/08870440902736964

Malle, B. F., Knobe, J. A., & Nelson, S. E. (2007). Actor-observer asymmetries in explanations of behavior: New answers to an old question. *Journal of Personality and Social Psychology, 93*(4), 491–514. doi:10.1037/0022-3514.93.4.491

Melzer, D., Buxton, J., & Villamil, E. (2004). Decline in common mental disorder prevalence in men during the sixth decade of life. Evidence from the National Psychiatric

Morbidity Survey. *Social Psychiatry and Psychiatric Epidemiology*, *39*(1), 33–38. doi:10.1007/s00127-004-0704-1

Miller, G. E., Chen, E., & Parker, K. J. (2011). Psychological stress in childhood and susceptibility to the chronic diseases of aging: Moving toward a model of behavioral and biological mechanisms. *Psychological Bulletin*, *137*(6), 959–997. doi:10.1037/a0024768

Morey, L. C., Hopwood, C. J., Gunderson, J. G., Skodol, A. E., Shea, M. T., Yen, S., . . . McGlashan, T. H. (2007). Comparison of alternative models for personality disorders. *Psychological Medicine*, *37*(7), 983–994. doi:10.1017/S0033291706009482

Mroczek, D. K., & Kolarz, C. M. (1998). The effect of age on positive and negative affect: A developmental perspective on happiness. *Journal of Personality and Social Psychology*, *75*(5), 1333–1349. doi:10.1037/0022-3514.75.5.1333

Mullins-Sweatt, S. N., Bernstein, D. P., & Widiger, T. A. (2012). Retention or deletion of personality disorder diagnoses for DSM-5: An expert consensus approach. *Journal of Personality Disorders*, *26*(5), 689–703.

Oltmanns, T. F., & Balsis, S. (2011). Personality disorders in later life: Questions about the measurement, course, and impact of disorders. *Annual Review of Clinical Psychology*, *7*, 321–349. doi:10.1146/annurev-clinpsy-090310-120435

Oltmanns, T. F., & Gleason, M. E. J. (2011). Personality, health, and social adjustment in later life. In L. B. Cottler (Ed.), *Mental health in public health: The next 100 years* (pp. 151–179). New York, NY: Oxford University Press.

Oltmanns, T. F., Rodrigues, M. M., Weinstein, Y., & Gleason, M. E. J. (2014). Prevalence of personality disorders at midlife in a community sample: Disorders and symptoms reflected in interview, self, and informant reports. *Journal of Psychopathology and Behavioral Assessment*, *36*(2), 177–188. doi:10.1007/s10862-013-9389-7

Oltmanns, T. F., & Turkheimer, E. (2006). Perceptions of self and others regarding pathological personality traits. In R. F. Krueger & J. L. Tackett (Eds.), *Personality and psychopathology* (pp. 71–111). New York, NY: Guilford.

Paris, J. (2003). Personality disorders over time: Precursors, course and outcome. *Journal of Personality Disorders*, *17*(6), 479–488. doi:10.1521/pedi.17.6.479.25360

Pfohl, B., Blum, N., & Zimmerman, M. (1997). *Structured Interview for DSM-IV Personality*. Washington, DC: American Psychiatric Press.

Powers, A. D., Gleason, M. E. J., & Oltmanns, T. F. (2013). Symptoms of borderline personality disorder predict interpersonal (but not independent) stressful life events in a community sample of older adults. *Journal of Abnormal Psychology*, *122*(2), 469–474. doi:10.1037/a0032363

Powers, A. D., & Oltmanns, T. F. (2012). Personality disorders and physical health: A longitudinal examination of physical functioning, healthcare utilization, and health-related behaviors in middle-aged adults. *Journal of Personality Disorders*, *26*(4), 524–538.

Powers, A. D., & Oltmanns, T. F. (2013a). Borderline personality pathology and chronic health problems in later adulthood: The mediating role of obesity. *Personality Disorders—Theory, Research, and Treatment*, *4*(2), 152–159. doi:10.1037/a0028709

Powers, A. D., & Oltmanns, T. F. (2013b). Personality pathology as a risk factor for negative health perception. *Journal of Personality Disorders*, *27*(3), 359–370.

Roberts, B. W., & DelVecchio, W. F. (2000). The rank-order consistency of personality traits from childhood to old age: A quantitative review of longitudinal studies. *Psychological Bulletin*, *126*(1), 3–25.

Roberts, B. W., Walton, K. E., & Viechtbauer, W. (2006). Patterns of mean-level change in personality traits across the life course: A meta-analysis of longitudinal studies. *Psychological Bulletin, 132*(1), 1–25. doi:10.1037/0033-2909.132.1.1

Samuel, D. B., Hopwood, C. J., Ansell, E. B., Morey, L. C., Sanislow, C., Markowitz, J. C., . . . Grilo, C. M. (2011). Comparing the temporal stability of self-report and interview assessed personality disorder. *Journal of Abnormal Psychology, 120*(3), 670–680. doi:10.1037/a0022647

Samuels, J. F., Eaton, W. W., Bienvenu, O. J., Brown, C. H., Costa, P. T., Jr., & Nestadt, G. (2002). Prevalence and correlates of personality disorders in a community sample. *British Journal of Psychiatry, 180*(6), 536–542. doi:10.1192/bjp.180.6.536

Shea, M. T., Edelen, M. O., Pinto, A., Yen, S., Gunderson, J. G., Skodol, A. E., . . . Morey, L. C. (2009). Improvement in borderline personality disorder in relationship to age. *Acta Psychiatrica Scandinavica, 119*(2), 143–148.

Shiner, R. L. (2005). A developmental perspective on personality disorders: Lessons from research on normal personality development in childhood and adolescence. *Journal of Personality Disorders, 19*(2), 202–210. doi:10.1521/pedi.19.2.202.62630

Singleton, N., Lee, A., & Melzer, H. (2001). *Psychiatric morbidity among adults living in private households.* doi:10.1080/0954026021000045967. Retrieved from www.statistics.gov.uk.

Skodol, A. E. (2008). Longitudinal course and outcome of personality disorders. *Psychiatric Clinics of North America, 31*(3), 495–503. doi:10.1016/j.psc.2008.03.010

Smith, T. W., Uchino, B. N., Berg, C. A., Florsheim, P., Pearce, G., Hawkins, M., . . . Yoon, H. C. (2008). Associations of self-reports versus spouse ratings of negative affectivity, dominance, and affiliation with coronary artery disease: Where should we look and who should we ask when studying personality and health? *Health Psychology, 27*(6), 676–684. doi:10.1037/0278-6133.27.6.676

Stepp, S. D., & Pilkonis, P. A. (2008). Age-related differences in individual DSM criteria for borderline personality disorder. *Journal of Personality Disorders, 22*(4), 427–432. doi:10.1521/pedi.2008.22.4.427

Torgersen, S. (2009). The nature (and nurture) of personality disorders. *Scandinavian Journal of Psychology, 50*(6), 624–632. doi:10.1111/j.1467-9450.2009.00788.x

Trull, T. J., Jahng, S., Tomko, R. L., Wood, P. K., & Sher, K. J. (2010). Revised Nesarc personality disorder diagnoses: Gender, prevalence, and comorbidity with substance dependence disorders. *Journal of Personality Disorders, 24*(4), 412–426.

Ullrich, S., & Coid, J. (2009). The age distribution of self-reported personality disorder traits in a household population. *Journal of Personality Disorders, 23*(2), 187–200.

Vazire, S. (2010). Who knows what about a person? The Self-Other Knowledge Asymmetry (SOKA) model. *Journal of Personality and Social Psychology, 98*(2), 281–300. doi:10.1037/A0017908

Vazire, S., & Carlson, E. N. (2011). Others sometimes know us better than we know ourselves. *Current Directions in Psychological Science, 20*(2), 104–108. doi:10.1177/0963721411402478

Verheul, R., & Widiger, T. A. (2004). A meta-analysis of the prevalence and usage of the personality disorder not otherwise specified (PDNOS) diagnosis. *Journal of Personality Disorders, 18*(4), 309–319. doi:10.1521/pedi.2004.18.4.309

Weinstein, Y., Gleason, M. E. J., & Oltmanns, T. F. (2012). Borderline but not antisocial personality disorder symptoms are related to self-reported partner aggression in late middle-age. *Journal of Abnormal Psychology, 121*(3), 692–698. doi:10.1037/a0028994

Whisman, M. A., Tolejko, N., & Chatav, Y. (2007). Social consequences of personality disorders: Probability and timing of marriage and probability of marital disruption. *Journal of Personality Disorders, 21*(6), 690–695. doi:10.1521/pedi.2007.21.6.690

Zanarini, M. C., Frankenburg, F. R., Reich, D. B., Silk, K. R., Hudson, J. I., & McSweeney, L. B. (2007). The subsyndromal phenomenology of borderline personality disorder: A 10-year follow-up study. *American Journal of Psychiatry, 164*(6), 929–935. doi:10.1176/appi.ajp.164.6.929

Zimmerman, M. (2011). A critique of the proposed prototype rating system for personality disorders in DSM-5. *Journal of Personality Disorders, 25*(2), 206–221. doi:10.1037/a0022108.

Biological Bases of Personality

10

Personality as Adaptation

Perspectives From Nonhuman Primates

JOHN P. CAPITANIO AND WILLIAM A. MASON ■

In this chapter, we examine personality in animals, with a focus on nonhuman primates. Our premise is that personality is a biological phenomenon, an emergent property of the central nervous system reflecting the organization within the individual of some fundamental psychological processes, such as approach/avoidance, activity/passivity, and social attraction/intolerance. We see personality as a dynamic, whole-organism phenomenon that is influenced by phylogeny, ecology, personal history, and developmental experience. At a fundamental level, personality is about adaptation: It describes how individuals interact with their world, and it permits prediction by others. In this view, personality can be disorganized and maladaptive to the individual's current situation; that is, there can be a poor fit between the individual's characteristics and the environment in which those characteristics are expressed. It is from this view that we suggest that a broader perspective on personality might have value in thinking about personality disorders in humans.

We begin by first describing two scenarios, which we will use to provide an overview of our approach to animal personality, and which also provide an opportunity to describe how personality is measured in nonhumans. We structure our overview by making four points.

> Scenario 1: Two adult male primates meet each other for the first time in an empty enclosure. The two eye each other warily and walk around each other for a few minutes. One of them looks at the other animal and flashes his eyebrows, and the second animal makes a facial expression that looks like a smile. The first animal smacks his lips together, mounts the second animal, and then both crouch on the ground, where the first animal begins to groom the second.

Scenario 2: Two adult male primates meet each other for the first time in an empty enclosure. The two males immediately begin to fight. Eventually one animal wins the series of encounters, but the second animal, though he repeatedly withdraws, continues to get chased every few minutes. Eventually the loser begins screaming, which is unusual behavior for an adult male. The next day, the loser is found huddled in the corner, refusing to eat.

Our first point is that variation in personality of animals can be described using many of the same terms that are used to describe human differences in personality. For example, if someone were asked to describe the characteristics of the individuals in the scenarios just described, one might use words like friendly, hostile, cautious, warm, sociable, and fearful. This seems natural to humans; we often describe dogs as friendly or bold, lions as fierce, cats as aloof, and so on. These descriptions can be used to generate quantifiable measures of personality, however. If our hypothetical person observed these individuals over a period of time and in a variety of situations, she might not only add other words to the list of descriptors (bold, vigilant, timid) but also adverbs, such as frequently, rarely, extremely, and occasionally. These adverbs can be easily converted to a Likert scale, resulting in an inventory that is able to quantify aspects of the individuals' personality (of course, there are other important issues, such as reliability and validity that must be addressed to avoid the specter of anthropomorphism). In 1938, Meredith P. Crawford, a psychologist at the Yale University Laboratories of Primate Biology, published a paper in which he had done just that. His subjects were chimpanzees, and this was one of the first scientific publications to use this "trait rating" approach in a nonhuman, an approach that remains valuable today (Capitanio, 1999; Stevenson-Hinde & Zunz, 1978).

A second point is that the same descriptors of personality within a species can be used to describe meaningful differences between species. In fact, the two scenarios described earlier are descriptions of two different species. The first scenario describes one outcome when well-socialized, but previously unfamiliar, adult male rhesus monkeys are put together for the first time. In our various research programs, we have done pairings just like this on dozens of occasions, and while the outcomes do vary, the one described here is not uncommon, especially if the animals are somewhat different in size. The second scenario is a description of a study conducted with patas monkeys at the Tulane National Primate Research Center several decades ago (Kummer, 1971). What accounts for the very different outcomes? Rhesus and patas monkeys are both monkeys of the Old World (Asia and Africa, respectively) and members of the same subfamily (Cercopithecinae) taxonomically. But patas monkeys are renowned for their extremely low levels of male-male tolerance; thus, the second scenario describes a common outcome for when unfamiliar adult males of this species meet. Thus, we might conclude that overall, rhesus monkeys are relatively more friendly and patas monkeys are relatively more hostile.

Our third point is that variations in personality between species can usefully be described in part as evolved adaptations that serve the individuals and the natural societies in which they usually live. Why are patas males far less friendly toward each other compared to rhesus males? In this particular case, the answer almost certainly has to do with sexual selection, and specifically with the adaptive value, for patas monkeys, of males competing with each other for access to females (Plavcan, 2001). Over evolutionary time, this intrasexual competition occurred to a much greater extent in patas monkeys than it did in rhesus monkeys. In fact, rhesus monkeys typically live in groups that contain multiple adult males, and patas monkeys typically live in groups that contain a single adult male. The greater role that male-male competition has played over evolutionary time in patas monkeys is also evidenced by the extreme sexual dimorphism in this species: males are nearly double the size of females (Galat-Luong et al., 1996), while among rhesus monkeys, males are only half again as large as females (Fooden 2000; Singh & Sinha 2004). Thus, from an evolutionary perspective, personality comprises a set of coevolved psychological characteristics that reflect how members of the species solved the many challenges in their environments over evolutionary time. In an important sense, personality is embedded in the biology of the species (including in the DNA of a species).

Our final point returns us to the study of variation within a species. We mentioned earlier that the first scenario describes one common outcome when unfamiliar, but well-socialized adult male rhesus monkeys meet. But there are other outcomes; not all adult male rhesus monkeys are as "friendly" as the ones described in the scenario. What accounts for the variation that one sees within a species? In fact, the second, more conflictual scenario can also describe an outcome when unfamiliar adult male rhesus monkeys meet—especially if one monkey was well socialized and the other monkey was reared in a highly restricted social environment, such as social isolation. In this situation (Mitchell, 1968), the isolate-reared animal can display extreme aggression, which does not seem to be assuaged by the normally reared monkey's display of submissive or fearful behavior. In the two decades during which such early rearing studies were conducted, a variety of outcomes were found; animals so reared can be described using words such as timid, fearful, vigilant, hostile, and the adverb that was often applied to these characteristics was "extremely" (Capitanio, 1986). While many of these effects are long-lasting, there is also evidence of plasticity—isolate-reared monkeys can be paired with normally reared infant "therapist" monkeys, and their behavior does normalize somewhat (Novak, 1979). The notion that personality organization has its roots in early development is, of course, not a new idea in psychology, nor is the idea that dysfunctional personalities can be somewhat remediated via therapeutic techniques. Animal studies, however, by virtue of the ability to manipulate and control early life conditions, provide some insights into the organizing role played by experience, and how plastic that organization is.

We believe that, to fully appreciate animal (including human) personality requires a perspective that is comparative, evolutionary, ecological, and developmental, and we will expand on these themes next. We note, however, that our biological approach to animal personality is not especially new. It has long been known that individuals within a species can differ from each other in important ways. The importance of this observation for biology was noted by Darwin more than 150 years ago, in chapter two of *The Origin of Species* (1859/1975):

> The many slight differences . . . being observed in the individuals of the same species inhabiting the same confined locality, may be called individual differences. No one supposes that all the individuals of the same species are cast in the same actual mould. These individual differences are of the highest importance for us, for they are often inherited . . . and they thus afford materials for natural selection to act on and accumulate. (p. 36)

Darwin also described, in his first chapter of *The Origin of Species*, how this knowledge had already been used by humans for millenia: this chapter was entitled "Variation Under Domestication." In it, Darwin discussed the selective breeding of individuals to illustrate how traits reflect, to a large extent, animals' adaptations to their environments. In the case of domestication, humans defined the environments and outcomes of interest, and over multiple generations, desired characteristics became more prevalent. One need only contrast domesticated animals with their wild counterparts to realize that the environments to which we adapted these animals has resulted in animals with very different temperaments,[1] often described as "placid" (Price, 1999).

In addition to natural history studies, and studies of domestication, animal temperament has been studied empirically for a century; one of the first published studies was reported by Utsurikawa (1917). As human studies of personality grew in number in the early part of the 20th century, however, a concern was raised that the study of personality was heading in a direction that emphasized only cultural influences on personality while ignoring personality's biological roots. Calvin Hall (1941) argued that animal studies of temperament could be valuable adjuncts to the study of personality in humans, because of the opportunity to employ rigorous experimental methods. Hall (1941) reviewed the literature on temperament in rodents, with an emphasis on identifying traits common to the various studies, describing how these traits had been operationalized, and addressing issues of reliability and validity. This was a masterful review, and it highlighted the second major approach to the study of personality that is still used today: studying individuals in well-controlled, standardized situations, and recording their behavior as they adapt to their circumstances. In contrast to the "trait rating" approach described earlier, this is referred to as a "behavior coding" approach (Weinstein et al., 2008).

Historically, then, individual variation in stable behavioral characteristics has been recognized (and exploited) for millenia, and its formal importance in biology dates back at least to the writings of Charles Darwin. The early studies in psychology that were focused on temperament presaged both the conceptual reasons for interest in personality (e.g., as models for human behavior, and as expressions of animals' adaptation to their environments) and the methods (behavior codings and trait ratings) that continue to be employed.

We next review some relevant literature in animal personality that we believe demonstrates the value of studying personality in species other than humans. Our focus is on comparative/ecological, developmental, and evolutionary perspectives.

A COMPARATIVE/ECOLOGICAL PERSPECTIVE: SPECIES DIFFERENCES IN PERSONALITY

Although members of all species have the same basic "problems" to solve—finding food, finding mates, staying healthy, not being preyed upon—the fact that species inhabit different ecological niches means that there will be variation in how these problems are dealt with. Consider two monkey species from the New World, squirrel monkeys and titi monkeys. These animals inhabit a relatively broad range in South America, and in parts of their range, overlap considerably, living in the same forests. Despite their living in proximity to each other, they show substantial differences in their life history. Titi monkeys live in small family groups, in which a single adult male and adult female show a pair bond to each other that is stronger than that seen between either of them and their offspring. They are socially monogamous, the father does the vast majority of the parental care, the male and female spend a substantial amount of time in close contact with each other, and they are territorial. Squirrel monkeys, on the other hand, are more gregarious, living in groups that usually contain multiple adult males and adult females. During the daytime, though, they often break up into smaller groups. Squirrel monkeys have larger home ranges, are not territorial, spend relatively little time grooming each other, and the father plays essentially no role in infant care. A long-standing research program by one of us (WAM) contrasted the behavioral and psychological characteristics of these two species. As a species, squirrel monkeys are more active than titi monkeys, a result consistent with their lifestyle that involves ranging over a larger area each day. Titi monkeys, on the other hand, are more selectively sociable, spending much more time in contact with each other. Again, this result makes sense in light of the facts that they live in small family groups, and that the male and female have a strong social bond. Moreover, the species differ in their responsiveness to novelty. Titi monkeys are somewhat neophobic, avoiding novel objects and situations; indeed, encounter with novel conditions can lead to something resembling a panic attack by titi monkeys. Squirrel monkeys, in contrast, seem more adaptable and less timid in response to novelty. Finally, the species differ in physiological organization. Squirrel monkeys show nearly five times higher basal levels of cortisol, the principal output of the hypothalamic-pituitary-adrenal system, as well as higher basal levels of sympathetic nervous system activity. Titi monkeys show greater parasympathetic activity, reflecting a species difference in autonomic balance. Together, the physiological data are again consistent with greater responsiveness and activity in squirrel monkeys; in response to challenge, they are likely to show a more active response, whereas titi monkeys' physiological organization is more appropriate to a lifestyle that is more sedentary and sociable (Mason 1966; 1971; Mason & Mendoza, 1993).

More broadly, primatologists have proposed various classification schemes over the years in an attempt to identify some common underlying themes reflecting similarities and differences in how species approach both their social and nonsocial worlds. Rarely have they been framed in explicitly "personality" terms, but overall, they present pictures at the species level that can be described in such terms. One scheme describes covarying traits in the 20 + species in the genus *Macaca* (the genus that includes rhesus, bonnet, and pigtailed macaques) relating to conflict management and dominance. The basic observation concerns how members of the various species exhibit aggressive behavior, and how much postaggression reconciliation there is. At one extreme, rhesus monkey aggression is highly asymmetric—when one animal starts a fight, the other animal typically flees—and postconflict friendly behavior between the former combatants is rare. In contrast, among Tonkean macaques, the target of an aggressive encounter usually counterattacks, and the aggressive exchange is usually pretty low-key, with little biting and few injuries. After the fight, the former combatants engage in a considerable amount of friendly behavior, seemingly "making up" for their earlier conflict. Thierry (2000) proposes four grades of macaque social organization. Beyond the simple observations of aggression asymmetry and occurrence of reconciliation, however, Thierry's four grades are also characterized by variation in maternal protectiveness (obviously much higher in the more "despotic" rhesus monkey, and less evident in the more "tolerant" Tonkean monkey), and other, more temperament-like characteristics. For example, the more tolerant species are generally less easy to arouse in stressful situations and are generally more exploratory, compared to the despotic species.

A second classification system is based upon feeding ecology, and it involves identifying so-called weed species (Richard et al., 1989). Weed macaques, like weed plants, thrive in environments that have been disturbed by humans. Rhesus monkeys may be the prototypical weed species, coexisting with humans in habitats as varied as forests, agricultural areas, temples, and inner cities. Their success in human environments suggested to Richard et al. (1989) that some defining traits of weed species are likely "curiosity, behavioral adaptability, an aggressive and gregarious temperament, and speed and agility on the ground" (p. 577). The aggressive and bold nature of these animals, combined with increasing human population and decreasing natural habitat, has resulted in a growing conflict between humans and monkeys in India, resulting in injuries, disease transmission, and even death (*Times of India*, 2014).

Together, these studies suggest that the concept of personality can be productively employed to describe species differences in biobehavioral organization. Indeed, there are active research programs specifically investigating species differences in personality (e.g., Morton et al., 2013; Sussman et al., 2013), with attempts to understand how such differences might be related to phylogeny, life history, and traditional socioecological factors such as predation pressure and food availability. What comes through clearly from these studies is the idea that personality, at the species level, is an evolved characteristic that not only contributes to a species's adaptation in its environment but is the psychological manifestation of that adaptation.

A DEVELOPMENTAL PERSPECTIVE: WITHIN-SPECIES DIFFERENCES IN PERSONALITY

The most common use of the construct "personality" in psychology is, of course, to describe individual differences within a species. Even within species, how-ever, subgroups have been characterized as showing differences in personality. In humans, for example, cross-cultural studies suggest that people in Northern Ireland are more extraverted than are Nigerians (McCrae & Terracciano, 2005). The adaptive value of this difference is unknown, but similar group differences have been identified within nonhuman primate species as well; some of the best evidence from natural populations is found in a series of papers from the 1960s that contrasted rhesus monkeys in India that were living in urban environments to those living in more remote, rural areas. Urban monkeys were much more ac-tive and manipulative compared to the shyer rural monkeys, and in social tests, the group formed from the urban monkeys was characterized by substantially more aggression and less affiliation, whereas the interactions among the rural monkeys appeared more relaxed. When members of the two sets of animals were tested together in a competitive situation, and later formed into a single group, it was clear that the urban monkeys dominated their rural counterparts and dis-played considerably more aggressive behavior (Singh, 1966, 1968)—a result sim-ilar to that described in scenario 2 earlier. Although the adaptive value of having a more active and aggressive temperament seems obvious for monkeys living in an urban environment, where resources may be scarcer and competition (including with humans) more intense, it is important to reiterate that, as with the human cross-cultural data on personality, within-group variation is typically much more substantial than between-group variation.

What might be the origins of differences in personality between individuals and groups within a species? One of the most obvious directions to pursue in an-swering this question is to examine development, and it is here that experimental animal studies can offer unique insights. An important early finding was that rhesus monkeys that were reared apart from their mothers in order to examine intellectual development were in fact impaired in many aspects of their person-ality, although they were in perfect physical health. These data were presented in a comprehensive series of reports in the early 1960s comparing wild-born rhesus monkeys with like-aged animals that had been reared in a laboratory setting with limited social experience. Compared to the feral animals, restricted animals were more aggressive, less gregarious, and more fearful in response to relatively benign conditions (Mason, 1960, 1961a, 1961b; Mason & Green, 1962).[2]

The early studies of social restriction during infancy in rhesus monkeys demonstrated a relatively consistent picture involving poor emotion regulation, extreme fear that can manifest itself as hyperaggressiveness, low social interest and competence, low interest in exploration, frequent display of abnormal behaviors, and a generally passive approach to their environment. Functionally, however, "early social restriction" actually involves a number of deficiencies. One is the absence of an attachment relationship. Provision of an inanimate object (a cloth surrogate, which provided "contact comfort") to which the infant monkeys could become attached resulted in some moderation of the consequences of early restriction, but deficits remained profound (Harlow & Zimmerman, 1959). A second deficiency in the environment of animals raised under restricted conditions is the experience of an interactive environment. Even with a cloth surrogate present, the environment that the animals lived in was completely predictable—sensory stimulation was experienced only when the individual animal moved its own sensory receptors, and there were no objects that initiated behavior to, or attempted to elicit behavior from, the animal. Finally, the characteristics of the interactive objects themselves likely matter; in normal development, social development involves access to other members of the same species, whose behavior is similar to one's own, and to members of multiple age-sex classes, the members of which might show different profiles of interaction. From a personality perspective, how might such experiences contribute to behavioral organization and personality characteristics that lead to more adaptive outcomes? Later research on socially restricted animals examined this question; we briefly describe three relevant sets of studies.

The first set of studies describes a variation on the usual surrogate that was typically present when animals were reared without access to conspecifics. What might be the outcome for personality if the surrogate moved? A set of papers described results from a study of infant rhesus monkeys that had been reared either with stationary or mobile surrogates. The surrogates themselves were identical, but the mobile surrogates were connected to a mechanism that was activated on an irregular schedule throughout the day and produced anywhere from 15 to 45 seconds of movement interspersed with stationary periods of up to 2 minutes. Importantly, the mobile surrogate could also move in the horizontal plane in response to an external force, such as the monkey jumping onto it. Thus, the mobile surrogate not only provided unexpected motion but also motion in response to the infant's initiation—a rudimentary form, perhaps, of "social interaction." Monkeys reared with the mobile surrogates showed many of the same behavioral disturbances seen of surrogate-reared monkeys from previous studies, except for one—none of the mobile monkeys developed rocking, whereas 9 of 10 stationary animals did. This result confirmed the original hypothesis that the rocking seen in isolate- or surrogate-reared monkeys appears to be a specific outcome attributable to what many would consider to be an inconsequential byproduct of living with a mother—the proprioceptive-kinesthetic stimulation that she provides. More important for our purposes, however, were the other outcomes from the two rearing conditions. In novel circumstances, stationary monkeys generally showed greater arousal, and in social situations, mobile monkeys showed less antagonistic behavior (Mason & Berkson, 1975). In tests of looking behavior, mobile monkeys spent more time looking at pictures of other monkeys and were more sensitive to differences between the stimuli, compared to stationary monkeys (Eastman & Mason, 1975), and by young adulthood, mobile monkeys showed greater social caution (i.e., less social impulsivity) and responsiveness (Anderson, Kenney, & Mason, 1977). What is it about movement of an inert object that leads to reduced emotionality and increased social interest, aspects of personality that persisted for years?

Additional insight was provided by a second series of studies, in which infant rhesus monkeys were raised individually in stimulus-rich environments with either an inanimate plastic hobbyhorse or a mongrel dog (Mason & Kenny, 1974). A dog takes the complexity of the rearing partner to another level—it provides for motion like the mobile surrogate does, but it also provides generalized social companionship as well as response-contingent feedback to the developing animal. Mothers do this as well, of course, although because mothers are also conspecifics, the contingent interactions and companionship with their infants are much more finely tuned than are those of dogs. So what are the consequences of being reared with an animate versus inanimate companion? Dog-reared (DR) monkeys were "more attentive to the environment, more responsive, less likely to be indifferent when confronted with change, and more likely to achieve an adaptive outcome by acting on the environment" compared to hobbyhorse-reared (HR) monkeys (Mason, 1978, p. 241). When presented with slides of complex visual stimuli, DR monkeys spent more time looking at the pictures and were more responsive to pictures based on their novelty or complexity. They also showed more physiological arousal: higher heart rate and higher concentrations of plasma cortisol (Wood, Mason, & Kenney, 1979). When placed in within-rearing-group social settings, DR animals continued to show a more active approach to the situations, a greater sensitivity to social cues, a more complex social network, and they were more often found in social configurations that were larger than simple dyads. DR monkeys were also more sensitive to changes in social context (Capitanio, 1984, 1985). It's important to note that members of both groups, DR and HR, showed deficiencies in specific behavior patterns—they were generally more aggressive than one would see in normally reared monkeys, they never showed the complete species-typical pattern of sexual behavior, and social grooming was virtually absent. Nevertheless, DR monkeys did seem to have a fundamentally different understanding of social objects, and overall their personality could be characterized as more social, more curious, and more likely to take an active approach to influence their surroundings, including their social surroundings.

A third set of data focused on outcomes when infants were given nonmaternal, but conspecific contact. In this case, monkeys were reared in a nursery setting, and by around 30 days of age were paired with another same-age peer 24 hours per day. At 6–12 months of age, pairs were put into social groups consisting of other pairs and, typically, one or two adult animals. Interestingly, the behavioral repertoire of these animals, when they are older, is reasonably normal. They groom, they have sex, and they are satisfactory parents, despite never having had parents themselves. They do show continued self-sucking of digits during stressful situations;

this may be a relic of not having had a nipple to suck on to reduce arousal (and the subsequent weaning from this response) when they were young. They also show more externalizing behavior; when challenged, they vocalize, they run around, and they defecate rather prodigiously (Capitanio et al., 2006).

Elsewhere (Mason & Capitanio, 2012), we have described an organismic perspective on development, emphasizing that individuals are active participants in their development, absorbing information (Oyama, 2000) from, and acting on, their environment and altering their organization as a consequence. The studies just described reflect that perspective: the organization of personality is affected by characteristics of the environment, some of which are often not even thought about by most people, such as the essential animate, interactive nature of our social world. This feature (operationalized as having a canine companion during development) can take the basic personality "program" that emerges in response to rearing without a surrogate (which can be described for rhesus monkeys as "nasty and asocial") and tune it into a more sophisticated form of organization in ways that were unexpected. Organisms whose social experience is no more sophisticated than the developing animal's own (as in the nursery/peer-rearing situation) can contribute to the organization of developing systems in ways that result in a close approximation to the normative pattern of personality.

AN EVOLUTIONARY PSYCHOLOGY PERSPECTIVE: WITHIN-SPECIES TRADE-OFFS

A more recent approach to understanding psychological phenomena can be subsumed under the heading of evolutionary psychology. This approach explicitly recognizes that species and individuals are the result of evolutionary processes, and that mental phenomena are subject to the same evolutionary processes as are physical phenomena (Tooby & Cosmides, 1989). This is, of course, the basic idea that Darwin conveyed in his writings. In fact, Buss (2009) has suggested how evolutionary psychology might productively be employed in understanding human personality. It is our opinion that this thinking need not be restricted to humans.

Evolutionary psychology borrows many concepts from the larger field of evolutionary biology. For our purposes, we wish to focus on one of these, namely, the idea of a trade-off. In psychology, the idea of a trade-off is often portrayed as a choice—does an individual "trade off" the possibility of getting a big reward in the future for the certainty of taking a smaller reward now? Obviously, the individual cannot have both. In evolutionary biology, the concept of a trade-off is similar in that it is tied to some outcome in the future, and it is based on the idea that one cannot optimize all aspects of one's life—if an individual is highly sociable, the individual may not be able to be, at the same time, highly active. Unlike in psychology, trade-offs in evolutionary biology do not typically reflect conscious choice. Moreover, biobehavioral mechanisms that drive evolutionary trade-offs have as their ultimate "goal" enabling an individual to achieve reproductive success under future conditions that are not known with certainty.

To illustrate the concept of a trade-off, consider an example. For the first few months of life, a young rhesus monkey will obtain all of its nutrition from its mother, in the form of breast milk, which contains energy, nutrients, hormones, immune factors, and so on. The infant could take the energy (in the form of kilocalories) that it receives from breast milk and put it toward growth. Or the animal could take the energy and put it toward behavior, showing high levels of activity, play, and exploration. But energy is a finite resource, and the animal cannot do both optimally; where does the animal preferentially "put" its resources: growth or behavior? What factors might affect this allocation? (Again, the word "put" is in quotes, because this is not likely to be a conscious choice.) Let's make the situation a bit more complicated. There is variation between rhesus monkey mothers in the quantity of each of the constituents in milk. A first-time mother, which, at our facility would deliver her first offspring when she was 3 years of age, is, herself, still growing; this fact, combined with the fact that her mammary glands are also somewhat underdeveloped, results in her producing milk with lower available energy across the period of lactation. Interestingly, the cortisol content of her milk is higher—and this is not simply because of her inexperience with motherhood. Recent data (Hinde et al., 2015) suggest that the concentrations of cortisol in mother's milk may serve as a signal to the infant about where to "put" the caloric resources that it will receive across lactation. In fact, cortisol concentrations in mother's milk were significantly associated with personality—monkeys whose mothers' milk contained more cortisol had faster weight gain but a more nervous temperament (characterized as timid and fearful), while monkeys whose mothers' milk had less cortisol had slower growth, but a more active, confident, and playful temperament. Presumably, a monkey whose mother produces high cortisol (which signals lower caloric resources in her milk across lactation) may be at a reproductive disadvantage if it puts those resources into an active temperament—perhaps it risks injury, malnutrition, or illness, which might impair its ability to be able to reproduce. The better strategy, for such an animal, may be to stay closer to home as an infant (i.e., be more timid in approaching the world) and to trade-off the benefits of having an active temperament for the benefits of faster growth—because there aren't sufficient resources to have both fast growth and an active temperament. In this way, a characteristic that may seem to be maladaptive, like a nervous temperament, may actually confer some advantage to the individual when one considers the broader pattern of that individual's life history.

An evolutionary psychology perspective on personality (human or nonhuman), then, places variation in personality into a broader evolutionary/ecological context that forces a focus on how a set of characteristics can benefit an individual's reproductive success. Trade-offs are not like choices in the sense that individuals probably do not consciously evaluate their current situation and actively attempt to predict whether they would thrive or fail under some anticipated future conditions. Rather, all that is required is that a relationship existed, over evolutionary time, between some particular cues (like cortisol in mother's milk) and successful reproduction.

We note, however, that the concept of a trade-off does not imply genetic determinism; in fact, trade-offs commonly illustrate the opposite, namely plasticity. We now know that the genome is not as static as we once thought but is, in fact, highly responsive to just the kind of cues indicated in our example: experiences (particularly experiences early in life such as, perhaps, the caloric content of mother's milk) can alter gene transcription through placement of epigenetic marks onto DNA. Thus, based on information in the environment that, over evolutionary time, was linked to fitness outcomes in individuals, a developmental trajectory can be established that gives an individual a "best shot" at surviving and thriving (and, of course, reproducing). Should such an individual find itself in circumstances that are different, however, from the ones in which it may have been epigenetically "prepared," it may have reduced chances of thriving and succeeding.

ANIMAL PERSONALITY AND PERSONALITY DISORDERS

Our goal in this chapter has been to discuss the phenomenon of personality in animals from comparative, developmental, and evolutionary perspectives with the hope that such perspectives may be useful in thinking about human personality disorders. Between species, personality, reflecting modal tendencies of responsiveness, reflects the broad, life-history outline of the species. There is considerable overlap in what the dimensions of personality are between different species (Gosling & John, 1999); what differs is where, within that multidimensional space, different species are situated. Within a species, there is variation around those modes, although again, broad intraspecific differences can reflect adaptations to local conditions (c.f., urban vs. rural rhesus monkeys). And even within individual social groups, variation in personality may be a reflection of adaptive processes: from the perspective of achieving reproductive success, individuals might trade-off one developmental trajectory for another, and these trade-offs can be reflected in personality differences.

We do not argue, however, that all variation is adaptive at all times in all situations. Consider the personality characteristic of sociability, which reflects a tendency to affiliate. There are documented health benefits of being socially connected for both human and nonhuman primates (e.g., House et al., 1988). If high sociability is so good, then one might ask why every member of a species is not "high sociable?" Why is variation in this (or any) personality characteristics still evident in populations? One can imagine situations, across evolutionary time, where being highly sociable could be a disadvantage, such as when a virus enters a population. Viruses are typically transmitted through direct contact between individuals; in the case of a severe respiratory virus, animals that are low in sociability might be at significantly lower risk of infection, illness, and death, and consequently be more successful in surviving and reproducing. Thus, one might trade-off the benefits of high sociability against lower risk of viral infection. Moreover, we've demonstrated experimentally that, under stable social conditions, there may be no health benefit of being high or low in sociability; but in socially unstable conditions, high-sociable animals do have an advantage (Capitanio et al., 2008, 2009). This example illustrates how variation can be maintained in a population: variation in this one trait can have little impact on survival and reproduction under benign conditions, but it can be an important influence on fitness under stressful conditions or when a viral pathogen enters the population.

What about human personality disorders? We are not clinicians, nor do we profess any deep understanding or insight into the phenomenon of personality disorders in humans. Rather, we conclude our discussion by emphasizing, and expanding upon, some relevant points raised in our review earlier.

First, we note that humans are remarkably social animals. Psychologists who only study humans almost certainly take for granted our highly social nature and how unusual we are as a mammalian species. We live our lives surrounded by multiple individuals of all age/sex classes, and we regularly interact—on the subway, in stores, at the office—with unfamiliar individuals of the same sex with no conflict. In contrast, the social unit for most mammalian species is a female with her immature offspring; other social interactions occur sporadically and are generally focused on particular "tasks," like mating or territorial defense. Many species of nonhuman primates, particularly monkeys of the Old World like rhesus monkeys, are also highly social, living 365 days per year in social groups containing multiple members of each age/sex class. It's not surprising then, that personality dimensions for both humans and rhesus monkeys include many items pertaining to social functioning—sociability, extraversion, and agreeableness, for example. Because our social life is so important to us, affecting patterns of health, mortality, and so on, we should not be surprised that many of the most problematic aspects of psychological functioning revolve around problems with social adaptation. Such problems seem to characterize personality disorders; in fact, others have suggested renaming "personality disorders" as "adaptation disorders" (Svrakic et al., 2009). This idea fits very well with the perspective on animal personality emphasized in this review.

The notion of "adaptation disorder" emphasizes the importance of the environment. Rural rhesus monkeys, with their shyer ways, are well adapted to their environment. But if they were transplanted to an urban setting, they would be at a competitive disadvantage and might be considered "maladapted." Inherent in the notion of adaptation is the idea of "fit" between the organism and the environment. Elsewhere, we've conceptualized stress as a state that can arise due to a "poor fit": a mismatch between an individual's characteristics and the affordances of the environment (Capitanio, 2011). Perhaps not surprisingly, dysregulation of stress response systems also seems to characterize at least some personality disorders, such as borderline (Scott, Levy, & Granger, 2013) and psychopathy (Thompson, Ramos, & Willett, 2014).

If personality (and personality disorder) are seen from the perspective of adaptation, the fact that personality disorders are relatively prevalent raises the question of whether there are circumstances under which a particular personality disorder (or, perhaps more precisely, the constituent personality traits that underlie a personality disorder) might be adaptive (Nettle, 2006). If so, then this could help explain why personality disorders are maintained in a population, much like the idea of why "low sociable" animals still exist in populations. Among humans, there does appear to be a cultural aspect to the definition (and prevalence) of certain personality disorders (Calliess et al., 2008). Beyond the broad context of different cultures, however, it's useful to remember that contingencies can change within an individual's lifetime. Are there subcultures or contexts in which traits reminiscent of personality disorder might be adaptive? What are the trade-offs in possessing a phenotype indicative of a personality disorder? Might they include trade-offs between short-term gains at the expense of long-term ones? Could they include exquisite adaptation to a narrow range of contexts, but poor adaptation to broader cultural contexts? Certainly, the popular (Bercovici, 2011) and professional (Rijsenbilt & Commandeur, 2013) literatures are replete with suggestions of a higher than usual prevalence of personality disorders among CEOs of large corporations; is this an environment where having a personality disorder can lead to success (either financial, social, or reproductive)?

Finally, the comparative/developmental/ecological approach we describe emphasizes the importance of early experience in promoting particular patterns of adaptation. The idea that early adverse experience is associated with later development of personality disorders has considerable support in the literature (Carr et al., 2013). We believe the experimental work described here suggests that variation in psychological functioning can arise from some surprising aspects of early life (e.g., the animate nature of one's companions). Other studies, which have examined gene–environment interactions in animals that experienced different rearing conditions (e.g., Karere et al., 2009), also indicate that the organizing effects of early experience can be contingent on other organismic factors, like genotype. Although early emotional abuse may be a risk factor for personality disorders (Carr et al., 2013), not everyone with personality disorders experienced emotional abuse, nor did everyone who experienced emotional abuse go on to develop a personality disorder. What contingent factors might be needed for adverse early environments to manifest as personality disorders?

CONCLUSION

The study of personality in nonhumans has a long history in psychology, dating back nearly 100 years. Although psychological studies of personality in animals have typically emphasized the role of experiential factors in the development of personality, studies with different species have suggested an important role for ecology and evolution—influences on behavior that operate in time frames much longer than that of a single individual's life span (Tinbergen, 1963). Regardless of which perspective one takes, however, a common theme in the study of animal personality is that personality is about adaptation—personality is viewed as a biological phenomenon that exists to help animals achieve reproductive success. But whether an individual achieves that ultimate evolutionary end point depends on whether the individual's characteristics mesh with the circumstances in which it finds itself: A rhesus monkey from the forest will flourish in the forest, but it will likely be at a competitive (and probably reproductive) disadvantage in an urban setting. We suggest that a broader, comparative approach to the study of personality, such as that described here, might provide some useful insight to understanding personality disorders.

NOTES

1. Historically, in animal behavior research, "personality" and "temperament" are terms that are used interchangeably, and we continue this tradition.
2. We note that studies from this era, by Mason, Harlow, Sackett, and others never used the words "personality" or "temperament," inasmuch as this was an era in which psychological research was still dominated by neobehaviorism. Nevertheless, these are apt descriptors of the pervasive alterations in biobehavioral organization induced by various types of early social restriction. This and related literature have been comprehensively reviewed elsewhere (Capitanio, 1986) and will not be repeated here.

REFERENCES

Anderson, C. O., Kenney, A. M., & Mason, W. A. (1977). Effects of maternal mobility, partner, and endocrine state on social responsiveness of adolescent rhesus monkeys. *Developmental Psychobiology, 10*, 421–434.

Bercovici, J. (2011). Why (some) psychopaths make great CEOs. *Forbes*, June 14, 2011. Retrieved from http://www.forbes.com/sites/jeffbercovici/2011/06/14/why-some-psychopaths-make-great-ceos/

Buss, D. M. (2009). How can evolutionary psychology successfully explain personality and individual differences? *Perspectives on Psychological Science, 4*, 359–366.

Calliess, I. T., Sieberer, M., Machleidt, W., & Ziegenbein, M. (2008). Personality disorders in a cross-cultural perspective: Impact of culture and migration on diagnosis and etiological aspects. *Current Psychiatry Reviews, 4*, 39–47.

Capitanio, J. P. (1984). Early experience and social processes in rhesus macaques (*Macaca mulatta*): I. Dyadic social interaction. *Journal of Comparative Psychology, 98*, 35–44.

Capitanio, J. P. (1985). Early experience and social processes in rhesus macaques (*Macaca mulatta*): II. Complex social interaction. *Journal of Comparative Psychology, 99*, 133–144.

Capitanio, J. P. (1986). Behavioral pathology. In G. Mitchell & J. Erwin (Eds.), *Comparative primate biology: Volume 2A. Behavior, conservation, and ecology* (pp. 411–454). New York, NY: Alan R. Liss.

Capitanio, J. P. (1999). Personality dimensions in adult male rhesus macaques: Prediction of behaviors across time and situation. *American Journal of Primatology, 47*, 299–320.

Capitanio, J. P. (2011). Nonhuman primate personality and immunity: Mechanisms of health and disease. In A. Weiss, J. E. King, & L. Murray (Eds.), *Personality and temperament in nonhuman primates* (pp. 233–255). New York, NY: Springer.

Capitanio, J. P., Mason, W. A., Mendoza, S. P., Del Rosso, L. A., & Roberts, J. A. (2006). Nursery rearing and biobehavioral organization. In G. P. Sackett, G. Ruppenthal, & K. Elias (Eds.), *Nursery rearing of nonhuman primates in the 21st century* (pp. 191–213). New York, NY: Springer.

Capitanio, J. P., Abel, K., Mendoza, S. P., Blozis, S. A., McChesney, M. B., Cole, S. W., & Mason, W. A. (2008). Personality and serotonin transporter genotype interact with social context to affect immunity and viral set-point in simian immunodeficiency virus disease. *Brain, Behavior, and Immunity, 22*, 676–689.

Capitanio, J. P., Mendoza, S. P., Mason, W. A., Lerche, N. W., Sloan, E. K., & Cole, S. W. (2009). Stress, coping, and AIDS: Insights from a monkey model. In P. P. Singh & R. M. Donahoe (Eds.), *Proceedings of the International Conference on Biotechnological Approaches to Neuroimmunomodulation and Infectious Diseases* (pp. 1–18). SAS Nagar: NIPER.

Carr, C. P., Severi Martins, C. M., Stingel, A. M., Lebgruber, V. B., & Juruena, M. F. (2013). The role of early life stress in adult psychiatric disorders: A systematic review according to childhood trauma subtypes. *Journal of Nervous and Mental Disorders, 201*, 1007–1020.

Crawford, M. (1938). A behavior rating scale for young chimpanzees. *Journal of Comparative Psychology, 26*, 79–92.

Darwin C. (1859/1975). *The origin of species*. Franklin Center, PA: Franklin Library.

Eastman, R. F., & Mason, W. A. (1975). Looking behavior in monkeys raised with mobile and stationary artificial mothers. *Developmental Psychobiology, 8*, 213–221.

Fooden, J. (2000). Systematic review of the rhesus macaque, Macaca mulatta (Zimmermann, 1780). *Fieldiana Zoology, 96*, 1–180.

Galat-Luong, A., Galat, G., Durand, J-P., & Pourrut, X. 1996. Sexual weight dimorphism and social organization in green and patas monkeys in Senegal. *Folia Primatologica, 67*, 92–3.

Gosling, S. D., & John, O. P. (1999). Personality dimensions in nonhuman animals: A cross-species review. *Current Directions in Psychological Science, 8*, 69–75.

Hall, C. S. (1941). Temperament: A survey of animal studies. *Psychological Bulletin, 38*, 909–943.

Harlow, H. F., & Zimmermann, R. R. (1959). Affectional responses in the infant monkey; orphaned baby monkeys develop a strong and persistent attachment to inanimate surrogate mothers. *Science, 130*(3373), 421–32.

Hinde, K. Skibiel, A. L., Foster, A. B., del Rosso, L., Mendoza, S. P., & Capitanio, J. P. (2015). Cortisol in mother's milk reflects maternal life history and predicts infant temperament. *Behavioral Ecology, 26*, 269–281.

House, J. S., Landis, K. R., & Umberson, D. (1988). Social relationships and health. *Science, 241*, 540–545.

Karere, G. M., Kinnally, E. L., Sanchez, J. N., Famula, T. R., Lyons, L. A., & Capitanio, J. P. (2009). What is an "adverse" environment? Interactions of rearing experiences and MAOA genotype in rhesus monkeys. *Biological Psychiatry, 65*, 770–777.

Kummer, H. (1971). *Primate societies*. Chicago, IL: Aldine.

Mason, W. A. (1960). The effects of social restriction on the behavior of rhesus monkeys: I. Free social behavior. *Journal of Comparative and Physiological Psychology, 53*, 582–589.

Mason, W. A. (1961a). The effects of social restriction on the behavior of rhesus monkeys: II. Tests of gregariousness. *Journal of Comparative and Physiological Psychology, 54,* 287–290.

Mason, W. A. (1961b). The effects of social restriction on the behavior of rhesus monkeys: III. Dominance tests. *Journal of Comparative and Physiological Psychology, 54,* 694–699.

Mason, W. A. (1966). Social organization of the South American monkey, *Callicebus moloch*: A preliminary report. *Tulane Studies in Zoology, 13,* 23–28.

Mason, W. A. (1971). Field and laboratory studies of social organization in Saimiri and Callicebus. In L. A. Rosenblum (Ed.), *Primate behavior: Developments in field and laboratory research* (Vol. 2, pp. 107–137). New York, NY: Academic Press.

Mason, W. A. (1978). Social experience and primate cognitive development. In G. M. Burghardt & M. Bekoff (Eds.), *The development of behavior: Comparative and evolutionary aspects* (pp. 233–251). New York, NY: Garland Press.

Mason, W. A., & Berkson, G. (1975). Effects of maternal mobility on the development of rocking and other behaviors in rhesus monkeys: A study with artificial mothers. *Developmental Psychobiology, 8,* 197–211.

Mason, W. A., & Capitanio, J. P. (2012). Basic emotions: A reconstruction. *Emotion Review, 4,* 238–244.

Mason, W. A., & Green, P. C. (1962). The effects of social restriction on the behavior of rhesus monkeys: IV. Responses to a novel environment and to an alien species. *Journal of Comparative and Physiological Psychology, 55,* 363–368.

Mason, W. A., & Kenney, M. D. (1974). Re-direction of filial attachments in rhesus monkeys: Dogs as mother surrogates. *Science, 183,* 1209–1211.

Mason, W. A., & Mendoza, S. P. (1993). Contrasting life modes in Cebidae: Titi monkeys (Callicebus) and squirrel monkeys (Saimiri). *Regional Proceedings of the American Association of Zoological Parks and Aquariums,* 715–722.

McCrae, R. R., & Terracciano, A. (2005). Personality profiles of cultures: Aggregate personality traits. *Journal of Personality and Social Psychology, 89,* 407–425.

Mitchell, G. D. (1968). Persistent behavior pathology in rhesus monkeys following early social isolation. *Folia primatologica, 8,* 132–147.

Morton, F. B., Lee, P. C., Buchanan-Smith, H. M., Brosnan, S. F., Thierry, B., Paukner, A., . . . Weiss, A. (2013). Personality structure in brown capuchin monkeys (Sapajus apella): comparisons with chimpanzees (Pan troglodytes), orangutans (Pongo spp.), and rhesus macaques (Macaca mulatta). *Journal of Comparative Psychology, 127,* 282–298.

Nettle, D. (2006). The evolution of personality variation in humans and other animals. *American Psychologist, 61,* 622–631.

Novak, M. A. (1979). Social recovery of monkeys isolated for the first year of life: II. Long-term assessment. *Developmental Psychology, 15,* 50–61.

Oyama, S. (2000). *The ontogeny of information. Developmental systems and evolution* (2nd ed.). Durham, NC: Duke University Press.

Plavcan, J. M. (2001). Sexual dimorphism in primate evolution. *Yearbook of Physical Anthropology, 44,* 25–53.

Price, E. O. (1999). Behavioral development in animals undergoing domestication. *Applied Animal Behaviour Science, 65,* 245–271.

Richard, A. F., Goldstein, S. J., & Dewar, R. E. (1989). Weed macaques: The evolutionary implications of macaque feeding ecology. *International Journal of Primatology, 10*, 569–594.

Rijsenbilt, A., & Commandeur, H. (2013). Narcissus enters the courtroom: CEO narcissism and fraud. *Journal of Business Ethics, 117*, 413–429.

Scott, L. N., Levy, K. N., & Granger, D. A. (2013). Biobehavioral reactivity to social evaluative stress in women with borderline personality disorder. *Personality Disorders: Theory, Research, and Treatment, 4*, 91–100.

Singh, M., & Sinha, A. (2004). Life history traits: Ecological adaptations or phylogenetic relics? In B. Thierry, M. Singh, & W. Kaumanns (Eds.), *Macaque societies: A model for the study of social organization* (pp. 80–83). Cambridge, UK: Cambridge University Press.

Singh, S. D. (1966). The effects of human rnvironment on the social behavior of rhesus monkeys. *Primates, 7*, 33–39.

Singh, S. D. (1968). Social Interactions between the rural and urban monkeys, *Macaca mulatta. Primates, 9*, 69–74.

Stevenson-Hinde, S., & Zunz, M. (1978). Subjective assessment of individual rhesus monkeys. *Primates, 19*, 473–482.

Sussman, A. F., Ha, J. C., Bentson, K. L., & Crockett, C. L. (2013). Temperament in rhesus, long-tailed, and pigtailed macaques varies by species and sex. *American Journal of Primatology, 75*, 303–313.

Svrakic, D. M., Lecic-Tosevskib, D., & Mirjana Divac-Jovanovicc, M. (2009). DSM Axis II: Personality disorders or adaptation disorders? *Current Opinion in Psychiatry, 22*, 111–117.

Thierry, B. (2000). Covariation of conflict management patterns across macaque species. In F. Aureli & F. B. M. de Waal (Eds.), *Natural conflict resolution* (pp. 106–128). Berkeley: University of California Press.

Thompson, D. F., Ramos, C. L., & Willett, J. K. (2014). Psychopathy: Clinical features, developmental basis and therapeutic challenges. *Journal of Clinical Pharmacy and Therapeutics, 39*, 485–495.

Times of India. (2014, September 17). Monkey menace continues, residents helpless. Retrieved from http://timesofindia.indiatimes.com/city/lucknow/Monkey-menace-continues-residents-helpless/articleshow/42654627.cms

Tinbergen, N. (1963). On aims and methods of ethology. *Zeitschrift für Tierpsychologie, 20*, 410–433.

Tooby, J., & Cosmides, L. (1989). Adaptation versus phylogeny: The role of animal psychology in the study of human behavior. *International Journal of Comparative Psychology, 2*, 175–188.

Utsurikawa, N. (1917). Temperamental differences between outbred and inbred strains of the albino rat. *Animal Behavior, 7*, 111–129.

Weinstein, T. A. R., Capitanio, J. P., & Gosling, S. D. (2008). Personality in animals. In O. P. John, R. W. Robins, & L. A. Pervin (Eds.), *Handbook of personality: Theory and research* (3rd ed., pp. 328–348). New York, NY: Guilford Press.

Wood, B. S., Mason, W. A., & Kenney, M. D. (1979). Contrasts in visual responsiveness and emotional arousal between rhesus monkeys raised with living and those raised with inanimate substitute mothers. *Journal of Comparative and Physiological Psychology, 93*, 368–377.

11

Molecular Trait Psychology

Advancing the Field by Moving From Gene Hunting to Tool Making

TURHAN CANLI ■

Biological studies of personality and other behavioral traits have always been defined by the tools available at the time. Twin studies established early on a significant role for both environmental and genetic factors. Noninvasive imaging technologies such as functional magnetic resonance imaging (fMRI) have motivated studies of individual differences in brain structure and function as a function of traits. Imaging genetics studies have begun to integrate information about individuals' genotype with brain-based endophenotypes.

Despite these advances, there is a sense that the search for genes associated with behavioral traits has stalled. This sentiment emerged as genome-wide association studies (GWAS) failed to discover the anticipated large numbers of novel candidate genes and showed poor replication results for those they did discover. The solution, which has yet to bear fruit, has been a progressive move toward ever-larger samples.

In this chapter, I will briefly recapitulate the current state of the link between genes, brains, and behavioral traits. I will then discuss a second potential solution to the shortcomings of GWAS trait studies: the development of next-generation molecular tools that were invented within the last decade (some as recently as 2013). These tools were conceived in the "postgenomic" era, that is, after the decoding of the human genome. As such, they are essentially designed from the ground up with genome-wide applications in mind.

GENE HUNTING

The Candidate Gene Approach

Building on prior work that established the heritability of behavioral traits (Defries, McClearn, McGuffin, & Plomin, 2000; Dilalla & Gottesman, 2004), particularly trait neuroticism (Bouchard et al., 1990; Eysenck, 1990; Floderus-Myrhed, Pedersen, & Rasmuson, 1980; Jang, Livesley, & Vernon, 1996; Tellegen et al., 1988), Lesch and colleagues were the first to show that a common variation (polymorphism) within the serotonin (5-hydroxytrypamine, or 5-HT) transporter gene (*5-HTT*, also referred to as *SERT* or *SLC6A4*) mapped onto individual differences in self-reported neuroticism (Lesch et al., 1996). The polymorphism is located in the gene's promoter region and is therefore named the serotonin transporter-linked polymorphic region, 5-HTTLPR. Individuals who carried one or two copies of the "short" allele, which contained a 44-basepair deletion, tended to score higher in neuroticism (and lower in agreeableness) than did individuals who carried two copies of the "long" allele. This was an exciting finding, because it bridged the wide gap between molecular-genetic and behavioral manifestations of neuroticism.

In the intervening years, this study has been subjected to a large number of replication attempts and meta-analyses (see, for example, meta-analyses by Clarke, Flint, Attwood, & Munafo, 2010; Munafo, Clark, & Flint, 2005; Munafo et al., 2009; Schinka, Busch, & Robichaux-Keene, 2004; Sen, Burmeister, & Ghosh, 2004), which converge on affirming a link between 5-HTTLPR genotype and self-reported neuroticism (when assessed with a particular questionnaire, the NEO PI-R; Costa & McCrae, 1992).

Although other candidate gene polymorphisms have since attracted the attention of researchers, their associations with any of the Big Five personality traits have been weak. Given that known candidate genes only account for a small percentage of genetic variance of these traits, expectations were high that the remaining missing genes would be discovered quickly with genome-wide discovery tools, such as gene arrays and next-generation sequencing technologies.

Genome-Wide Association Studies

The arrival of molecular probes covering the entire human genome enabled genome-wide association studies (GWAS). The successes of GWAS in medical genetics gave rise to the expectation that this technology would also quickly identify the large sets of genes presumed to contribute to individual differences in behavioral traits. Yet results so far have fallen short of expectations, as illustrated by several GWAS that examined possible associations with neuroticism.

One of these GWAS (van den Oord et al., 2008) used a discovery sample of 1,227 individuals, and a replication sample of 1,880 individuals, and reported a significant association with neuroticism for only one gene: *MAMDC1* (also known as *MDGA2*; MAM-Meprin/A5-protein/PTPmu-domain containing glycosylphosphatidylinositol anchor 2). However, a follow-up GWAS by the same group based on 2,686 individuals failed to replicate this finding (Hettema et al., 2009), as did a GWAS of 2,235 individuals by another group (Calboli et al., 2010). One independent group did replicate this association, albeit in a much smaller sample of 541 healthy and 199 depressed individuals (Heck et al., 2011).

Another GWAS focused on extreme scorers (Shifman et al., 2008). The discovery cohort consisted of 2,054 individuals who were drawn from extremely concordant or discordant sibling pairs; a second set of 1,534 singletons comprised the replication sample. Again, only one probe, a single-nucleotide polymorphism (SNP) (rs702543) in the phosphodiesterase 4D gene (*PDE4D*), survived statistical significance testing in both samples. However, when these investigators added three more replication samples of 761, 1,022, and 417 individuals, respectively, replication failed. The authors pointed out that nonreplication may have been due to differences in the measurement instruments to assess neuroticism that were used across these cohorts. In support of their initial finding, a later GWAS replicated an association between neuroticism and *PDE4D* (Calboli et al., 2010).

Another GWAS was conducted for each of the Big Five traits (Terracciano et al., 2010); it was based on a discovery sample of 3,972 individuals and two replication sets of 923 and 1,158 individuals, respectively. Although the discovery set produced significant SNP associations with each of the Big Five, only one replicated (Agreeableness was associated with a SNP, rs 6832769, in the CLOCK gene).

A set of eight European cohorts, ranging in size from 546 to 1,338 individuals and totaling 6,268 participants, was studied by applying a meta-analytic approach to the individual cohort results (Luciano et al., 2012). These investigators identified a set of five genes (*LCE3C, POLR3A, LMAN1L, ULK3, SCAMP2*) with SNPs that were significantly associated with neuroticism. Two of these genes (*LMAN1L* and *SCAMP2*) were also significantly associated with neuroticism in a replication sample of 6,032 Australian individuals.

Finally, the most recent GWAS was conducted in 2,748 individuals with a specific focus on neuroticism and antisocial personality disorder (Aragam, Wang, Anderson, & Liu, 2013). This study reported 32 SNPs that had a "suggestive association" (defined as better than alpha = 10^{-4}, but not reaching significance of alpha = 10^{-7}, based on Wellcome Trust Case Control 2007) with neuroticism, although none reached the defined threshold for claiming significance.

Looking at these GWAS studies in aggregate, one result is striking: There is practically no overlap in reported results. Indeed, when investigators compiled the largest personality GWAS to date—by using a meta-analytic approach based on data from more than 17,000 individuals—they failed to replicate *any* associations with neuroticism (de Moor et al., 2012). Why can we not find this "missing heritability"? One common answer is that GWAS datasets in personality research still are too small.

One creative approach to increasing sample sizes for personality trait GWAS is the application of item-response theory (IRT), as illustrated in a recent study by the Genetics of Personality Consortium (van den Berg et al., 2014). The study focused on neuroticism and extraversion, two personality traits that are commonly assessed across research groups with different personality inventories. Items from different self-report measures were then "harmonized," using IRT to map items across inventories onto the same underlying constructs. This method was applied to data collected from more than 160,000 individuals from 23 study cohorts. A power analysis demonstrated that this harmonizing procedure increased statistical power to detect genetic variants associated with personality: IRT-based neuroticism and extraversion scores showed heritability estimates of 48% and 49%, which were largely due to nonadditive genetic factors.

Large-scale GWAS have been conducted outside personality psychology: 60,000 cases for colorectal cancer (Liao et al., 2015), 86,000 for Alzheimer's (N. Shen et al., 2014b), 94,000 for height (He et al., 2014), and 100,000 for major depressive disorder (Major Depressive Disorder Working Group of the Psychiatric et al., 2013). Yet these larger samples still did not produce large bounties of newly discovered genes. In fact, the depression study reported that "[n]o SNPs achieved genome-wide significance in the MDD discovery phase, the MDD replication phase or in pre-planned secondary analyses" (p. 497) and concluded that "[a]lthough this is the largest genome-wide analysis of MDD yet conducted, its high prevalence means that the sample is still underpowered to detect genetic effects typical for complex traits." (p. 497) Aside from ever-larger GWAS samples, what else can be done to improve the prospect for discovering genes associated with behavioral traits?

Improving Genome-Wide Association Studies

BETTER PHENOTYPING

Ebstein and colleagues have written a blistering critique of GWAS based on self-reported questionnaires (Ebstein et al., 2015), in which they state that

> it is crucial that a meticulous definition of the phenotype be employed, with no shortcuts. Otherwise, there is a danger of a garbage-in garbage-out GWAS based on poorly constructed and biologically distant and implausible phenotypes that are badly matched at the molecular level. Such a phenotype-weak study is likely to lead to false-negative findings and an overly pessimistic view that impedes future progress. (p. 184)

There are alternatives to self-report-based phenotypes. Ebstein and colleagues have argued for extensive lab-based behavioral assessments, at least when applied to studies of decision making. Another approach is the measurement of neural endophenotypes, which has given rise to the field of imaging genetics (see the second section). Conventional wisdom says that both are too difficult and too expensive to lend themselves to large-scale genomic studies, but see the second section for recent developments toward such study designs.

EXPERIMENTS

GWAS results should be evaluated in the context of plausible biological mechanisms. For example, the conflicting results of GWAS studies linking neuroticism to *MAMDC1/ MDGA2* reviewed earlier should be viewed in light of this gene's actual biological function. This gene regulates the development of inhibitory synapses (Lee et al., 2013; Pettem et al., 2013). Animal studies, perhaps using optogenetics (see the third section) could address whether inactivation of such synapses alters fear behavior in rodents.

The gene has also been shown to regulate rostral growth of commissural axons in chicken embryos (Joset et al., 2011). Given the existence of large-scale datasets of structural MRIs, along with corresponding genome-wide SNP data (see next section), it should be easy to test whether variation within the *MAMDC1/MDGA2* maps onto individual differences in commissural volume or fiber integrity. A secondary analysis could then address whether such structural variation correlates with trait neuroticism. These types of studies would help shape plausible models of how this gene may play a role in neuroticism or quickly discard *MAMDC1/ MDGA2* as contributing to this trait.

CURRENT TRENDS IN IMAGING GENETICS

Following the first report of amygdala activation as a function of 5-HTTLPR genotype (Hariri et al., 2002), early imaging genetics studies converged on the view that presence of the 5-HTTLPR short allele is associated with increased amygdala activation to negative stimuli (Bertolino et al., 2005; Furmark et al., 2004; Hariri et al., 2005; Heinz et al., 2005; Pezawas et al., 2005). This interpretation was challenged by fMRI data using multiple baselines conditions (Canli et al., 2005) and arterial spin labeling using absolute measures of blood flow (Canli et al., 2006), which suggested that carriers of the 5-HTTLPR short allele were characterized by elevated resting "tonic activation" of the amygdala and other regions (Canli & Lesch, 2007). Replications of the fMRI baseline results (Heinz et al., 2007) and the arterial spin labeling (ASL) resting activation results (Brockmann et al., 2011; Rao et al., 2007) were consistent with the tonic model. However, another large-scale ASL study failed to replicate (Viviani et al., 2010) and therefore suggests that other factors may further affect amygdala resting activation. Indeed, we had already shown that resting activation varied as a function of an interaction with life stress history, in the first gene–environment imaging study of 5-HTTLPR function in the brain (Canli et al., 2006), which was replicated in subsequent studies (Alexander et al., 2012; Hermann et al., 2012).

The first imaging genetics studies used relatively small sample sizes of tens to a few dozen subjects. The current trend clearly follows the example set by GWAS toward ever-larger samples that are accumulated either by meta-analysis or consortia or both. One of the largest examples is the ENIGMA (Enhancing NeuroImaging Genetics through Meta-Analysis) Consortium, which includes data from over 25,000 individuals and 70 institutions (Thompson et al., 2014). ENIMGA also has genome-wide SNP data, which can be integrated with MRI data. One study reported on genome-wide SNPs associated with hippocampal volume, based on a discovery sample of 7,795 scans and a total replication dataset of 13,356 scans (Stein et al., 2012).

NEXT-GENERATION MOLECULAR TOOLS

The previous two sections illustrate the direction toward "Big Science" in genetics and in neuroimaging. Although larger datasets are statistically more powerful, and rich mines for future explorations, there are drawbacks: They are extremely costly; phenotypes of interest are defined by the lowest common denominator across a multitude of participating labs; they do not lend themselves to quick changes in experimental design; and they demand high-throughput analysis pipelines.

Any causal test of gene contributions to traits requires experimental manipulation of gene function, ideally in a behaving organism or the brain. Yet this approach is also very costly and time consuming. For example, the production of transgenic animals is largely limited to mice, manipulates only single genes, and takes generations of breeding. Thus, current experimental techniques represent a bottleneck to the analysis of large-scale datasets generated by GWAS. Next-generation molecular techniques, which were conceived in the period after the decoding of the human genome and therefore came into existence with genomic data in mind, have the potential to address the bottleneck limitation, as I will discuss in the next sections.

Optogenetics

FOUNDATIONS AND CURRENT APPLICATIONS

Optogenetics was developed by Deisseroth and Boyd and colleagues in 2005 (Boyden et al., 2005). It is based on the principle that light-sensitive molecules called "opsins" can be attached by means of viral vectors to other cellular constituents, such as neuronal ion channels. The viral vectors can be programmed such that infection occurs in very precisely defined subsets of neuronal populations. As a result, lasers can be used to activate opsins that can excite or inhibit precisely defined sets of neurons with millisecond temporal specificity (Bernstein & Boyden 2011; Kramer, Mourot, & Adesnik, 2013; Packer, Roska, & Hausser, 2013; Tye & Deisseroth, 2012; Williams & Deisseroth, 2013; Zhang et al., 2007). More specifically, channelrhodopsins (ChRs) were developed first and are cation-selective ion channels that are responsive to blue light and act to depolarize neurons (Boyden et al., 2005; Nagel et al., 2003). Later developments were halorhodopsins (NpHRs; chloride pumps) and Archaerhodopsins (Archs; proton pumps) that are responsive to yellow light and act to inhibit neurons (Chow et al., 2010; Gradinaru et al., 2010; Zhang et al., 2007).

Relevant to trait psychology, optogenetic applications include studies of behaving animals that were implanted with guide cannulae for fiberoptic strands to deliver laser light into the brain. Such studies have addressed a number of behaviors, including trait-related ones such as anxiety, depression, and social and reward-motivated behaviors (for recent reviews, see Allsop et al., 2014; Nieh, Kim, Namburi, & Tye, 2013).

The value of the optogenetic approach is illustrated by studies that investigated brain regions with diverse sets of neurons. For example, the ventral tegmental area (VTA) contains neurons responsive to GABA, glutamate, or dopamine, and optogenetic techniques were developed to selectively target and activate each set of neurons independently with millisecond precision (reviewed in Nieh and colleagues [2013]). Furthermore, these studies could differentiate functional features within each set of neurons, such as dopaminergic neurons that were responsive not only to reward (a function expected in this brain region) but also to aversive stimuli, as well as their respective projection patterns. These results have begun to erode classic theories that were based on brain region and neurotransmitters alone, by revealing intrastructure circuitry and functional diversity within brain regions and neuron sets.

HUMAN APPLICATIONS

For those interested in studying the biology of traits in humans, optogenetics appears ill suited for human applications. Yet there is keen interest in developing tools for human applications, such as novel neuropsychiatric treatments (Huang, Tang, & Jiang, 2013; Tourino, Eban-Rothschild, & de Lecea, 2013), which I have discussed in detail elsewhere (Canli, 2015). A critical aspect of current optogenetics is the invasive nature of the procedure, which requires, at minimum, injection of a genetically modified viral vector into the brain and implantation of fiber-optic wires or guide cannulae. Hence, there is intense interest in developing noninvasive methods.

The development of noninvasive alternatives to viral vector injection into the brain is driven by advanced clinical studies using gene therapy for neurological diseases in human patients (Chtarto et al., 2013). For example, some viral vectors have been developed that can cross the blood-brain barrier and can therefore reach brain targets by simply being injected intravenously (Duque et al., 2009). These vectors still have limited capabilities; for example, they can only carry small genetic loads to modify brain cells, they currently target astrocytes rather than neurons, and they evoke a stronger immune reaction than do traditional viral vectors (Bevan et al., 2011; Foust et al., 2010; Samaranch et al., 2012).

A noninvasive alternative to brain implants for fiber-optic wires is being developed by Tsien and his laboratory. They recently engineered a novel opsin (red-activatable Channelrhodopsin, ReaChR) that is responsive to orange-to-red light. It turns out that light of this frequency can penetrate the intact skull, because it is less subject to tissue scatter and blood absorption. Using awake mice, this group demonstrated that light shining through the intact skull could activate ReaChR-expressing cells in the vibrissa motor cortex to drive vibrissa movements (Lin et al., 2013).

I don't expect to see the optogenetic human applications purely for research purposes and discussed the ethical implications elsewhere (Canli, 2015). But I think that future trait studies might recruit psychiatric or neurological patients who will be treated with gene therapy approaches.

Genome Editing

FOUNDATIONS AND CURRENT APPLICATIONS

Genome editing refers to techniques that are aimed at altering specific sites within genomes. Previous genome editing tools were technically challenging, requiring highly sophisticated protein design, synthesis, and validation, which have hampered widespread adoption (reviewed by Doudna & Charpentier, 2014). This has dramatically changed with the development of a new tool in 2012, which has produced more than 1,300 published applications in the following 2 years.

This new tool is referred to as the CRISPR-CAS9 system. CRISPRs are "clustered regularly interspaced palindromic repeats," which were first discovered in 1987 in the bacterium *Escherichia coli* (Ishino et al., 1987) and later proposed to represent part of a bacterial defense system against plasmid and phage infection (Makarova et al., 2006), along with Cas9 (CRISPR-associated gene 9) (Barrangou et al., 2007; Deltcheva et al., 2011). In 2012, Jinek and colleagues engineered CRISPR-Cas9 such that researchers now had a two-component system consisting of a single guide RNA (sgRNA) to direct Cas9 to any DNA sequence of choice, by simply altering the nucleotide sequence within the sgRNA to match the desired DNA target (Jinek et al., 2012).

Applications of CRISPR-Cas9 have been extensive (see reviews by Hsu et al., 2014; Mali et al., 2013; Sander & Joung, 2014). One application of potential relevance to behavioral scientists is the in vivo use in the mammalian brain. This was first accomplished in 2015 by Zhang's group in mice (Swiech et al., 2015), who packaged a sgRNA and a Cas9 into two separate adeno-associated viral (AAV) vectors that are commonly used in gene therapies directed at the brain. The RNA sequences they used were designed to target the *MeCP2* (methyl CpG-binding protein 2) gene, which is widely expressed by neurons, and when deficient contributes to the etiology of Rett syndrome (Chahrour & Zoghbi, 2007). Injection of these viral vectors into the dentate gyrus (DG) of hippocampus was shown to produce mutations in the gene in 68% of targeted cells, with a corresponding MeCP2 protein reduction of more than 60%.

Next, these investigators assessed behavioral sequelae. Building on prior work that implicated MeCP2 in contextual fear learning (Moretti et al., 2006), and that assigned the DG a critical role in the acquisition of contextual fear (Kheirbek et al., 2013), they showed that CRISPR-Cas9–mediated inactivation of MeCP2 in the DG impaired contextual memory. Furthermore, they demonstrated behavioral specificity, as experimental animals did not exhibit impaired performance in other cognitive or affective tests (open field testing, novel object recognition, elevated plus maze).

Additional behavioral testing of these animals could be of great interest to trait psychologists: overexpression of MeCP2 in transgenic mice can alter aggressive and social interactive behavior (Moretti et al., 2005; Tantra et al., 2014), and schizophrenic patients genotyped for two SNPs within this gene exhibited allele-specific differences in aggressive behavior (based on patients' readouts of the PANSS; positive and negative syndrome scale) in a discovery cohort of 1,052 patients and a replication cohort of 385 patients (Tantra et al., 2014).

Also in 2015, the CRISPR-Cas9 system was empowered to potentially modify any human protein-coding gene in a "multiplexed" (i.e., affecting multiple genes simultaneously) experimental design. This feat was accomplished by Konermann and colleagues from Zhang's lab (Konermann et al., 2015); they used the RefSeq database to build a massive library of sgRNAs, which were designed to cover all known 70,290 human protein-coding mRNA sequences. Furthermore, they engineered a CRISPR-Cas9 complex that could activate 10 genes simultaneously (multiplexing had previously been accomplished in nonhuman organisms and in much smaller gene sets; see Cong et al., 2013; Niu et al., 2014; Wang et al., 2013). This is a breakthrough technology, because it will allow for experimental designs to probe the functions of entire networks of human genes.

HUMAN APPLICATIONS

The CRISPR-Cas9 system has already been applied to the study of human cells (Cong et al., 2013; Hou et al., 2013). Of particular interest has been the potential application to treat infectious pathogens. For example, the technology has already been used to mutate the HIV-1 virus and to even remove viral genes from infected cells (Ebina et al., 2013; Hu et al., 2014).

More relevant to trait psychologists, the CRISPR-Cas9 system has been applied to the parasite *Toxoplasma gondii*, which is capable of remarkable behavioral changes in rodents and, possibly, in humans. *T. gondii* is a parasite that lives and mates in feline intestines, and that has been linked to schizophrenia in humans (Mortensen et al., 2007; Torrey & Yolken, 2003; Torrey et al., 2007, 2012). When *T. gondii's* eggs are released into the environment through feline excretions, they can come into contact with rodents. Infected rats show accumulation of *T. gondii* cysts in the prefrontal cortex, hippocampus, and amygdala (Berenreiterova et al., 2011; Vyas et al., 2007). In a remarkable feat of neural reprogramming, *T. gondii* causes a reduction in stress hormones and dendritic retraction in the basolateral amygdala (Mitra et al., 2013) and increases activation in regions associated with sexual arousal (House et al., 2011). These neural changes are accompanied by a dramatic change in behavior: Infected rats become sexually attracted to the scent of cat urine (Berdoy et al., 2000; House et al., 2011). Amorously seeking the proximity to roaming felines, these infected rodents then become prey and the *T. gondii* they carried set up residence in the predating cat to start their life cycle anew.

A staggeringly large proportion of humans, about one third of the world's population (Montoya & Liesenfeld 2004), are infected with *T. gondii*. Across 20 European countries, *T. gondii* prevalence rates correlate significantly with national suicide rates (Lester, 2010).

T. gondii infection has been linked to personality traits, based on a variety of personality assessments. For example, *T. gondii* infection is associated with reduced Novelty Seeking scores (Flegr et al., 2003; Skallova et al., 2005) and increased Self-Transcendence (Novotna et al., 2005; Skallova et al., 2005) in Cloninger's

Temperament and Character Inventory; and changes in several of Cattel's factors (superego strength; protension: suspicion and jealousy; affectothymia: reserved, detached, critical; guilt-proneness) (Flegr et al., 2000; Flegr, 2007, 2010). Based on the NEO-PI-R, *T. gondii* infection is associated with higher levels of extroversion and lower levels of conscientiousness (Flegr, 2013). Relevant to Lester's reported association of *T. gondii* with suicide, infection is also associated with trait-reactive aggression in women and with higher disinhibition in men (Cook et al., 2015).

Lafferty (2006) correlated national *T. gondii* seroprevalence data with estimated national neuroticism data. Seroprevalence data were based on national statistics obtained from women of childbearing age (who are commonly tested for *T. gondii* to determine the prospective mother's immunity to infection which would harm the fetus). Neuroticism data were based on two independent assessments of national aggregate personality: one was based on the NEO-PI-R (McCrae et al., 2005); the other was based on the author's own methodology which is statistically independent from the NEO-PI-R (Lester, 2000). Controlling for national GDP, the analysis revealed a significant positive correlation between *T. gondii* prevalence and national neuroticism levels with either measure across 31 (NEO-PI-R: $R^2 = 0.30$) and 25 (Lafferty aggregate: $R^2 = 0.28$) nations, respectively.

These data, though suggestive, do not prove a causal link between *T. gondii* infection and neuroticism or other behavioral traits. Recent work has begun to use CRISPR-Cas9 system in *T. gondii*-infected cells (Ohshima et al., 2014; B. Shen et al., 2014a; Sidik et al., 2014). Disruption of *T. gondii* genes is a first step toward developing a cure for this parasitic infection. It would be fascinating to assess whether an eventual successful treatment for *T. gondii* infection would be accompanied by lowered levels of neuroticism.

CONCLUDING THOUGHTS

Nonreplication across GWAS rests on a fundamental question: What constitutes a significant result? Statistical significance is an arbitrary threshold, set by the conventions of the field. But underlying such conventions is a calculation: What is the cost of a false-positive versus a false-negative result? If replication of, or the experimental follow-up work to, a positive GWAS result is expensive, that is, requires a great deal of money, time, lab space, personnel, and so on, then one would want to err on the side of caution and minimize the risk of reporting false-positive results. That reflects the current approach to reporting GWAS results. But there is the risk of missing important, if perhaps subtle, biological information: committing a false-negative error. However, if replication and follow-up experimental work is cheap, that is, is technically easy to implement, high-throughput, fast, and cost-effective, then the bias should shift toward lowering statistical thresholds to maximize the opportunity for discovery. I think we are beginning to approach this new phase, as novel molecular tools with the potential for genome-wide, high-throughput screening become more widely available.

REFERENCES

Alexander, N., Klucken, T., Koppe, G., Osinsky, R., Walter, B., Vaitl, D., . . . Hennig, J. (2012). Interaction of the serotonin transporter-linked polymorphic region and environmental adversity: Increased amygdala-hypothalamus connectivity as a potential mechanism linking neural and endocrine hyperreactivity. *Biol Psychiatry*, *72*(1), 49–56. doi:10.1016/j.biopsych.2012.01.030

Allsop, S. A., Vander Weele, C. M., Wichmann, R., & Tye, K. M. (2014). Optogenetic insights on the relationship between anxiety-related behaviors and social deficits. *Front Behav Neurosci*, 8, 241. doi:10.3389/fnbeh.2014.00241

Aragam, N., Wang, K.-S., Anderson, J. L., & Liu, X. (2013). TMPRSS9 and GRIN2B are associated with neuroticism: a genome-wide association study in a European sample. *Journal of Molecular Neuroscience: MN*, *50*(2), 250–256.

Barrangou, R., Fremaux, C., Deveau, H., Richards, M., Boyaval, P., Moineau, S., . . . Horvath, P. (2007). CRISPR provides acquired resistance against viruses in prokaryotes. *Science*, *315*(5819), 1709–1712. doi:10.1126/science.1138140

Berdoy, M., Webster, J. P., & Macdonald, D. W. (2000). Fatal attraction in rats infected with Toxoplasma gondii. *Proceedings Biological sciences/The Royal Society*, *267*(1452), 1591–1594.

Berenreiterova, M., Flegr, J., Kubena, A. A., & Nemec, P. (2011). The distribution of Toxoplasma gondii cysts in the brain of a mouse with latent toxoplasmosis: implications for the behavioral manipulation hypothesis. *PLoS One*, *6*(12), e28925.

Bernstein, J. G., & Boyden, E. S. (2011). Optogenetic tools for analyzing the neural circuits of behavior. *Trends Cogn Sci*, *15*(12), 592–600. doi:10.1016/j.tics.2011.10.003

Bertolino, A., Arciero, G., Rubino, V., Latorre, V., De Candia, M., Mazzola, V., . . . Scarabino, T. (2005). Variation of human amygdala response during threatening stimuli as a function of 5'HTTLPR genotype and personality style. *Biol Psychiatry*, *57*(12), 1517–1525.

Bevan, A. K., Duque, S., Foust, K. D., Morales, P. R., Braun, L., Schmelzer, L., . . . Kaspar, B. K. (2011). Systemic gene delivery in large species for targeting spinal cord, brain, and peripheral tissues for pediatric disorders. *Mol Ther*, *19*(11), 1971–1980. doi:10.1038/mt.2011.157

Bouchard, T. J., Jr., Lykken, D. T., Mcgue, M., Segal, N. L., & Tellegen, A. (1990). Sources of human psychological differences: The Minnesota study of twins reared apart. *Science*, *250*, 223–228.

Boyden, E. S., Zhang, F., Bamberg, E., Nagel, G., & Deisseroth, K. (2005). Millisecond-timescale, genetically targeted optical control of neural activity. *Nat Neurosci*, *8*(9), 1263–1268. doi:10.1038/nn1525

Brockmann, H., Zobel, A., Schuhmacher, A., Daamen, M., Joe, A., Biermann, K., . . . Boecker, H. (2011). Influence of 5-HTTLPR polymorphism on resting state perfusion in patients with major depression. *J Psychiatr Res*, *45*(4), 442–451. doi:S0022-3956(10)00260-8 [pii] 10.1016/j.jpsychires.2010.08.016

Calboli, F. C., Tozzi, F., Galwey, N. W., Antoniades, A., Mooser, V., Preisig, M., . . . Balding, D. J. (2010). A genome-wide association study of neuroticism in a population-based sample. *PLoS One*, *5*(7), e11504. doi:10.1371/journal.pone.0011504

Canli, T. (2015). Neurogenethics. In T. Canli (Ed.), *The Oxford Handbook of Molecular Psychology*. New York, Oxford: Oxford University Press.

Canli, T., & Lesch, K.-P. (2007). Long story short: the serotonin transporter in emotion regulation and social cognition. *Nature Neuroscience*, *10*(9), 1103–1109.

Canli, T., Omura, K., Haas, B. W., Fallgatter, A., Constable, R. T., & Lesch, K. P. (2005). Beyond affect: a role for genetic variation of the serotonin transporter in neural activation during a cognitive attention task. *Proceedings of the National Academy of Sciences of the United States of America*, *102*(34), 12224–12229.

Canli, T., Qiu, M., Omura, K., Congdon, E., Haas, B. W., Amin, Z., . . . Lesch, K. P. (2006). Neural correlates of epigenesis. *Proceedings of the National Academy of Sciences of the United States of America*, *103*(43), 16033–16038.

Chahrour, M., & Zoghbi, H. Y. (2007). The story of Rett syndrome: from clinic to neurobiology. *Neuron*, *56*(3), 422–437. doi:10.1016/j.neuron.2007.10.001

Chow, B. Y., Han, X., Dobry, A. S., Qian, X., Chuong, A. S., Li, M., . . . Boyden, E. S. (2010). High-performance genetically targetable optical neural silencing by light-driven proton pumps. *Nature*, *463*(7277), 98–102. doi:10.1038/nature08652

Chtarto, A., Bockstael, O., Tshibangu, T., Dewitte, O., Levivier, M., & Tenenbaum, L. (2013). A next step in adeno-associated virus-mediated gene therapy for neurological diseases: regulation and targeting. *Br J Clin Pharmacol*, *76*(2), 217–232. doi:10.1111/bcp.12065

Clarke, H., Flint, J., Attwood, A. S., & Munafo, M. R. (2010). Association of the 5-HTTLPR genotype and unipolar depression: a meta-analysis. *Psychological Medicine*, *40*(11), 1767–1778.

Cong, L., Ran, F. A., Cox, D., Lin, S., Barretto, R., Habib, N., . . . Zhang, F. (2013). Multiplex genome engineering using CRISPR/Cas systems. *Science*, *339*(6121), 819–823. doi:10.1126/science.1231143

Cook, T. B., Brenner, L. A., Cloninger, C. R., Langenberg, P., Igbide, A., Giegling, I., . . . Postolache, T. T. (2015). "Latent" infection with Toxoplasma gondii: Association with trait aggression and impulsivity in healthy adults. *J Psychiatr Res*, *60*, 87–94. doi:10.1016/j.jpsychires.2014.09.019

Costa, P. T., & McCrae, R. R. (1992). *Revised NEO personality inventory: Professional manual.* Odessa, FL: Psychological Assessment Resources.

de Moor, M. H., Costa, P. T., Terracciano, A., Krueger, R. F., de Geus, E. J., Toshiko, T., . . . Boomsma, D. I. (2012). Meta-analysis of genome-wide association studies for personality. *Mol Psychiatry*, *17*(3), 337–349. doi:10.1038/mp.2010.128

Defries, J. C., McClearn, G. E., McGuffin, P., & Plomin, R. (Eds.). (2000). *Behavioral Genetics* (4th edition ed.). New York: Worth Publishers.

Deltcheva, E., Chylinski, K., Sharma, C. M., Gonzales, K., Chao, Y., Pirzada, Z. A., . . . Charpentier, E. (2011). CRISPR RNA maturation by trans-encoded small RNA and host factor RNase III. *Nature*, *471*(7340), 602–607. doi:10.1038/nature09886

Dilalla, L. F., & Gottesman, I. I. (Eds.). (2004). Behavior Genetics Principles: Perspectives in Development, Personality, and Psychopathology American Psychological Association.

Doudna, J. A., & Charpentier, E. (2014). Genome editing. The new frontier of genome engineering with CRISPR-Cas9. *Science*, *346*(6213), 1258096. doi:10.1126/science.1258096

Duque, S., Joussemet, B., Riviere, C., Marais, T., Dubreil, L., Douar, A. M., . . . Barkats, M. (2009). Intravenous administration of self-complementary AAV9 enables transgene delivery to adult motor neurons. *Mol Ther*, *17*(7), 1187–1196. doi:10.1038/mt.2009.71

Ebina, H., Misawa, N., Kanemura, Y., & Koyanagi, Y. (2013). Harnessing the CRISPR/Cas9 system to disrupt latent HIV-1 provirus. *Sci Rep*, *3*, 2510. doi:10.1038/srep02510

Ebstein, R. P., Zhong, S., Chark, R., San Lai, P., & Chew, S. H. (2015). Genetics of Social Cognition in the Laboratory: Definition, Measurement, and Association. In T. Canli (Ed.), *The Oxford Handbook of Molecular Psychology*. New York, Oxford: Oxford University Press.

Eysenck, H. J. (1990). Genetic and environmental contributions to individual differences: the three major dimensions of personality. *J Pers*, *58*(1), 245–261.

Flegr, J. (2007). Effects of toxoplasma on human behavior. *Schizophr Bull*, *33*(3), 757–760. doi:10.1093/schbul/sbl074

Flegr, J. (2010). Influence of latent toxoplasmosis on the phenotype of intermediate hosts. *Folia Parasitologica*, *57*(2), 81–87.

Flegr, J. (2013). Influence of latent Toxoplasma infection on human personality, physiology and morphology: pros and cons of the Toxoplasma-human model in studying the manipulation hypothesis. *The Journal of Experimental Biology*, *216*(Pt 1), 127–133. doi:10.1242/jeb.073635

Flegr, J., Kodym, P., & Tolarova, V. (2000). Correlation of duration of latent Toxoplasma gondii infection with personality changes in women. *Biol Psychol*, *53*(1), 57–68.

Flegr, J., Preiss, M., Klose, J., Havlicek, J., Vitakova, M., & Kodym, P. (2003). Decreased level of psychobiological factor novelty seeking and lower intelligence in men latently infected with the protozoan parasite Toxoplasma gondii Dopamine, a missing link between schizophrenia and toxoplasmosis? *Biol Psychol*, *63*(3), 253–268.

Floderus-Myrhed, B., Pedersen, N., & Rasmuson, I. (1980). Assessment of heritability for personality, based on a short-form of the Eysenck Personality Inventory: a study of 12,898 twin pairs. *Behavior Genetics*, *10*(2), 153–162.

Foust, K. D., Wang, X., McGovern, V. L., Braun, L., Bevan, A. K., Haidet, A. M., . . . Kaspar, B. K. (2010). Rescue of the spinal muscular atrophy phenotype in a mouse model by early postnatal delivery of SMN. *Nat Biotechnol*, *28*(3), 271–274. doi:10.1038/nbt.1610

Furmark, T., Tillfors, M., Garpenstrand, H., Marteinsdottir, I., Langstrom, B., Oreland, L., & Fredrikson, M. (2004). Serotonin transporter polymorphism related to amygdala excitability and symptom severity in patients with social phobia. *Neurosci Lett*, *362*(3), 189–192.

Gradinaru, V., Zhang, F., Ramakrishnan, C., Mattis, J., Prakash, R., Diester, I., . . . Deisseroth, K. (2010). Molecular and cellular approaches for diversifying and extending optogenetics. *Cell*, *141*(1), 154–165. doi:10.1016/j.cell.2010.02.037

Hariri, A. R., Drabant, E. M., Munoz, K. E., Kolachana, B. S., Mattay, V. S., Egan, M. F., & Weinberger, D. R. (2005). A susceptibility gene for affective disorders and the response of the human amygdala. *Arch Gen Psychiatry*, *62*(2), 146–152.

Hariri, A. R., Mattay, V. S., Tessitore, A., Kolachana, B., Fera, F., Goldman, D., . . . Weinberger, D. R. (2002). Serotonin transporter genetic variation and the response of the human amygdala. *Science*, *297*(5580), 400–403.

He, M., Xu, M., Zhang, B., Liang, J., Chen, P., Lee, J. Y., . . . Qi, L. (2014). Meta-analysis of genome-wide association studies of adult height in East Asians identifies 17 novel loci. *Hum Mol Genet*. doi:10.1093/hmg/ddu583

Heck, A., Pfister, H., Czamara, D., Muller-Myhsok, B., Putz, B., Lucae, S., . . . Ising, M. (2011). Evidence for associations between MDGA2 polymorphisms and harm avoidance: replication and extension of a genome-wide association finding. *Psychiatric Genetics, 21*(5), 257–260. doi:10.1097/YPG.0b013e3283457bfb

Heinz, A., Braus, D. F., Smolka, M. N., Wrase, J., Puls, I., Hermann, D., . . . Buchel, C. (2005). Amygdala-prefrontal coupling depends on a genetic variation of the serotonin transporter. *Nat Neurosci, 8*(1), 20–21.

Heinz, A., Smolka, M. N., Braus, D. F., Wrase, J., Beck, A., Flor, H., . . . Weinberger, D. R. (2007). Serotonin Transporter Genotype (5-HTTLPR): Effects of Neutral and Undefined Conditions on Amygdala Activation. *Biological Psychiatry, 61*(8), 1011–1014.

Hermann, A., Kupper, Y., Schmitz, A., Walter, B., Vaitl, D., Hennig, J., . . . Tabbert, K. (2012). Functional gene polymorphisms in the serotonin system and traumatic life events modulate the neural basis of fear acquisition and extinction. *PLoS One, 7*(9), e44352. doi:10.1371/journal.pone.0044352

Hettema, J. M., van den Oord, E. J., An, S. S., Kendler, K. S., & Chen, X. (2009). Follow-up association study of novel neuroticism gene MAMDC1. *Psychiatric Genetics, 19*(4), 213–214. doi:10.1097/YPG.0b013e32832cec22

Hou, Z., Zhang, Y., Propson, N. E., Howden, S. E., Chu, L. F., Sontheimer, E. J., & Thomson, J. A. (2013). Efficient genome engineering in human pluripotent stem cells using Cas9 from Neisseria meningitidis. *Proc Natl Acad Sci U S A, 110*(39), 15644–15649. doi:10.1073/pnas.1313587110

House, P. K., Vyas, A., & Sapolsky, R. (2011). Predator cat odors activate sexual arousal pathways in brains of Toxoplasma gondii infected rats. *PLoS One, 6*(8), e23277. doi:10.1371/journal.pone.0023277

Hsu, P. D., Lander, E. S., & Zhang, F. (2014). Development and applications of CRISPR-Cas9 for genome engineering. *Cell, 157*(6), 1262–1278. doi:10.1016/j.cell.2014.05.010

Hu, W., Kaminski, R., Yang, F., Zhang, Y., Cosentino, L., Li, F., . . . Khalili, K. (2014). RNA-directed gene editing specifically eradicates latent and prevents new HIV-1 infection. *Proc Natl Acad Sci U S A, 111*(31), 11461–11466. doi:10.1073/pnas.1405186111

Huang, F., Tang, B., & Jiang, H. (2013). Optogenetic investigation of neuropsychiatric diseases. *Int J Neurosci, 123*(1), 7–16. doi:10.3109/00207454.2012.728651

Ishino, Y., Shinagawa, H., Makino, K., Amemura, M., & Nakata, A. (1987). Nucleotide sequence of the iap gene, responsible for alkaline phosphatase isozyme conversion in Escherichia coli, and identification of the gene product. *J Bacteriol, 169*(12), 5429–5433.

Jang, K. L., Livesley, W. J., & Vernon, P. A. (1996). Heritability of the big five personality dimensions and their facets: a twin study. *J Pers, 64*(3), 577–591.

Jinek, M., Chylinski, K., Fonfara, I., Hauer, M., Doudna, J. A., & Charpentier, E. (2012). A programmable dual-RNA-guided DNA endonuclease in adaptive bacterial immunity. *Science, 337*(6096), 816–821. doi:10.1126/science.1225829

Joset, P., Wacker, A., Babey, R., Ingold, E. A., Andermatt, I., Stoeckli, E. T., & Gesemann, M. (2011). Rostral growth of commissural axons requires the cell adhesion molecule MDGA2. *Neural Dev, 6*, 22. doi:10.1186/1749-8104-6-22

Kheirbek, M. A., Drew, L. J., Burghardt, N. S., Costantini, D. O., Tannenholz, L., Ahmari, S. E., . . . Hen, R. (2013). Differential control of learning and anxiety along the dorso-ventral axis of the dentate gyrus. *Neuron, 77*(5), 955–968. doi:S0896-6273(13)00046-9 [pii] 10.1016/j.neuron.2012.12.038

Konermann, S., Brigham, M. D., Trevino, A. E., Joung, J., Abudayyeh, O. O., Barcena, C., . . . Zhang, F. (2015). Genome-scale transcriptional activation by an engineered CRISPR-Cas9 complex. *Nature, 517*(7536), 583–588. doi:10.1038/nature14136

Kramer, R. H., Mourot, A., & Adesnik, H. (2013). Optogenetic pharmacology for control of native neuronal signaling proteins. *Nat Neurosci, 16*(7), 816–823. doi:10.1038/nn.3424

Lafferty, K. D. (2006). Can the common brain parasite, Toxoplasma gondii, influence human culture? *Proc Biol Sci, 273*(1602), 2749–2755. doi:R8663292G0L526V6 [pii] 10.1098/rspb.2006.3641

Lee, K., Kim, Y., Lee, S. J., Qiang, Y., Lee, D., Lee, H. W., . . . Ko, J. (2013). MDGAs interact selectively with neuroligin-2 but not other neuroligins to regulate inhibitory synapse development. *Proc Natl Acad Sci U S A, 110*(1), 336–341. doi:10.1073/pnas.1219987110

Lesch, K. P., Bengel, D., Heils, A., Sabol, S. Z., Greenberg, B. D., Petri, S., . . . Murphy, D. L. (1996). Association of anxiety-related traits with a polymorphism in the serotonin transporter gene regulatory region. *Science, 274*(5292), 1527–1531.

Lester, D. (2000). National differences in neuroticism and extraversion. *Pers Indiv Differ, 28*, 35–39.

Lester, D. (2010). Brain parasites and suicide. *Psychol Rep, 107*(2), 424.

Liao, M., Wang, G., Quan, B., Qi, X., Yu, Z., Feng, R., . . . Liu, G. (2015). Analyzing large-scale samples confirms the association between rs16892766 polymorphism and colorectal cancer susceptibility. *Sci Rep, 5*, 7957. doi:10.1038/srep07957

Lin, J. Y., Knutsen, P. M., Muller, A., Kleinfeld, D., & Tsien, R. Y. (2013). ReaChR: a red-shifted variant of channelrhodopsin enables deep transcranial optogenetic excitation. *Nat Neurosci, 16*(10), 1499–1508. doi:10.1038/nn.3502

Luciano, M., Huffman, J. E., Arias-Vasquez, A., Vinkhuyzen, A. A., Middeldorp, C. M., Giegling, I., . . . Deary, I. J. (2012). Genome-wide association uncovers shared genetic effects among personality traits and mood states. *Am J Med Genet B Neuropsychiatr Genet, 159B*(6), 684–695. doi:10.1002/ajmg.b.32072

Major Depressive Disorder Working Group of the Psychiatric, G. C., Ripke, S., Wray, N. R., Lewis, C. M., Hamilton, S. P., Weissman, M. M., . . . Sullivan, P. F. (2013). A mega-analysis of genome-wide association studies for major depressive disorder. *Mol Psychiatry, 18*(4), 497–511. doi:10.1038/mp.2012.21

Makarova, K. S., Grishin, N. V., Shabalina, S. A., Wolf, Y. I., & Koonin, E. V. (2006). A putative RNA-interference-based immune system in prokaryotes: computational analysis of the predicted enzymatic machinery, functional analogies with eukaryotic RNAi, and hypothetical mechanisms of action. *Biol Direct, 1*, 7. doi:10.1186/1745-6150-1-7

Mali, P., Esvelt, K. M., & Church, G. M. (2013). Cas9 as a versatile tool for engineering biology. *Nat Methods, 10*(10), 957–963. doi:10.1038/nmeth.2649

McCrae, R. R., Terracciano, A., & Pro, P. P. C. (2005). Personality profiles of cultures: Aggregate personality traits. *Journal of Personality and Social Psychology, 89*(3), 407–425. doi:Doi 10.1037/0022-3514.89.3.407

Mitra, R., Sapolsky, R. M., & Vyas, A. (2013). Toxoplasma gondii infection induces dendritic retraction in basolateral amygdala accompanied by reduced corticosterone secretion. *Disease Models & Mechanisms, 6*(2), 516–520. doi:10.1242/dmm.009928

Montoya, J. G., & Liesenfeld, O. (2004). Toxoplasmosis. *Lancet, 363*(9425), 1965–1976. doi:10.1016/S0140-6736(04)16412-X

Moretti, P., Bouwknecht, J. A., Teague, R., Paylor, R., & Zoghbi, H. Y. (2005). Abnormalities of social interactions and home-cage behavior in a mouse model of Rett syndrome. *Hum Mol Genet, 14*(2), 205–220. doi:10.1093/hmg/ddi016

Moretti, P., Levenson, J. M., Battaglia, F., Atkinson, R., Teague, R., Antalffy, B., . . . Zoghbi, H. Y. (2006). Learning and memory and synaptic plasticity are impaired in a mouse model of Rett syndrome. *J Neurosci, 26*(1), 319–327. doi:10.1523/JNEUROSCI.2623-05.2006

Mortensen, P. B., Norgaard-Pedersen, B., Waltoft, B. L., Sorensen, T. L., Hougaard, D., Torrey, E. F., & Yolken, R. H. (2007). Toxoplasma gondii as a risk factor for early-onset schizophrenia: analysis of filter paper blood samples obtained at birth. *Biol Psychiatry, 61*(5), 688–693. doi:S0006-3223(06)00710-4 [pii] 10.1016/j.biopsych.2006.05.024

Munafo, M. R., Clark, T. G., & Flint, J. (2005). Does measurement instrument moderate the association between the serotonin transporter gene and anxiety-related personality traits? A meta-analysis. *Mol Psychiatry, 10*(4), 415–419.

Munafo, M. R., Freimer, N. B., Ng, W., Ophoff, R., Veijola, J., Miettunen, J., . . . Flint, J. (2009). 5-HTTLPR genotype and anxiety-related personality traits: a meta-analysis and new data. *Am J Med Genet B Neuropsychiatr Genet, 150B*(2), 271–281. doi:10.1002/ajmg.b.30808

Nagel, G., Szellas, T., Huhn, W., Kateriya, S., Adeishvili, N., Berthold, P., . . . Bamberg, E. (2003). Channelrhodopsin-2, a directly light-gated cation-selective membrane channel. *Proc Natl Acad Sci U S A, 100*(24), 13940–13945. doi:10.1073/pnas.1936192100

Nieh, E. H., Kim, S. Y., Namburi, P., & Tye, K. M. (2013). Optogenetic dissection of neural circuits underlying emotional valence and motivated behaviors. *Brain Res, 1511*, 73–92. doi:10.1016/j.brainres.2012.11.001

Niu, Y., Shen, B., Cui, Y., Chen, Y., Wang, J., Wang, L., . . . Sha, J. (2014). Generation of gene-modified cynomolgus monkey via Cas9/RNA-mediated gene targeting in one-cell embryos. *Cell, 156*(4), 836–843. doi:10.1016/j.cell.2014.01.027

Novotna, M., Hanusova, J., Klose, J., Preiss, M., Havlicek, J., Roubalova, K., & Flegr, J. (2005). Probable neuroimmunological link between Toxoplasma and cytomegalovirus infections and personality changes in the human host. *BMC Infect Dis, 5*, 54. doi:10.1186/1471-2334-5-54

Ohshima, J., Lee, Y., Sasai, M., Saitoh, T., Su Ma, J., Kamiyama, N., . . . Yamamoto, M. (2014). Role of mouse and human autophagy proteins in IFN-gamma-induced cell-autonomous responses against Toxoplasma gondii. *J Immunol, 192*(7), 3328–3335. doi:10.4049/jimmunol.1302822

Packer, A. M., Roska, B., & Hausser, M. (2013). Targeting neurons and photons for optogenetics. *Nat Neurosci, 16*(7), 805–815. doi:10.1038/nn.3427

Pettem, K. L., Yokomaku, D., Takahashi, H., Ge, Y., & Craig, A. M. (2013). Interaction between autism-linked MDGAs and neuroligins suppresses inhibitory synapse development. *J Cell Biol, 200*(3), 321–336. doi:10.1083/jcb.201206028

Pezawas, L., Meyer-Lindenberg, A., Drabant, E. M., Verchinski, B. A., Munoz, K. E., Kolachana, B. S., . . . Weinberger, D. R. (2005). 5-HTTLPR polymorphism impacts human cingulate-amygdala interactions: a genetic susceptibility mechanism for depression. *Nat Neurosci, 8*(6), 828–834.

Rao, H., Gillihan, S. J., Wang, J., Korczykowski, M., Sankoorikal, G. M., Kaercher, K. A., . . . Farah, M. J. (2007). Genetic variation in serotonin transporter alters resting brain function in healthy individuals. *Biol Psychiatry, 62*(6), 600–606.

Samaranch, L., Salegio, E. A., San Sebastian, W., Kells, A. P., Foust, K. D., Bringas, J. R., . . . Bankiewicz, K. S. (2012). Adeno-associated virus serotype 9 transduction in the central nervous system of nonhuman primates. *Hum Gene Ther, 23*(4), 382–389. doi:10.1089/hum.2011.200

Sander, J. D., & Joung, J. K. (2014). CRISPR-Cas systems for editing, regulating and targeting genomes. *Nat Biotechnol, 32*(4), 347–355. doi:10.1038/nbt.2842

Schinka, J. A., Busch, R. M., & Robichaux-Keene, N. (2004). A meta-analysis of the association between the serotonin transporter gene polymorphism (5-HTTLPR) and trait anxiety. *Mol Psychiatry, 9*(2), 197–202.

Sen, S., Burmeister, M., & Ghosh, D. (2004). Meta-analysis of the association between a serotonin transporter promoter polymorphism (5-HTTLPR) and anxiety-related personality traits. *American Journal of Medical Genetics, 127B*(1), 85–89.

Shen, B., Brown, K. M., Lee, T. D., & Sibley, L. D. (2014). Efficient gene disruption in diverse strains of Toxoplasma gondii using CRISPR/CAS9. *MBio, 5*(3), e01114–01114. doi:10.1128/mBio.01114-14

Shen, N., Chen, B., Jiang, Y., Feng, R., Liao, M., Zhang, L., . . . Liu, G. (2014). An Updated Analysis with 85,939 Samples Confirms the Association Between CR1 rs6656401 Polymorphism and Alzheimer's Disease. *Mol Neurobiol.* doi:10.1007/s12035-014-8761-2

Shifman, S., Bhomra, A., Smiley, S., Wray, N. R., James, M. R., Martin, N. G., . . . Flint, J. (2008). A whole genome association study of neuroticism using DNA pooling. *Mol Psychiatry, 13*(3), 302–312. doi:4002048 [pii] 10.1038/sj.mp.4002048

Sidik, S. M., Hackett, C. G., Tran, F., Westwood, N. J., & Lourido, S. (2014). Efficient genome engineering of Toxoplasma gondii using CRISPR/Cas9. *PLoS One, 9*(6), e100450. doi:10.1371/journal.pone.0100450

Skallova, A., Novotna, M., Kolbekova, P., Gasova, Z., Vesely, V., Sechovska, M., & Flegr, J. (2005). Decreased level of novelty seeking in blood donors infected with Toxoplasma. *Neuro Endocrinol Lett, 26*(5), 480–486.

Stein, J. L., Medland, S. E., Vasquez, A. A., Hibar, D. P., Senstad, R. E., Winkler, A. M., . . . Schmidt, R. (2012). Identification of common variants associated with human hippocampal and intracranial volumes. *Nature Genetics, 44*(5), 552–561.

Swiech, L., Heidenreich, M., Banerjee, A., Habib, N., Li, Y., Trombetta, J., . . . Zhang, F. (2015). In vivo interrogation of gene function in the mammalian brain using CRISPR-Cas9. *Nat Biotechnol, 33*(1), 102–106. doi:10.1038/nbt.3055

Tantra, M., Hammer, C., Kastner, A., Dahm, L., Begemann, M., Bodda, C., . . . Ehrenreich, H. (2014). Mild expression differences of MECP2 influencing aggressive social behavior. *EMBO Mol Med, 6*(5), 662–684. doi:10.1002/emmm.201303744

Tellegen, A., Lykken, D. T., Bouchard, T. J., Jr., Wilcox, K. J., Segal, N. L., & Rich, S. (1988). Personality similarity in twins reared apart and together. *Journal of Personality and Social Psychology, 54*(6), 1031–1039.

Terracciano, A., Sanna, S., Uda, M., Deiana, B., Usala, G., Busonero, F., . . . Costa, P. T., Jr. (2010). Genome-wide association scan for five major dimensions of personality. *Mol Psychiatry, 15*(6), 647–656. doi:10.1038/mp.2008.113

Thompson, P. M., Stein, J. L., Medland, S. E., Hibar, D. P., Vasquez, A. A., Renteria, M. E., . . . Drevets, W. (2014). The ENIGMA Consortium: large-scale collaborative analyses of neuroimaging and genetic data. *Brain Imaging Behav.* doi:10.1007/s11682-013-9269-5

Torrey, E. F., Bartko, J. J., Lun, Z. R., & Yolken, R. H. (2007). Antibodies to Toxoplasma gondii in patients with schizophrenia: a meta-analysis. *Schizophr Bull, 33*(3), 729–736. doi:sbl050 [pii], 10.1093/schbul/sbl050

Torrey, E. F., Bartko, J. J., & Yolken, R. H. (2012). Toxoplasma gondii and other risk factors for schizophrenia: an update. *Schizophr Bull, 38*(3), 642–647. doi:sbs043 [pii]10.1093/schbul/sbs043

Torrey, E. F., & Yolken, R. H. (2003). Toxoplasma gondii and schizophrenia. *Emerg Infect Dis, 9*(11), 1375–1380. doi:10.3201/eid0911.030143

Tourino, C., Eban-Rothschild, A., & de Lecea, L. (2013). Optogenetics in psychiatric diseases. *Curr Opin Neurobiol, 23*(3), 430–435. doi:10.1016/j.conb.2013.03.007

Tye, K. M., & Deisseroth, K. (2012). Optogenetic investigation of neural circuits underlying brain disease in animal models. *Nat Rev Neurosci, 13*(4), 251–266. doi:nrn3171 [pii] 10.1038/nrn3171

van den Berg, S. M., de Moor, M. H., McGue, M., Pettersson, E., Terracciano, A., Verweij, K. J., . . . Boomsma, D. I. (2014). Harmonization of Neuroticism and Extraversion phenotypes across inventories and cohorts in the Genetics of Personality Consortium: an application of Item Response Theory. *Behavior Genetics, 44*(4), 295–313. doi:10.1007/s10519-014-9654-x

van den Oord, E. J. C. G., Kuo, P.-H., Hartmann, A. M., Webb, B. T., Moller, H.-J., Hettema, J. M., . . . Rujescu, D. (2008). Genomewide association analysis followed by a replication study implicates a novel candidate gene for neuroticism. *Archives of General Psychiatry, 65*(9), 1062–1071.

Viviani, R., Sim, E. J., Lo, H., Beschoner, P., Osterfeld, N., Maier, C., . . . Kirchheiner, J. (2010). Baseline brain perfusion and the serotonin transporter promoter polymorphism. *Biol Psychiatry, 67*(4), 317–322. doi:10.1016/j.biopsych.2009.08.035

Vyas, A., Kim, S. K., Giacomini, N., Boothroyd, J. C., & Sapolsky, R. M. (2007). Behavioral changes induced by Toxoplasma infection of rodents are highly specific to aversion of cat odors. *Proc Natl Acad Sci U S A, 104*(15), 6442–6447. doi:10.1073/pnas.0608310104

Wang, H., Yang, H., Shivalila, C. S., Dawlaty, M. M., Cheng, A. W., Zhang, F., & Jaenisch, R. (2013). One-step generation of mice carrying mutations in multiple genes by CRISPR/Cas-mediated genome engineering. *Cell, 153*(4), 910–918. doi:10.1016/j.cell.2013.04.025

Wellcome Trust Case Control, C. (2007). Genome-wide association study of 14,000 cases of seven common diseases and 3,000 shared controls. *Nature, 447*(7145), 661–678. doi:10.1038/nature05911

Williams, S. C., & Deisseroth, K. (2013). Optogenetics. *Proc Natl Acad Sci U S A, 110*(41), 16287. doi:10.1073/pnas.1317033110

Zhang, F., Aravanis, A. M., Adamantidis, A., de Lecea, L., & Deisseroth, K. (2007). Circuit-breakers: optical technologies for probing neural signals and systems. *Nat Rev Neurosci, 8*(8), 577–581. doi:nrn2192 [pii] 10.1038/nrn2192

Tables, figures, and boxes are indicated by an italic t, f, and b following the page/paragraph number